Th   ley

Known from her day to ours as "the Author of *Frankenstein*," Mary Shelley in-deed created one of the central myths of modernity. But she went on to survive all manner of upheaval – personal, political, and professional – and to pro-duce an *oeuvre* of bracing intelligence and wide cultural sweep. *The Cambridge Companion to Mary Shelley* helps readers to assess for themselves her remark-able body of work. In clear, accessible essays, a distinguished group of scholars places Shelley's works in several historical and aesthetic contexts: literary his-tory, the legacies of her parents William Godwin and Mary Wollstonecraft, and of course the life and afterlife, in cinema, robotics, and hypertext, of *Frankenstein*. Other topics covered include Mary Shelley as a biographer and cultural critic, as the first editor of Percy Shelley's works, and as travel writer. This invaluable volume is complemented by a chronology, a guide to further reading, and a select filmography.

THE CAMBRIDGE
COMPANION TO

MARY SHELLEY

EDITED BY

ESTHER SCHOR

Princeton University

CAMBRIDGE
UNIVERSITY PRESS

CAMBRIDGE UNIVERSITY PRESS
Cambridge, New York, Melbourne, Madrid, Cape Town,
Singapore, São Paulo, Delhi, Tokyo, Mexico City

Cambridge University Press
The Edinburgh Building, Cambridge CB2 8RU, UK

Published in the United States of America by Cambridge University Press, New York

www.cambridge.org
Information on this title: www.cambridge.org/9780521007702

First published 2003

A catalogue record for this publication is available from the British Library

Library of Congress Cataloguing in Publication Data
The Cambridge companion to Mary Shelley / edited by Esther Schor.
p.   cm. – (Cambridge companions to literature)
Includes bibliographical references and index.
ISBN 0 521 80984 3 – ISBN 0 521 00770 4 (pbk.)
1. Shelley, Mary Wollstonecraft, 1797–1851 – Criticism and interpretation.
2. Women and literature – England – History – 19th century.
I. Schor, Esther H.   II. Series
PR5398.c36   2003
823'.7–dc21   2003046266

ISBN 978-0-521-80984-9 Hardback
ISBN 978-0-521-00770-2 Paperback

For the next generation:

Daniel, Jordy, Susannah in Princeton
Noemi, Shayna, Rafaella in Millburn
Adam in Atlanta
Gabriel and Zachary in Stamford
Annabelle in White Plains
and
Jake in Seattle

CONTENTS

Part 2. Fictions and myths

Part 3. Professional personae

ILLUSTRATIONS

BETTY T. BENNETT is Distinguished Professor of Literature at American University, Washington, D.C. Her books include her edition of *The Letters of Mary Wollstonecraft Shelley* (1980–88), *Mary Diana Dods: A Gentleman and a Scholar* (1991; paper 1994), and *Mary Wollstonecraft Shelley: An Introduction* (1998). She is currently completing a biography of Mary Shelley.

JAY CLAYTON is Professor of English at Vanderbilt University, Tennessee. He is the author of *Romantic Vision and the Novel* (1987), *The Pleasures of Babel: Contemporary American Literature and Theory* (1993), and *Charles Dickens in Cyberspace* (2002).

PAMELA CLEMIT is Reader in English at the University of Durham, UK. She is the author of *The Godwinian Novel* (1993, rpt. 2001). She has edited numerous scholarly and critical editions of Godwin's writings, two volumes in *Novels and Selected Works of Mary Shelley* (1996), and, most recently, "Life of William Godwin" in *Mary Shelley's Literary Lives and Other Writings* (2002). She is writing a two-volume study of Godwin's life, works, and contexts.

STUART CURRAN, Vartan Gregorian Professor of English at the University of Pennsylvania, has been writing on Mary and Percy Shelley for three decades. His edition of *Valperga: or, The Life and Adventures of Castruccio, Prince of Lucca* was published in 1997, and he is currently completing a hypertext edition of *Frankenstein*, surrounding the two principal texts of the novel with intellectual and literary contexts and criticism. Having edited the poetry of Charlotte Smith (1993), he currently serves as general editor of a forthcoming complete works.

KATE FERGUSON ELLIS is an Associate Professor at Rutgers University in New Brunswick, New Jersey. She is the author of *The Contested Castle: Gothic Novels and the Subversion of Domestic Ideology* (1989) and, more recently, a memoir, *Crossing Borders* (2001). She makes her home in New York City and Nigeria, and is currently working on the next installment of her memoir project.

DIANE LONG HOEVELER is Professor of English and Coordinator of Women's Studies at Marquette University, Wisconsin. She is author of *Romantic Androgyny* (1990) and *Gothic Feminism* (1998); co-author of *Charlotte Brontë* (1997) and *The Historical Dictionary of Feminism* (1996); and co-editor of *Approaches to Teaching Jane Eyre* (1993), *Comparative Romanticisms* (1998), and *Women of Color* (2001). In addition, she has edited *Wuthering Heights* (2001) and is currently editing *Jane Eyre*. Her *Approaches to Teaching Gothic Fiction* will be published in 2003.

GREG KUCICH is Associate Professor of English at the University of Notre Dame, Indiana. His publications include *Keats, Shelley, and Romantic Spenserianism* (1991) and, co-edited with Jeffrey N. Cox, the forthcoming edition of *The Selected Writings of Leigh Hunt*. He is also co-editor of *Nineteenth-Century Contexts: An Interdisciplinary Journal*. He is currently completing a book on Romanticism and women's historiography.

KARI E. LOKKE, Professor of English and Comparative Literature at the University of California, Davis, is the author of *Gérard de Nerval: The Poet as Social Visionary* (1987) and co-editor of *Rebellious Hearts: British Women Writers and the French Revolution* (2001). She is currently completing a book entitled *Romantic Abandon: Gender and Transcendence in Staël, Shelley, Arnim and Sand*. A related essay entitled "'Children of Liberty': Three Women Writers of Romanticism and Idealist Historiography" appeared in *PMLA*, May 2003.

DEIDRE LYNCH teaches in the Department of English at Indiana University. She is the author of *The Economy of Character: Novels, Market Culture, and the Business of Inner Meaning* (1998) and the editor, most recently, of *Janeites: Austen's Disciples and Devotees* (2000). She is currently at work on a cultural history of the love of literature, which bears the tentative title *At Home in English: "Loving" Literature, in the Eighteenth Century and After*.

ANNE K. MELLOR is Professor of English and Women's Studies at the University of California, Los Angeles. She is the author of numerous books and articles in the field of British Romanticism, and has co-edited both an anthology of British literature 1780–1840 and several collections of essays. Her books include *Blake's Human Form Divine* (1974), *English Romantic Irony* (1980), *Mary Shelley: Her Life, Her Fiction, Her Monsters* (1988), *Romanticism and Gender* (1993), and *Mothers of the Nation: Women's Political Writing in England, 1780–1830* (2000; paper, 2002). She is currently working on the intersection of race and gender in British Romantic writing.

TIMOTHY MORTON is Professor of Literature and the Environment at the University of California, Davis. He is the author of four books: *Radicalism in British Literary Culture, 1650–1830* (2002), *The Poetics of Spice* (2000), *Radical Food* (2000), and *Shelley and the Revolution in Taste* (1995). He writes on relationships between food, eating, and literature, and issues in ecology and literature.

JEANNE MOSKAL is Professor of English at the University of North Carolina at Chapel Hill. She authored *Blake, Ethics, and Forgiveness* (1994) and edited Volume VIII, *Travel Writing*, in *The Novels and Selected Works of Mary Shelley* (1996). She is working on four books: *Reading and Teaching Eighteenth- and Nineteenth-Century British Women Writers*, co-edited with Shannon R. Wooden (forthcoming 2004), *Travel, Mariana Starke, and Britain's Two Empires* (forthcoming 2005), a book on British women travel writers of the Napoleonic Wars, and another on British and American women missionaries, 1792–1945.

JUDITH PASCOE teaches at the University of Iowa. She is the author of *Romantic Theatricality: Gender, Poetry, and Spectatorship* (1997) and the editor of *Mary Robinson: Selected Poems* (2000). She is currently at work on a book-length study of Romantic-era collectors.

ESTHER SCHOR, Professor of English at Princeton University, is the author of *Bearing the Dead: The British Culture of Mourning from the Enlightenment to Victoria* (1993) and co-editor of *The Other Mary Shelley: Beyond "Frankenstein"* and *Women's Voices: Visions and Perspectives* (1990). She is now completing a study of nineteenth-century British writers and the Risorgimento and a biography of the American poet, Emma Lazarus. Her most recent publication is a book of poems, *The Hills of Holland* (2002).

CHARLOTTE SUSSMAN is Associate Professor of English at the University of Colorado. She is the author of *Consuming Anxieties: Consumer Protest, Gender and British Slavery, 1713–1833* (2000), as well as articles on Aphra

Behn, Samuel Richardson, Charlotte Smith, and Walter Scott. She is currently researching the cultural impact of demographic theory during the long eighteenth century.

SUSAN J. WOLFSON, Professor of English at Princeton University, is the author of *The Questioning Presence: Wordsworth, Keats, and the Interrogative Mode in Romantic Poetry* (1986) and *Formal Charges: The Shaping of Poetry in British Romanticism* (1998); and editor of *Felicia Hemans: Selected Poems, Letters, and Reception Materials* (2000). She is also on the editorial board of the Longman Anthology of British Literature. She is currently finishing *Figures on the Margin: The Languages of Gender in British Romanticism,* and is at work on *Romantic Conversations: Social Action and the Turns of Literature,* which includes an essay on Mary Shelley's editing of her husband's works.

ACKNOWLEDGMENTS

Great appreciation is due to those who labored to produce modern editions of Mary Shelley's works. This list, which includes several contributors to this volume, comprises: Charles E. Robinson; James Rieger; Betty T. Bennett; Paula Feldman and Diana Scott-Kilvert; Pamela Clemit, Jane Blumberg, Doucet Devin Fischer, Fiona Stafford, and Jeanne Moskal; Stuart Curran; Clarissa Campbell Orr, Tilar Mazzeo, Arnold Markley, and Lisa Vargo. Special thanks go to Nora Crook for her editions of both the *Novels and Selected Works of Mary Shelley* and *Mary Shelley's Literary Lives and Other Writings*; not only for those, but also for help in a pinch with citations. Susan J. Wolfson and Claudia L. Johnson generously shared their expertise as Companion editors for Cambridge University Press; U. C. Knoepflmacher, both in person and in print, has been an invaluable resource. Talking with Denise Gigante and Christopher Rovee about Mary Shelley was both a pleasure and a help, while Aileen Forbes provided excellent research assistance. I could never make enough chicken sandwiches to thank Andrew Krull for his timely aid with the front matter and bibliography. Shanon Lawson's *Mary Wollstonecraft Shelley Chronology & Resource Site* (a Romantic Circles website), was most helpful (http://www.rc.umd.edu/reference/mschronology/mws.html). Thanks of a different kind to Ewa Whitlock for running interference upstairs while I worked downstairs.

I am grateful for support from the Princeton University Department of English, especially Michael Wood, and from the Humanities Research Council of Princeton University. For help capturing images, thanks to Michael Muzzie and Lance Herrington of the New Media Center of Princeton University. The staff of Firestone Library was invaluable.

Linda Bree of Cambridge University Press proved to be the incisive, knowledgeable editor I had always heard she was. I am grateful for her excellent guidance and advice. Thanks also to Rachel De Wachter for her kind and efficient editorial assistance and to Audrey Cotterell and Alison Powell for their help seeing the typescript into print.

Walter Greenblatt brewed the coffee every morning and stayed up with me till all hours of the night. *Sine te non.*

1797: (Aug. 30) Mary Wollstonecraft Godwin born in London, daughter of William Godwin and Mary Wollstonecraft.

(Sept. 10) Wollstonecraft dies of puerperal fever.

1801: (Dec. 21) Godwin remarries, to Mary Jane Clairmont. Mary Godwin is raised in Somers Town (near London); her family household consists of her father, stepmother, half-sister (Fanny Imlay, daughter of Wollstonecraft and Gilbert Imlay), and step-siblings Mary Jane (Claire) Clairmont and Charles Clairmont.

1808: Publishes first story, "Mounseer Nongtongpaw" (M. J. Godwin and Co.).

1812: (June 7) Travels to Dundee to live with the Baxter family until the following spring.

(Nov. 11) Briefly meets Percy Bysshe Shelley (b. Aug. 4, 1792) and his wife, Harriet Westbrook Shelley.

1814: (May) Meets Percy Shelley again; a friendship develops.

(June 28) Elopes with Percy Shelley to the Continent, with Claire Clairmont.

(July–Aug.) Travels in France, Germany, Switzerland, Holland.

(Sept.) They return to England. During the next two months, Percy Shelley resides in London, dodging creditors.

1815: (Feb. 22) Gives birth to her first daughter, who dies March 6.

(Aug.) Moves to Bishopsgate, Windsor.

1816: (Jan. 24) Gives birth to a son, William.

(May) Travels with Percy Shelley and Claire Clairmont, who is pregnant with Byron's child, to Geneva. They live near Byron and Polidori.

(June 16) Begins writing *Frankenstein*.

(July) Visit to Chamonix.

(Sept.) Returns to London, with Percy Shelley and Claire Clairmont in Bath.

(Oct. 9) Fanny Imlay commits suicide.

(Dec. 10) Harriet Shelley's pregnant body is found in the Serpentine, Hyde Park, London; five days later, Percy Shelley is informed about her suicide.

(Dec. 30) Marriage to Percy Shelley in St. Mildred's Church, London.

1817: (Jan. 12) Claire Clairmont gives birth to Alba, later Allegra, Byron.

(Mar.) Percy Shelley loses custody of his children, Charles and Ianthe. Mary Shelley moves to Marlow.

(May 14) Completes *Frankenstein*.

(Sept. 2) Gives birth to a daughter, Clara.

(Nov.) Publishes *History of a Six Weeks' Tour*, a collaboration with Percy Shelley (T. Hookham and C. and J. Ollier).

1818: (Jan. 1) *Frankenstein; or, The Modern Prometheus* published (Lackington, Hughes, Harding, Mavor, & Jones).

(Mar. 11) Family departs for Continent; arrives in Milan April 4.

(June) At Bagni di Lucca.

(Sept. 24) Clara Shelley dies in Venice.

(Nov.–Dec.) Travel to Rome and Naples; they remain in Naples until the following February.

1819: (Mar. 5–June) In Rome, where William Shelley dies of malaria on June 7.

(June 17) Move to Livorno (Leghorn).

(Aug.) Begins writing *Matilda*.

(Oct. 2) Move to Florence.

(Nov. 12) Gives birth to Percy Florence.

1820: (Jan. 26) Move to Pisa.

(Feb.) Finishes *Matilda*.

(Mar.) Begins *Castruccio, Prince of Lucca*; Godwin later renames it *Valperga*.

(Apr.–May) Composes *Proserpine* and *Midas*.

(Oct.) After relocating several times, move to Pisa.

1821: (Aug.–Dec.) Finishes and revises [*Valperga: or,*] *Castruccio*.

1822: (Apr. 19) Allegra Byron dies from typhus.

(June 16) Miscarriage; hemorrhage arrested when Percy Shelley places her in a vat of icy water.

(July 8) Percy Shelley drowns in the Gulf of Spezia.

(Sept.) Moves to Genoa.

1823: (Feb.) Publishes *Valperga* (Henry Colburn and Richard Bentley).

(Apr. 23) "Madame d'Houtetôt" appears in *The Liberal*, 3, 67–83.

(July 29) Opening night of *Presumption, or, The Fate of Frankenstein*, a play by Richard Brinsley Peake; Mary Shelley sees it on August 28.

(July 30) "Giovanni Villani" appears in *The Liberal*, 4, 281–97.

(Aug. 25) With Percy Florence, returns to London.

(Aug.) Second (unrevised) edition of *Frankenstein* appears.

1824: (Mar.) "On Ghosts" appears in *London Magazine*, 9, 253–56.

(Apr. 19) Byron dies at Missolonghi in Greece.

(Spring) Begins *The Last Man*.

(June) Publishes her edition of Percy Shelley's *Posthumous Poems*; enraged, Sir Timothy Shelley threatens to withdraw Percy Florence Shelley's allowance if she again brings Percy Shelley's name before the public.

1825: (June 25) Refuses marriage proposal from American dramatist John Howard Payne.

1826: (Jan. 23) Publishes *The Last Man* (Henry Colburn).

(Oct.) "The English in Italy" appears in *Westminster Review*, 6, 325–41.

(Dec.) "A Visit to Brighton" appears in *London Magazine*, n.s. 6, 460–66.

1827: (June) Agrees to help Thomas Moore with his biography of Byron.

(July) Helps secure passports for friends Isabel Robinson, her illegitimate child, and her partner, "Sholto Douglas" (Mary Diana Dods); the three elope to Paris.

1828: (Jan.) Begins *The Fortunes of Perkin Warbeck*.

(Mar.) Begins writing for the *Keepsake*, to which she will contribute for ten years.

(Apr.) In Paris with Douglases; meets Prosper Mérimée; contracts smallpox.

1829: (Jan.) "Illyrian Poems – Feudal Scenes," review of works by Mérimée, published in *Westminster Review*, 10, 71–81.

1830: (Jan. 18) Moore publishes Volume I of his *Letters and Journals of Lord Byron: With Notices of his Life*.

(May 13) *Perkin Warbeck, A Romance* published (Colburn and Bentley).

(Nov.–Dec.) "Transformation" in the *Keepsake for* MDCCCXXXI (18–39).

1831: (Jan.) Begins *Lodore*. Volume II of Moore's *Byron* published.

(Nov.) Publishes revised third edition of *Frankenstein*, with "Author's Introduction," in Bentley's Standard Novels series (Colburn and Bentley).

1832: (Sept. 8) William Godwin, Jr. (born Mar. 28, 1803, son of William and Mary Jane Clairmont Godwin) dies of cholera.

(Sept. 29) Percy Florence enters Harrow; the following May, Mary Shelley moves there.

1835: (Feb.) Publishes volume I of *Lives of the Most Eminent Literary and Scientific Men of Italy, Spain and Portugal* (Longman).

(Apr.) Publishes *Lodore* (Richard Bentley).

(Oct.) Publishes volume II of *Lives of . . . Men of Italy, Spain and Portugal.*

1836: (Mar. 23) Removes Percy Florence Shelley from Harrow; together, they relocate to Regent's Park, London.

(Apr. 7) William Godwin dies.

1837: (Feb.) Publishes *Falkner, A Novel* (Saunders and Otley)

(Sept.–Oct.) Publishes volume III of *Lives of . . . Men of Italy, Spain and Portugal.*

(Oct. 10) Percy Florence Shelley enters Trinity College, Cambridge.

1838: (Aug.) Publishes volume I of *Lives of the Most Eminent Literary and Scientific Men of France* (Longman). Sir Timothy Shelley relents, allowing publication of his son's poems, but not a biographical memoir. Mary Shelley instead writes extensive notes.

1839: (Jan.–May) Her four-volume edition of Percy Shelley's *Poetical Works* appears, with prefaces and notes (Moxon).

(Aug.) Publishes volume II of *Lives of . . . Men of France.*

(Nov.) One-volume edition of Percy Shelley's *Poetical Works* (Moxon).

(Dec.) Publishes two-volume edition of Percy Shelley's *Essays and Letters from Abroad, Translations and Fragments* (Moxon).

1840: (June 22) Arrives in Paris with her son and his Cambridge friends for continental tour; travel through Germany and Switzerland, summer in Italian lakes; arrive Milan on Sept. 11. Late September, Percy Florence Shelley and friends depart for England; Mary Shelley travels to Paris, where she remains through December.

1841: (Jan.) Returns to London.

(Feb.) Percy Florence Shelley graduates from Cambridge.

(June 17) Death of Mary Jane Godwin.

1842: (June 30–Aug.) With her son and friends, second tour of Continent: Kissingen (baths), Berlin, Dresden, Venice, Florence, Rome, Paris.

(July–Aug.) In Paris; meets Ferdinando Luigi Gatteschi and other Italian exiles.

1844: (Apr. 24) Death of Sir Timothy Shelley; Percy Florence Shelley inherits baronetcy and estate.

(July) Publishes two-volume *Rambles in Germany and Italy in 1840, 1842, and 1843* (Moxon).

1845: (Sept.) Gatteschi threatens to expose her letters to him; blackmail attempt foiled.

1846: (Mar.) "Attack," probably of severe back pain; possibly also chest pain.

1848: (June 22) Percy Florence Shelley marries Jane St. John, a young widow.

(Oct.) Complains of headaches; probably symptoms of a brain tumor. Intermittently ill until her death.

1850: (Dec. 17) Diagnosis of brain tumor.

1851: (Feb. 1) Mary Shelley dies at age fifty-three at home in London.

(Feb. 8) Buried in Bournemouth with her parents, who were exhumed from St. Pancras at Lady Jane Shelley's request.

ABBREVIATIONS

Most citations to Mary Shelley's works appear in the text. For ease of reference, several works available in multiple editions, including the 1818 *Frankenstein*, *The Last Man*, and *Valperga*, are cited by volume, chapter, and page numbers; the 1831 *Frankenstein* is cited by chapter and page numbers. Works in multi-volume, modern editions are cited by volume and page numbers.

CTS: *Mary Shelley: Collected Tales and Stories*, Charles E. Robinson (ed.), Baltimore: Johns Hopkins University Press, 1976.

EF: Knoepflmacher, U. C. and Levine, George (eds.), *The Endurance of "Frankenstein": Essays on Mary Shelley's Novel*, Berkeley: University of California Press, 1979.

EL: [Shelley, Percy Bysshe.] *Essays, Letters from Abroad, Translations and Fragments*, 2 vols., London: Moxon, 1840 [1839].

F [or *F* 1818]: *Frankenstein: The 1818 Text*, J. Paul Hunter (ed.), New York: Norton, 1996.

F 1831: *Frankenstein, or The Modern Prometheus*, Maurice Hindle (ed.), Harmondsworth: Penguin, 1985.

ID: Conger, Syndy M., Frank, Frederick S., and O'Dea, Gregory (eds.), *Iconoclastic Departures: Mary Shelley after Frankenstein: Essays in Honor of the Bicentenary of Mary Shelley's Birth*, Madison, NJ: Fairleigh Dickinson University Press, 1997.

J: *The Journals of Mary Shelley, 1814–44*, Paula R. Feldman and Diana Scott-Kilvert (eds.), 2 vols., Oxford: Oxford University Press, 1987.

KSJ: *Keats–Shelley Journal*.

L: *The Letters of Mary Wollstonecraft Shelley*, Betty T. Bennett (ed.), 3 vols., Baltimore: Johns Hopkins University Press, 1980–83.

LF: *Lives of the Most Eminent Literary and Scientific Men of France*, 2 vols., London: Longman, 1838, 1839.

LISP: *Lives of the Most Eminent Literary and Scientific Men of Italy, Spain and Portugal*, 3 vols., London: Longman, 1835–37.

LL: *Mary Shelley's Literary Lives and Other Writings*, Nora Crook (ed.), 4 vols., London: Pickering and Chatto, 2002.

LM: *The Last Man*, Hugh J. Luke, Jr. (ed.); Anne K. Mellor (intro.), Lincoln: University of Nebraska Press, 1993.

MST: Bennett, Betty T. and Curran, Stuart (eds.), *Mary Shelley in Her Times*, Baltimore: Johns Hopkins University Press, 2000.

NSW: *The Novels and Selected Works of Mary Shelley*, Nora Crook (gen. ed.) with Pamela Clemit, Betty T. Bennett (cons. ed.), 8 vols., London: William Pickering, 1996.

OMS: Fisch, Audrey A., Mellor, Anne K., and Schor, Esther H. (eds.), *The Other Mary Shelley: Beyond Frankenstein*, New York: Oxford University Press, 1993.

PBSL: *The Letters of Percy Bysshe Shelley*, Frederick L. Jones (ed.), 2 vols., Oxford: Oxford University Press, 1964.

PP: *Posthumous Poems of Percy Bysshe Shelley*, ed. Mary W. Shelley, London: John and Henry L. Hunt, 1824.

PW: *Poetical Works of Percy Bysshe Shelley*, 4 vols., ed. Mrs. [Mary] Shelley, London: Moxon, 1839.

PWPBS: *Poetical Works of Percy Bysshe Shelley*, ed. Mrs. [Mary] Shelley, London: Moxon, 1840 [1839].

SiR: *Studies in Romanticism*.

SPP: *Shelley's Poetry and Prose*, Donald H. Reiman and Neil Fraistat (eds.), 2nd edn., New York: Norton, 2002.

V: *Valperga: or, The Life and Adventures of Castruccio, Prince of Lucca*, Stuart Curran (ed.), New York: Oxford University Press, 1997.

ESTHER SCHOR

Introduction

Mary Shelley well knew that books can make good companions. In the Preface to *Rambles in Germany and Italy in 1840, 1842, and 1843*, she writes: "I have found it a pleasant thing while travelling to have in the carriage the works of those who have passed through the same country . . . If alone, they serve as society; if with others, they suggest matter for conversation" (*NSW* VIII 65). With this "if," Shelley gives us two images of her life: first, a lonely, widowed life of reading and writing, isolation and anxiety; and second, a convivial life of adventurous friendship. It was Shelley's way to live both lives at once. In Italy, in the tight embrace of the Shelley circle, she withdrew after losing two children to the vagaries of an itinerant, expatriate life. Soon her dejection was compounded by marital estrangement and by 1822, she was left a widow. After she returned to England in 1823, however, her long widowhood was punctuated by enduring friendships, a proposal of marriage, nights at the theatre and opera, endless correspondence with editors and publishers, and two continental journeys taken with her beloved son and his Cambridge friends. In one of the great ironies of the era, the daughter of Mary Wollstonecraft and William Godwin, two visionaries of social renovation, invented in *Frankenstein* the loneliest character in the English novel. But this is no more ironic, perhaps, than that Shelley conceived her great novel of loneliness in a writer's game, among the flamboyant companions of her youth.

According to a study of the early 1990s,[1] more than half of all students of Romanticism read *Frankenstein*; since then, the novel has also become a staple in courses as different as "The Gothic," "The Nineteenth-Century Novel," "Women's Literature," and "The Post-Human." Both of the leading undergraduate anthologies – Norton and Longman's – offer *Frankenstein* either between their covers or in a package deal. The momentum generated by critical interest in *Frankenstein* has finally propelled several of Shelley's other novels into affordable paperback editions, among them, *Valperga, The Last Man* (both in multiple editions), *Lodore,* and *Matilda;* paperbacks of

Betty T. Bennett and Charles E. Robinson's *Mary Shelley Reader* as well as Robinson's *Collected Tales and Stories* are at our fingertips. In our research libraries are the eight hefty volumes of Nora Crook, Pamela Clemit, and Bennett's edition of the *Novels and Selected Works of Mary Shelley*, as are the four volumes of Crook's edition of *Mary Shelley's Literary Lives and Other Writings*. Now, it seems, Mary Shelley is writing for the screen; on the Internet Movie Database (http://www.imdb.com), she receives a writing credit on some forty-four films which, as I argue in chapter 4, hardly reflects the influence of *Frankenstein* on cinema. Shelley Jackson's *Frankenstein*-pastiche, *Patchwork Girl*, is widely considered the first hypertext "classic." Today, whether she is found between staid cloth covers, in paperback, on the screen or in cyberspace, Mary Shelley is everywhere, and clearly the time is right for her to have a Cambridge Companion.

For most students, Mary Shelley is either represented by a single work or read in relation to Percy Bysshe Shelley, Byron, and the so-called Satanic school of British Romanticism. These essays, however, read Mary Shelley on her own account as a figure who survived all manner of upheaval, personal, political, and professional, to produce an oeuvre of bracing intelligence and wide cultural sweep. Having written the century's most blistering critique of Romantic egotism in *Frankenstein*, she unsettles familiar literary-historical periods. Her career, along with those of L.E.L. (Letitia Elizabeth Landon) and Felicia Hemans, demands that we pause over the critically neglected 1820s and 1830s as a distinct period; these writers, rather than moving ever more surely toward psychological realism, the hallmark of the Victorian novel, take the novel and the lyric to sensational and extreme destinies. Also like Landon and Hemans, Shelley refused to isolate Britain from the Continent; she shares with them a distinctive worldliness that informs their writing long after the end of the Revolutionary-Napoleonic period. Thus, this book places her achievement in a multiplicity of contexts: the Enlightenment novel of ideas; British Jacobinism; Romantic lyricism; Scott and the historical novel; Romantic and early Victorian women writers; and the nineteenth-century struggle between national movements and imperial powers.

The sixteen chapters in the *Cambridge Companion to Mary Shelley* are divided into three parts. Part I, "The author of *Frankenstein*," brings readers face to face with the novel *Frankenstein* as well as its "hideous progeny" in literary theory, film, and popular culture. In chapter 1, "Making a 'monster': an introduction to *Frankenstein*," Anne K. Mellor offers a feminist orientation to the novel, its complex narrative structure, and its textual history. Mellor concludes by looking closely at Mary Shelley's informed critique of the cutting-edge science of her day. Next, in "*Frankenstein, Matilda*, and the legacies of Godwin and Wollstonecraft," Pamela Clemit examines Shelley's conflicted attitudes toward the intellectual inheritance of her illustrious parents. In both *Frankenstein* and *Matilda*, a novella about father–daughter incest, Clemit finds the power and passion of revolutionary idealism even as these forces wreak havoc on the lives of Shelley's characters.

The legacy of *Frankenstein* in the nineteenth century is still debated. As William St. Clair points out, the stage adaptations had a far wider influence than the novel: "Every single night one of the Frankenstein plays was performed, it brought a version of the story to more men and women than the book had in ten or twenty years."[2] And the melodramatic versions encountered in theatres typically honed the story on a sharply moral blade. Thus popularized, as St. Clair argues, the myth of Frankenstein became a conservative caricature of a progressive novel, an alarmist cliché. On the other hand, Chris Baldick's important book, *In Frankenstein's Shadow: Myth, Monstrosity, and Nineteenth-Century Writing*, argues that in numerous literary works of the Victorian period, the Frankenstein myth "turns repeatedly upon these new problems of an age in which humanity seizes responsibility for re-creating the world, for violently reshaping its natural environment and its inherited social and political forms, for remaking itself."[3] In the twentieth century, the Frankenstein myth has been just as malleable, alternately a monitory fable, an allegory of alienation, an ontology of "the other." Chapters 3 through 5 take up the fate of *Frankenstein* in the twentieth century and beyond. First, Diane Long Hoeveler traces the deep impact of *Frankenstein* on feminism and literary and cultural studies, surveying the literature on *Frankenstein* from Ellen Moers's landmark essay in *Literary Women* (1976) to recent invocations of the novel in disability studies, queer theory, and cultural studies. "*Frankenstein* and film," chapter 4, asks what cinema may have to show us about Shelley's Creature – in particular, the expressionist animation sequences of James Whale's *Frankenstein* and *Bride of Frankenstein*. This chapter then considers three films that demote the animation sequence in order to show us a decidedly different face of the "monster." Next, Jay Clayton's "*Frankenstein's* futurity: replicants and robots" takes stock of recent allusions to the Frankenstein myth in treatments of robots, cyborgs, and replicants. In readings of Ridley Scott's *Blade Runner*, Shelley Jackson's hypertext *Patchwork Girl*, and Steven Spielberg's *AI: Artificial Intelligence*, Clayton notes that these writings are far less monitory than earlier twentieth-century uses of the myth.

Part 2, "Fictions and myths," connects "The author of *Frankenstein*" with her subsequent fiction, some of it equally bold, heterodox, and experimental. In his essay on Shelley's *Valperga*, Stuart Curran examines Shelley's counterpoint between the "public" and "private" histories of her two protagonists: the historical Castruccio Castracani and Euthanasia, the fictional Countess of Valperga. Although Euthanasia's democratic, feminist alternative falls to Castruccio's cruel ambition, Curran conveys the "radical force" with which *Valperga* confronted its contemporary reviewers. In Shelley's next novel, *The Last Man*, she undertakes an even broader survey of political systems, from imperialism to republicanism, theocracy to anarchy. In chapter 7, Kari E. Lokke finds this novel balancing a sweeping social criticism with a pessimistic view of the human psyche. Pessimistic; but not nihilistic, for Lokke claims that the novel ultimately affirms the redemptive capacities of art. Shelley's historicism again becomes the focus in chapter 8 on *The Fortunes of Perkin Warbeck; A Romance*. Deidre Lynch argues that Shelley eschews Scott's "vision of national history as a smooth synthesis of differences"; moreover, Perkin, as a pretender to the English throne, becomes a crux through which Shelley asks what "counts" as history. In chapter 9, Kate Ferguson Ellis considers Shelley's high claims for her last novel, *Falkner*. Ellis argues that Shelley at last delivers a female character who, unlike the heroines of *Lodore* and *Matilda*, manages to derail the agendas of dominant men, placing in their stead an ideal of "feminine fosterage." Writing on Shelley's contributions to the gift-book annuals in chapter 10, Charlotte Sussman finds a "gendered intersection of the human form and the commodity form," in which wasting women become the grim sign of their attenuated value in the marriage market. As Judith Pascoe argues in chapter 11, transformation and loss are also central themes of Shelley's two mythological plays, *Proserpine* and *Midas*. Pascoe reads them not as closet drama, but as works that "approach the stage," showing us how Shelley, like the playwright Joanna Baillie, uses the resources of theatre to probe the inner lives of her characters.

Part 3, "Professional personae," surveys Shelley's impressive career as a professional writer. In chapter 12, Susan J. Wolfson tells us how Mary Shelley as editor constructed, "[b]y fragments and wholes . . . 'Percy Bysshe Shelley.'" While Sir Timothy Shelley sought to efface his son's name from the public domain, Mary Shelley's several editions indelibly reinscribed it, shaping the poet's reception – and her own, as the poet's best reader – for decades. Next, Betty T. Bennett, editor of the three-volume *Letters of Mary Wollstonecraft Shelley*, claims that Shelley used the letter genre "not only to bridge public and private concerns, but to link them in bold, original ways." In chapter 13, Bennett shows how gleanings from Shelley's letters become charged symbols in her later publications. Public and private meet also in Shelley's six volumes of biographical essays, originally written for Dionysius Lardner's *Cabinet Encyclopaedia*. Greg Kucich, in chapter 14, shows how Shelley, along with several other women biographers and historians of her era, "escalat[ed] . . . sentimental and private elements into the center of historical consciousness." While Kucich and other contributors assess the implicit politics of Shelley's writings, Jeanne Moskal's chapter on the travel writing shows how the explicit liberal ideals of her *History of a Six Weeks' Tour* (a youthful collaboration with Percy Bysshe Shelley) are sustained more than thirty-five years later in *Rambles in Germany and Italy in 1840, 1842 and 1843*, albeit in the narrower sphere of Italian nationalism. Finally, Timothy Morton gives us Mary Shelley not only as a novelist, essayist, and reviewer, but also as a sophisticated theorist of culture. In a fresh view of Shelley's achievement, Morton finds her imagining a neutral space for the discourse of culture, one free of both the incursions of egotism and those of prejudice.

Since controversies continue to swirl around Mary Shelley's oeuvre, they swirl, too, among these essays. We find varied responses to the following questions: What are the limits of Shelley's liberalism? Of her feminism? How can she be alternately a proponent of the incursive ego and its most ferocious critic? Is she a social visionary, like her parents, or a bitter satirist, for whom humanity is incapable of rising above its own imperial drive for power? Why is it so difficult, finally, to capture *Frankenstein*'s philosophical orientation? Is it moral? ethical? epistemological? political? Why, having written *Matilda*, did she refuse to write about the incestuous Cenci? How do we account for the mixed mode of her novels, so acutely attuned to the realpolitik of post-Napoleonic Europe, but so deeply claimed by romance? And why, if Shelley's skeptical historicism is so trenchant, so consistent from novel to novel, life to life, is she still best known as a Gothic sensationalist?

Finally, how will posterity encounter her? In the children's section of my local public library are two biographies of Mary Shelley. The first, *Shelley's Mary* by Margaret Leighton, dates itself; though published in the heyday of women's liberation, 1973, here "Mary" remains in every sense *Shelley's*. Indeed, Percy Bysshe Shelley drowns on page 189, and Mary Shelley lasts only another thirty-odd pages to nurse his surviving poems. On the jacket, a demure young woman with sausage curls, posing sideways, gazes off to our right, clutching a nameless tome with long, graceful fingers. *My book*, she seems to say through clenched teeth; *mine*. The alluring young woman portrayed on the cover of Joan Kane Nichol's recent biography, at first glance, appears strikingly similar: we see the same regency neckline, the curls, the sideways pose. Only now it is 1998 and she looks us square in the eye; she has the pouty, pink mouth of a teen gymnast and sports blue eye-shadow. Apparently we have interrupted her, for, with a flourish of a feather pen, she has just committed a single word to a vellum page: *Frankenstein*. Even so, the book's title – *Mary Shelley, Frankenstein's Creator* – has her once again possessed, once again *his*.

All of us who write about Mary Shelley have sought to free her from possession, both by her poet-husband and by her "hideous progeny," along with its ghoulish spawn of images. Yet in wanting to give her back to the public and on to posterity, we risk possessing her anew. Whether taken up for feminist politics and theory, for liberalism, for alarmism about reproductive technology, or to champion the post-human, Mary Shelley is finally not ours, to speak and write for us; not ours to hand down to those who follow. Now that virtually all her published works are widely available, Mary Shelley can at last speak for herself. This is a good thing for us, her readers, or any companion, to bear in mind.[4]

NOTES

1 Harriet Kramer Linkin, "The Current Canon in British Romantics Studies," *College English* 53.5 (1991), 548–70.
2 William St. Clair, *MST* 52.
3 Chris Baldick, *In Frankenstein's Shadow: Myth, Monstrosity, and Nineteenth-Century Writing* (Oxford: Oxford University Press, 1987), p. 5.
4 A recent discovery suggests that we may have more to learn; a fragment from the mid-1840s thought to be Shelley's own fiction has been identified by Nora Crook as Shelley's translation of a portion of *Cecil*, a novel by Ida von Hahn-Hahn, known in her day as the "German George Sand." Not only was Shelley's German better than she claimed, but she found Hahn-Hahn's themes – "surrogate parenting, female education, maternal attachment" – to resonate with those of her own novels of the 1830s, *Lodore* and *Falkner*. See Nora Crook, "Germanizing in Chester Square: Mary Shelley, *Cecil*, and Ida von Hahn-Hahn," *TLS*, June 6, 2003, p. 14.

I

"THE AUTHOR OF
FRANKENSTEIN"

I

ANNE K. MELLOR

Making a "monster": an introduction to *Frankenstein*

Mary Shelley's waking nightmare on June 16, 1816, gave birth to one of the most powerful horror stories of Western civilization. *Frankenstein* can claim the status of a myth so profoundly resonant in its implications that it has become, at least in its barest outline, a trope of everyday life. The condemners of genetically modified meats and vegetables now refer to them as "Frankenfoods," and the debates concerning the morality of cloning or stem cell engineering constantly invoke the cautionary example of Frankenstein's monster. Nor is the monster-myth cited only in regard to the biological sciences; critics of nuclear, chemical, and biological weapons alike often make use of this monitory figure. Of course, both the media and the average person in the street have frequently and mistakenly assigned the name of Frankenstein not to the maker of the monster but to his creature. But as we shall see, this "mistake" actually derives from a crucial intuition about the relationship between them. *Frankenstein* is our culture's most penetrating literary analysis of the psychology of modern "scientific" man, of the dangers inherent in scientific research, and of the horrifying but predictable consequences of an uncontrolled technological exploitation of nature and the female.

Let us begin, then, with the question of origins: why did the eighteen-year-old Mary Shelley give birth to this particular idea on this particular night? How did it come about that she produced so prescient, powerful, and enduring a myth? In attempting to answer these questions, we must also take into account the various ways in which Mary Shelley responded to the philosophical ideas and literary influences of her mother, Mary Wollstonecraft, and her father, William Godwin; these particular influences are taken up at length in the following chapter. But as we shall see, in *Frankenstein*, Shelley also turns a skeptical eye on the Enlightenment celebration of science and technology and, no less critically, on her husband, the Romantic poet Percy Bysshe Shelley, and their friend, Lord Byron.

Origins of the text

From the feminist perspective which has dominated discussions of *Franken-stein* in the last decade (see chapter 3), this is first and foremost a book about what happens when a man tries to procreate without a woman. As such, the novel is profoundly concerned with natural as opposed to un-natural modes of production and reproduction. In Shelley's introduction to the revised 1831 edition, she tells a story, of how she, Percy Bysshe Shelley, Byron, and Byron's doctor, William Polidori, after reading ghost stories to-gether one rainy evening near Geneva in June, 1816, agreed each to write a thrilling horror story; how she tried for days to think of a story, but failed; and finally, how on June 15, after hearing Byron and her husband discussing experiments concerning "the principle of life," she fell into a waking dream in which she saw "the pale student of unhallowed arts kneeling beside the thing he had put together" (*F* 1831, Intro. 55). In this reverie, she felt the terror *he* felt as the hideous corpse he had reanimated with a "spark of life" stood beside his bed, "looking on him with yellow, watery, but speculative eyes" (*F* 1831, Intro. 55).

As critic Ellen Moers pointed out in her classic essay on *Frankenstein* (1974),[1] only eighteen months earlier, Mary Shelley had given birth for the first time to a baby girl, a baby whose death two weeks later produced a recurring dream that she recorded in her journal: "Dream that my little baby came to life again – that it had only been cold & that we rubbed it by the fire & it lived – I awake & find no baby" (*J* 70). Six months before, on January 24, 1816, her second child, William, was born. She doubtless expected to be pregnant again in the near future, and indeed, she conceived her third child, Clara Everina, only six months later in December. Mary Shelley's reverie unleashed her deepest subconscious anxieties, the natural fears of a very young woman embarking on the processes of pregnancy, giving birth, and mothering. As many such newly pregnant women have asked, What if my child is born deformed, in Shelley's phrase, a "hideous" thing? Could I still love it, or would I wish it had never been born? What will happen if I cannot love it? Am I capable of raising a healthy, normal child? One reason Shelley's novel reverberates so strongly with its readers, especially its female readers, is that it articulates in unprecedented detail the most powerfully felt anxieties about pregnancy and parenting.

Mary Shelley's dream thus gives rise to a central theme of the novel: Victor Frankenstein's total failure as a parent. The moment his child is "born," Frankenstein rejects him in disgust, fleeing from his smiling embrace, and completely abandoning him. Victor's horror is caused both by his crea-ture's appearance – his yellow skin which "scarcely covered the work of muscles and arteries underneath," his "shrivelled complexion, and straight black lips" (*F* I iv 34)[2] and by his tremendous size. For in an effort to simplify the process of creation, Frankenstein has chosen to work with larger-than-normal human and animal body parts, constructing a being who is of "gigantic stature, that is to say, about eight feet in height" (at a time when the average male was only 5'6" tall) and "proportionably large" (*F* I iv 32). Never once has Frankenstein asked himself whether such a gigantic creature would wish to be created, or what his own responsibilities toward such a creature might be.

Mary Shelley's novel relentlessly tracks the consequences of such parental abandonment: Victor's unloved "child," after desperately seeking a home and family with the De Laceys and, later, with a mate, is rejected on both counts; Felix de Lacey flees in terror and Frankenstein cruelly reneges on his promise to create an Eve for this Adam. In time, the creature turns to violence and revenge, killing not only Victor's brother William but also his bride Elizabeth and his best friend Clerval. Here Shelley presciently reveals a now-familiar paradigm: the abused child who becomes an abusive, battering adult and parent; note that the creature's first victim, William Frankenstein, is a child that he had hoped to adopt as his own. That Shelley modeled this child both in name and appearance on her own son William suggests even deeper anxieties about herself as a mother.

"My hideous progeny"

Mary Shelley's anxiety surrounding birth and parenting also resonates in her representations of her own literary authority. In the 1831 Introduction, she refers to *Frankenstein* as her "hideous progeny" (*F* 1831, Intro. 56). This metaphor of book as baby suggests Shelley's anxieties about giving birth to her self-as-author. But Shelley's anxiety about her authorship did not derive from what Sandra Gilbert and Susan Gubar have famously called a female "anxiety of authorship," the fear of speaking in public in a literary culture that systematically denigrated women's writing.[3] Rather, her anxiety was produced by both Godwin's and Percy Shelley's expectation that she would become a writer like her mother. Alone among the participants in the ghost-story writing contest, she felt a compulsion to perform, but at the same time, as she later recalled, "that blank incapability of invention which is the greatest misery of authorship, when dull Nothing replies to our anxious invocations" (*F* 1831, Intro. 54); apparently, she feared the trauma of barrenness as much as the trauma of birth. As Barbara Johnson has trenchantly observed, *Frankenstein* is "the story of the experience of writing *Frankenstein*."[4] And since the book represents her authorial self, Mary Shelley dedicated it to her father, William Godwin, even though he had disowned her after her elopement with the already-married Percy Shelley.

Accordingly, the events of the novel mirror the dates of Mary Shelley's own conception and birth. *Frankenstein* is narrated in a series of letters written by the sea-captain Robert Walton to his sister, Margaret Walton Saville (whose initials, M. W. S., are those Mary Wollstonecraft Godwin coveted and gained when she married the widowed Percy Shelley on December 30, 1816). The novel's first letter is dated December 11, 17–; the last, September 12, 17–. Exactly nine months enwomb the telling of the history of Frankenstein; moreover, these nine months correspond almost exactly with Mary Shelley's third pregnancy, for Clara Everina was born on September 2, 1817. Based on the internal calendar in the novel and on manuscript evidence garnered by Charles E. Robinson,[5] we can reliably date Walton's letters to December 1796 – September 1797; Mary Shelley was born on August 30, 1797, and her mother died on September 10, 1797, two days before Walton's final epistle. Thus, Victor Frankenstein's death, the creature's promised suicide, and Wollstonecraft's death from puerperal fever can all be seen as the consequences of the same creation, the birth of Mary Godwin-the-author.

Our focus on birth, reproduction, and authority, raises a provocative question: if Victor Frankenstein's ambition is to "give birth" asexually, what is the fate of sexual desire in this novel? One possible answer – that it is repressed – aligns *Frankenstein* with the genre of the Gothic novel. As David Punter has shrewdly observed, the Gothic novel deals centrally with paranoia, the taboo, and the barbaric, with everything that a given culture most fears and tries hardest to repress.[6] The male-authored masterpieces of the genre – Horace Walpole's *The Castle of Otranto* (1765), William Beckford's *Vathek* (1786 [English edn.]), Matthew Lewis's *The Monk* (1796), Charles Robert Maturin's *Melmoth the Wanderer* (1820), and Bram Stoker's *Dracula* (1897), all written by avowed homosexuals or bisexuals – uncover the damage caused by compulsory heterosexuality. By contrast, the female-authored Gothic novel, most notably in the works of Ann Radcliffe, Charlotte Dacre, Sophia Lee, and Emily Brontë, explores the cultural repression of all female sexual desire in the name of the chaste, modest, proper lady – a lady confined within a patriarchal bourgeois domesticity and often menaced by a looming threat of incest. Mary Shelley's novel diverges in at least two respects from the Gothic genre: first, her central protagonist is not a woman; second, she eschews the simple assignment of villainy to a malicious (usually Catholic) male figure. Indeed, as we shall see, the novel revolves around a penchant for violence shared between creator and creature. But in *Frankenstein*, we do find that hallmark of the Gothic – the denial of all overt sexuality – as well as a recurring hint of incest. Walton is alone, writing to his beloved . . . sister;

Victor Frankenstein regards his bride-to-be as his cousin/sister; Victor's mother marries her father's best friend, to whom she becomes a devoted and dutiful daughter/wife; even the lovers Felix and Safie meet only in a public, chaste space. But when Elizabeth Lavenza Frankenstein meets her death on her wedding night, the repressed erotic desires in the novel erupt in violence. Indeed, Victor Frankenstein's close, emotional relationships with males – with Walton, the creature, and Clerval – dominate the novel.

It may be that these charged homosocial relationships are meant to suggest the perversity of denying female sexuality. Indeed, Victor's ambition to create a literally larger and more beautiful male "object of affection"[7] has been read as a displacement of his repressed homoerotic attraction to the handsome Henry Clerval. The passion and admiration with which Walton regards Victor further extends this homosocial theme to the frame narrative. But the case of Victor Frankenstein, whose main partner is *his own creation*, suggests rather that Mary Shelley offers here a bleak parody of Romantic love, theorized by Percy Shelley as a triumph of the visionary imagination. Specifically, she takes issue with Percy Shelley's notion (later articulated in the fragment "On Love") that the lover imagines an idealized form of himself, then sets out to find its "antitype" in the world. That such a strategy pits women against a masculine ideal that is sublimely egotistical is only part of Mary Shelley's point. For she also suggests that the lover's idealizations represent a deep-seated fear of female sexual desire. Perhaps the most striking example of this fear lies in Frankenstein's brutal destruction of the female creature, a potential sexual partner for the creature. After surmising that the female creature might have a will of her own, Frankenstein, "[T]rembling with passion, tore to pieces the thing on which I was engaged . . . I almost felt as if I had mangled the living flesh of a human being" (*F* II iii 115, 118). Though this violent scene suggests rape, Frankenstein's strange identification with the female creature has curious consequences. For as he sets sail to drown the female's mangled body parts, he too feels torn apart, sea-sick, and nearly drowns. Only by imagining the subjectivity of the female creature does Frankenstein intuit that the original creature is an image of his own desires. For Frankenstein, this knowledge is very nearly fatal.

Like Frankenstein, Walton, too, is driven far afield by heady Romantic ideals of fame and fortune. Certainly Walton's desire to conquer nature, to tread where no man has gone before, and to tear open a Northeast Passage through the Polar ice to China, is cognate with Frankenstein's Promethean attempt to steal the principle of life from nature. But unlike Victor, Walton remains answerable to a feminine presence, his sister, and is finally persuaded by his crew to give up his egotistical quest and return to domesticated civility (Margaret Saville). It may well be that Shelley's elaborate narrative structure is a defensive gesture, building a series of concentric screens that obscure her originating voice. But one important effect of this structure is to slow down the narrative, allowing time for extended meditations by both the creature and Frankenstein on the nature of morality, the responsibilities of God and parents, and the very principle of life itself. By using three male narrators, Mary Shelley explores in minute detail the outsized, inhuman Romantic ambitions shared by Frankenstein and Walton, and scrutinizes their effects on the creature at the novel's core.[8]

The texts of *Frankenstein*

If Shelley's frame narrative is a self-censoring gesture, a similar gesture occurred when she gave the manuscript of *Frankenstein* to her husband to edit. Percy Shelley made numerous revisions and corrections to his wife's manuscript, which has recently been analyzed in detail and published both with and without Percy's emendations by Charles E. Robinson.[9] Percy Shelley's editorial revisions often improved the novel by correcting misspellings, using more precise technical terms, and clarifying the narrative and thematic continuity of the text, but on several occasions he misunderstood his wife's intentions and distorted her ideas. I have discussed these revisions at length elsewhere;[10] here let me briefly summarize my findings. By far the greatest number of Percy Shelley's revisions attempt to elevate his wife's prose style into a more Latinate idiom. He typically changed her simple Anglo-Saxon diction and straightforward or colloquial sentence structures into their more complex and stylistically heightened equivalents. He is thus largely responsible for the stilted, ornate, putatively Ciceronian prose style about which so many readers have complained. Her own voice tended to utter a sentimental, rather abstract, and generalized rhetoric, but typically energized this with a brisk stylistic rhythm. Here is Mary Shelley on Frankenstein's fascination with supernatural phenomena:

> Nor were these my only visions, the raising of ghosts or devils was also a favorite pursuit and if I never saw any attributed it rather to my own inexperience and mistake, than want of skill in my instructors.   (*F Notebooks* I 23)

And here is Percy Shelley's revision:

> Nor were these my only visions. The raising of ghosts or devils was a promise liberally accorded by my favourite authors; the fulfillment of which I most eagerly sought; & if my incantations were always unsuccessful, attributed the failure rather to my own inexperience and mistake, than to a want of skill or fidelity in my instructors.   (*F* I i 22)

Percy Shelley consistently preferred more learned, polysyllabic terms, as the following lists indicate:

Mary Shelley's manuscript	Percy Shelley's revision
have	possess
wish	desire, purpose
cause	derive their origin from
place	station
time	period
felt	endured
hope	confidence
stay	remain
we were all equal	neither of us possessed the slightest pre-eminence over the other
do not wish to hate you	will not be tempted to set myself in opposition to thee
what to say	what manner to commence the interview

Perhaps more important, Percy Shelley on several occasions distorted the meaning of his wife's text. He tended to see the creature as more monstrous and less human, changing her word "wretch" to "devil" (*F* III vii 141, line 17) and introducing the description of the creature as "an abortion" (*F* III vii 155, line 6). Conversely, Percy Shelley tended to see Victor Frankenstein more positively than did Mary Shelley. When Frankenstein fails to remain in contact with Elizabeth during his scientific researches at the University of Ingolstadt, Mary Shelley presents his self-justification in these terms: "I wished, as it were, to procrastinate my feelings of affection, untill the great object of my affection was compleated" (*F Notebooks* 91). Percy Shelley, anxious to avoid the repetition of the word "affection," revised this: "I wished, as it were, to procrastinate all that related to my feelings of affections until the great object which swallowed up every habit of my nature should be compleated" (*F* I iii 33). Percy Shelley here underestimated his wife's rhetorical subtlety, for her wording alerts us to the fact that Frankenstein is more sexually attracted to his male creature than he is to his fiancée. Furthermore, in a fine piece of dramatic irony, she anticipates Frankenstein's failure to feel any affection whatsoever for his newborn, living creature.

Most important, Percy Shelley changed the last line of the novel in a way that potentially alters its meaning. Here is Mary Shelley's version of Walton's final view of the creature: "He sprung from the cabin windows as he said this on to an ice raft that lay close to the vessel & pushing him self off he was carried away by the waves and I soon lost sight of him in the darkness &

distance" (*F Notebooks* II 817). Percy Shelley changed this to: "He sprung from the cabin-window, as he said this, upon an ice-raft which lay close to the vessel; he was soon borne away by the waves, & lost in the darkness of distance" (*F* III vii 156). Mary Shelley's version, by suggesting that Walton has only "lost sight of" the creature, preserves the possibility that the creature may still be alive, a threatening reminder of the danger released when men presume to transgress the laws of nature. Percy Shelley's revision, by rendering the creature passive ("borne away" instead of her more assertive "pushing himself away") and by flatly asserting that the creature is "lost in the darkness of distance," provides a comforting reassurance to the reader that the creature is now powerless and completely gone. Beyond accepting Percy Shelley's stylistic changes, particularly of the novel's final sentences, Mary Shelley also allowed him to write the Preface, in which he misleadingly defined the novel's chief concern as "the exhibition of the amiableness of domestic affection, and the excellence of universal virtue" (*F* Preface 6). Why did she do this? Mary looked upon Percy, five years older and already a published novelist and poet, as a literary mentor, who was well qualified to edit and improve her writing. That he felt "authorised to amend" her text (*PBSL* I 553), suggests that he concurred.

In 1831, when Mary Shelley revised *Frankenstein* for republication in Colburn and Bentley's Standard Novel Series, she rewrote it into a significantly different text. Since the first edition is far closer to her originating dream-inspiration, biographical experiences, and early political and philosophical convictions, it has become the text of choice in the classroom and in this *Companion*. Still, we should recognize the important ways in which the 1831 text differs from that of 1818.

By 1831, Mary Shelley had endured countless losses: the deaths of Percy Shelley, of three of her four children, and of Byron; and the betrayal of her closest friends Jane Williams and Thomas Jefferson Hogg, who condemned her for having been an unloving wife. Her journals of the 1820s repeatedly record episodes of depression. She had become convinced that human events are decided not by personal choice or free will but by material forces beyond the control of human agency. As she confessed to Jane Williams Hogg in August, 1827: "The power of Destiny I feel every day pressing more & more on me, & I yield myself a slave to it, in all except my moods of mind" (*L* I 572). Into the 1831 *Frankenstein*, Mary Shelley introduced the powerful influence of what she called "Destiny." In the 1818 text, Frankenstein's free will, his capacity for meaningful moral choice, is paramount: he *could* have abandoned his quest for the "principle of life," *could* have cared for his creature, *could* have protected Elizabeth. But in the fatalistic and surprisingly unChristian vision of the 1831 edition, such moral choices are denied to him.

His decision to study chemistry is now attributed to "Chance – or rather the evil influence, the Angel of Destruction, which asserted omnipotent sway over me" (*F* 1831, iii 94). The deaths of both William Frankenstein and Justine are now represented by Victor as a curse imposed by "inexorable fate" (*F* 1831, viii 135). Not only Victor but also Elizabeth and Justine now attribute their fates to "immutable laws" (*F* 1831, vi 113) or an omnipotent "will" to which mankind must "learn . . . to submit in patience" (*F* 1831, viii 134).

In the 1831 text, Mary Shelley replaces her earlier conception of nature as organic, benevolent, and maternal with a mechanistic view of nature as a mighty juggernaut, impelled by unconscious, amoral force. Since fate or an "imperial Nature" (*F* 1831, x 142) now controls human lives, Victor Frankenstein is decidedly less responsible for his actions; in the best light, he seems almost a tragic hero suffering for an understandable hubris.[11] At the same time, Walton and Clerval, his alter-egos in the novel, are portrayed in ways that reflect more positively on Victor; Walton is more remorseful, while Clerval is no longer a moral touchstone against whom we measure Victor's failures, but rather an equally ambitious colonial imperialist, eager to work for the East India Company (*F* 1831, vi 116, xix 203).[12]

Crucially, Mary Shelley now undercuts the positive ideal of a loving, egalitarian family, embodied in the De Laceys, which had undergirded the 1818 edition of *Frankenstein*. There she had suggested that if the creature had been mothered by his maker; if he had been accepted into the loving De Lacey family unit, as Safie had been; or if he had been given a female mate and thus enabled to begin his own family, then he might indeed have become the perfected man of whom Victor dreamed. But in the 1831 edition, Shelley portrays the bourgeois family far more negatively, as the site where women are oppressed, silenced, even sacrificed, and racial prejudices are formed.[13] Emblematically, even Ernest Frankenstein, who in 1818 desired to become a farmer, now imagines himself living a soldier's life (*F* 1831 vi 112).

A feminist critique of science

Mary Shelley based her myth of the scientist who creates a monster he cannot control upon an extensive understanding of the cutting-edge science of her day. Said to initiate the genre of science fiction, *Frankenstein* is a thought-experiment based directly on the work of three scientists: Humphry Davy, the first President of the Royal Society of Science; Erasmus Darwin, author of *The Botanic Garden, or, Loves of the Plants* (1789, 1791); and Luigi Galvani (and his nephew/assistant). From Davy's pamphlet *A Discourse, Introductory to a Course of Lectures on Chemistry* (1802) (which Shelley read in October 1816), and his textbook, *Elements of Chemical Philosophy* (1812), she derived her portrait of Professor Waldman, her use of chemical terminology, and most important, Victor's belief that the "master" chemist is one who attempts, in Davy's words: "to modify and change the beings surrounding him, and by his experiments to interrogate nature with power, not simply as a scholar, passive and seeking only to understand her operations, but rather as a master, active with his own instruments."[14] From Erasmus Darwin, who first theorized the process of botanical and biological evolution through sexual selection, Mary Shelley derived her belief that a good scientist attempts, not to alter the workings of nature, but rather to observe her processes closely in order to understand her. Bearing in mind Darwin's theory that dual-sex propagation is more highly evolved than asexual reproduction, we see the pitfalls of Frankenstein's science. Not only is he a bad scientist for tampering with nature, but he also moves *down* rather than *up* the evolutionary ladder, suturing his creature from both human and animal body parts (he obtains his materials from cemeteries and charnel-houses, from "the dissecting room and the slaughter-house" [*F* 1 iii 32]). Moreover, Frankenstein tries to create a "new species" rather than allowing one to evolve randomly through sexual selection.

From the work of Luigi Galvani, the Italian scientist who attempted to prove that electricity was the life force by reanimating dead frogs with electrical charges, Mary Shelley derived Victor Frankenstein's experiment. In December, 1802, in London, Galvani's nephew Giovanni Aldini attempted to restore to life a recently hanged criminal named Thomas Forster. When volatile alkali was smeared on Forster's nostrils and mouth before the Galvanic electrical stimulus was applied, Aldini reported, "the convulsions appeared to be much increased . . . and extended from the muscles of the head, face, and neck, as far as the deltoid. The effect in this case surpassed our most sanguine expectations," Aldini exulted, concluding that "vitality might, perhaps, have been restored, if many circumstances had not rendered it impossible."[15] Aldini's attempt, widely reported in the British press, is the scientific prototype for Frankenstein's attempt to reanimate a human corpse with the "spark of being" (*F* 1 iv 34).

Through the work of Victor Frankenstein, Mary Shelley mounts a powerful critique of the early modern scientific revolution: of scientific thinking as such, of the psychology of the modern scientist, and of the commitment of science to discover the "objective" truth, whatever the consequences. Inherent in seventeenth-century scientific thought was a ruthless gender politics. As Francis Bacon had announced of the modern scientist, "I am come in very truth leading to you Nature with all her children to bind her to your service and make her your slave."[16] Both Waldman and Frankenstein share this desire to "penetrate into the recesses of nature, and show how she works in her hiding places" (*F* I ii 28). Indeed, Victor's quest is precisely to usurp from nature the female power of biological reproduction, to become a male womb.

Further, Waldman and Frankenstein share with early modern science the assumption that nature is only matter, particles that can be rearranged at the will of the scientist. They thus defy an earlier Renaissance world-view that perceived nature as a living organism, Dame Nature or Mother Earth, with whom humans were to live in a cooperative, mutually beneficial communion. Frankenstein thus opposes ecology with egotism, with his own yearning to command the worship only a God receives:

> Life and death appeared to me ideal bounds, which I should first break through and pour a torrent of light into our dark world. A new species would bless me as its creator and source; many happy and excellent natures would owe their being to me. No father could claim the gratitude of his child so completely as I should deserve their's.
>
> (*F* I iii 32)

But Victor's scientific experiment, as the world knows by now, does not succeed. This is not merely because the creature turns on him, but also because "Mother Nature" fights back. She destroys Victor's health (he is frequently sick with both physical and mental diseases and dies of "natural" causes at the age of twenty-five); prevents him from creating a "normal" creature by denying him the maternal instinct or the emotional capacity for empathy; and stops him from engendering his own natural child by diverting his desire for his bride on their wedding night into a desire for revenge. Pointedly, Nature pursues Frankenstein with the very electricity – that "spark of being" with which he animated his creature – that this "modern Prometheus" has stolen from her. As Victor works, lightning flashes around him, storms rage on land and sea, rain falls. Like Percy Shelley in his poem *Mont Blanc*, Mary locates Nature's sublime, elemental power in the Alpine peaks of Mont Blanc; unlike her husband, though, she explicitly genders this power as female (*F* III iii 134). Ultimately, in *Frankenstein*, as in Percy Shelley's poem *Alastor, Or The Spirit of Solitude*, the penalty for pursuing Nature to her hiding places is death.

Problems of perception

My discussion of Mary Shelley's conception of nature raises two basic philosophical questions, questions explored in depth by the Enlightenment French *philosophes* Rousseau and Voltaire and by the German philosopher Immanuel Kant. First, a question of ontology: What, in Shelley's view, *is* nature, both the external world and human nature? Put otherwise, what is *being*? Second, a question of epistemology: how do we know what we know? These are the bristling questions Victor Frankenstein pursues when he asks, "Whence did the principle of life proceed?" (*F* I iii 30). And these are the questions that the creature asks so hauntingly again and again: "Who was I? What was I? Whence did I come? What was my destination?" (*F* II vii 86).

As its characters wrestle with these ontological and epistemological questions, Shelley's novel presents two diametrically opposed answers. On the one hand, the creature, following the French *philosophes* Rousseau and Condorcet, insists that human nature is innately good: "I was benevolent and good; misery made me a fiend" (*F* II ii 66) and later, "My vices are the children of a forced solitude that I abhor; and my virtues will necessarily arise when I live in communion with an equal" (*F* II ix 100). By contrast, Frankenstein, following a more traditional Christian doctrine of original sin, insists that the creature is innately evil: "Abhorred monster! fiend that thou art! the tortures of hell are too mild a vengeance for thy crimes. Wretched devil!" (*F* II ii 65–66).

Is the creature, frequently referred to as "Being," innately good or innately evil? This question resonates in the emblematic scene in which the creature first sees himself mirrored in a pond in the woods: "[H]ow was I terrified, when I viewed myself in a transparent pool! At first I started back, unable to believe that it was indeed I who was reflected in the mirror; and when I became fully convinced that I was in reality the monster that I am, I was filled with the bitterest sensations of despondence and mortification" (*F* II iv 76). Here, knowing oneself (cognition) is a matter of seeing oneself reflected in a mirror; in other words, that cognition is always a secondary, derivative perception or image of oneself. The creature is at first "unable to believe" that what he knows (feels, experiences) himself to be is what he sees, but then he becomes "convinced" that he is "in reality" what he sees, a "monster." Here Shelley follows the eighteenth-century idealist philosopher Berkeley: to be is to be perceived.

But *how* should the creature be perceived? For he enters the novel as the sign of the unknown, the never-before-perceived. How is he to be fit into our culture's existing codes of signification? All the characters in the novel assume that his outer appearance is a valid index to his inner nature (a phenomenon probed in the many cinematic versions of the novel; see chapters 4 and 5, below). Here, again, Mary Shelley is abreast of the scientific theories of her day, for this semiotics of the face implicitly endorses late eighteenth-century theories that physiognomy and character are closely related. Johann Casper Lavater's physiognomical theory, for example, held that a person's inner soul or moral character produces his or her outer appearance, while Spurzheim and Gall's phrenological theory held that the contours of the skull determines character and moral nature.

In Shelley's novel, with only two exceptions, the characters read the creature's gigantic, yellow-skinned body as monstrous, as *evil*. Victor Frankenstein takes one peremptory look at his animated creation – "I beheld the wretch – the miserable monster whom I had created" (F I iv 35) – and flees. When the creature sets forth alone into the world, everyone he encounters assumes that he is a threat. The crippled old man in the hut, the villagers, the rustic whose drowning girlfriend he rescues, Felix, Safie, Agatha, even the innocent William Frankenstein – all immediately read his countenance as that of an "ogre" (F II viii 96).

That such readings are arbitrary and perhaps mistaken is clarified when Frankenstein encounters his creature a second time. After denouncing him as a "devil," a "vile insect," and an enemy (F II ii 65), Frankenstein commands him to "Begone! relieve me from the sight of your detested form." The creature, having asserted his innate goodness, replies, "'Thus I relieve thee, my creator,' . . . and placed his hated hands before my eyes" (F II ii 67). By momentarily blinding Victor, the creature cautions us lest our own acts of perception prove faulty. Significantly, the only character who listens to his tale of suffering and then feels sympathy for him, is the blind, old father of the De Laceys.

Shelley's reader, who listens to the creature's voice as recorded in Walton's letters, has a rare opportunity to judge the creature through the ear, not the eye. But is Walton, who only glimpses the creature after listening carefully to both stories, to guide us in this act of judgment? His response to the creature is deeply ambivalent: "Never did I behold a vision so horrible as his face, of such loathsome, yet appalling hideousness. I shut my eyes voluntarily, and endeavoured to recollect what were my duties with regard to this destroyer. I called on him to stay" (F III vii 152). Walton feels anger and revulsion, but at the same time – by shutting his eyes – he recalls the creature's suffering, acknowledges his remorse, and tries to assess his "duties" toward both Victor and his creation. Instead of moving from perplexity to judgment, however, Walton loses sight of him "in the darkness & distance," as Mary Shelley originally wrote, suggesting not only that the creature is still alive but also that his nature, his *meaning*, remains unfixed, ever available to new interpretations.

Thus, the question remains open: how are we to see or read the creature? From one perspective, Shelley endows her creature with the features of sublimity, a word used to describe the human mind's confrontation with the unknowable, the overwhelming, the infinite. As we have already noted, she sets him free among the archetypal landscapes of the sublime: among the Alps, in the frozen wastes of the North Pole. And like power itself, he has superhuman strength. But Shelley's novel outstrips the eighteenth-century idiom of sublimity, powerfully anticipating the insights of Jacques Derrida and Michel Foucault: human knowledge is the product of invented or linguistically constructed forms or grammars which societies have imposed over time on an unknowable (or, as Derrida would put it, absent) ontological being. In the 1831 Introduction, Mary Shelley linked the creature directly to the unknowable elements of the universe: "Invention, it must be humbly admitted, does not consist in creating out of void, but out of chaos; the materials must, in the first place, be afforded: it can give form to dark, shapeless substances, but cannot bring into being the substance itself" (F 1831, Introduction 54). What we call knowledge, truth, or culture are only a collection of "discourses," linguistic readings of what is essentially a "chaos." Since the creature is by definition unique, a "new species," he cannot be known, but once he enters the social realm, he will inevitably be named. In 1826, finding the creature listed on a playbill as "xxxxx," Shelley commented wryly, "this nameless mode of naming the unnameable is rather good" (L I 378; see chapter 4 below).

But Mary Shelley's literary purposes are primarily ethical rather than epistemological; she wants us to understand the *moral* consequences of our ways of reading or seeing the world, of our habit of imposing meanings on that which we cannot truly know. In *Frankenstein*, human beings typically construe the unfamiliar, the abnormal, the unique as dangerous or evil, a construction given form in their language. As Foucault suggested in *Madness and Civilisation*, language is an instrument of power, establishing and policing a myriad of boundaries between "us" and "them," in a desperate effort to protect human societies from the terrors of the unknown.

What we find in Shelley's novel is that such linguistic definitions of other beings as "monsters" create the very evils that they imagine. It is significant in this context that the creature is yellow-skinned and black-lipped (F I iv 34). These features are usually read either as a marker of disease (the creature may have jaundice or yellow fever), of his liminal status between the living and the dead (he is the color of a "mummy" [F III vii 152] or one of the undead), or of his anatomical incompleteness. But it is also a marker of his racial otherness; as Walton observes, the creature is not a European but a "savage inhabitant" of some "undiscovered island" north of the "wilds of Russia and Tartary" (F I, Letter iv 13). And to read such a member of another race as "savage" or monstrous is to participate in the cultural production of racist stereotypes.

Doubling Frankenstein

Mary Shelley suggests that if we concur with her characters in reading the creature as a monster, then we write the creature as a monster and become ourselves the authors of evil; as the poet William Blake put it, "we become what we behold." In her novel, Victor Frankenstein literally becomes the monster he linguistically constructs: "I considered the being whom I had cast among mankind . . . nearly in the light of my own vampire, my own spirit let loose from the grave" (*F* I vi 49). This identification of Victor with his creature is textually reinforced by the repeated association of both Victor and his creature with both Milton's Satan (*F* III vii 146; II ii 66) and his fallen Adam (*F* III v 131; II ii 66). Here, too, Mary Shelley's response to a precursor is distinctive. Whereas Blake, Byron, and Shelley revised Milton's epic by aligning themselves with the revolutionary energies of Satan, Mary Shelley explores the ambiguities of the fallen condition, whether human or Satanic.

Victor and his creature are virtually fused into one being, almost one consciousness, during their final race across the icy wastes of the North Pole. Here, the hunter becomes the hunted, the pursued the pursuer. The creature leaves food for the pursuing Victor so that they can finally reunite. And when each boards Walton's ship, each articulates the same feelings of intermingled revenge, remorse, and despair. As the creature observes to the corpse of Victor, in Shelley's manuscript, "Miserable as you were my wretchedness is superior to yours for remorse is the bitter sting that rankles in my wounds & tortures me to madness" (*F Notebooks* II 817). Victor has become his creature, his creature has become his maker; they are each other's double. Hence naming the creature "Frankenstein" – as popular folklore would have it – uncovers a profound truth within the novel's narrative.

Perhaps Mary Shelley's most profound critique of the divine Romantic imagination celebrated by Percy Shelley, Byron, Blake, Wordsworth, and Coleridge lies in her conviction that an unfettered imagination is more likely to create forms based on fear than on love. As the rationalist Theseus warns in Shakespeare's *Midsummer Night's Dream*, the poet, like the lover and the lunatic, sees "more devils than vast hell can hold" or in the night, "imagining some fear," supposes every bush a bear. Thus, Shelley's strikingly modern, even post-modern, answer to the philosophical questions raised in *Frankenstein* is both a radical skepticism and a categorical moral imperative. When we write the unfamiliar as monstrous, we literally create the evil, the injustice, the racism, sexism, and class prejudice, that we arbitrarily imagine. Throughout the first edition of her novel, Shelley implicitly endorses a redemptive alternative to Frankenstein's egotistical attempt to penetrate and manipulate nature. This is an ethic of care that would sympathize with and protect all living beings, that would live in beneficial cooperation with nature, and that would bring about social reform not through a violent French-style revolution but rather through peaceful, gradual evolution. Such an ideal flickers in the happy domesticity of the loving De Lacey family, where Felix (whose name means happiness) and Agatha (whose name means goodness) eagerly embrace the racial other, the Turkish/Christian Safie (whose name means wisdom). And when the De Laceys flee in horror from the gift-bearing, beneficent Creature, they leave the reader stranded in the terrifying nightmare of Victor Frankenstein's single-minded, egotistical attempt to steal the secrets of nature. But, as the chapters that follow will suggest, the survival of Frankenstein's creature, in story, film, myth, and literary criticism opens the way for ever new, possibly more constructive readings of Shelley's "monster."

NOTES

1 Ellen Moers, *Literary Women* (Garden City, NY: Doubleday, 1976), pp. 91–99. For later feminist readings of *Frankenstein*, see Anne K. Mellor, *Mary Shelley: Her Life, Her Fiction, Her Monsters* (New York: Methuen, 1988).

2 Unless otherwise noted, all references are to the 1818 edition of *Frankenstein*.

3 Sandra Gilbert and Susan Gubar, *The Madwoman in the Attic* (New Haven: Yale University Press, 1979), pp. 45–92.

4 Barbara Johnson, "My Monster/My Self," *Diacritics* 12.2 (1982), 7.

5 See Mellor, *Mary Shelley*, pp. 54–55; this date has since been confirmed by Charles Robinson, editor of Mary Wollstonecraft Shelley, *The Frankenstein Notebooks, A Facsimile Edition of Mary Shelley's Manuscript Novel, 1816–17* (New York: Garland, 1996), I lxv–lxvi.

6 David Punter, *The Literature of Terror* (London: Longman, 1980; rpt. 1996); see esp. pp. 183–88.

7 In Shelley's manuscript, Victor Frankenstein refers to his creature as "the great object of my affection"; see discussion below.

8 See Richard J. Dunn, "Narrative Distance in Frankenstein," *Studies in the Novel* 6 (1974), 408–17.

9 See Robinson, *Frankenstein Notebooks*, throughout. Subsequent references to the *Notebooks* appear in parentheses.

10 See Mellor, *Mary Shelley*, pp. 57–69; reprinted in part in F 1818 160–66.

11 Working with the 1831 edition of Frankenstein, Robert Kiely interprets Victor Frankenstein as a tragic hero in *The Romantic Novel in England* (Cambridge, MA: Harvard University Press, 1972).

12 See Gayatri Chakravorty Spivak, "Three Women's Texts and a Critique of Imperialism," *Critical Inquiry* 12 (1985), 243–61; and Joseph W. Lew, "The Deceptive Other: Mary Shelley's Critique of Orientalism in *Frankenstein*," *SiR* 30.2 (1991), 255–83.

13 On the positive portrayal of the bourgeois nuclear family in the 1818 edition of Frankenstein, see Mellor, *Mary Shelley*, pp. 1–37, 117–18, 125–26, and throughout; on the more negative view of the nuclear family represented in the 1831

edition, see Kate Ferguson Ellis, "Monsters in the Garden: Mary Shelley and the Bourgeois Family," *EF* 123–42, and Adam Komisaruk, "'So Guided by a Silken Cord': *Frankenstein*'s Family Values," *SiR* 38.3 (1999), 409–41.

14 Sir Humphry Davy, *A Discourse, Introductory to A Course of Lectures on Chemistry* (London: Joseph Johnson, 1802), p. 16.

15 Giovanni Aldini, *An Account of the Late Improvements in Galvanism* (London: Cuthell and Martin, and J. Murray, 1803), p. 54.

16 Francis Bacon, "'Temporis Partus Masculus': An Untranslated Writing of Francis Bacon," trans. Benjamin Farrington, *Centaurus* 1 (1951), 197.

2

PAMELA CLEMIT

Frankenstein, Matilda, and the legacies of Godwin and Wollstonecraft

[My mother's] greatness of soul & my father high talents have perpetually reminded me that I ought to degenerate as little as I could from those from whom I derived my being . . . my chief merit must always be derived, first from the glory these wonderful beings have shed [?*around*] me, & then for the enthusiasm I have for excellence & the ardent admiration I feel for those who sacrifice themselves for the public good.   (*L* II 4)

In this letter of September 1827 to Frances Wright, the Scottish-born author and social reformer, Mary Shelley reveals just how much she felt her life and thought to be shaped by the social and political ideals of her parents, William Godwin, the leading radical philosopher of the 1790s, and his wife, the proto-feminist writer Mary Wollstonecraft. The multiple literary, political, and philosophical influences of Godwin and Wollstonecraft may be traced in all six of Mary Shelley's full-length novels, as well as in her tales, biographies, essays, and other shorter writings. Yet while she consistently wrote within the framework established by her parents' concerns, she was no mere imitator of their works. Writing with an awareness of how French revolutionary politics had unfolded through the Napoleonic era, Mary Shelley extends and reformulates the many-sided legacies of Godwin and Wollstonecraft in extreme, imaginatively arresting ways. Those legacies received their most searching reappraisal in *Frankenstein; or, The Modern Prometheus* (1818), Mary Shelley's remarkable first novel, and were reexamined a year later in *Matilda*, a novella telling the story of incestuous love between father and daughter, which, though it remained unpublished until 1959, has now become one of her best-known works.

Though *Frankenstein* appeared anonymously, Mary Shelley advertised her primary intellectual allegiance in the dedication of the first edition, "To William Godwin, Author of Political Justice, Caleb Williams, &c." Reviewers, piqued by the absence of the author's name, were quick to draw parallels with Godwin's writings, but could not agree on the nature of those parallels. Sir Walter Scott, in a long, insightful piece in *Blackwood's Magazine*, declared that *Frankenstein* was a novel on the same plan as Godwin's *St. Leon: A Tale of the Sixteenth Century* (1799), in which "the author's principal object . . . is less to produce an effect by means of the marvels of the narrations, than to open new trains and channels of thought."[1] He surmised that the author was Percy Bysshe Shelley, Godwin's son-in-law. The liberal *Scots* (later, *Edinburgh*) *Magazine*, owned by Archibald Constable, Godwin's friend and publisher, was torn between admiration and censure: "Here is one of the productions of the modern school in its highest style of caricature and exaggeration. It is formed on the Godwinian manner, and has all the faults, but likewise many of the beauties of that model." Again invoking *St. Leon*, the reviewer confessed himself fascinated as well as repelled by "this wild fiction" and attributed its "monstrous conceptions" to "the wild and irregular theories of the age."[2] In contrast, J. W. Croker, writing in the Tory *Quarterly Review*, compared *Frankenstein* to Godwin's latest novel, *Mandeville: A Tale of the Seventeenth Century* (1817), a confessional account of spiraling religious obsession:

> [*Frankenstein*] is piously dedicated to Mr. Godwin, and is written in the spirit of his school . . . Mr. Godwin is the patriarch of a literary family, whose chief skill is in delineating the wanderings of the intellect . . . His disciples are a kind of *out-pensioners of Bedlam*, and, like "Mad Bess" or "Mad Tom," are occasionally visited with paroxysms of genius and fits of expression, which make sober-minded people wonder and shudder.[3]

While these early reviewers identified Mary Shelley's major intellectual affiliation, they did not grasp its full significance. What did it mean to be brought up and educated in the Godwin "school"? From her birth on August 30, 1797, Mary Shelley was indissolubly linked to her parents' controversial writings and reputations. Wollstonecraft, who had married Godwin earlier that year, died on September 10, 1797 from complications following the birth. The story of her life was disclosed to all when Godwin published *Memoirs of the Author of A Vindication of the Rights of Woman* in January 1798.[4] This was a work of unprecedented biographical frankness, which covered every phase of Wollstonecraft's unorthodox career. It documented her friendship with the married artist Henry Fuseli, her residence in revolutionary France, her liaison with the American merchant Gilbert Imlay (to whom she bore a child, Fanny), her two attempts at suicide, her domestic "experiment" with Godwin, and, finally, her slow, painful death.[5] From Godwin's point of view, such candor was an attempt to enact in the public sphere the revolutionary doctrine of sincerity he had advocated in his works of the early 1790s: frank information about Wollstonecraft's unconventional domestic circumstances was necessary to make her individual history an effective agent of historical change. Contemporary readers, however, were shocked rather than liberated by what they perceived as cold-hearted revelations of Wollstonecraft's immorality, and *Memoirs* provoked widespread hostility from the conservative press.

Even before the publication of *Memoirs*, Godwin was regarded as a dangerously subversive "disturber of the status quo."[6] *An Enquiry concerning Political Justice*, his great work of philosophical anarchism, appeared in February 1793. Here Godwin argued that individuals, by the exercise of reason and judgment, have the power to emancipate themselves from the false opinion on which government is based, leading to the gradual dissolution of all legislative restraints.[7] This substantial philosophical treatise became an immediate success among revolutionary sympathizers of all persuasions. Despite Godwin's principled opposition to the use of force, his vigorous criticism of all forms of political authority seemed to offer leaders of the democratic reform movement a philosophical justification for their practical demands, and this may have prompted the government to debate his prosecution.[8] The view that Godwin's theories posed a threat to social stability was reinforced by his next two works: *Things As They Are; or, The Adventures of Caleb Williams* (1794), a novel dramatizing the impact of aristocratic corruption on the individual; and *Cursory Strictures* (1794), a pamphlet written in defense of twelve leading radicals charged with high treason in October 1794. Indeed, by late 1797, Godwin's teachings were felt to be so dangerous that the *Anti-Jacobin*, a satirical journal supported by government funds, launched a popular campaign to discredit him.[9] That campaign found a new focus after the publication of *Memoirs*, in which Godwin not only politicized Wollstonecraft's arguments in favor of women's rights to equality and self-determination, but also conceptualized her as an agent of revolutionary social change. The ensuing reaction against the advanced social theories of Godwin and Wollstonecraft lasted well into the nineteenth century.

Whatever the legacy of fame or notoriety surrounding her parents, Mary Shelley was brought up to share their central belief in the duty of engagement in public debate on all pertinent moral, social, and political issues as a means of contributing to the general welfare. Apart from attending a local day school at the age of four and a boarding school at Ramsgate at the age of thirteen, Mary Shelley was educated at home.[10] The household in which she grew up comprised five children with no two parents in common: in addition to herself and Fanny Imlay, it included Jane Clairmont (later known as Claire) and her half-brother Charles, the two children of

Godwin's second wife, Mary Jane Clairmont; William Godwin, Jr. was born in 1803, fifteen months after his parents' marriage. Apparently domestic complications did not inhibit the family's vibrant intellectual life. From his background in eighteenth-century Protestant Dissent, Godwin derived a lasting belief in education as the key to social change, and sought to put his enlightened pedagogical theories into practice in raising his children. Mary Shelley's early reading included her father's works of reformist history, classical literature, and English grammar, written for the children's bookshop established by the Godwins in 1805.[11] In these works, he developed a mode of writing designed to encourage children to think for themselves, and sought to cultivate the reader's imagination as a means of fostering moral autonomy. In addition, Mary Shelley read extensively in Godwin's library, which included his own books and her mother's, along with a wealth of literature, history, science, and philosophy in both French and English Enlightenment traditions. Godwin also took the children on regular outings to public lectures, plays, and art galleries, and encouraged them to meet the many distinguished writers, artists, scientists, and medical men – such as Anthony Carlisle, Coleridge, Humphry Davy, Fuseli, Hazlitt, Charles and Mary Lamb, and Wordsworth – who visited him at home. The Godwin household thus provided Mary Shelley with an unusually wide-ranging education, in which different forms of knowledge, scientific as well as literary, were equally available as intellectual and literary resources.

When in July 1814 Mary Shelley, then aged sixteen, eloped to the Continent with another of her father's visitors, Percy Bysshe Shelley, and accompanied by Claire Clairmont, her Godwinian education continued to flourish. As she recalled in October 1838: "To be something great and good was the precept given me by my father: Shelley reiterated it" (J II 554). Percy Bysshe Shelley's successive readings of *Political Justice* laid the foundations for his own political philosophy. Three areas of Godwin's early teachings became central aspects of the younger man's thought: Godwin's insistence on the connection between politics and morality; his belief in the individual's potential for rational improvement; and his attacks on monarchy, aristocracy, and all the forms of internalized values for which Percy Bysshe Shelley adopted the term "Custom."[12] Percy Bysshe Shelley also sought to fashion his life in terms of Godwin's early theories. When in January 1812 he wrote to introduce himself to Godwin as his intellectual heir, he conceptualized his upbringing in terms of his mentor's analysis of the corrupting effects of aristocracy, to which, he declared, "your inestimable book on 'Political Justice'" provided an antidote.[13] Moreover, Percy Bysshe Shelley's elopement with Mary Shelley, despite his marriage to Harriet Westbrook, was planned in the light of Godwin's early arguments against marriage as "the most odious of all monopolies"[14] – though in practice it led to a two-year estrangement from Godwin. Over the next few years, up to and including the writing of *Frankenstein*, Mary Shelley and her lover embarked on a shared, intensive course of reading, which included all of Godwin's and Wollstonecraft's works, documenting their progress in a collaborative journal designed to emulate the intellectual reciprocity of Mary Shelley's parents.

While Mary Shelley and Percy Bysshe Shelley turned to her parents' works partly in order to legitimate their own experiment in revolutionary domesticity, they also sought to emulate her parents' roles as social and cultural critics. Just as Godwin and Wollstonecraft felt the events of the French Revolution on their pulses, so too the Shelleys bore witness to the impact of the "great and extraordinary events" (*History of a Six Weeks' Tour*, NSW VIII 21) of Napoleon's meteoric career, culminating in his defeat and the restoration of despotical governments in Europe. In August 1814, they traveled through French countryside ravaged just months earlier by Cossack troops, the final result of Napoleon's unsuccessful Russian campaign. In June 1816, their second continental tour took them to Geneva, the birthplace of Jean-Jacques Rousseau, which prompted Mary Shelley to reflect on the whole course of "that revolution, which his writings mainly contributed to mature, and which, notwithstanding the temporary bloodshed and injustice with which it was polluted, has produced enduring benefits to mankind, which all the chicanery of statesmen, nor even the great conspiracy of kings, can entirely render vain" (*History of a Six Weeks' Tour*, NSW VIII 46). Later that year, the Shelleys' attention shifted to the disturbing events at home, notably the savage government response to the last phase of Luddite uprisings (1811–16), in which workers in the manufacturing industries united to destroy the machines which threatened their livelihood, and to the Spa Fields riot of December 1816.[15]

In their reading, the Shelleys sought an intelligible explanation of how the progressive ideals of the French Revolution had collapsed in despotism, both at home and abroad.[16] Alongside Godwin's philosophical theory of revolution in *Political Justice* and Wollstonecraft's eye-witness account, *An Historical and Moral View of . . . the French Revolution* (1794), they studied counter-revolutionary theories of intellectual conspiracy, such as the Abbé Barruel's *Memoirs, Illustrating the History of Jacobinism* (1797–98). They gave special attention to autobiographical and biographical writings, which highlighted the inseparability of personal and historical experience. As well as reading Godwin's philosophical biographies, *Life of Chaucer* (1803) and *Lives of Edward and John Philips, Nephews and Pupils of Milton* (1815), they studied biographical sketches of revolutionary leaders, such as the loyalist John Adolphus's *Biographical Memoirs of the French Revolution* (1799), and the self-justifying memoirs of persecuted Girondins (the moderate faction in the French Legislative Assembly), such as Jean-Baptiste Louvet de Couvray's *Narrative of the Dangers to which I have been Exposed* ... (1795). After reading Wollstonecraft's autobiographical work of revolutionary instruction, *Letters Written* . . . *in Sweden, Norway, and Denmark* (1796), they turned to the two works that had provided a model for her politicized language of sensibility, Rousseau's *Confessions* (1782–89) and *Reveries of the Solitary Walker* (1782). Finally, and most important, the pair read widely in Godwin's novels, which employed a Rousseauvian confessional form to explore the contradictory relations between the self and society. In addition to Wollstonecraft's unfinished Godwinian tale, *The Wrongs of Woman; or, Maria* (1798), they read and reread Godwin's four mature novels, *Caleb Williams, St. Leon, Fleetwood; or, The New Man of Feeling* (1805), and *Mandeville*, in which he continuously modified and reformulated his political principles in response to the historical and cultural changes of the post-revolutionary era.[17]

Frankenstein's central, flawed aspiration to create "a new species," which "would bless [him] as its creator and source" (*F* I iii 32), has often been read as a specific critique of Godwin's utopian idealism, as set out in the first edition of *Political Justice*.[18] Such readings take their cue from Godwin's tentative speculations concerning a future state of rational beings, which are based on Benjamin Franklin's "sublime conjecture . . . that 'mind will one day become omnipotent over matter'" (*PJ* 460). Godwin writes:

> The men . . . will cease to propagate, for they will no longer have any motive, either of error or duty, to induce them. In addition to this they will perhaps be immortal. The whole will be a people of men, and not of children . . . There will be no war, no crime, no administration of justice as it is called, and no government.
>
> (*PJ* 465)

Such projections concerning the regeneration of the individual and of society were by no means unique to Godwin, but were also present in the writings and speeches of French revolutionary ideologues. For example, Saint-Just and Robespierre each described the making of himself into a new man, devoted to the Rousseauvian principle of "public virtue"; each announced plans for the creation of a "new race" of socially autonomous citizens, educated by the state, whose attachment to family life would be broken.[19] Additionally, by the time that Mary Shelley began writing *Frankenstein* in 1816, Godwin had reformulated his early account of moral action to incorporate the private affections, and had dramatized the socially and psychologically destructive effects of revolutionary aspirations in *St. Leon*.[20] *Frankenstein*, as a critical reassessment of the politics of the French revolutionary era which provides "a retrospect on the whole process . . . through Waterloo,"[21] has more in common with Godwin's and Wollstonecraft's fictions of historical and cultural reappraisal than has been allowed.

As in the best-known Godwinian novels of the 1790s, *Caleb Williams* and *Maria*, *Frankenstein* achieves a balance between psychological and social concerns, and between personal and political allegory.[22] The central, highly charged relationship between creator and creature reenacts the complex bond of fear and fascination between the aristocrat Falkland and his servant Caleb. In the earlier novel, Caleb is cast as a "monster" for daring to challenge Falkland's social authority, but it is Falkland who becomes an inhuman tyrant. Mary Shelley builds on Godwin's use of the pursuit motif to destabilize conventional moral values: in *Frankenstein*, the abandoned creature returns to confront his "monstrous" father, and the pair act out a drama of enticement and threat that leads to widespread social destruction. In her choice of a multiple narrative mode, Mary Shelley was also influenced by *Maria*, in which Wollstonecraft presents several first-person narratives telling the same, mutually reinforcing story of the social oppression of women in different classes of society. Mary Shelley similarly presents several versions of the same tale, but this time the stories are told from competing angles, highlighting her dissolution of moral and cultural certainties.

Yet Mary Shelley's skeptical treatment of revolutionary idealism is partly anticipated by Godwin's cosmopolitan historical novel, *St. Leon*, in which he paid tribute to Wollstonecraft's influence on his thought. In *St. Leon* as in *Frankenstein*, overweening public ambitions, symbolized by secret occult practices, lead to the breakdown of family life. The conversations between the French aristocrat St. Leon and his endlessly sympathetic wife Marguerite (an idealized portrait of Wollstonecraft) reflect the opposition of public and private values found in *Letters from Norway*, in which Wollstonecraft explores the destructive impact of "the chase after wealth" on domestic relationships.[23] The plot of *St. Leon* is structured as a series of bondings and separations. Each experience of shared domestic tranquillity is disrupted by St. Leon's obsessive striving for wealth, honor, and fame, which leads only to an unbearable social isolation: "I possessed the gift of immortal life," recalls St. Leon, "but I looked on myself as a monster that did not deserve to exist."[24] Yet St. Leon, like all of Godwin's protagonists, is an unreliable interpreter of his own history, and the novel's final message is equivocal: while St. Leon warns against the neglect of domestic ties in pursuit of the ideal, he is still fascinated by the prospect of wealth and social power. Similarly, Frankenstein is ultimately unwilling to abandon his misguided revolutionary ambitions, despite their human cost.

The subtitle of *Frankenstein*, "The Modern Prometheus," further suggests that Mary Shelley's study of revolutionary aspirations is specifically concerned with the question of Rousseau's influence. Rousseau, with his dual reputation as one of the intellectual fathers of French republicanism and as, in Wollstonecraft's phrase, "the true Prometheus of sentiment," was a central, ambivalent presence in her parents' post-revolutionary writings.[25] This ambivalence is especially evident in *Fleetwood*, where Godwin contrasts the philanthropist Macneil, who presides over a patriarchal idyll modeled on Rousseau's novel, *The New Eloise* (1761), with the misanthropic "new man of feeling" of his subtitle, Fleetwood, who resembles Rousseau's autobiographical persona in the *Confessions*. Macneil, a former friend of Rousseau, volunteers an analysis of his character, in which he admits that Rousseau, toward the end of his life, was deluded and "lived . . . in a world of his own." Yet, Macneil declares, "he had such resources in his own mind . . . his vein of enthusiasm was so sublime . . . It was difficult for me to persuade myself that the person I saw at such times, was the same as at others was beset with such horrible visions."[26] This ambivalent attitude to Rousseau was shared not only by Mary Shelley but also by other writers of her generation.[27] Byron, for example, provided a highly equivocal portrait of Rousseau in *Childe Harold's Pilgrimage* (hereafter *CHP*), Canto the Third, transcribed in part by Mary Shelley at the Villa Diodati in 1816. Like Napoleon, another revolutionary overreacher undone by a Promethean "fire / And motion of the soul" (*CHP* III, lines 371–72), Rousseau is both praised for his passionate sensibility and blamed for his inability to control the forces it unleashed: "as a tree / On fire by lightning; with ethereal flame / Kindled he was, and blasted" (*CHP* III, lines 734–36). Such images of simultaneous creativity and destruction underscore Mary Shelley's rewriting of the Prometheus legend as a critique of Rousseauvian "enthusiasm," in which the use of competing first-person narratives assigns the task of evaluation to the reader in Godwin's manner.

To begin with, Mary Shelley's use of symbolic European locations highlights the associations between Frankenstein and the autobiographical Rousseau. The novel's action centers on the republic of Geneva, where Rousseau was born and where the Frankenstein family is established as a pillar of bourgeois society, celebrated for its devotion to public affairs, in the era of the French Revolution.[28] However, it is at the University of Ingolstadt, famed as the birthplace of the Illuminati,[29] a secret society pledged to spread egalitarian principles and infidelity (or atheism), that Frankenstein begins his revolutionary education. Here Frankenstein's affinity with Rousseau is underlined by his "primitivist" reluctance to abandon the ancient alchemical dream of "immortality and power" (*F* I ii 27) in favor of "progressive" science.[30] It is only after hearing M. Waldman echo this ancient ideal, in his lecture on the "new and almost unlimited powers" (F I ii 28) of modern chemists to control and shape nature, that Frankenstein is persuaded of the validity of modern scientific endeavors. Under M. Waldman's tutelage, he is inspired with "an almost supernatural enthusiasm" (F I iii 30) for scientific enquiry, culminating in his project of solitary creation.

Moreover, Frankenstein's rejection of his creature makes him guilty of a crime that made Rousseau notorious: parental abandonment. Just as Rousseau in the *Confessions* and *Reveries* repeatedly defended leaving his five children by Thérèse Levasseur at a Paris orphanage,[31] so too Frankenstein seeks to justify his negligence by depicting the creature as a malignant "devil," "monster," and "fiend" (F II ii 67). Instead of acknowledging the creature's independent rights and needs, Frankenstein depicts him as a projection of his own worst qualities, adapting images of monstrosity drawn from anti-Jacobin propaganda: "I considered the being whom I had cast among mankind . . . nearly in the light of my own vampire, my own spirit let loose from the grave, and forced to destroy all that was dear to me" (F I vi 49). Frankenstein's final retreat into an imaginary world of dead friends – "How did I cling to their dear forms . . . and persuade myself that they still lived!" (F III vii 142) – further recalls the moral solipsism of Rousseau, who, dissatisfied with social reality, took refuge in "an ideal world . . . peopled with beings after my own heart."[32] Such parallels with Rousseau's life story establish Frankenstein as another disappointed egotist in the manner of St. Leon and Fleetwood, whose self-justifying confessional narrative collapses into unwitting self-condemnation.

Mary Shelley's most powerful critique of Frankenstein occurs when she allows the creature to tell his own story. In contrast to Frankenstein's melodramatic outbursts, the creature's measured eloquence reflects a Rousseauvian sensibility, tempered by Godwinian logic. Like Caleb Williams in his final courtroom meeting with Falkland, the creature seeks an alternative to "human laws, bloody as they may be" by appealing directly to Frankenstein's sympathies: "Let your compassion be moved, and do not disdain me. Listen to my tale: when you have heard that, abandon or commiserate me, as you shall judge that I deserve. But hear me" (F II ii 66–67). Yet the creature is repeatedly frustrated in his efforts to find an unprejudiced listener within the novel. Though the blind De Lacey's response to the creature's story is the opposite to that of Frankenstein – "there is something in your words," he says, "which persuades me that you are sincere" (F II vii 91) – the younger De Laceys are unable to acknowledge a being so different from themselves. The role of the true arbiter of political justice is reserved for the reader of the novel.

The creature's life history is both the tale of a beleaguered individual surviving against the odds and an allegorical account of the progress of the human race. It is broadly structured as a narrative of natural goodness corrupted by civil society in the manner of Rousseau's *Discourse . . . on Inequality among Men* (1755). Yet the creature speedily outgrows Rousseau's notion of happiness that arises from the satisfaction of physical passions, and his developing moral and intellectual awareness reflects Godwin's and Wollstonecraft's shared emphasis on the formative power of education and circumstances. Moreover, unlike the essentially solitary man in Rousseau's state of nature, Frankenstein's creature instinctively seeks society. Thus he learns to read by listening to the cross-cultural exchanges between Felix De Lacey and Safie, themselves fugitives from injustice in revolutionary Paris. As he secretly shares in the De Laceys' patriarchal idyll, his lack of biological origins is offset by a comprehensive cultural education. His program of vicarious instruction begins with Volney's *The Ruins; or, A Survey of the Revolutions of Empires* (1791–92), a powerful Enlightenment critique of ancient and modern governments as tyrannical and supported by religious fraud. This work gives him insight into the mixed nature of humankind and into systematized social inequality: "Was man, indeed, at once so powerful, so virtuous, and magnificent, yet so vicious and base? . . . I heard of the division of property, of immense wealth and squalid poverty; of rank, descent, and noble blood" (*F* II v 80). The books that he finds by chance, Plutarch's *Parallel Lives*, Milton's *Paradise Lost*, and Goethe's *The Sorrows of Young Werther* (1774), complement Volney's historical overview by focusing on issues of individual morality at different stages of Western civilization.

Such progressive reading-matter not only transforms the creature's sense of himself, but also equips him to launch a vigorous critique of Frankenstein's actions in both public and private spheres. While the creature's Godwinian reading of *Paradise Lost* as "a true history . . . of an omnipotent God warring with his creatures" leads him to curse Frankenstein as a tyrannical God, he also reproaches his creator for denying him full humanity: "I was benevolent and good; misery made me a fiend. Make me happy, and I shall again be virtuous" (*F* II vii 87, ii 66).[33] When Frankenstein reneges on his promise to create a female companion, his offspring's campaign of vengeful murders acts out Frankenstein's own withholding of love and drives home the arbitrary nature of the justice meted out to himself. As Percy Bysshe Shelley wrote in a review of *Frankenstein*, intended for the *Examiner*: "Treat a person ill, and he will become wicked . . . divide him, a social being, from society, and you impose upon him the irresistible obligations – malevolence and selfishness."[34] Yet the creature's history is more ambiguous than this reading allows. In his final, grief-stricken speech over his creator's corpse, he exclaims, "Oh

Frankenstein! generous and self-devoted being!" (*F* III vii 153), and blames himself for the failure of his creator's revolutionary experiment.

This ambiguity toward Frankenstein and his project is reinforced by the attitude of Robert Walton, whose narrative of a failed voyage of discovery, addressed to his sister Margaret Saville, frames that of Frankenstein and of his creature. At first glance, Walton's life history provides a corrective to Frankenstein's tale of overreaching ambition. Though Walton, like Frankenstein, dreams of "the inestimable benefit which I shall confer on mankind to the last generation," his framing narrative seems to relegate Frankenstein's story to a cautionary tale: "Learn from me, if not by my precepts, at least by my example" (*F* I, Letter I 8, iii 31). Similarly, Walton's longing for society appears to provide a critical gloss on Frankenstein's story of solitary egotism: whereas Frankenstein laments what he perceives as his irrevocable destiny, Walton recognizes the insufficiency of the individual and laments the absence of a friend.

Yet Walton's narrative is full of contradictions. He longs for a companion, yet he has put himself in the situation where he seems least likely to find one. When he meets Frankenstein, he quickly begins to "love him as a brother," idolizing him as a figure of persecuted benevolence who resembles the autobiographical Rousseau: "I never saw a more interesting creature: his eyes have generally an expression of wildness, and even madness; but there are moments when, if any one performs an act of kindness towards him . . . his whole countenance is lighted up, as it were, with a beam of benevolence and sweetness that I never saw equalled" (*F* I, Letter IV 14). Their final exchange is deeply ambivalent. Though Walton forgoes his hopes of "utility and glory" in compliance with the will of the sailors, who seek to return to society, this decision is presented in negative terms: "Thus are my hopes blasted by cowardice and indecision; I come back ignorant and disappointed" (*F* III vii 150). Frankenstein, though chastened, is even more unwilling to relinquish his ambitions. While he admits that his project was impelled by "a fit of enthusiastic madness," he exonerates himself of blame for his treatment of the creature, and his last words to Walton leave open the possibility of the future success of similar quests for knowledge: "Seek happiness in tranquillity, and avoid ambition, even if it be only the apparently innocent one of distinguishing yourself in science and discoveries. Yet why do I say this? I have myself been blasted in these hopes, yet another may succeed" (*F* III vii 151, 152).

The effect of these mixed messages from all three principal narrators – creator, creature, and explorer – is to present the reader with a moral choice: as in earlier Godwinian novels, do we collude with the flawed protagonist's version of events, or learn from his tale? Mary Shelley's attitude toward revolutionary "enthusiasm" is anything but straightforward. While she presents a critical study of Frankenstein's self-centered ambition, dramatizing the disastrous consequences of his neglect of the domestic affections, she also emphasizes the social origins of the creature's "monstrous" deeds. Such ambivalence is compounded by the use of a Rousseauvian confessional narrative, with its inbuilt drive toward self-justification. Just as Frankenstein ends his story by claiming that his ideal was not unworthy, even if historical circumstances were unpropitious, so too the creature, in his last speech to Walton, asserts his fundamentally benevolent nature, thwarted by an unjust society: "Once I falsely hoped to meet with beings, who, pardoning my outward form, would love me for the excellent qualities which I was capable of bringing forth" (F III vii 154). Significantly, this notional image of sympathetic community is momentarily enacted through Walton's willingness to "pardon" the creature's "outward form" and listen to his tale. But, as in *Caleb Williams*, this ideal social transformation is unaffordable within the constraints of "things as they are," and the creature's extravagant plans for self-immolation complete the novel's breakdown of meaning. Even so, Mary Shelley posits an alternative to Frankenstein's misguided attempt to force the pace of historical change, outside the novel, by encouraging a gradual transformation in moral consciousness through the experience of reading.

In *Matilda*, Mary Shelley abandons the multiple narrative mode of *Frankenstein* in favor of a confessional account of the motherless heroine's troubled relations with her father and her would-be lover, Woodville, a Shelleyan poet-figure. The autobiographical format of *Matilda* (Mary Shelley spelled the novel's title *Matilda* and the heroine's name, "Mathilda"), together with its emotionally intense language, has traditionally led critics to read the work as an uncontrolled expression of Mary Shelley's psychological anxieties following the deaths in September 1818 and June 1819 of her two young children.[35] Yet to read *Matilda* merely as an expression of psychic crisis is to overlook her self-consciousness as a literary artist. The exploitation of autobiographical material and the use of a self-dramatizing, histrionic narrator are established generic features of the Godwinian novel: *Maria, St. Leon*, and *Frankenstein*, for example, all contain extreme, displaced renderings of the author's personal experience. In *Matilda*, as in earlier works in the Godwin "school," authorial experience is redeployed in the service of a larger ethical and political design.[36]

Indeed, the manuscripts of *Matilda* reveal that Mary Shelley deliberately chose the form of an autobiographical memoir after rejecting other narrative modes. The rough draft, entitled *The Fields of Fancy*, shows that Mary Shelley originally conceived of the novella as a cautionary tale of the errors of unchecked passion. In chapter one, she sets up an intricate narrative frame based on Platonic and Dantean allegories of the soul's journey through suffering to union with the divine.[37] An unnamed narrator, mourning the loss of her loved ones, is conducted by Fantasia, a mythical figure, to the Elysian Fields, where the narrator overhears Mathilda, now immortal, telling her tale of earthly sufferings to the prophetess Diotima, the instructor of Socrates in Plato's *Symposium*. Diotima responds to Mathilda's story in overtly didactic terms: "It is by the acqiurement [*sic*] of wisdom and the loss of the selfishness that is now attatched to the sole feeling that possesses you that you will at last mingle in that universal world of which we all now make a divided part" (*NSW* II 407). Yet at the end of her narrative, Mathilda substitutes for Diotima's goal of collective wisdom a wish for individual reunion with her father. This discrepancy between the instructive tenor of the frame and the wish-fulfillment of the inset narrative reveals the unreliability of Mathilda's account and establishes her story as a warning of the dangers of excessive feeling. Mary Shelley's abandonment of the frame narrative indicates her rejection of overtly didactic fiction in favor of the indirect educative purpose of the Godwinian confessional mode.

In *Matilda*, the story is told by the heroine on her deathbed and addressed to Woodville. Like other self-justifying Godwinian protagonists, Mathilda presents herself as the victim of "a hideous necessity," presided over by "malignant fate" (*NSW* II 6, 49). Just as Godwin's use of the flawed narrator invites the reader to play an active interpretative role, so too the ambiguities and contradictions of Mathilda's narrative assign to the reader the task of evaluating her guilt or innocence. Again, Mary Shelley follows Godwinian precedents in structuring *Matilda* as a psychologically intense narrative of temptation and fall. In fact Mathilda's story involves two scenes of temptation, which are placed on either side of the two central chapters dealing, respectively, with her prophetic dream of her father's death and with the pursuit ending in her discovery of his actual death. In the first temptation sequence, Mathilda successfully persuades her father to reveal the secret of his mysterious, brooding behavior, which results in his declaration of his incestuous love for her. In the second, she unsuccessfully tempts Woodville to join her in a suicide pact by drinking laudanum. Yet the coherence of this two-part narrative is not merely a matter of structural symmetry: it also reflects the troubled psychology of the flawed protagonist. Mathilda, cheated by her father's suicide of the deathly union she might have chosen, tries to achieve a similar outcome with Woodville instead.

As in *Frankenstein*, Mary Shelley's debt to her parents' writings is not simply a matter of basic similarities of plot and technique: at the heart of the novella is a reappraisal of specific aspects of Godwin's social theories.

In particular, Mary Shelley reevaluates Godwin's early belief in the unrestrained exercise of private judgment, the basis of the theory of gradual social improvement set out in *Political Justice*,[38] which formed the core of Percy Bysshe Shelley's political thought.

The first half of *Matilda* is modeled on the central scenes of Godwin's most celebrated narrative of revolutionary change, *Caleb Williams*. Like the inscrutable aristocrat Falkland, whose position is based on hypocrisy and imposture, Mathilda's father maintains a dignified public reserve but suffers secret paroxysms of frenzy. Like Caleb, conjecturing the source of his master's agonies, Mathilda is fascinated by "the diseased yet incomprehensible state of [her father's] mind" (*NSW* II 20), and determined to seek out the cause. After listening to the account of her father's behavior by his servant, she wonders, "Could there be guilt in it?" (*NSW* II 24), directly echoing Caleb's conjecture about Falkland's suffering: "Is this . . . the fruit of conscious guilt . . .?"[39] Just as Caleb is hurried on by a "fatal impulse," Mathilda declares, "I hardly know what feelings resis[t]lessly impelled me"; while her father's criticism of her "frantic curiosity" resembles Falkland's castigation of Caleb's "foolish inquisitive humour" (*CW* 110, *NSW* II 27, *CW* 123).

Moreover, in the scene when Mathilda confronts her father and demands the truth, Mary Shelley exploits the conventional language of Godwinian gradualism. "[L]et him receive sympathy . . . Let him confide his misery" (*NSW* II 25), Mathilda says to herself before meeting him, invoking the values extolled in Godwin's notional vision of transformed human relations at the end of *Caleb Williams*. When she first addresses her father, she claims to speak "although with the tender affection of a daughter, yet also with the freedom of a friend and equal" (*NSW* II 26), gesturing toward that erosion of parent–child distinctions which Godwin saw as an essential preliminary to social change.[40] "[P]ermit me to gain your confidence," she continues, alluding to "the forbearance that man is entitled to claim from man" which Godwin argued should be exercised toward all men and women as a means of fostering moral autonomy, and which Caleb and Falkland fail to exercise toward each other.[41] When her father continues to resist her entreaties, she exclaims, "You do not treat me with candour," invoking the Dissenting principle which formed the moral underpinning of Godwin's notion of the duty of private judgment.[42]

Yet Mathilda's plea for unrestricted frankness and sincerity leads to disaster. Like those other flawed, historically premature revolutionaries, Caleb and Frankenstein, Mathilda starts out with benevolent intentions but ends up unleashing forces beyond her control. Her father's revelation of his incestuous feelings, rather than leading to an imagined egalitarian partnership, results in the breakdown of community, and, finally, death. "A mighty revolution had taken place with regard to me," she says: "the natural work of years had been transacted since the morning" (*NSW* II 30). In the reversal that follows, both parties flee from the intimacy they formerly sought. Initially Mathilda's father assumes the role of a Godwinian social outcast, but after his death she too takes on this identity. In the second half of the novella, she replicates her father's early mysterious behavior, only this time the story of disabling guilt, like Caleb's, is told from the inside.

In *Matilda*, Mary Shelley also sought to question Percy Bysshe Shelley's poetic assimilation of Godwin's theories. At first glance, Mathilda's rejection of Woodville's consolation seems to repudiate the utopian vision of human potential articulated by Percy Bysshe Shelley in *Prometheus Unbound* (1820), his grand reworking of the Prometheus myth, begun in 1818. Certainly Woodville, the spokesman for Shelleyan optimism, is ambivalently portrayed. On the one hand he is an ideal poet-figure, compared to Plato and Christ, but at the same time he is morally naive: "He seemed incapable of conceiving of the full extent of the power that selfishness & vice possesses in the world" (*NSW* II 48). To some extent Woodville appears as a figure of admonishment, since he too, like both Mathilda and her father, has suffered the premature loss of a loved one – his fiancée Elinor – but, unlike Mathilda and her father, he is consoled by his Godwinian faith in gradual but irresistible progress. Yet for all his visionary insight into human ordering schemes, he is unable to respond sufficiently to Mathilda's human need.

The clash between Woodville's idealizing temperament and Mathilda's experience of "dreary reality" (*NSW* II 56) is most evident when she tries to persuade him to join her in a suicide pact. In an effort to counteract Mathilda's despair, Woodville puts forward an argument based on Godwin's belief in the individual's duty to exercise his or her talents in pursuit of the general good: "If you can bestow happiness on another," he urges Mathilda, "if you can give one other person only one hour of joy ought you not to live to do it?" (*NSW* II 60).[43] Yet his optimistic theories are undercut by the context in which they occur. Though his lessons momentarily comfort Mathilda, they also provoke her most extreme expression of social alienation. Adopting the vocabulary of Frankenstein's creature, she describes herself as "this outcast from human feeling; this monster with whom none might mingle in converse and love . . . a marked creature, a pariah, only fit for death" (*NSW* II 61).

While this impasse may suggest the limitations of utopian social theories in the face of individual suffering, it also raises the question of whether Mathilda is beyond all help. As well as expressing skepticism concerning the visionary idealism of *Prometheus Unbound*, Mary Shelley challenges Percy Bysshe Shelley's darker vision of "sad reality" (*SPP* 140) in *The Cenci* (1819). This play, subtitled "A Tragedy," represents the story of Beatrice Cenci, a beautiful young Italian aristocrat who was raped by her father, then conspired to kill him, and was executed for parricide in 1599. Though Mary Shelley praised the fifth act of this play as "the finest thing he [Percy Bysshe Shelley] ever wrote" (*NSW* II 286),[44] in *Matilda* she took issue with his representation of Beatrice's experience. While he, in the Preface to *The Cenci*, describes Beatrice's story as a moral problem – since she, unlike Prometheus, reacts to her wrongs by doing evil – in the play itself, Beatrice is dramatized as a victim of domestic and social tyranny, who is "violently thwarted from her nature by the necessity of circumstance and opinion" (*SPP* 141).[45] In Mathilda's story, however, the role of Godwinian "circumstance and opinion" is by no means clear-cut: instead Mary Shelley focuses on the disabling ambiguities of the heroine's predicament. Though Mathilda's experience centers on incestuous feelings rather than on the physical act of incest, it is nevertheless one from which she is unable to recover: "say not to the lily laid prostrate by the storm arise, and bloom as before. My heart was bleeding from its death's wound; I could live no otherwise" (*NSW* II 45). It is this state of psychological arrest that sets her apart from Woodville, and, she feels, from all humanity, and renders her incapable of responding to new experiences. Each time Woodville leaves her, "despair returned; the work of consolation was ever to begin anew" (*NSW* II 55).

This disquieting perception that suffering may be, in Wordsworth's phrase, "permanent, obscure, and dark" (*The Borderers* [1797–98], III v 64), confirms Mary Shelley's fundamental literary affiliation with Godwin, not so much as the author of the 1790s, but as the creator of *Mandeville*, which she later praised as superior to all his works in "forcible developement of human feeling" (*NSW* II 250). In *Mandeville*, Godwin takes as his subject an unstable, self-dramatizing protagonist traumatized by past experiences of loss and betrayal. Pursuing his analysis of the disjunction between the self and society to a new extreme, he allows that the individual could be thwarted as much by psychological impulse – in this case, the repressed passion of sibling incest – as by unfavorable historical circumstances. Mary Shelley's appropriation of this dark vision in *Matilda* reveals that she continued to extend, modify, and develop her parents' imaginative concerns beyond *Frankenstein*, and prepares for her further transmutations of their multiform, ambivalent legacies in her subsequent novels.

NOTES

This chapter was written during my tenure, mainly for other purposes, of an Arts and Humanities Board Research Leave Award, held in conjunction with a term's sabbatical granted by the University of Durham. I am grateful to both institutions for their material support in this and in other areas of my research. My personal thanks are due to Doucet Devin Fischer, Michael Rossington, and Lisa Vargo, for valuable comments on a draft of this chapter.

1 [Sir Walter Scott], "Remarks on *Frankenstein*," *Blackwood's Edinburgh Magazine* 2 (1818), 614.
2 Review of *Frankenstein, Edinburgh [Scots] Magazine*, 2nd ser. 2 (March 1818), 249, 252, 253.
3 [J. W. Croker], review of *Frankenstein, Quarterly Review* 18 (Jan. 1818), 382.
4 For details, see Pamela Clemit and Gina Luria Walker, Introduction to William Godwin, *Memoirs of the Author of A Vindication of the Rights of Woman* (Peterborough: Broadview Press, 2001), pp. 11–36.
5 Godwin, *Memoirs*, p. 106.
6 Edward W. Said, *Representations of the Intellectual: The 1993 Reith Lectures* (London: Vintage, 1994), p. x.
7 The best account of Godwin's philosophical arguments is in Mark Philp, *Godwin's Political Justice* (London: Duckworth, 1986).
8 Mary Shelley, "Life of William Godwin" [1836–40], *Godwin*, ed. Pamela Clemit, LL iv 74, 86 (London: Pickering & Chatto, 2002); but there is no report of such a debate in the official minutes of the Privy Council (Philp, *Godwin's Political Justice*, p. 105).
9 See Peter H. Marshall, *William Godwin* (New Haven: Yale University Press, 1984), pp. 211–33.
10 Sources drawn on include Emily W. Sunstein, *Mary Shelley: Romance and Reality* (Boston: Little, Brown, 1989; rpt. Baltimore: Johns Hopkins University Press, 1991), pp. 29–61; and Betty T. Bennett, *Mary Wollstonecraft Shelley: An Introduction* (Baltimore: Johns Hopkins University Press, 1998), pp. 7–16.
11 For details, see Pamela Clemit, "Philosophical Anarchism in the Schoolroom: William Godwin's Juvenile Library, 1805–25," *Biblion: The Bulletin of The New York Public Library*, 9. 1/2 (Fall 2000 / Spring 2001), 44–70.
12 The most useful accounts of Percy Bysshe Shelley's debts to Godwin remain Kenneth Neill Cameron, *The Young Shelley: Genesis of a Radical* (London: Victor Gollancz, 1951), pp. 61–70; and P. M. S. Dawson, *The Unacknowledged Legislator: Shelley and Politics* (Oxford: Oxford University Press, 1980), pp. 76–133.
13 Shelley to Godwin, January 3, 1812, *PBSL* 1 227.
14 Godwin, *An Enquiry concerning Political Justice* [1793 edn.], *Political and Philosophical Writings of William Godwin*, gen. ed. Mark Philp, 7 vols. (London: Pickering & Chatto, 1993), iii 453. (Hereafter *PJ*.)
15 See E. P. Thompson, *The Making of the English Working Class* (London: Victor Gollancz, 1963; rev. edn., Harmondsworth: Penguin, 1980), pp. 627–28, 691–700; cf. Mary Shelley to Leigh Hunt, March 2, 1817, *L* 1 29.
16 For the Shelleys' reading lists through 1814–17, see *J* 1 85–103; my account is also indebted to Gerald McNiece, *Shelley and the Revolutionary Idea* (Cambridge, MA: Harvard University Press, 1969), pp. 10–41.
17 For details, see Pamela Clemit, *The Godwinian Novel: The Rational Fictions of Godwin, Brockden Brown, Mary Shelley* (New York: Oxford University Press, 1993, rpt. 2001), pp. 35–102.
18 Eg., Lee Sterrenburg, "Mary Shelley's Monster: Politics and Psyche in *Frankenstein*," *EF* 143–71.

19 My account is indebted to Carol Blum, *Rousseau and the Republic of Virtue: The Language of Politics in the French Revolution* (Ithaca, NY: Cornell University Press, 1986), pp. 133–52, 182–203.

20 See Philp, *Godwin's Political Justice*, pp. 142–53, 202–09; Clemit, *The Godwinian Novel*, pp. 70–79, 88–95.

21 Ronald Paulson, *Representations of Revolution, 1789–1820* (New Haven: Yale University Press, 1983), p. 239.

22 The following account of *Frankenstein* expands my arguments in *The Godwinian Novel*, pp. 139–74. Other sources drawn on include David Marshall, *The Surprising Effects of Sympathy: Marivaux, Diderot, Rousseau, and Mary Shelley* (Chicago: University of Chicago Press, 1988), pp. 178–227; and Gregory Dart, *Rousseau, Robespierre and English Romanticism* (Cambridge: Cambridge University Press, 1999), pp. 1–15, 43–75.

23 Mary Wollstonecraft, *Letters Written during a Short Residence in Sweden, Norway, and Denmark*, *The Works of Mary Wollstonecraft*, eds. Janet Todd and Marilyn Butler, 7 vols. (London: Pickering & Chatto, 1989), VI 342.

24 Godwin, *St. Leon: A Tale of the Sixteenth Century*, *Collected Novels and Memoirs of William Godwin*, gen. ed. Mark Philp, 8 vols. (London: Pickering & Chatto, 1992), IV 294.

25 Mary Wollstonecraft, *The Wrongs of Woman; or, Maria*, *Works*, I 96; see Gary Kelly, "'The Romance of Real Life': Autobiography in Rousseau and William Godwin," *Man and Nature/L'Homme et La Nature* I (1982), 93–101; Dart, *Rousseau, Robespierre*, pp. 118–38.

26 Godwin, *Fleetwood; or, The New Man of Feeling*, *Collected Novels*, V 159.

27 See Edward Duffy, *Rousseau in England: The Context for Shelley's Critique of the Enlightenment* (Berkeley: University of California Press, 1979), pp. 71–85.

28 I am grateful to Patrick Vincent for making available to me his unpublished paper, "'This Wretched Mockery of Justice': *Frankenstein* and Geneva," delivered at *Geneva: An English Enclave*, University of Geneva, November 1–2, 2001.

29 Abbé Augustin Barruel, *Memoirs, Illustrating the History of Jacobinism*, trans. Robert Clifford, 4 vols. (London, 1797–8), III 444.

30 Dart, *Rousseau, Robespierre*, pp. 1–2.

31 Eg. Jean-Jacques Rousseau, *The Confessions*, trans. J. M. Cohen (Harmondsworth: Penguin, 1953), pp. 333–34; and *The Reveries of the Solitary Walker*, trans. Peter France (Harmondsworth: Penguin, 1979), pp. 139–40.

32 Rousseau, *Confessions*, p. 398.

33 For Godwin's view of Milton's Satan, see *PJ* 146; cf. Wollstonecraft's emphasis in *Maria* on Jemima's lack of parental, especially maternal, care (*Works*, I 108–10).

34 Percy Bysshe Shelley, "On 'Frankenstein; or, the Modern Prometheus'" [1818], *The Prose Works of Percy Bysshe Shelley*, ed. E. B. Murray (Oxford University Press, 1993), I 283.

35 Eg., U. C. Knoepflmacher, "Thoughts on the Aggression of Daughters," *EF* 113–15; Terence Harpold, "'Did You Get Mathilda from Papa?': Seduction Fantasy and the Circulation of Mary Shelley's *Mathilda*," *SiR* 28 (Spring 1989), 49–67; for biographical details, see Sunstein, *Mary Shelley*, pp. 168–79.

36 For a fuller statement of the argument developed in the rest of this chapter, see my "From *The Fields of Fancy* to *Matilda*: Mary Shelley's Changing Conception of her Novella," *Romanticism* 3.2 (1997), 152–69, rpt. in *MST* 64–75.

37 Mary Shelley transcribed her husband's translation of Plato's *Symposium* from July 20 to August 6, 1818, and the pair read Dante's *Purgatorio* together in February and August 1819 (*J* I 220–22, 248, 294–95).

38 See Philp, *Godwin's Political Justice*, pp. 16–23.

39 Godwin, *Things As They Are; or, The Adventures of Caleb Williams, Collected Novels*, III 101. (Hereafter *CW*.)

40 Cf. *PJ* 18.

41 Godwin, *The Enquirer, Political and Philosophical Writings*, V 134; *CW* 273.

42 Philp, *Godwin's Political Justice*, pp. 24, 95.

43 Cf. *PJ* 53.

44 For Mary Shelley's involvement in the composition of *The Cenci*, see her 1839 "Note on The Cenci" (*NSW* II 282–83) and Bennett, *Mary Wollstonecraft Shelley*, pp. 47–48.

45 For details, see Michael Rossington, "Shelley, *The Cenci* and the French Revolution," in *Revolution in Writing: British Literary Responses to the French Revolution*, ed. Kelvin Everest (Buckingham and Bristol: Open University Press, 1991), pp. 138–57.

3

DIANE LONG HOEVELER

Frankenstein, feminism, and literary theory

Cave ab homine unius libri, as the Latin epigram warns us: "beware the author of one book." *Frankenstein* has so overshadowed Mary Shelley's other books in the popular imagination that many readers believe – erroneously – that she is a one-book author. While this is decidedly not the case, *Frankenstein* has figured more importantly in the development of feminist literary theory than perhaps any other novel, with the possible exception of Charlotte Brontë's *Jane Eyre*. This essay will discuss the major feminist literary interpretations of the novel, beginning with Ellen Moers's landmark reading in *Literary Women*[1] and then move to the more recent approaches taken by critics engaged in post-colonial theory, cultural studies, queer theory, and disability studies. In the process we will explore the provocative claim made by Fred Botting, who noted, "*Frankenstein* is a product of criticism, not a work of literature."[2]

Let us begin by describing briefly the three major strands in feminist literary criticism: American, French, and British. American feminist literary critics (represented best perhaps by Sandra Gilbert and Susan Gubar) understand "women's experiences" to be the basis of the differences in women's writings. American feminist critics of the 1970s and 1980s tended to discuss recurring patterns of themes (i.e., the valorization of the quotidian value of domestic life, human community and relationships) or imagery (i.e., houses, claustrophobia, food and eating disorders, insanity, fetishizing of clothing, body image, etc.) in works by women. Led by the pioneering work of Elaine Showalter, such critics also took pains to rediscover "lost" women writers and to demonstrate the continuities of a women's literary tradition.

By contrast, French feminist critics of this period (i.e., Julia Kristéva, Luce Irigaray, and Hélène Cixous, among others) were concerned with the way the masculine-dominated system of language produces meanings that tend to objectify or erase women's voices. In such a linguistic situation, women can rebel either through the strategic use of silence or by using *l'écriture feminine*, a specifically feminine form of language that is based on female subjectivity and the physiology and bodily instincts of women. French feminism identifies *l'écriture feminine* with the pleasures (*jouissance*) of living in and writing out of a female body in harmony with the voice and body of the mother. Such writing seeks to resist the patriarchal system by which man has sought to objectify and dominate the external world by reclaiming the voice of the mother and the prelinguistic potentiality of the unconscious.

British feminists (for example, Michele Barrett, Cora Kaplan, and Juliet Mitchell, among others) have criticized both the American and French approaches as essentialist, that is, for understanding "masculine" and "feminine" as essential categories rather than as qualities shaped by social class and economics. British feminists of the 1970s and 1980s maintained that no woman can write outside of the constraints and oppressions that dominate the social and economic systems she inhabits. Influenced by Marxian literary criticism, British feminists are concerned with the material conditions under which literature is produced, while at the same time viewing literature largely as a manifestation of the dominant cultural ideologies operating invisibly in the society. As we will see, all three schools of feminist criticism are well represented in the critical work on *Frankenstein*, the novel itself appropriated as a sort of template by feminist critics with diverse approaches.

Feminist readings: the 1970s and 1980s

In her *Literary Women*, Ellen Moers first coined the term "female gothic" to define what she called a genre written by women, centering on a "young woman who is simultaneously persecuted victim and courageous heroine." Moers's emphasis on the heroine's body is significant, for it signals a new theme in feminist criticism, a reading of literature not as a purely cerebral activity, but as one based in the pleasures and pains of the body. Moers was one of the first critics to recognize that *Frankenstein* evolved out of Shelley's own tragic experience as a young, unwed mother of a baby who would live only a few weeks. For Moers, *Frankenstein* is a "birth myth" that reveals the "revulsion against newborn life, and the drama of guilt, dread, and flight surrounding birth and its consequences." Mary Wollstonecraft, as her daughter well knew, was killed by puerperal fever, contracted when she was unable to expel the placenta after Mary Shelley's birth in 1797. Moers reads Shelley's novel as a sublimated afterbirth, in which the author expels her own guilt both for having caused her mother's death and for having failed to produce a healthy son and heir for Percy (as his legal wife Harriet had done three months earlier). For Moers, the novel's strength was to present the "abnormal, or monstrous, manifestations of the child–parent tie" and in so doing, "to transform the standard Romantic matter of incest, infanticide, and patricide into a phantasmagoria of the nursery."[3] Moers died shortly after the publication of her major work, but her approach was elaborated and sustained when, three years later, U. C. Knoepflmacher as well as Gilbert and Gubar were making similar assessments of the novel's focus on parenting – more often than not, inadequate parenting.

Knoepflmacher's own essay in his important collection, *The Endurance of "Frankenstein,"* explores Shelley's conflicted and ambivalent relationship to both her parents, one dead and the other very much alive. Knoepflmacher states: "*Frankenstein* resurrects and rearranges an adolescent's conflicting emotions about her relation both to the dead mother she idealized and mourned and to the living, 'sententious and authoritative' father-philosopher she admired and deeply resented for his imperfect attempts at 'moulding' Mary Wollstonecraft's two daughters."[4] His psycho-biographical approach to the work widened its readership by aligning it with the psychomachias written by such canonical male romantic poets as Percy Shelley, William Blake, and even Samuel Taylor Coleridge. By seeing the novel as essentially a "war within the mind" of the central character, in this case Victor functioning as a stand-in for Mary Shelley herself, literary critics like Knoepflmacher placed the work clearly within a recognizable Romantic framework.

In 1979, Sandra M. Gilbert and Susan Gubar also published their groundbreaking study of nineteenth-century women writers, *The Madwoman in the Attic*. Gilbert and Gubar interpret *Frankenstein* as a "Romantic 'reading' of *Paradise Lost*," with Victor alternately playing the roles of Adam, Satan, and Eve. The first two roles had become fairly standard topics of discussion in the criticism of the novel, but the last role, "Victor-as-Eve," was to assume a distinctly important function in the evolution of American feminist approaches to the work. Gilbert and Gubar's theory about the anxieties that plague a woman writer informs their approach to *Frankenstein* as "a waking dream . . . a Romantic novel about – among other things – Romanticism, as well as a book about books and perhaps, too, about the writers of books." With this approach, the specter of Mary Wollstonecraft – a woman plagued by her attempts to reconcile the needs of her mind with her body – begins to haunt their account: "For this orphaned literary heiress, highly charged connections between femaleness and literariness must have been established early, and established specifically in relation to the controversial figure of her dead mother." Gilbert and Gubar coin the term "bibliogenesis" to capture their sense of Shelley's "fantasy of sex and reading," that she brought herself to birth not through a human mother, but through the reading and consumption of books which "functioned as her surrogate parents." The chief contribution of Gilbert and Gubar, however, lies in their recognition that Victor's role "is paradigmatic, like the falsely creative fallen angel, of the female artist, whose anxiety about her own aesthetic activity is expressed in Mary Shelley's deferential introductory phrase about her 'hideous progeny,' with its plain implication that in her alienated attic workshop of filthy creation she has given birth to a deformed book, a literary abortion or miscarriage."[5] In Gilbert's and Gubar's work, we find both the pragmatic wisdom and the limitations of American feminist literary criticism, which often sidesteps a rigorous examination of the specific historical contexts in which the literature was written.

In the 1980s, the increasingly explicit discussion of bodily issues in the novel – one manifestation of the influence of French feminist theory – was counterbalanced by a more textually oriented approach to this highly allusive and literary novel. In her influential book, *The Proper Lady and the Woman Writer*, Mary Poovey locates the tension between sexuality and textuality within the novel. Poovey focuses on the conflict between proper, conduct-book femininity identity and improper female, original, Romantic self-assertion: "[T]he narrative strategy of *Frankenstein*, like the symbolic presentation of the monster, enables Shelley to express and efface herself at the same time and thus, at least partially, to satisfy her conflicting desires for self-assertion and social acceptance."[6] Poovey's analysis focuses on Shelley's ambivalent responses to the ideology of motherhood, as well as on her condemnation of masculine Romantic egotism, epitomized in her husband's naively idealistic – perhaps cavalier – attitude to marriage vows, family responsibility, and societal conventions.

As we have seen, feminist criticism has never been monolithic; not surprisingly, some feminist critics have been keenly influenced by the assumptions and strategies of post-structuralist criticism, especially deconstruction. For feminism, the appeal of deconstruction lies in its capacity to explode the foundational assumptions of patriarchy. Once the human subject is decentered and viewed as a social construction, gender itself can be viewed as an artificial construct, a play of signifiers. As adapted from the work of Jacques Derrida, deconstruction became a technique of reading that stressed not the unity and wholeness of a text, but instead its gaps, fissures, or breaks in structure. Deconstruction further empowered feminists who had already undertaken to denounce Western culture's crucial binary oppositions – culture/nature; male/female – and embrace the belief that there are no determinate bounds to a text or a gender.

The emphasis on textuality that we see in Poovey and later Barbara Johnson was clearly indebted not simply to deconstruction, but also to the theories of Michel Foucault, who defined some of the dominant strategies practiced by literary critics working in a post-structuralist mode. Foucault claims that power operates throughout society through the manipulation of "discourse systems" that control how ideologies are disseminated. Feminists who have adapted Foucault's theories have studied literary genres as species of "discourse systems" that control and dominate how women function in a society that prescribes how they appear and behave. Hence, feminists and critics working in cultural studies have been interested in *Frankenstein* as a particularly potent discourse system, a manifestation of conflicted ideologies, working sometimes in league with its society's repressive attitudes towards women and sometimes arguing against society's negative stereotypes about the proper roles of mothers, daughters, servants, and friends.

One of the first American critics to link feminism and deconstruction, Barbara Johnson adopts a self-conscious and self-reflexive literary approach to the novel by analyzing it as an autobiographical record of the "struggle for feminine authorship": "*Frankenstein* can be read as the story of the experience of writing *Frankenstein*." Most interesting in Johnson's discussion, however, is her recognition of the novel as dominated by its "description of a primal scene of creation . . . where do babies come from? And where do stories come from? In both cases, the scene of creation is described, but the answer to these questions is still withheld."[7] As we shall see shortly, these questions about *Frankenstein* would be developed in the 1990s by Peter Brooks and Fred Botting.

In addition to deconstruction and post-structuralist theories, feminist literary criticism has also had to wrestle with the legacy of Sigmund Freud, particularly with his theories of gender, of the development of sexuality, of object choice, of the parents' role in gender formation, of repression and sublimation, and of the girl's transition from maternal to paternal identifications. Feminists such as Juliet Mitchell, in *Psychoanalysis and Feminism*,[8] have sought to rethink such Freudian concepts as "the Oedipus complex," "penis envy," and "infantile sexuality," rather than merely reject them wholesale. In this influential study, Mitchell takes a shrewd look at "the ideology of the biological family," a subject of endless interest to feminist readers of *Frankenstein*.

A variety of psychoanalytical approaches to the novel increasingly came to dominate the feminist criticism of the 1980s. Mary Jacobus's 1982 article, "Is There a Woman in This Text," offers one of the most influential observations made on the novel: "A curious thread in the plot focuses not on the image of the hostile father (Frankenstein/God) but on that of the dead mother who comes to symbolize to the monster his loveless state. Literally unmothered, he fantasizes acceptance by a series of women but founders in imagined rebuffs and ends in violence."[9] By bringing into the forefront the need to recognize the importance of the representation of women within the absences, gaps, or fissures of a work, Jacobus situated women as a category of significance within the deconstructive methodology. Her syncretic approach, feminist-deconstructive, informed by psychoanalysis, helped to make this among the most widely cited of all critical essays on *Frankenstein*. In the same year, Kate Ellis published "Monsters in the Garden: Mary Shelley and the Bourgeois Family," an article that explores the constraining and claustrophobic sex-roles in the novel. For Ellis, the work is an attack on the oppressiveness of domesticity and the doctrine of separate spheres (public vs. private) for men and women.

Devon Hodge, in her 1983 essay "*Frankenstein* and the Feminine Subversion of the Novel," adapts French feminist theoretical positions to explain the use of three male narrators in the text: "But perhaps in adopting a male voice, the woman writer is given the opportunity to intervene from within, to become an alien presence that undermines the stability of the male voice."[10] Hodge's use of the terms "lack" and "absence" reveals the influence of another towering figure in feminist psychoanalytic theory: the French analyst Jacques Lacan. Lacan revised Freud's basic positions by claiming that the true subject of psychoanalysis was language and the unconscious mind, not the ego and its relation to the body, as Freud had asserted. For Lacan, psycho-sexual development could be understood by charting the stages that human beings undergo as they learn to process language. Lacan saw the so-called symbolic realm of language as the realm of the law of the father, in which the "phallus" (the symbol of the father's power) was the "privileged signifier" for all discourse. Lacan further asserted that all discourse was driven by a "desire" for a lost and unachievable object, as if moving incessantly along a chain of unstable signifiers without any possibility of coming to any final point of meaning or fixed significance. For Lacan, this hole within the self was a "lack," an "absence," hence the heavy use of the term by feminist critics influenced by his theories about development.

Another influential Lacanian reading belongs to Peter Brooks, who claims that the creature's monstrosity is the result of his inability to enter the signifying chain and language and thereby to gain meaning as a transcendental signified. Brooks's "What is a Monster? (According to *Frankenstein*)" relies on Lacan's theory of the "mirror stage," during which individual subjectivity is formed when the child sees itself reflected in the mother's eyes. According to Brooks, the motherless creature can only find what he thinks is human identity through the acquisition of language and the mastery of texts in the De Lacey household. Such a narrative displays, then, the constructed nature of bodies, and, ultimately, of cultures. As he notes, whatever else the monster might be, it "may also be that which eludes gender definition."[11]

But Lacan's most famous student in Paris, the Bulgarian emigrée Julia Kristéva, countered his theory of patriarchal language with a prelinguistic, pre-oedipal signifying process centered on the infant's complete immersion and oneness with the body of the mother. This so-called semiotic stage of the completely unified mother and child is typically repressed when we acquire patriarchal language and enter the realm of the "symbolic." But Kristéva believes that the semiotic can always break out in revolutionary ways – particularly in avant-garde poetry – as a "heterogeneous destructive causality" that assaults the stable "subject." This revolutionary assault undermines the rationality of phallic discourse and the power of the "law of the Father," the patriarchal system that keeps women in a marginal status. Since language acquisition, the body of the mother, and the assault on the father are all central themes in *Frankenstein*, we can see why her influence continues to figure importantly.

A recent example of Kristéva's influence in the work of British critic Marie Mulvey-Roberts (2000) makes the point nicely. For Kristéva, in order to become a separate and speaking subject apart from the mother, the individual must reject everything associated with the mother's body and see it as "unacceptable, unclean or anti-social."[12] But the mother's body, now called "the abject," can never be completely expelled from one's consciousness and instead always exists on the borders of one's identity – like a corpse or bodily waste: "the most sickening of wastes . . . a border that has encroached upon everything . . . It is death infecting life. Abject. It is something rejected from which one does not part, for which one does not protect oneself as from an object. Imaginary uncanniness and real threat, it beckons to us and ends up engulfing us."[13] For Mulvey-Roberts, the creature represents the "spectre of the maternal body as well as Frankenstein's monstrous child." Hence, "the quest for the expelled abject and reunion with it are another form of catharsis for matricidal guilt; in Shelley, this quest converges with the Female Gothic quest for the missing mother and the Romantic quest for lost origins."[14] The abjected maternal also comes into focus in "Bearing Demons: *Frankenstein*'s Circumvention of the Maternal," a crucial chapter in Margaret Homans's 1986 book *Bearing the Word*. For Homans, the novel "portrays the situation of women obliged to play the role of the literal in a culture that devalues it . . . [T]he novel is simultaneously about the death and obviation of the mother and about the son's quest for a substitute object of desire."[15]

Perhaps because of Kristéva's influence, a key episode for psychoanalytic critics has been Victor's dream of seeing the youthful Elizabeth walking in the street, only to watch her turn into his dead mother, worms crawling over her decaying flesh (*F* I iv 34–35). Such critics read the dream as the "moment of desire" in the novel, with its conflation of the sexualized Elizabeth ("desire") and the dead mother ("lack"). Victor's rejection of his creature has been seen as one manifestation of the child's sense of abandonment and betrayal by the dead mother. He blames Elizabeth for spreading the disease that killed his mother, at the same time he blamed his younger brother and Justine for stealing his mother's affections from him, the first child and rightful love object of the mother. In creating the monster, Victor attempts to undo the death of his mother. The monster is, so to speak, the first run on an experiment that Victor intends to eventually undertake on his dead mother's corpse. To psychoanalytic critics, all of this points to Shelley's own inability to accept her mother's death, as well as her baby's. And all of this suggests that the writing of literature was, for Shelley as for so many others, one way of denying the power of death.

Another key scene in the text for feminist critics is the creation and then destruction of the female creature's body, the "mate" that Victor had promised the creature in return for their exile from humanity. The fact that Victor constructs the body and then, when contemplating the realities of sexuality, desire, and reproduction, rips that body apart, suggests that the female body is for Victor infinitely more threatening and "monstrous" than was the creature's male body. As Homans notes:

> [T]he impossibility of Frankenstein giving [his creature] a female demon, an object of its own desire, aligns the demon with women, who are forbidden to have their own desires. But if the demon is really a feminine object of desire, why is it a he? I would suggest that this constitutes part of Shelley's exposure to the male romantic economy that would substitute for real and therefore powerful female others a being imagined on the model of the poet's own self. By making the demon masculine, Shelley suggests that romantic desire seeks to do away, not only with the mother, but also with all females so as to live finally in a world of mirrors that reflect a comforting illusion of the male self's independent wholeness.[16]

The theme of the masculine Romantic ego in love with only versions of itself writ large is a topic that Shelley would have encountered in her husband's early poem *Alastor, or The Spirit of Solitude*. But Victor's inability to allow the female creature to live is, for feminist critics, more than narcissism; it is another instance of the misogyny and fear of female sexuality that Shelley exposes and condemns.

But even psychoanalytic critics continue to be informed by the pragmatic legacy of American feminist criticism, for there are many who focus on the novel's female presences, rather than female absences. William Veeder's *Mary Shelley & Frankenstein: The Fate of Androgyny* dissects Shelley's psyche in a more traditional Freudian manner to explore her female characters. For Veeder, "Mary Shelley's very sense of the weakness in herself and womanhood makes her defensive in *Frankenstein*."[17] By reading Shelley's personal life back into the text, Veeder concludes that the motivating force in the work is a "negative Oedipus" compulsion, or the need to destroy the father, not the mother. For Veeder, Mary's real rage in her life was toward her distant and emotionally unavailable father, and so the victims of the creature move inexorably back through the alphabet of names to "Alphonse," the father, the Alpha of the Universe.

Perhaps the most provocative essay to focus on the female body is Susan Winnett's "Coming Unstrung: Women, Men, Narrative, and Principles of Pleasure," which begins with the invitation, "first, let us return to the question of orgasm." Boldly, Winnett reinterprets the three male-narrated sections of the novel according to "the different narrative logic – and the very different possibilities of pleasure – that emerge when issues such as incipience, repetition, and closure are reconceived in terms of an experience of the female body." The central bodily experiences conveyed in *Frankenstein*, according to Winnett, are giving birth and breast-feeding:

> Shelley's use of the rhythms and dynamics of the experience of birth criticizes the culture's association of detumescence and "significant discharge" with ending and sense making. In its unrelenting insistence on the demands made by the figure whose existence turns the scientist's triumphant *consummatum est* into a new beginning, Shelley's narrative poses questions not accommodated in a *Master*plot and gestures toward an economy in which another consideration of the relations among beginning, middles, and ends would yield different results.[18]

Winnett's emphasis on the pleasures of the female body suggests the influence of French feminists Cixous and Irigaray. This focus on the female body (if not on its pleasures) is sustained in Paul Youngquist's 1991 article, "*Frankenstein*: The Mother, the Daughter, and the Monster," which argues that it is not the father who was the target of Mary's critique in the novel, but the mother – specifically, Mary Wollstonecraft's rationalist, almost bodiless, form of feminism: "[O]ne of Shelley's central tenets is that her mother's feminism reduces the human to a rational corpse."[19] Clearly, writing on *Frankenstein* from a biographical perspective has led feminist critics to a new assessment of Wollstonecraft's life and work, and one of the results of the work on Shelley has been a renaissance in studies of her mother's influence on cultural and literary history.

As we turn to more recent approaches, it is worth noting Fred Botting's reflexive study of *Frankenstein* criticism, *Making Monstrous: "Frankenstein," Criticism, Theory*. Botting ventures that the dialectical relationship between Victor and his creature reveals "a partial glance away from the repetitions of opposition and difference, of this hidden law of textuality, that offers no mastery and confers precious little authority." Reading the novel through one critical approach can only lead, according to Botting, to a recognition of the "monstrous differences of the text . . . *Frankenstein* seems to foreground the contradictions and conflicts of and between positions." Because Botting's reading responds to Mary Jacobus's and Margaret Homans's attempts to locate the feminine, he reconsiders the same scene that they focused on – Victor's destruction of the unfinished female creature:

> The destruction of the female binds the monster closely to humanity, and Victor in particular, and foregrounds the need for a monster to haunt the margins of those networks of signification which define humanity . . . The monster's marginal place, neither outside nor inside, is thus the place of differences, of others whose monstrousness is that they cannot be finally fixed in one place alone. Indeed, the system in which meaning is produced could not function without such monstrous elements.

Reviewing theories of political monstrosity from Hobbes to Burke, Botting concludes that monstrosity represents "a complex and changing resistance to established authority."[20] As befits a critic who posits the critically constructed nature of *Frankenstein*, Botting's work on the novel cannot be neatly categorized. It veers from political to psychoanalytical to linguistic; as we shall see, it also anticipates the approaches of cultural studies and disability studies. Notwithstanding Botting's epigram – "*Frankenstein* is a product of criticism" – there must be few novels that could occasion such a diversity of approaches in a single study.

Recent views: cultural studies, queer theory, and disability studies

So what is the difference that gender makes? continues to be the dominant question in feminist, psychoanalytical, and materialist readings of the novel. And clearly the critical discussions have centered on the realities of Shelley's life as a daughter, a wife, and a mother herself. Critics have gone back and forth, assigning the mother or the father, the husband, siblings, or children the central position of importance in her creative work. The decade of the 1990s, however, which began with the publication of Stephen Behrendt's *Approaches to Teaching Shelley's "Frankenstein"* (containing an excellent essay by Susan J. Wolfson on feminist approaches) saw feminist readings expand to include the insights of post-colonial theory, queer theory, cultural studies, and disability studies. Many of the critics working in these latter and newer areas have been deeply indebted to the feminist approaches of the 1980s.

Post-colonial theory, propelled by Edward Said's seminal study, *Orientalism*,[21] has been used fruitfully to explore the complicated class, race, and gender issues raised by *Frankenstein*, as well as a number of other works. Gayatri Chakravorty Spivak's oft-cited "Three Women's Texts and a Critique of Imperialism," focusing on *Jane Eyre* and *Wide Sargasso Sea* in addition to *Frankenstein*, reads the latter work as "a text of nascent feminism that remains cryptic."[22] Sketching out the Orientalist ideology operating in the novel, Spivak briefly analyzes the objectification of Safie as an eroticized Other, and compares her to the similarly fetishized dark women in Brontë's and Rhys's novels. But in a 1992 postscript, Spivak at last states explicitly what was only implicit in the earlier version: "The feminist dimension of [*Frankenstein*] provides a frame that is critical of the effort to construct a creature without womb-life and infancy. But when it comes to the colonial subject's pre-history, Shelley's political imagination fails. (We have seen that in postcoloniality, the subject mourns the unlamented death of this previous history.")[23] This remarkably suggestive observation positions post-colonialism within a psychoanalytical framework, implying that colonized subjects mourn the loss of their oppressors, much as children mourn the death of their abusers, much as the creature mourns the death of Victor. Spivak indicts *Frankenstein*, then, for being complicitous with its cultural, social, and historical conditions, rather than standing apart from that history and condemning its use and abuse of others (women, creatures, children).

Another important practice of post-colonial criticism, one indebted to the new historicism, is to locate the meaning of the text in the socio-political context in which it was composed. H. L. Malchow examines the material and historical contexts of African emigration into Britain and the West Indies, arguing that Frankenstein's creature needs to be read within the "tradition in which the mixed-race person was often represented as an ambivalent creature torn between different cultures and loyalties, an outcast, a misfit, and a biological unnatural."[24] D. S. Neff invokes the growing Anglo-Indian population and their awkward presence in England to suggest that fascination and repugnance toward dark-skinned or half-caste peoples alternates in the novel.

Safie, the dark-skinned daughter of a Muslim father and a Coptic (Christian) mother, figures prominently in several post-colonial readings. Most recently, Ronald Bush has focused on one of the central issues in post-colonial theory – the diaspora – or the forced dispersal of people from their native land. Bush claims that the creature's speech "is unintelligible outside a colonial context. In case the horror of the monster viewing himself through the eyes of his European neighbors was not pointed enough for her readers, Shelley explicitly aligns his anguish with Europe's relations to the Orient." Comparing the creature to Safie's father, Bush concludes that "after their rejection, the monster, like Safie's father before him, turns to the wickedness that has been expected of him,"[25] by Western racial stereotypes of the "evil" Oriental. Elizabeth Bohls's 1994 article explores not only the use of late eighteenth-century British theories of race, but also the influence of Edmund Burke's aesthetic theories. Placing *Frankenstein* in the context of other popular travel literature of the day: Mungo Park's *Travels in the Interior Districts of Africa*, Thomas Pennant's *View of Hindoostan*, Bryan Edwards's *History of the West Indies*, Bohls sees Shelley's work not as an endorsement of Western hegemony, but instead as an indictment of Burkean aesthetics, an "inherently imperial discourse, structured by principles of hierarchy and exclusion."[26]

Cultural studies is an approach to literature that examines both popular and literary works in relation to a larger cultural matrix of other writings – historical, political, or commercial. For instance, *Frankenstein* might be examined in light of contemporary conduct books on the proper behavior of parents or children, or in relation to newspaper accounts of mixed-race peoples, or in juxtaposition to other popular literary genres of its day – the sentimental romance, the scientific fantasy, or the educational treatise. Again, one can see how feminist criticism has influenced such an approach, as feminism has long posited that "high" culture is a system that favors males and that acts to ensure the continued power and status of the patriarchy. By examining what has traditionally been considered "low" cultural artifacts, feminists have opened up and made available many works written by women and neglected by the literary establishment.

Class issues frequently form the basis of cultural studies readings. As early as 1983, Anca Vlasopolos located the novel's "hidden logic" in the author's "fusion of the socio-political forces used to ensure the survival of the aristocracy with the private drama of a man who sees himself as ineluctably driven to incest." Vlasopolos also argues that another subtext of the novel concerns its indictment of a class system that has created "an aesthetics of exclusion to perpetuate its ascendancy," hence explaining why the novel was banned in her native South Africa in 1955. In an intelligent analysis of the work's subversive sympathies, Vlasopolos claims: "Class selection, namely the survival of the upper class and its will-to-power, appears in incident after incident throughout the novel and acts as the barely visible crack which in the end causes the collapse of the house of Frankenstein."[27] More recently, the Italian critic Franco Moretti has analyzed the creature in the novel as informed by Marx's theory of the alienation of the proletariat. In an influential chapter in his book *Signs Taken for Wonders*,[28] Moretti has discussed

the creature alongside Dracula, the displaced aristocrat, as the two archetypal and intensely anxiety-producing class-based figures in nineteenth-century
British culture.

Cultural studies criticism has drawn on, and in turn responded to, Ellen
Moers's politically charged notion of the "female gothic." Most recently, my
essay, "Fantasy, Trauma, and Gothic Daughters: *Frankenstein* as Therapy,"[29]
places the novel within the framework of the female Gothic tradition, labeled
"Gothic feminism." I differ from Moers in seeing the true woman in the
text as "Victor," a Gothic feminist who manipulates others to do "his"
bidding, all the way washing "his" hands of responsibility for the elimination
of his family – rivals for the lost mother's love. Lee Heller distinguishes
among three different types of Gothic: horror, sentimental-educational, and
philosophical. Each variety of Gothic does different "cultural work" on its
specific audience, each of whom came from a different class of readers. A
further cultural studies approach has been to analyze the varieties of popular
cultural adaptations of the novel, including the myriad film productions
inspired by it (see chapters 4 and 5).

Cultural studies readings also juxtapose literary works with nonliterary,
even ephemeral, texts, for instance, scientific beliefs or superstitions current
at the time of a novel's composition. Anne K. Mellor's critical biography,
Mary Shelley: Her Life, Her Fiction, Her Monsters, argues that Shelley criticizes the scientific discoveries and increasing technological advancements
that were taking place in her own day, advocating instead a more humane,
sympathetic, and nurturing use of science to improve human life. For Mellor,
the novel charts how Nature, a specifically feminine power, avenges herself
on Victor's benighted – rational, objective, Enlightenment – masculinity.

But in addition to working in a feminist-cultural studies mode, Mellor
was one of the earliest critics to recognize the homosocial dynamic operating in the text, writing that Victor's "most passionate relationships are with
men rather than with women . . . In the place of a normal heterosexual attachment to Elizabeth, Victor has substituted a homosexual obsession with
his creature, an obsession that in his case is energized by a profound desire
to reunite with his dead mother, by becoming himself a monster."[30] Such
a recognition lies at the center of numerous queer-theory readings of the
novel, which are in part motivated by the feminist analysis of gender as a
cultural construct. One of the central concerns of queer studies has been the
heretofore unrecognized issue of "male homosocial desire," a concept initially defined by Eve Sedgwick. Her pioneering work, *Between Men*, identifies
masculinity, paranoia, and homophobia as the bases of male Gothic texts.
According to Sedgwick, British patriarchy is predicated on "male homosocial desire," or the bonds both of competition *and attraction* that arise in the

heretofore masculine arenas of sports, military service, and the professions. Even so, men are encouraged to experience "homophobia" or "homosexual panic" at the thought of physical contact with another man. For Sedgwick, *Frankenstein* is one of the texts that explores the ambivalences of what she calls "paranoid Gothic": "Romantic novels in which a male hero is in a close, usually murderous relation to another male figure, in some respects his 'double,' to whom he seems to be mentally transparent."[31] For Sedgwick, Victor and his creature/double are engaged in the classic homosocial dyad gone horribly wrong so that the murderous rejection of the bond between them can only end in both their deaths.

Jonathan Dollimore, another queer-studies theorist, offers a suggestive theory of the "perverse" that directs us to moments when the binary structures that give meaning to society (male/female; heterosexual/homosexual) break down without being totally dissolved or eradicated.[32] According to this approach, Victor enters the realm of the perverse when he begins to create his monster, knowing that by so doing, he is rupturing his society's normative codes of behavior and binary structures (male/female; God/man). For James Holt McGavran, Victor is driven to create a giant male who would adore him because of his own unconscious "homoerotic desire" – desire that turns quickly to panic. Alternatively, in a recent lesbian reading, Frann Michel sees in the novel a series of gaps, absences, and contradictions when the subject of same-sex desire between women occurs. Michel criticizes feminists like Homans for her heterosexist bias and her refusal to recognize desire between women in the novel. Similarly, Bette London criticizes the heterosexist bias in Veeder, whom she accuses of failing to recognize the homosexuality implicit in the narcissistic fetishizing of the male body. For London, "a feminist critique might best fulfill its project by . . . reading the presence of the novel's self-consciously male texts to illuminate the absences they cover, to expose the self-contradictions they repress."[33] And finally there is also a transgendered reading of *Frankenstein*, written by the transgendered writer Susan Stryker. In an autobiographical narrative that parallels the creature's own narrative within the novel, Stryker reveals the anger she has experienced because of her pain and rejection, comparing it to the ostracism that "Frankenstein's monster felt in its enmity to the human race."[34] But it is not simply anger that Stryker describes. She also compares the reconstruction of her new female body to Victor's assembly of the monster's, noting that both operations bespeak the conservative attempt to stabilize gender in the service of heterosexism.

It is interesting, then, to observe in a transgendered woman's reference to physical "disfigurement," a clear link to disability-studies approaches to the novel. Disability studies, another relatively new and growing field of literary criticism, also owes a good deal of its impetus to the influence of feminist and post-structuralist approaches to literary criticism. The purpose of disability studies, according to Simi Linton, is to criticize the constricted, inaccurate, and inhumane concepts of disability that have dominated academic inquiry, in particular the notion that disability is primarily a medical category. As Linton explains:

> [T]he medicalization of disability casts human variation as deviance from the norm, as pathological condition, as deficit, and significantly, as an individual burden and personal tragedy. Society, in agreeing to assign medical meaning to *disability*, colludes to keep the issue within the purview of the medical establishment, to keep it a personal matter and "treat" the condition and the person with the condition rather than "treating" the social processes and policies that constrict disabled people's lives . . . [Our goal] is the reinterpretation of *disability* as a political category and to the social changes that could follow such a shift.[35]

From this definition, then, one can see how the creature could be interpreted as "disabled" in a society that values external beauty (as defined by the aesthetic theories of Edmund Burke), conformity, and stable gender and class determinacy. Not surprisingly, therapists, social workers, and educators have used film versions of *Frankenstein* to stimulate discussion among the disabled.

Thus far, a few critics have seized on *Frankenstein* as a paradigmatic text that expresses the "otherness" of living as differently abled in a world of able, hostile, or indifferent people. In "The Monster's Human Nature," the biologist Stephen Jay Gould places the novel within this context by exploring the nature/nurture debate in regard to the evolution of the monster. Gould argues that "the creature becomes a monster because he is cruelly ensnared by one of the deepest predispositions of our biological inheritance – our aversion toward seriously malformed individuals." For Gould, it is a "mammalian pattern" to inherit an "instinctive aversion to serious malformation," which needs to be tempered by "learning and understanding." The creature in Shelley's novel represents, for Gould, the disabled person who is born into a society that is genetically programmed to reject and persecute him for his physical differences. For Gould, Shelley uses an extreme case to explore the nature versus nurture debate: "[N]ature can only supply a predisposition, while culture shapes specific results . . . [we must all] judge people by their qualities of soul, not by their external appearances."[36] More recently, Denise Gigante, in her article "Facing the Ugly: The Case of *Frankenstein*,"[37] traces the etymology and history of the term "ugly," placing Shelley's use of an "ugly" character in its historical, social, and political contexts. In treating ugliness as a disability, Shelley's novel reveals the philosophical, psychological, and aesthetic bases for the cruelty we heap on others not like ourselves. The "otherness" of the creature, founded in its physical appearance and size, is yet another manifestation of disability, a permanent physical condition that the subject can never alter. The responses that the monster experiences from his creator and society – rejection, fear, hatred, and punishment – can all be compared to those described by other disabled writers or characters.

So is it valid to claim, as Botting has, that Frankenstein is a "product of criticism, not a work of literature"? Clearly, one has to wonder what status and reputation *Frankenstein* would have now if feminist literary critics had not "rediscovered" the book with such passion and imagination in the 1970s. The fact that the novel proved to be such fertile ground for so many different critical schools has no doubt led to its installation as the most frequently taught canonical novel written by a woman in the early nineteenth century. But to imply that literary critics "created" the novel as a work of literature is not fair to the work's artistry or complexity. *Frankenstein* may be, in the words of one of its most acute readers, a "flawed" novel, but its power as a literary work is undeniable. It is the "mother-lode" of feminist criticism, as well as the text on which many literary critics have tested their assumptions and theories. It continues to entrance, irritate, and puzzle readers and critics alike because it speaks at once – in so many different contradictory voices – to so many issues that are central to what we make of being "human."

NOTES

1 Ellen Moers, *Literary Women* (Garden City, NY: Doubleday, 1976).
2 Fred Botting, ed., *Frankenstein/Mary Shelley* (New York: St. Martin's, 1995), p. 1.
3 Moers, *Literary Women*, pp. 91, 93, 99, 99.
4 U. C. Knoepflmacher, "Thoughts on the Aggression of Daughters," *EF* 91.
5 Sandra Gilbert and Susan Gubar, *The Madwoman in the Attic* (New Haven: Yale University Press, 1979), pp. 222, 222, 223, 223.
6 Mary Poovey, *The Proper Lady and the Woman Writer* (Chicago: University of Chicago Press, 1984), p. 131.
7 Barbara Johnson, "My Monster/My Self," *Diacritics* 12.2 (1982), 3, 7, 7.
8 Juliet Mitchell, *Psychoanalysis and Feminism* (London: Penguin, 1974).
9 Mary Jacobus, "Is There a Woman in This Text," *New Literary History* 14.1 (1982), 132–33.
10 Devon Hodges, "*Frankenstein* and the Feminine Subversion of the Novel," *Tulsa Studies in Women's Literature* 2.2 (1983), 157.
11 Peter Brooks, *Body Work: Objects of Desire in Modern Narrative* (Cambridge, MA: Harvard University Press, 1993), p. 219.

12 Elizabeth Gross, "The Body of Signification," in *Abjection, Melancholia and Love: The Works of Julia Kristéva*, eds. John Fletcher and Andrew Benjamin (London: Routledge, 1990), p. 86.

13 Julia Kristéva, *Powers of Horror: An Essay on Abjection*, trans. Leon S. Roudiez (New York: Columbia University Press, 1982), pp. 3–4.

14 Marie Mulvey-Roberts, "The Corpse in the Corpus: *Frankenstein*, Rewriting Wollstonecraft and the Abject," in *Mary Shelley's Fictions: From Frankenstein to Falkner*, ed. Michael Eberle-Sinatra (New York: Macmillan, 2000), pp. 199, 204.

15 Margaret Homans, "Bearing Demons: *Frankenstein*'s Circumvention of the Maternal," *Bearing the Word: Language and Female Experience in Nineteenth-Century Women's Writing* (Chicago: University of Chicago Press, 1986), p. 100.

16 *Ibid.*, p. 107.

17 William Veeder, *Mary Shelley & Frankenstein: The Fate of Androgyny* (Chicago: University of Chicago Press, 1986), p. 182.

18 Susan Winnett, "Coming Unstrung: Women, Men, Narrative, and Principles of Pleasure," *PMLA* 105.3 (1990), 505, 509, 510–11.

19 Paul Youngquist, "*Frankenstein*: The Mother, the Daughter, and the Monster," *Philological Quarterly* 70.3 (1991), 342.

20 Fred Botting, *Making Monstrous: "Frankenstein," Criticism, Theory* (New York: St. Martin's, 1991), pp. 136, 136, 113, 131.

21 Edward Said, *Orientalism* (New York: Vintage, 1979).

22 Gayatri Chakravorty Spivak, "Three Women's Texts and a Critique of Imperialism," *Critical Inquiry* 12 (1985), 254, 258.

23 Gayatri Chakravorty Spivak, "*Frankenstein* and a Critique of Imperialism," in *F 1818*, p. 269.

24 H. L. Malchow, *Gothic Images of Race in Nineteenth-Century Britain* (Stanford, CA: Stanford University Press, 1996), pp. 198–99.

25 Ronald Bush, "Monstrosity and Representation in the Postcolonial Diaspora: *The Satanic Verses, Ulysses, and Frankenstein*," in *Borders, Exiles, Diasporas*, eds. Elazar Barkan and Marie-Denise Shelton (Stanford, CA: Stanford University Press, 1998), p. 245, 245.

26 Elizabeth Bohls, "Standards of Taste, Discourses of 'Race,' and the Aesthetic Education of a Monster: Critique of Empire in *Frankenstein*," *Eighteenth-Century Life* 18.3 (1994), 34.

27 Anca Vlasopolos, "*Frankenstein*'s Hidden Skeleton: The Psycho-Politics of Oppression," *Science-Fiction Studies* 10 (1983), 125, 125.

28 Franco Moretti, "Dialectic of Fear," in *Signs Taken For Wonders* (London: Verso, 1988), pp. 83–108.

29 Diane Long Hoeveler, "Fantasy, Trauma, and Gothic Daughters: *Frankenstein* as Therapy," *Prism(s)* 8 (2000), 7–28.

30 Anne K. Mellor, *Mary Shelley: Her Life, Her Fiction, Her Monsters* (New York: Methuen, 1988), pp. 121–22.

31 Eve Kosofsky Sedgwick, *Between Men: English Literature and Male Homosocial Desire* (New York: Columbia University Press, 1985), p. 186n.

32 Jonathan Dollimore, *Sexual Dissidence: Augustine to Wilde, Freud to Foucault* (Oxford: Oxford University Press, 1991), pp. 229–30.

33 Bette London, "Mary Shelley, *Frankenstein*, and the Spectacle of Masculinity," *PMLA* 108.2 (1993), 260.

34 Susan Stryker, "My Words to Victor Frankenstein above the Village of Chamounix: Performing Transgender Rage," in *States of Rage: Emotional Eruption, Violence, and Social Change*, eds. Renée R. Curry and Terry L. Allison (New York: New York University Press, 1996), p. 201.

35 Simi Linton, *Claiming Disability: Knowledge and Identity* (New York: New York University Press, 1998), pp. 2, 11.

36 Stephen Jay Gould, "The Monster's Human Nature," *Natural History* 103 (July 1994), 20, 20, 21.

37 Denise Gigante, "Facing the Ugly: The Case of *Frankenstein*," *ELH* 67.2 (2000), 565–87.

4

ESTHER SCHOR

Frankenstein and film

On Friday, August 29, 1823, Mary Shelley went to the theatre to see *Presumption, or, The Fate of Frankenstein*, by Richard Brinsley Peake. To Leigh Hunt, she wrote:

> [A]t the end of the Ist Act. The stage represents a room with a staircase heading to *F* workshop – he goes to it and you see his light at a small window, through which a frightened servant peeps, who runs off in terror when F. exclaims "It lives . . ." I was much amused, & it appeared to excite a breathelss [*sic*] eagerness in the audience – . . . & all stayed till it was over. (*L* I 378)

The scene Mary Shelley singles out here would become the sine qua non of countless cinematic versions of *Frankenstein* and one of the most cherished clichés of the horror-film genre: the crucial animation scene, in which both Frankenstein and the audience perceive the first motions of the creature. The theatrical "It lives," of course, would become the cinematic "It's alive!," an exclamation caught between horror and exultation.

Readers who arrive at Shelley's novel by way of the cinematic Frankenstein – which, today, includes nearly everyone – are inevitably surprised by the quietness and dimness of the creature's animation. There are no lightning bolts, no thunder, no celebratory ejaculation; it occurs silently, to the accompaniment of a sputtering candle and pattering rain, observed only by Victor Frankenstein: "It was already one in the morning; the rain pattered dismally against the panes, and my candle was nearly burnt out, when, by the glimmer of the half-extinguished light, I saw the dull yellow eye of the creature open; it breathed hard, and a convulsive motion agitated its limbs" (*F* I iv 34). It was for Peake and other dramatists, given only the merest of motions by the novel, to bring the creature's animation to the eyes and ears of an audience.[1] The licensed theatres of Mary Shelley's day, some of which held as many as three thousand spectators, were vast and dimly lit, with mediocre acoustics. In this milieu, Frankenstein's shriek, "It lives!" had to substitute for the creature's "hard breath"; a fleeing servant, for the creature's convulsive twitch.

The spectacular animation scenes of so many Frankenstein films clearly owe a debt to the early theatrical adaptations. But cinema as an art form is as distinct from theatre as it is from fiction and poetry; in fact, film theorists have variously identified the origins of cinema with popular art forms such as magic shows and comic strips.[2] Filmmakers, whether or not they adapt literary works, make use of film's particular visual and aural resources, among them, all the films that have gone before. And unlike most novels, films are a product of collaboration, a fact that applies as much to star vehicles as it does to films by directorial *auteurs*. Furthermore, films both reflect and refract their own historical moment, a phenomenon that becomes increasingly obvious as we peer into the cinematic legacy of Shelley's novel. In the history of Frankenstein films, we can trace a Rohrschach – a psychologist's inkblot – of our collective fears. Critics have explored the implication of racism and lynching in the 1931 *Frankenstein*; of eugenics and the threat of a "master race" in Whale's 1935 *Bride of Frankenstein*; of nuclear danger in the 1957 *Curse of Frankenstein* (dir. Terence Fisher) and the Hammer Studios sequels of the 1950s and 1960s; of organ transplants in various films of the 1960s and 70s; of sexual perversity in *Andy Warhol's Frankenstein* (dir. Antonio Margheriti and Paul Morrissey, 1974); of the post-modern subject in Kenneth Branagh's *Mary Shelley's Frankenstein* (1994); and of replicants, cyborgs, and artificial intelligence in such films as Ridley Scott's *Blade Runner* (1982) and Steven Spielberg's *Artificial Intelligence: AI* (2001; see chapter 5). But such a history lies beyond the scope of this essay. Instead, I will pursue here a question: how do the visions of cinema return us – horrified? optimistic? saddened? – to Shelley's dark novel?

From page to screen

As I have already suggested, there are certain features of Shelley's novel that filmmakers have typically found unamenable. *Frankenstein*, as we have seen in chapter 1, is a series of impacted narratives, either written, as in the case of Walton's letters to his sister; or told, as in the case of both Frankenstein's narrative and that of the creature. In most cases, the epistolary frame of the novel is missing from Frankenstein films, though other sorts of framing devices are sometimes used. But the ironies that ride the impacted narratives are thrown off when filmmakers tell the story, as it were, in the third person and in sequence. Perhaps the most extraordinary undocumented theft of the twentieth century is cinema's theft of the creature's eloquent language, forcing him to speak through his body and through his actions. Even the intertitles of the first known film version, the Edison Company's silent 1910 *Frankenstein* (dir. J. Searle Downey), feature Frankenstein's histrionic speeches but, apparently, not the creature's. Since James Whale's 1931 *Frankenstein*, adapted from a London stage hit by Peggy Webling, the creature's virtual muteness has been an adjunct of Boris Karloff's huge, lumbering, deep-browed, flat-topped, monster, with conduction bolts protruding from his neck. With Jack Pierce's makeup (based on Whale's sketches and revived for the 1935 *Bride*) and forty-eight pounds of costume, the creature becomes, for ever and anon, a monster.[3] As Paul O'Flinn wrote in a seminal essay on film adaptations of *Frankenstein,* this representation of Shelley's creature as an abnormal, degenerate, malicious fiend "upend[s]" the novel by canceling entirely the creature's pathetic predicament,[4] as he describes it to Victor Frankenstein: "If I have no ties and no affections, hatred and vice must be my portion; the love of another will destroy the cause of my crimes . . . My vices are the children of a forced solitude that I abhor; and my virtues will necessarily arise when I live in communion with an equal" (*F* II ix 100).

But this reckoning of losses from page to screen neglects the crucial issue of what might be gained – not for the novel itself, but for our ongoing reading of it – from a closer look at the cinematic *Frankenstein*. The heart of the matter is what movies do that the novel cannot do: show us the monster. Chris Baldick's *In Frankenstein's Shadow* notes that the term "monster" derives from the Latin term for a "divine portent or warning," that is, a warning that only works when the brutish, ugly body is understood to signify evil.[5] But Shelley's novel departs from this convention by putting the creature's persona under a rather large question mark.[6] The question, of course, is not merely ours, but also his: "But where were my friends and relations? No father had watched my infant days, no mother had blessed me with smiles and caresses . . . I had never yet seen a being resembling me, or who claimed any intercourse with me. What was I?" (*F* II vi 81). If we are to trust the 1831 Introduction, this question mark is the seed of the entire story, for Shelley's creature also baffles Byron's call for a ghost story. To offer a creature in lieu of a ghost is to transform the terms of the game radically, for if a ghost is a spirit disembodied, then the monster is a body whose spirit is – what? Put differently, what is the meaning of the signifying body? Indeed, the creature finds it hard to understand his own significance; to Frankenstein, he remarks: "I ought to be thy Adam; but I am rather the fallen angel" (*F* II ii 66). While his first encounter with his reflection induces a horror at his "deformity" (*F* II iv 76), shortly after, he interprets his deformity as his difference from man: "I saw and heard of none like me" (*F* II v 81). In Shelley Jackson's hypertext "Patchwork Girl" (see chapter 5), the composite body signifies an unwitting community of persons, each of whom gets a brief soliloquy. On another reading, the creature's body is construed as a soulless mechanism, an interpretation explored in the following chapter on "*Frankenstein*'s futurity."[7]

Clearly the creature's body, in its imposing, yet occult, significance, is monstrous. But in the novel, the manner in which it signifies is neither spontaneous, nor transparent. Instead, its meaning is revealed gradually through the monster's narrative, when he takes us through his first sensory perceptions, through his strivings for language, through his ardent attentions to the De Laceys, through his inchoate desires, through his first self-conscious reflections (literal and figurative), through his interpretations of signs and later books, all the way to the coalescence of his attitudes and opinions. In Mary Shelley's novel, far more hinges on the creature's capacities than on his nature, especially since the creature's essential plea to Frankenstein is that his moral formation remains radically unfinished.

I am not among the critics for whom cinema inevitably demeans and diminishes Shelley's creature into a vicious, aberrant criminal. Films, by putting before us the body of the monster projected and magnified beyond all reason, radicalize the question that hangs over the monster's physical being. They do so by setting in motion an interplay between his looming, opaque body, and the revelation of his character to our eye over time. And the crucial scene of animation is the moment when that interplay begins. Hence, cinema's fascination with the scene of animation is not simply a throwback to the days of cavernous regency theatres; on the contrary, it is the scene in which cinema explores, most acutely, its power to realize a conundrum the novel merely glimpses.

Moving fragments: from James Whale to Kenneth Branagh

The first known motion picture called *Frankenstein*, a silent film of 1910 long thought to be lost, was discovered in the 1960s to exist in a private archive. As Wheeler Winston Dixon notes (having seen, like most critics, only a few clips from the film), Frankenstein pours an alchemical mixture into a cauldron and leaves his laboratory, to watch the creature materialize through a keyhole: "[W]e see flesh compose on bone, eyes find sockets, limbs take on human aspect: the sequence proceeds like a magical ritual."[8] This reverse-motion sequence endows Frankenstein with the power to deny the naturalistic process of decay and degeneration; yet he is also, like the viewer, a spectator. A prophet Ezekiel in the valley of dry bones, Frankenstein watches as what was dead miraculously resumes life.

In a later sequence, however, Frankenstein is forced to own up to his role as creator. According to the pressbook,[9] when the creature glimpses himself in the mirror, he spontaneously fades out, as if this self-recognition evaporates him. When Frankenstein enters the room and looks in the same mirror, it is the creature's reflection that looks back at him; hence, what he had previously glimpsed at a remove, as a spectator, he must now acknowledge as his own creation. But Frankenstein repudiates this reflection and before our eyes, the reflection fades, leaving in its stead a vision of "his young manhood"[10] in the mirror. In this moralized melodrama, Frankenstein, by forfeiting the power to regenerate life, redeems his own and joins his bride – presumably to make new life the old-fashioned way.

If the magical, visionary propensities of film are affirmed in the 1910 silent version, the 1931 *Frankenstein*, directed by James Whale, reveals a complementary view of film as a medium of moving fragments pierced by light. In the 1931 *Frankenstein*, William Nestrick perceives "a continued ambivalence toward film itself . . . Sometimes the mechanical medium is allowed to wind down or shift gears so that we can see the machine; sometimes the motif of 'coming to life' reasserts the possibility that the medium can bridge the polarities of technology and human nature and art."[11] As Nestrick remarks, *Frankenstein* appeared in the infancy of talking pictures; provocatively, he reads the creature as "a vestigial embodiment of the film conceived as having its own childhood, growth, adulthood and education." In his sutured parts, jerky movements, stumbling speech, and hunger for light, the "Monster" (as he is billed in the credits) does indeed make a plausible allegory of cinema.

As we shall see, however, the reflexivity of the animation scene, which is all spectacle, competes with the film's extraordinarily intimate introduction of the Monster. The first of these sequences is set in the remarkable laboratory designed by Kenneth Strickfaden. Once Frankenstein predicts that the storm will reach its height in fifteen minutes, the remainder of the scene unfolds in real time. When the scientist is interrupted by a trio of visitors knocking below, an audience is suddenly admitted to the spectacle. Halfway up the stairs, Frankenstein pauses to ask menacingly, "Are you quite sure you want to come in?" – a question that alludes to the opening of the film, where Edward van Sloan, the actor playing Waldman, comes out from behind a stage curtain to warn away the faint of heart; accordingly, the first to assent, with a nod of the head, is Waldman.

Where Frankenstein in the 1910 film was a spectator, here he plays the leading role, remarking, "Quite a good scene, isn't it? One man crazy, three very sane spectators." The spectacle that follows hardly needs rehearsing: as the storm builds, filaments in bulbs of all shapes and sizes begin pulsing with current, and Frankenstein, with much buzzing and gear-grinding, sends a platform bearing the huge, mummy-like, inert body up to a small trap-door opening in the roof of the tower. Indeed, the scenery fairly chews the

Figure 1 Colin Clive as Frankenstein, *Frankenstein*, dir. James Whale (1931)

actors, but so invested is Frankenstein in the aparatus, that it seems almost an extension of his body. Throughout, the camera cannot shift quickly enough between the blinding lightning, the cowering spectators, and the fevered attentions of Frankenstein to his gauges and levers (figure 1). Only once the platform is lowered and all is quiet, does the camera focus on the bandaged fingers of the creature, which move ever so slightly. Throwing himself on the body hysterically, Frankenstein fills both lens and sound track, crying in a hoarse crescendo, "It's moving, it's alive, it's alive, it's moving." To move, in the laboratory of cinema, is to live.

Not until two scenes later, do we actually perceive the creature. In a sly form cut, the film takes us from Frankenstein's baronial father, comically smoking from a long cigarette holder, to Frankenstein himself, puffing at a cigarette in his study with Waldman. Their brief exchange pits two views of the creature against one another. When Frankenstein genially notes that "his brain must be given time to develop . . . He's only a few days old, remember," Waldman counters with the revelation that the brain stolen from his laboratory was abnormal. Before Frankenstein can fully register the news, a shuffle of footsteps is heard, and Frankenstein yells, "turn off the light." In the dimmed room, a door slowly opens: the immense creature stands framed in the doorway, with his back to us. In a close-up, framing head

Figure 2 Boris Karloff as the Monster, *Frankenstein*, dir. James Whale (1931)

and shoulders, he slowly turns to the left, and pauses as we catch his broad, overhanging brow in profile. He continues to swivel toward us and, just as we get our first glimpse of his face, the camera jumps to a tighter close-up (figure 2), then finally to a close-up that shows, beneath the precipitous brow, a pair of gruesome eyes that seem just about to roll back into oblivion. They seem to want to take us with them.

The effect of these sequential, tightening close-ups is paradoxical. While what our eye sees is preternaturally restricted by the camera, the effect is to liberate the film, if temporarily, from the theatrical structure of actor and audience, spectacle and spectator. After this unrevealing close-up of the Monster's eyes, it is hardly surprising that even when Frankenstein gingerly tests the creature's reaction to light, the camera's interest swerves from the Monster's eyes to his hands. What ensues is a pantomime of heartbreaking yearning. A large, square shade in a rooftop windowframe is pulled back to reveal the creature in a close-up, turning instinctively toward the light. In the following shot, a very low camera shows him standing at full height, and reaching toward the light; this time the close-up is on his huge, sutured hands nakedly jutting from too-short sleeves, attempting futilely to grasp light. When the shade is returned, the creature lowers his arms in the direction of Frankenstein; as the camera closes in on the palms of his upturned hands, he

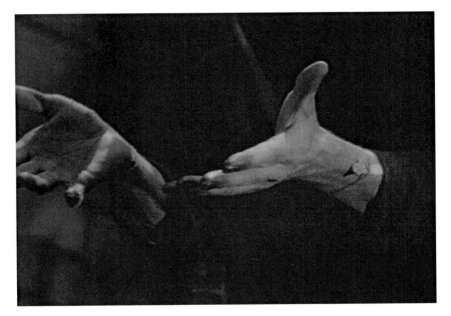

Figure 3 Boris Karloff as the Monster, *Frankenstein*, dir. James Whale (1931)

rashes his hands gently, imploringly, through the air in tiny circles (figure 3).
Between each circular movement, he pauses for an instant, as if half-awaiting
a response. These are the hands that gave the first sign of life, which, well
before they learn to throttle, bludgeon, or hurl, open to make a harmless, but
unheeded, request. While the sinister, lowered brow may intimate a vicious
destiny, the Monster's open, upturned hands suggest innocence, receptivity,
helplessness.

A rather different request (as well as the runaway success of the 1931 film)
animates Whale's 1935 sequel, *The Bride of Frankenstein*: the Monster's request for a companion. A brief framing sequence features a young Mary
Shelley (Elsa Lanchester), flanked by Byron (Gavin Gordon) and Shelley
(Douglas Walton), who blandly ask how her youthful beauty can accompany such a horrific imagination. The question neatly inverts the Monster's
problem, where a horrific appearance belies a benevolent spirit; Lanchester's
reappearance later on as the Bride may not answer the poets' question
(a question which poets should not have to ask), but does give it some point.

In *The Bride of Frankenstein*, we meet the fey, campy Dr. Praetorius (Ernst
Thesiger), an old professor of Frankenstein's, who makes the notion of their
collaboration on a female monster sound altogether lascivious. Throughout the film, the strained partnership between the two scientists is a foil for
the creature's attempts to garner a companion, an attempt which acquires

Christian dimensions in the blind hermit scene. Whereas in the 1931 film, Frankenstein performs for spectators, here the two scientists labor jointly to birth the new creature. It might even be said that their pairing generates "electricity"; certainly the animation scene, running about five minutes longer than that of the 1931 film, is far more visually explosive, more stylized, busier, noisier. The camera studies the faces of Frankenstein and Praetorious in increasingly bizarre, very tight shots, some backlit, some lit from below, some framed on a diagonal. In the transaction between them, sparks fly; the platform rises a full storey above the top of the tower as a series of odd kites are let out, Ben Franklin-style. A lush score by Franz Waxman barely covers the familiar grinding and buzzing.

Whereas the 1931 film introduces the Monster by leaving his hands an open matter, here the question of capacity sits instead on the heart. Again, there is a fatal ambiguity. For while the Bride is designed expressly to love the male Monster, the two scientists are palpably anxious lest their plan goes awry. And their anxieties are well founded; for Waxman's score provides a loud *da-dum da-dum* ostinato throughout this scene, an ironic reminder that the heart, minus the projections of romance and sentimentalism, is but a muscle. As in the earlier picture, the hand moves, but at once the bandage is torn away to reveal two wide-open, startled eyes. When the platform is rotated, we see a bandaged, unmistakably female form. And a quick dissolve allows Praetorious formally to present the Bride, now sporting a Nefertiti coiffure and draped in nuptial (shroudlike) white, to the accompaniment of wedding bells. A series of close-ups magnifies the creature's face; but instead of having her swivel round to greet us, Whale cuts quickly from profile to profile, emphasizing her convulsive twitch (figure 4). A chasm opens between her bizarre beauty and her mechanical movements; once she rejects the infuriated Monster, she even serves up a fierce, snaky hiss. Ultimately, no matter how attentively the male creators fashion her female form and her heart, her capacity for love and friendship lies well beyond their control.

Sixty years would pass before a filmmaker would visualize the creation of the female creature with Whale's gusto. Branagh's film, its title lamely mimicking Coppola's successful *Bram Stoker's Dracula*, was neither a critical nor a box office success. The film's chief pitfall lies not in its unscary, sophomoric gore and slime, but in its reductive, oedipal reading of Frankenstein's motives. Here, the sight of his mother dying in childbed, smeared with afterbirth and blood, sets a bereft Victor (Branagh) on his quest to defy the limits of life. Accordingly, the lengthy animation sequence finds the Creature (as he is billed – Robert De Niro) in an enclosed chamber filled with amniotic fluid; as he nears birth, rending the metal womb, its "water breaks," flooding the large laboratory. The Creature's body (though still not his face) appears

Figure 4 Elsa Lanchester as The Bride, *The Bride of Frankenstein*, dir. James Whale (1935)

neither bandaged, nor badly dressed, but naked and slippery, an enormous infant (figure 5). In Branagh's film, we find a strange amalgam of the magically whole 1910 monster, and his counterpart in the 1931 *Frankenstein*, a sutured misfit. As Bouriana Zakharieva has observed, one glimpse of the creature's face, scarred and patched, puts the lie to the conceit of artificial birth;[12] this Creature's body, quite emphatically, is a composite. With a nod to Nestrick, Zakharieva claims that, for the nineties, not "animation" but "montage" is "the word that bridges the world of film and man (or monster)."

If the creature's face reveals the secret, betraying patchwork within the scientist's pseudo-birth, the female creature is *spectacularly* composite (figure 6). In fact, she is a composite not of anonymous corpses, but of two rather familiar ones: that of Elizabeth (Helena Bonham-Carter), whose heart has just been murderously ripped out by the Creature; and that of Justine (Trevyn McDowell), hanged for a crime she did not commit. By following Elizabeth's death with the creation of the female creature, Branagh curiously deforms the plot of both the novel and *The Bride of Frankenstein*, in both of which Frankenstein only undertakes this task to prevent the murder of Elizabeth. In the novel, Frankenstein cancels the work-in-progress in response to the following "train of reflection" (*F* III iii 114):

Figure 5 Robert De Niro as the Creature and Kenneth Branagh as Victor Frankenstein, *Mary Shelley's Frankenstein*, dir. Kenneth Branagh (1994)

Figure 6 Helena Bonham Carter as the female creature, *Mary Shelley's Frankenstein*, dir. Kenneth Branagh (1994)

[S]he might become ten thousand times more malignant than her mate, and delight, for its own sake, in murder and wretchedness. He had sworn to quit the neighbourhood of man, and hide himself in deserts; but she had not . . . They might even hate each other; the creature who already lived loathed his own deformity, and might he not conceive a greater abhorrence for it when it came before his eyes in the female form? She also might turn with disgust from him to the superior beauty of man . . . (*F* III iii 114)

Seesawing between misogyny and identification, Frankenstein supposes that "the superior beauty of man" – presumably himself – might prove a fatal attraction. But in Branagh's revision, Frankenstein not only wants to be desired by a female monster, but he also harbors a necrophiliac desire for the dead.

In this female creature is writ large the necrophiliac destiny of Frankenstein's oedipal desire – larger even than it is in the novel when Frankenstein dreams, upon the completion of his work: "I thought I saw Elizabeth, in the bloom of health . . . but as I imprinted the first kiss on her lips, they became livid with the hue of death; her features appeared to change, and I thought that I held the corpse of my dead mother in my arms" (*F* I iv 34). But where Shelley's Frankenstein dreams this transformation, Branagh's acts it out, spinning his new creature in a wild *danse macabre* before the Creature, now cast in the role of spectator. Thus, when Branagh deforms Shelley's plot to bring Frankenstein's oedipal trauma face to face with the Creature's ravishing jealousy, the monstrosity of human affections meets the humanity of the Creature's desires. That Branagh refuses to choose between them is far more important than the female creature's blazing rejection of both.[13] The tragedy of this film is that neither creator nor Creature perceives the commonality of their pain. In this single instance, Branagh's film becomes animated by ambitions well beyond the oedipal "explanation" of Frankenstein's work.

In the final section of this chapter, I turn to a trio of films in which the ordeal of animation is parodied, displaced, or eliminated entirely. To revisit my argument, the animation sequence brings to life not only the creature, but also the looming question of what he or she may yet become or accomplish. In Whale's *Frankenstein* and *The Bride of Frankenstein*, the camera visualizes this indeterminacy as ambiguity, taking the hands, or alternately, the heart, as a metonymy for the body. In Branagh's film, the question of what the female creature might become is a question each rival answers differently. What is foiled is less *her* potential, than *their* potential for empathy and companionship. In the films to which I now turn, the animation scene becomes redundant when the creature's potential for kindness and benevolence becomes, at last, a given. As we shall see, the drama of animation is displaced by the drama of empathy.

Parody and empathy

When Universal Pictures released *Frankenstein* in 1931, Mel Brooks was a five-year-old boy; by the time *The Bride of Frankenstein* was released, he was on the verge of puberty. The title of his 1974 masterpiece, *Young Frankenstein*, refers to young Frederick Frankenstein, the modern medical grandson of Victor von Frankenstein, who wears his pedigree so reluctantly that he pronounces his name *FRONK-en-steen*. But the title evokes as well Mel Brooks's own young *Frankenstein*, an impressionable boy's mesmerized, anxious, and jokey encounter with both of James Whale's classic films. In the black and white *Young Frankenstein*, Brooks exquisitely captures the gloomy luminosity of Whale's films, aping both Strickfaden's sets and Jack Pierce's makeup (minus the precipitous brow). For transitions between sequences, Brooks uses nostalgic iris-in shots (beginning with a point of light and expanding gradually to a large circle) and iris-out shots (a circular shot that gradually diminishes to a point); in some cases, he uses a campy heart shape in lieu of a circle. He also recalls the cinema of the 1930s with vertical wipes, gradually replacing one shot with another, as though wiping the previous shot away from right to left or left to right. But this is "*Young*" *Frankenstein*, and Brooks crosscuts his visual mimicry with a virtuosic naughtiness obsessed with, in the memorable locution of the nubile lab assistant, Inga (Teri Garr), the dimensions of the Monster's "shlangschtücke" (Peter Boyle).

While Shelley gives us a Frankenstein who is sexually repressed (if not oedipally arrested), both of Whale's films limply affirm the marriage of Frankenstein and Elizabeth; in the first, "the House of Frankenstein" is roundly toasted. But Brooks rings a signal change: he gives us a sexually frustrated Frankenstein caught between his wealthy fiancée (or "financier" as he says in a slip of the tongue), Elizabeth (Madeline Kahn), and Inga, sexy, available, and charitably inclined. In the course of the film, not only Frankenstein and Inga, but indeed Elizabeth and the creature itself, will all become wildly, blissfully reanimated by sex, which is operatically proclaimed, to the strains of the old Jeanette McDonald song, the "sweet mystery of life."

Not surprisingly, two of the film's three animation scenes focus on the sexual arousal of the repressed Frederick. By following the old notebooks of his grandfather (which include direct quotations from the novel), Frederick attempts to make good on his forerunner's aborted project in the very same laboratory. When his ghoulish, bugeyed assistant, Igor (pronounced, of course, EYE-gore [Marty Feldman]) asks amid the pulsing current and showering sparks, "Are you *sure* this is how they did it?" we are reminded that, as any ten-year-old kid knows, this is not at all how they "do it." As the storm rises, Frederick suddenly demands of Inga, "Elevate me"; her tickled, embarrassed response – "Not here . . ." – alerts us that Frederick craves more than scientific glory. Indeed, his need for animation is so great that unlike all his predecessors, Frederick Frankenstein hops on the platform and rides it all the way to the roof. Needless to say, the procedure fails to animate the creature, but perhaps it is more efficacious for Frederick. In a brief reprise of this scene, Frederick is sought in the laboratory by his housekeeper, Frau Blucher (Cloris Leachman); from the roof, the platform creakily lowers to reveal Frederick and Inga naked beneath the sheets, sharing a post-coital cigarette.

But the virility he boasts with Inga contrasts sharply with his timidity before Elizabeth, who spits, "no tongues!" when he tries to kiss her good-night. At his worst moments, young Frederick is heard to wail, desperately, "Mommy!" Accordingly, Frederick finally intuits that what his miserable, violent creature needs is precisely a mother's care. And, quite remarkably, he undertakes to supply it: "Love is the only thing that can save this poor creature, and I'm going to convince him that he is loved, even at the cost of my own life." Entering the creature's locked cell, he calls out, "Hello, handsome!" and praises his "boyish face," "sweet smile," and "physical strength"; "You are not evil; you are *good*," he asserts. Unable to resist, the tearful creature embraces Frederick, who says with a distinct Yiddish into-nation, "This is a *nice* boy. This is a *good* boy. This is a mother's *angel*!" and vows to "teach you . . . [to] show you how to walk, how to speak, how to move, how to think" (figure 7). As a good Jewish mother, Frederick takes his Monster well beyond walking, speaking, moving, and thinking, teaching him to sing and tap dance. To show the Monster's accomplishments off to the public, the two perform – unforgettably – a top hat and tails tap routine to "Puttin' on the Ritz." Toward the end of the film, in a double-platform labo-ratory scene, animation is replaced by maternal self-sacrifice. Frederick gives up both his brain and his bride so that the Monster might attain, in his own delicate phrase, "a somewhat more sophisticated way of expressing myself." Having ceded Elizabeth to the Monster, Frederick ends up with Inga, from whose wedding-night astonishment, we surmise that he has acquired the creature's formidable "shlangschtücke." That Frederick's conversion from man of science to Jewish mother should affirm his virility says much about Brooks's comic optimism; emblematically, as the "mother's angel" sequence closes, he owns up to his patronymic for the first time, yelling, "My name is *Frank*enstein!" At the same time, this denouement suggests what Daniel Boyarin has called "Jewish Masochism," a style of masculinity that amalga-mates male potency and "femminine" masochism.[14]

Figure 7 Gene Wilder as Frederick Frankenstein and Peter Boyle as the Monster, *Young Frankenstein*, dir. Mel Brooks (1974)

In Susan Seidelman's blithe Miami comedy *Making Mr. Right* (1987), however, the roles of scientist-creator and nurturer are split apart along familiar gender lines. The scientist is Dr. Jeff Peters (John Malkovich, in a double role as the nerdy Peters and Ulysses, his innocent, benign, and infinitely suggestible android), and the nurturer is one Frankie Stone (Ann Magnuson), a female public relations executive. *Making Mr. Right* may be the first cinematic *Frankenstein* to dispense with the animation sequence entirely. Frankie meets Ulysses when he is already animated, but still full of bugs; he walks oddly, he spills, but in fact his awkwardness exceeds that of Peters only by a couple of degrees. In several senses, he is made in his creator's image.

While Chemtec hires Frankie to work on Ulysses's image (before his first space mission), she teaches Ulysses how to offer the kind of empathy and affection she desires but cannot manage to eke out of her self-promoting, politician boyfriend, Steve Marcus. In the first session with Ulysses, for instance, she tells him to make eye contact, to listen as if everything depended on it, to show both confidence and concern (figure 8). Interrupted by a visitor, Frankie leaves Ulysses alone with two items: a televsion on which talk-show host Phil Donahue interviews thirtysomething women looking – in vain – for "Mr. Right"; and Frankie's overstuffed purse. In the antic scene that follows, Ulysses explores the accouterments of late twentieth-century American

Figure 8 Ann Magnuson as Frankie Stone and John Malkovich as Ulysses, *Making Mr. Right*, dir. Susan Seidelman (1987)

femininity: a paperback copy of *Smart Women, Foolish Choices*, pantyhose, a blowdrier, a diaphragm (which the curious android pokes, jiggles, bites, listens to, and finally inflates), and lipstick. Suddenly Ulysses's attention is taken by a promotional ad for Marcus, whose slogan, evidently composed by Frankie, is "It takes a man this sensitive to know your needs." Dr. Peters bursts into the room, and in a direct allusion to Whale's *Frankenstein*, Seidelman's android slowly swivels in his chair to greet his maker; Ulysses, his mouth blooming with Frankie's Chinese red lipstick, parrots, "It takes a man this sensitive to meet your needs." So much for his creator's image (figure 9). In *Making Mr. Right*, Frankie's patient "making," a sentimental education, is readily distinguished from Peters's laboratory production of Ulysses. And when Frankie rescues Ulysses from an eternity in outer space, it is clear that his destiny has become (Frankie's?) inner space, for Seidelman leaves us in no doubt that Ulysses's empathic powers reside in an emphatically masculine body.

Both Brooks and Seidelman entitle their monsters to education, nurturing, and companionship, all under the aegis of an aggressive, gratified sexuality. But notably, this gratification is bounded by the perquisites of heterosexual desire. Bill Condon's 1998 film *Gods and Monsters*, based on Chrisopher Bram's novel, *Father of Frankenstein* (1995), takes up the drama of empathy in a different key, exploring the ambiguous friendship between the aging, debilitated James Whale (Ian McKellan) and his young gardener Clayton Boone (Brendan Fraser). In the course of this friendship, set in 1957,

Figure 9 John Malkovich as Ulysses, *Making Mr. Right*, dir. Susan Seidelman (1987)

Whale reveals to Clayton his impoverished, miserable childhood ("I was an aberration . . . a giraffe") and war trauma, while Clayton is forced to see past the aging, effete "homo" to a man in intense, irremediable suffering.

At the heart of the film, lies a sustained sequence in which Clayton and Whale – the former in a bar, the latter in his living room – each watch a television screening of *The Bride of Frankenstein*. As a foil for their developing friendship, each watches in the company of a woman (Clayton with an ex-girlfriend, Betty [Lolita Davidovich]; Whale with his housekeeper, Hannah [Lynne Redgrave]) who finds the film emotionally unpersuasive: Betty finds it comical, while Hannah finds it disgusting. Clayton, however, is clearly moved by the plot – "The Monster's lonely – he wants a friend" – while Whale watches his creation with a father's pride and pleasure. Condon's careful editing moves us through the plot of *Bride* in six well-chosen scenes, which focus on the Monster's request for companionship, on the animation sequence, and on the Bride's rejection of the Monster; deftly, he leaves the impression that the two men have shared a viewing of the film.

Afterwards, Whale drowsily recalls directing a scene just quoted on the diminutive television screen. Condon suddenly takes us to a voluminous soundstage where, in living color, Thesiger (Arthur Dignam) as Praetorius and Lanchester (Rosalind Ayres) as the Bride are taking up their marks. When the Bride appears, her hairdo is apparently news to both cast and crew, and their delighted banter is campy, high-spirited, full of in-jokes: "Are they to understand that Colin and I *have done her hair*?" asks Thesiger with feigned

Figure 10 Rosalind Ayres as Elsa Lanchester and Arthur Dignam as Ernest Thesiger, *Gods and Monsters*, dir. Bill Condon (1998)

astonishment (figure 10), while Lanchester coyly advises Whale to make a film with a female scientist who would create her own Gary Cooper. Whale's pleasure in this campy repartee is palpable; in fact, the odd man out is the humorless Colin Clive (Matt McKenzie) who takes Whale aside to complain of a flu. Putting his arm around Clive, Whale leers, "Praetorius is a little bit in love with Frankenstein" and Clive's discomfort mounts.

When Whale calls "Action," paradoxically, the giddy animation on the set is magically stilled, all eyes on the Bride's silent twitching. Where Whale's 1935 camera sidles up for close-ups of the Bride (some shot from very low angles), Condon's camera does the opposite, drawing way back in a long, slow dolly shot. The visual strangeness of this scene is compounded by the absence of Waxman's sonorous wedding bells; instead, the score features several deep chords struck, then suspended. Condon's film belies Nestrick's dichotomy between the magical illusions of cinema and the exhibition of its technology; here, the very exposure of gay theatricality and companionship behind the scenes enables this transfigured scene to cast its spell.

Whale's friendship with Clayton pales in comparison to the idyll of theatrical companionship we glimpse in this scene. In fact, the film thrives on the ambiguity of their friendship, coming to rest not on Whale's nostalgia, but on Clayton's awakened hopes and strong misgivings. While the friendship originates in Whale's invitation to Clayton to model for a sketch, the muscular Clayton gradually rejects the role of admired object.[15] This rejection at first comes about by virtue of Clayton's deepening perspective; the more augmented his subjectivity, the less comfortable he is being objectified. But it is also true that Whale's doting gaze raises Clayton's self-regard; we catch him looking in a mirror, becoming enraged when Betty calls him a "loser." Clayton's empathy alternates with a reservoir of resentment, and Whale's intentions for him remain obscure until the film climaxes in Clayton's impassioned exclamation: "*I am not your monster.*" In fact, Whale's unconscious directs Clayton in both roles; even as he seeks monstrosity in Clayton, he dreams of Clayton in a surgical gown removing Whale's own brain. Still, on his last night on earth, Whale dreams of Clayton as the most benevolent of monsters, one who kindly and irrevocably leads him beyond suffering; one who understands the likeness between a grave and a trench.

As so many critics have observed, Boris Karloff's impersonation of the monster looms over all later visualizations of him, and it seems no coincidence that the filmmakers most eager to address the Monster's wrongs are most oblique in their rendering of the Frankenstein story: in Brooks's case, through sublime pastiche; in Seidelman's, by invoking the missing female nurturer; in Condon's, by reclaiming the trials of companionship, fraught with the ambiguities of homosociality. This obliqueness is a strategy of indirection, for in pointing both toward and away from the horror genre, these filmmakers frankly identify with the Monster, who, not surprisingly, becomes infinitely more pleasing to our eye: think of Peter Boyle's pained nobility, John Malkovich's open-faced innocence, Brendan Fraser's movie-star glamour. When the Frankenstein myth is brought to bear on the experience of being a Jew, a woman, or a gay man, the alien – once a figure of horror and disgust – becomes a figure of beauty and pathos.

At this writing, a title search under "Frankenstein" in the Internet Movie Database (http://www.imdb.com) lists exactly one hundred films in English, French, Italian, Spanish, Japanese (*Furankenshutain no kaiju* [*Frankenstein's Monsters*], 1966, for example) and several other languages, including about twenty made for television or video. This does not include a spate of films about Mary Shelley and the Shelley circle in the mid- to late-1980s, including Ken Russell's *Gothic* (1986), Ivan Passer's *Haunted Summer* (1988), and Gonzalo Suarez' awful *Remando al Viento* (*Rowing with the Wind*, 1987); nor does it include so-called adult films of necrophilia and sadism, which draw liberally on Frankenstein imagery. Nor, for that matter, does it include the films encountered in chapter 5, when cinema's embrace of the Monster takes new forms and dimensions to grapple with a new generation of artificial creatures. However comprehensive, the list takes no notice of Seidelman's and Condon's revisions of the Frankenstein myth, nor of such treasures as Victor Erice's *El Espíritu de la Colmena* (*The Spirit of the Beehive*, 1973), which follows Karloff's monster out of film, into the imaginations of two small girls in Franco's Spain. But for Shelley's creature, as I have argued here, these other habitations may be the most revelatory. In our own day, cinema has taken him well beyond the garish laboratories of animation into the shadowy recesses where he is most himself, pursuing what he needs and wants and deserves. Most himself; and perhaps, most alive.

NOTES

1 For Peake's play and its sequel, see Steven Early Forry, *Hideous Progenies: Dramatizations of "Frankenstein" from Mary Shelley to the Present* (Philadelphia: University of Pennsylvania Press, 1990), pp. 135–76; and Albert J. LaValley, "The Stage and Film Children of *Frankenstein*: A Survey," *EF* 243–89.

2 In a classic essay, Erwin Panofsky points out that "the imitation of stage performances [in film] was a comparatively late and thoroughly frustrated development"; see "Style and Medium in the Motion Pictures," in *Film Theory and Criticism*, eds. Gerald Mast and Marshall Cohen, 3rd edn. (Oxford: Oxford University Press, 1985), p. 217. See also William Nestrick, "Coming to Life: *Frankenstein* and the Nature of Film Narrative," *EF* 291.

3 LaValley, "Stage and Film Children," 263.

4 Paul O'Flinn, "Production and Reproduction: The Case of *Frankenstein*," *Literature and History*, 9.2 (1983), 205.

5 Chris Baldick, *In Frankenstein's Shadow: Myth, Monstrosity, and Nineteenth-Century Writing* (Oxford: Oxford University Press, 1987), p. 10. The point is also made in James A. W. Heffernan, "Looking at the Monster: *Frankenstein* and Film," *Critical Inquiry* 24.1 (1997), 148 n57. On the aesthetics of ugliness in the novel, see Denise Gigante, "Facing the Ugly: The Case of *Frankenstein*," *ELH* 67.2 (2000), 565–87.

6 In the opening credits for James Whale's 1931 *Frankenstein*, a question mark appears after "The Monster." "Karloff," the stage name of English actor William Henry Pratt, is supplied in the closing credits.

7 See Bouriana Zakharieva, "Frankenstein of the Nineties: The Composite Body," *Canadian Review of Comparative Literature* 23.3 (1996), 742.

8 See Wheeler Winston Dixon, "The Films of *Frankenstein*," in *Approaches to Teaching Shelley's "Frankenstein,"* ed. Stephen C. Behrendt (New York: Modern Language Association, 1990), p. 167. I am grateful for Dixon's detailed description of the 1910 film.

9 Quoted in *ibid.*, p. 168.

10 *Ibid.*, p. 168.

11 As Nestrick argues, "Since 'life' in film is movement, the word that bridges the worlds of film and man is animation – the basic principle by which motion is imparted to the picture." See Nestrick, "Coming to Life," 295, 296.

12 Zakharieva, "Frankenstein of the Nineties," 745, 741.

13 Zakharieva describes this rejection as "a sort of modern-woman gesture of independence"; see *ibid.*, 750.

14 Boyarin uses the coinage "femminization" to suggest a male mimesis of the feminine, rather than femininity per se; see Daniel Boyarin, "Jewish Masochism: On Penises and Politics, Power and Pain," *Unheroic Conduct* (Berkeley: University of California Press, 1997), pp. 111–24.

15 I would like to acknowledge a helpful talk with Gideon Schor on the Clayton–Whale friendship.

5

JAY CLAYTON

Frankenstein's futurity: replicants and robots

> If the power of reflecting on the past, and darting the keen eye of contemplation into futurity, be the grand privilege of man, it must be granted that some people enjoy this prerogative in a very limited degree. Every thing new appears to them wrong; and not able to distinguish the possible from the monstrous, they fear where no fear should find a place, running from the light of reason, as if it were a firebrand.
>
> (Mary Wollstonecraft, *A Vindication of the Rights of Woman* [1792])[1]

The Creature's descendants

In an age of reproductive technology, cloning, artificial intelligence, and robotics, has *Frankenstein*'s futurity come to pass? Are we living in the time Mary Shelley foreshadowed? Perhaps so, although the author did not think of her work as prophesying the future. Shelley was much more interested in the science of her own day than in looking ahead. She uses the word "futurity," an old-fashioned noun meaning a time to come, only once in the novel, and it has nothing to do with fearful prophecies. Rather, it appears in a letter Elizabeth Lavenza writes to reassure Victor that she still wants to marry him; he plays a lead role, she tells him, in all her "airy dreams of futurity" (*F* 1818, III v 130). Though Mary Shelley, writing in 1816, set her novel in the late eighteenth century, *Frankenstein*, perhaps more than any other novel, has been interpreted as a warning about impending events. As a cautionary tale, *Frankenstein* has had an illustrious career; virtually every catastrophe of the last two centuries – revolution, rampant industrialism, epidemics, famines, World War I, Nazism, nuclear holocaust, clones, replicants, and robots – has been symbolized by Shelley's monster.[2] If Shelley's work is the first futuristic novel, as some critics have claimed, then the genre of science fiction was inaugurated as a warning, not a promise, about the world of tomorrow.[3]

In recent years, however, something has changed. Against all odds, a few influential writers and artists have begun to interpret Shelley's tale of a modern Prometheus as promising things they would like to see happen in real life. These people make up an eclectic collection, including Hollywood filmmakers such as Ridley Scott, George Lucas, and Steven Spielberg; science fiction writers Nancy Kress and Octavia A. Butler; pioneers of robotics Hans Moravec and Rodney A. Brooks; the visionary inventor Ray Kurzweil; the feminist theorist of science studies Donna Haraway; the hypertext author Shelley Jackson, and others. Each of these figures uses the legacy of *Frankenstein*, either implicitly or explicitly, to register some positive views of a future containing artificial creatures. In this chapter I explore these new conceptions, tracing the way they transform Shelley's vision through several key works – Ridley Scott's *Blade Runner* (1982; rev. 1992), Shelley Jackson's *Patchwork Girl* (1995), Hans Moravec's *Robot* (1999), Steven Spielberg's *A.I.: Artificial Intelligence* (2001), and Rodney Brooks's *Flesh and Machines* (2002). Sympathetic descendants of Frankenstein's Creature remain a tiny minority, almost lost among the multitude of demons stalking popular culture, but their emergence today is worth analyzing.

This development takes two forms: first, revisions that explore genetic and reproductive technology; second, those that reimagine *Frankenstein* in a world of cyborgs, artificial intelligence (AI), artificial life (AL), and robotics. In terms of genetics, the influence of *Blade Runner* has been unparalleled. The "replicants" in this movie are entirely biological creatures, designed by genetic engineers in the early twenty-first century to be "off-world" slaves on space colonies. When four stage a violent escape and return to earth to find their maker, they are hunted down and killed as dangerous monsters. The movie powerfully evokes *Frankenstein*, but concludes by converting its hero to the replicants' cause. The artificial creatures end up seeming more "human" than the people who stalk them.

The second line of descendants from *Frankenstein* are characterized by mechanical components and computer intelligence. Though the Creature in Shelley's novel was made up entirely of flesh and blood, filmmakers, and, later, science fiction novelists, have added a mechanical dimension of increasing complexity to her creation (see chapter 4). Most of these later creatures continued to be viewed as monstrous, in keeping with their horror genre roots, but a different attitude began to take shape in the 1940s when Isaac Asimov's long-running and popular robot series gave a positive spin to the idea of intelligent machines. Since then, scientists in the fields of AI and robotics have striven mightily to alter *Frankenstein*'s legacy by crossing it with that of Asimov. Spielberg too invokes Asimov's *I, Robot* in interviews about *A.I.*, and the screenplay of another recent film, *Bicentennial Man* (1999), is adapted from an Asimov story. If asked, these recent exponents of artificial life would no doubt repudiate Shelley's cautionary vision, but they are her heirs nonetheless. As I shall show, affirmative visions of artificial life, no less than dire warnings against scientific hubris, possess strong ties to *Frankenstein*.

It is easy to see how the novel serves the cause of those concerned that science has overstepped its bounds. In the biological arena, critics routinely label genetically modified agriculture "Frankenfood" and conjure up the specter of Shelley's monster to fight against reproductive cloning. In response to robotics, the monster still turns up in debates about automated machinery displacing workers (just as it did in nineteenth-century Luddite protests), and hostile computers in movies, from *2001: A Space Odyssey* to the *Terminator* series and *The Matrix*, mine the Frankenstein complex for some prophetic touches.

Demonstrating how affirmative perspectives on artificial life emerge from Shelley's text requires more detailed attention to the original work. Today's positive interpretations draw on an undercurrent in *Frankenstein*, to which feminist critics of the 1970s and 1980s first drew attention: the novel's sympathy for the Creature (see chapter 3). Contemporary advocates of AI emphasize many of the same things Shelley did: the emotional vulnerability of this new being, its abandonment in a hostile world, existentially alone, its sheer *creatureliness*. Turning its artificial origins from a liability to a virtue, writers and filmmakers focus on what humans owe to the things they create. For example, a scientist in Spielberg's *A.I.* remarks, "If a robot could genuinely love a person, what responsibility does that person hold toward that Mecha in return?" Ridley Scott in *Blade Runner* follows Shelley in associating the replicants both with Adam, fallen and in exile from his proper home, and with a Romantic version of Satan, noble in his defiance of the creator who has deserted him.[4] Further, all of the filmmakers and writers considered here follow Shelley in using images of slavery, abandoned children, spurned love, and bitter loneliness to arouse fellow feeling in the public at large.

The most interesting parallel, however, exists because of a little-appreciated aspect of Shelley's text: its complex attitude toward the science of her own day. Shelley was hardly an unthinking opponent of what was then called "natural philosophy." As Anne K. Mellor has shown in chapter 1 and elsewhere, Shelley distinguishes between "good" and "bad" science, the former epitomized by what she saw as Erasmus Darwin's respect for nature, the latter by Humphry Davy, Luigi Galvani, and Adam Walker's interventionist approaches.[5] Like her mother, Mary Wollstonecraft, Shelley viewed favorably many forms of natural science, and she shared her mother's

Enlightenment belief in intellectual progress, the virtue of education, and the rationality of women. The epigraph for this chapter captures something of Wollstonecraft's faith in futurity and her hope that the light of reason might disentangle the worthwhile from the monstrous in new ideas.

Similar positive views toward progress, including technological progress, are visible in *Frankenstein*, particularly in the first edition of 1818, alongside the indictments of scientific overreaching. Shelley's portrait of the ideal "man of science" – Frankenstein's admired professor Waldman – is sympathetically drawn: it combines an aversion to pedantry, dogmatism, and "petty experimentalis[m]" with frankness, good nature, and a commitment to a well-rounded, liberal approach to learning (*F* 1818, I ii 27–28). In two passages that were cut from the 1831 version of the novel (that which most readers encountered, until the 1970s), Victor's father teaches him the properties of electricity by imitating Benjamin Franklin's experiment with a kite, and Victor himself works hard to acquire the main scholarly languages of the age and to master practical scientific advances such as distillation, the steam engine, and the air pump (*F* 1818, I i 22–23).

Still, despite these favorable assessments of science, most readers come away from the book with an overwhelming impression of the dangers of scientific hubris. What makes matters confusing is that even the Enlightenment attitudes found in the 1818 version contain critiques of scientific inquiry. The rhetoric, however, is often different from the 1831 text. Notice the balanced cadence of an eighteenth-century moralist in this warning Frankenstein gives to Walton in the 1818 text: "Learn from me, if not by my precepts, at least by my example, how dangerous is the acquirement of knowledge, and how much happier that man is who believes his native town to be the world, than he who aspires to become greater than his nature will allow" (*F* 1818, I iii 31). Now compare it with this typical addition to the 1831 edition that dramatizes scientific overreaching: "So much has been done, exclaimed the soul of Frankenstein – more, far more, will I achieve: treading in the steps already marked, I will pioneer a new way, explore unknown powers, and unfold to the world the deepest mysteries of creation" (*F* 1831, iii 96). In these additions, one finds all the Romantic motifs of madness and guilt, impenetrable mysteries, the tumult of the swelling heart, clearly marked as evidence of Frankenstein's terrible error.

A careful reader can trace both Enlightenment and Romantic versions of the author's indictments of her scientist hero. Frankenstein's scientific "enthusiasm" is condemned as self-centered and isolating in the 1818 version (*F* 1818, I iii 30). The dangers of enthusiasm is a common Enlightenment theme, found throughout the works of Samuel Johnson or Jane Austen, to pick two writers who have rarely been identified with Shelley. In the 1831 text, Shelley adds the language of madness, obsessive questing, and uncontrollable ambition. Here, in one such insertion, is Frankenstein warning Walton about scientific aspiration: "a groan burst from his heaving breast . . . at length he spoke, in broken accents – 'Unhappy man! Do you share my madness? Have you drunk also of the intoxicating draught? Hear me – let me reveal my tale, and you will dash the cup from your lips!'" (*F* 1831, Letter IV 77). The final text stresses Frankenstein's "fervent longing to penetrate the secrets of nature" (*F* 1831, ii 88), to rend the veil of this world with a violence that is identified as willful and characteristically masculine.

By eliminating many positive comments about science and by exaggerating Frankenstein's Romantic spirit, the 1831 text makes it difficult to distinguish between Shelley's measured critique of nineteenth-century science and her more flamboyant denunciations of the Romantic male ego. Although related, these two dimensions of the book can be distinguished. Shelley's target was never a thoughtful natural philosophy, especially when it was balanced by other branches of learning. When Shelley takes aim at Frankenstein's research, she criticizes the excesses of an overwrought sensibility, not natural philosophy itself. The craving for immortality, the hubris of trying to rival God, a foolish regard for alchemy, or a desire to usurp women's power of creation – these passions afflict other possessed souls in nineteenth-century literature, from Faust and Cain to Melville's Ahab, and are hardly confined to mad scientists. Shelley's purpose in intensifying her rhetoric in the 1831 version is not to amplify the critique of science but to lay bare the dangers of Romantic egotism.

The replicant's tears: Ridley Scott's *Blade Runner*

All but the most utopian works considered here share with Shelley's *Frankenstein* the ambitions both of criticizing the methods of science and yet producing sympathy for the living creations of science. The next two sections discuss works that present their artificial beings as wholly biological constructions: Ridley Scott's *Blade Runner* and Shelley Jackson's *Patchwork Girl*. Scott's film, a techno-thriller set in the permanent twilight of Los Angeles in 2019, brings Shelley's story into the era of genetic engineering. Its portrait of ecological disaster and urban poverty, of a visual and aural landscape saturated with advertising, of a polyglot population immersed in a Babel of competing cultures, of decadence and homelessness, of technological achievement and social decay, has appeared to many people as foreshadowing imminent social conditions. Its indictment of irresponsible genetic tampering has seemed equally prescient. Yet, just as in Shelley's case, the film's ultimate point concerns how one should treat other beings, not the evils of science per se.

Scott's film invokes *Frankenstein* from its opening sequence, in which a disembodied eye stares down on an aerial view of Los Angeles at night. In Shelley's novel, disembodied eyes terrify Frankenstein repeatedly. Indeed, eyes seem to hold a special place among the bodily organs the novel assembles. From the first moment that Frankenstein sees "the dull yellow eye of the creature open," he is repelled by this feature, by the "watery eyes, that seemed almost of the same colour as the dun white sockets in which they were set" (*F* 1818, I iv 34). That night, when the creature visits Frankenstein's bed chamber, what disturbs him most is the fact that the creature's "eyes, if eyes they may be called, were fixed on me" (*F* 1818, I iv 35). Ultimately, Frankenstein has a vision of eyes watching him wherever he goes: "I saw around me nothing but a dense and frightful darkness, penetrated by no light but the glimmer of two eyes that glared upon me" (*F* 1818, III iv 126).

Blade Runner emphasizes eyes fully as much.[6] From the pupil-dilation test that police administer to determine if a person is a replicant to the various mediated gazes the film highlights to the gruesome murder committed by a replicant, who pushes his thumbs through his victim's eyes, the organs of vision symbolize both the vulnerable materiality of the creatures and their human capacity for sight. One scene combines both of these dimensions in a particularly graphic way. Two of the escaped replicants, trying to locate their creator, stop at a genetic engineering outlet called "Eye World." While Roy (Rutger Hauer), the leader of the replicants, questions the genetic technician, the other replicant picks up two exceedingly watery and yellow eyeballs, and delicately places one on each of the technician's shoulders. The terrified worker, an Asian-American caught in an economy of specialization that prevents him from knowing the answers the replicants seek, realizes that he was the one who made Roy's eyes. So informed, Roy answers: "If only you could see what I have seen with your eyes," amplifying a prominent motif in the movie: the creature *sees*[7] (figure 11). This episode raises questions about racial stereotypes, post-industrial outsourcing of parts – here, body parts – an allusion to Blake, and more. I bring it up, however, to show how Scott's film, like Shelley's novel, uses the embodied character of its creatures both to horrify and to humanize.

Embodiment and power are at stake in other motifs these two works share. Both compare their creatures to slaves driven by desperation to turn on their masters, and both show the creatures glorying in their life-and-death power over their former masters. Frankenstein's Creature exults over him: "Slave . . . Remember that I have power . . . You are my creator, but I am your master; – obey!" (*F* 1818, III iii 116). When Roy holds in his hand the life of his human antagonist Deckard (Harrison Ford), a similar taunt springs to the replicant's lips: "Quite an experience to live in fear, isn't it?

Figure 11 James Hong as Hannibal Chew, *Blade Runner*, dir. Ridley Scott (1982/1992)

That's what it is to be a slave." Both works explore the emotional dynamics between a creator and his creation, and both attend closely to the created being's feelings of thwarted love, anger, and thirst for revenge. The climax of the second volume of Shelley's novel is the Creature's confrontation with his maker and his resolution to wreak havoc on humanity: "if I cannot inspire love, I will cause fear; and chiefly towards you my arch-enemy, because my creator, do I swear inextinguishable hatred" (*F* 1818, II ix 98). In a climactic scene of *Blade Runner*, Roy, too, confronts his creator, Dr. Tyrell, the genius who has designed the replicants and created Tyrell Corporation to exploit them commercially.[8] Roy opens their tense dialogue with the line: "It's not an easy thing to meet your maker," a canny pun, since the idea of meeting his maker refers as much to Roy's impending death as to facing proof of his artificial origin. Like Frankenstein's Creature, Roy presents his maker with an ultimatum. The replicant's demand, however, is not for a mate (he already has a replicant partner, Pris [Daryl Hannah]) but for an extension of life beyond the four years that the replicants are designed to last. "Can the maker repair what he makes?" Roy asks ominously. Tyrell claims he cannot – whether truthfully or not viewers have no way of knowing. In response, Roy exacts a murderous revenge. Although Roy destroys Tyrell rather than Tyrell's family, the parallel with *Frankenstein* is unmistakable.

The climactic struggle between Roy and Deckard takes place in the nearly abandoned Bradbury building, where Deckard has gone to find Pris in the apartment of J. F. Sebastian, one of the Tyrell Corporation's genetic designers, who "makes friends" in the form of mechanical toys. This macabre sequence echoes a diverse range of films and fictions of monstrosity. The

Figure 12 Rutger Hauer as Roy Batty, *Blade Runner*, dir. Ridley Scott (1982/1992)

slowly revolving fans on the building's rooftop evoke the windmills from James Whale's classic film *Frankenstein* (1931); Roy's stiff-legged lope echoes Karloff's monster, while his wolf-like howling picks up on the werewolf sub-genre; Sebastian's collection of mechanical toys reaches back to a whole range of nineteenth- and early-twentieth-century automata that came after Shelley, including those in the tales of E. T. A. Hoffman, *Pinocchio*, and even *The Thief of Bagdad*; Pris's disguise as a mechanical ballerina ironically plays on her artificiality, while recalling *The Nutcracker* and *Petrushka*. When Deckard slowly removes Pris's veil, the scene turns into a violent parody of the Galatea myth, with the frozen woman coming to life not as a lover, but as an acrobatic killer.

The fight between Deckard and Roy alludes, above all, to Frankenstein's attempt to "close with [the Creature] in mortal combat" (*F* 1818, II ii 65) and Deckard, like Frankenstein, fails to kill his adversary. Roy, however, knows he is dying anyway, and out of newfound pity for another mortal being, spares Deckard's life. Roy's dying words echo the final pages of *Frankenstein*, where the Creature resolves to sacrifice himself: "I shall no longer see the sun or stars, or feel the winds play on my cheeks. Light, feeling, and sense, will pass away . . . I shall die" (*F* 1818, III vii 155–56). Roy's last words also express a lyrical grief: "I've seen things you people wouldn't believe. Attack ships on fire off the shoulder of Orion. I watched c-beams glitter in the dark near the Tannhäuser Gate. All those moments will be lost in time like tears in the rain. Time to die" (figure 12). These elegiac speeches in each work humanize the creature, demanding recognition of the other as a living, feeling, and sentient being.

Shelley Jackson's piecework: *Patchwork Girl*

Shelley Jackson's *Patchwork Girl* takes as its premise that Mary Shelley's second creature, the female companion that Frankenstein began making but then destroyed, was secretly finished by Mary Shelley herself. The artificial creature becomes the lover of this fictive Mary Shelley, then travels to America, where she goes through numerous adventures until her death in the 1990s. Describing these events, Jackson frequently weaves quotations from *Frankenstein* directly into her account, creating a variegated patchwork of "original" writing and borrowed phrases, including passages from L. Frank Baum, Donna Haraway, Jacques Derrida, and many others. Jackson's hypertext, one of the most successful efforts in this new medium, consists of 323 lexias (or screens of text), varying in length from a single sentence to some 300 or so words. The lexias are joined to one another by 462 links, which create multiple pathways through the text. Like most hypertexts, *Patchwork Girl* has no proper beginning or end, but it does have numerous narrative characteristics, including characters, settings, flashbacks, recognition scenes, shifting points of view, and consecutive temporal sequences.

Because many readers are unfamiliar with this work, I shall take a moment to describe its structure. Written with Storyspace software and published by Eastgate Systems, the premier source for stand-alone hypertexts, it is distributed on disk and equipped with maps that allow readers to visualize the structure of the crisscrossing network of lexias.[9] The narrative core of the work – the chronological arrangement of events, not the order of the lexias, which is determined by the reader – is contained in two long sections. The first, "Journal," contains "Mary Shelley's" diary of her construction of the female creature and of their initial, halting attempts at a relationship. Their bond culminates in a dramatically convincing act of lovemaking, which finely captures the characters' blend of fear and exploratory passion. The other section, "Story," is subdivided into six further parts: "M/S," which explores the love affair from the creature's point of view; "Severance," which recounts their mutual but painful decision to separate and includes a strong scene in which the creator and creation exchange skin-grafts, so that each will contain a living fragment of the other; "Seagoing" and "Seance," which follow the creature across the Atlantic and narrate various adventures involving crossdressing, an encounter with a circus freak, and the purchase of a false identity; and, finally, "Falling Apart" and "Rethinking," in which her 175-year-old body begins to decompose into its component pieces. The narrative core culminates in the creature's decision to wander off into the desert of Death Valley, an effective counterpoint to the fate of Frankenstein's Creature, who disappears into the ice floes of the Arctic.

Flanking the narrative core, yet interspersed in most readings, are three nonlinear sections. "Body of the Text" and "Crazy Quilt" contain meditations on hypertext writing, lyrical passages, dreams, irreverent remarks, and fragmentary musings in various voices (the author's, the creature's, the text's itself). "Graveyard," the most haunting of the sections, gives voice to the creature's individual body parts. In lexias titled "eyeballs," "lips," "left breast," and "heart," for example, Jackson tells the stories of the dead women from whom the organs were harvested. Macabre and witty, sometimes forming tiny interpolated narratives, these passages literalize the post-structuralist dictum that the subject is always multiple. The creature's eyes, for example, give her the traits of the person from whom they were acquired: a woman named Tituba, which is also the name of a West Indian slave jailed in the Salem witch trials. This origin underlines the slavery theme, which *Patchwork Girl* presents in more explicitly racial terms than either *Frankenstein* or *Blade Runner*, for the creature in Jackson's hypertext is sewn together from the skins of people from different races.

The creature's eyes also open a hidden level of Jackson's text. In a lexia that has no entry or exit, a passage unlinked to any other in the hypertext and hence inaccessible except by using the software's search engine, the Patchwork Girl thanks her maker for giving her life. "Hideous progeny: yes, I was both those things, for you, and more. Lover, friend, collaborator. It is my eyes you describe – with fear, yes, but with fascination: yellow, watery, but speculative eyes" ("thanks"). This impulse to thank rather than hate one's creator marks the hypertext's largest thematic departure from Shelley's novel. The difference stems from the loving, nurturing embrace Jackson imagines her character "Mary Shelley" bestowing on the creature she has made.

In fact, Jackson's "Mary Shelley" uses a technique for creating an artificial person that more closely resembles Frankenstein's methods than Tyrell's genetic engineering. In an age of biotechnology, sewing parts together seems anachronistic, a throwback to the nineteenth century when scientific creation of life was conceptualized in terms of assembling already existent pieces. But Jackson associates this older kind of creativity with feminine crafts and values – weaving, collaborating, conserving, reusing. The notion of sewing internal organs into place implies meticulous care, a time-consuming total-body operation: kidneys tucked in place, intestines wound into their cavity, veins sewn one by one along their proper paths. Such patient piecework contrasts vividly with the high tech procedures of contemporary genetics.

This contrast forms a part of Jackson's sustained critique of technoscience. Yet like Shelley before her, Jackson is no mindless opponent of science. In fact, she obviously admires what she calls the creature's "techy bent" ("am I mary"), and she draws frequent metaphors from genetics and cyborg theory.

An interest in science is virtually mandatory for the affirmative pressure she puts on the Frankenstein myth. And it works best when Jackson is most true to her maternal origin – most faithful to Mary Shelley's novel – endowing her artificial creature with the pathos of life.

The robot child: Steven Spielberg's *A.I.*

The final section of this chapter turns to some of the numerous works that reinterpret Shelley's legacy in mechanistic rather than biological terms. The most famous recent work in this vein is Steven Spielberg's movie *A.I.*, but readers need some groundwork in contemporary robotics to see where Spielberg culled his ideas about artificial life.

The two most radical proponents of intelligent machines are Hans Moravec, founder of the world's largest robotics program at Carnegie Mellon University, and Rodney A. Brooks, director of the MIT Artificial Intelligence Laboratory. Although Moravec and Brooks have profound differences in their approaches to building robots, they share a fundamental belief that the future belongs to silicon rather than carbon-based life forms. In numerous scientific publications and two popular books, Moravec has predicted that by 2040 robots will have equaled humans in intelligence and gained consciousness; thereafter they will move beyond humans, controlling their own evolution as their mental and physical capabilities transcend anything now imaginable. Moravec does more than predict such developments, however – he devotes his life to bringing them about. Moravec works to build the very future Frankenstein fears when he shudders at the prospect that "a race of devils would be propagated upon the earth, who might make the very existence of the species of man a condition precarious" (*F* 1818, III iii 114). Moravec and Brooks, by contrast, welcome the idea of a new species supplanting humanity entirely. Moravec regards robots as the legitimate heirs of our niche on earth, and he argues that we should see them as our "mind children," sacrificing for them as we would for our biological children.[10] Brooks agrees, arguing that we already are machines, just as much as any robot: "I believe myself and my children all to be mere machines. Automatons at large in the universe. Every person I meet is also a machine – a big bag of skin full of biomolecules interacting according to describable and knowable rules."[11]

Moravec and Brooks's utilitarian acceptance of humanity's eventual extinction resembles the stern rationalism advocated by Shelley's father William Godwin, to whom she dedicated *Frankenstein*. In *Political Justice* (1793), Godwin notoriously contends that one should value most highly the life of a being who "will be most conducive to the general good" even at the cost of sacrificing oneself or one's closest relative.[12] Godwin intends this argument to apply to different species as well, for he contrasts the superior value of a human life to that of a beast. In a comparable argument, Moravec exhorts us to sacrifice ourselves in favor of our mechanical descendants:

> Robots will displace humans from essential roles. Rather quickly, they could displace us from existence. I'm not as alarmed as many by the latter possibility, since I consider these future machines our progeny . . . Like biological children of previous generations, they will embody humanity's best chance for a long-term future. It behooves us to give them every advantage and to bow out when we can no longer contribute.[13]

Spielberg's *A.I.* unites the latest preoccupations of artificial intelligence researchers with Shelleyan themes. The movie begins in a distant future, in which humanity has become extinct and benign aliens have inherited the planet earth. Through an elegiac voiceover, the narrative moves back in time to a near future, when New York and other coastal cities have been drowned by melting ice caps, and reasoning, humanoid robots called "Mechas" perform most of the essential tasks of life. The story concerns a robot child named David (Haley Joel Osment), who is the first intelligent machine designed to have feelings. Spielberg's interest in artificial intelligence brings him full circle back to the place where Shelley began – to the understanding that a creature with feelings acquires personhood, even if it is not of the same species as humans. As Professor Hobby (William Hurt), head of Cybertronics Corporation, explains, "Love will be the key by which they acquire a kind of subconsciousness, never before achieved. An inner world of metaphor, of intuition, of self-motivated reasoning, of dreams."[14] David is an experimental prototype, given to an employee in Cybertronics whose child, Martin, is in a coma. Only later do viewers discover that Professor Hobby has lost a child of his own named David, who died at age eleven, the same age that this robot will remain forever (figure 13).

Much to everyone's surprise, Martin awakens from his coma, creating the conditions for an intense sibling rivalry. When Martin returns home, he is confined to a mechanized wheelchair, and later he wears computer-assisted leg braces, and these prostheses illustrate a point Brooks makes explicitly: that humans already are kin to machines.[15] It is not long before Martin is sadistically taunting David as "the new Supertoy" – not much better than their mechanical bear Teddy – and getting his mother to read *Pinocchio* out loud before bed. This last torment initiates David's lifelong quest to become "a real boy," as Pinocchio did in the story, and thus to reclaim his mother's love. As in *Patchwork Girl*, David never turns against his human creators, no matter how much he is persecuted. This revision of the *Frankenstein* myth inevitably makes the artificial creature even more sympathetic. Once Martin

Figure 13 Haley Joel Osment as David, *A.I.: Artificial Intelligence*, dir Steven Spielberg (2001)

and David's rivalry turns violent, their mother is pressured to get rid of the Mecha child. Finding she cannot bear to return him to the factory to be destroyed, she secretly abandons him in a forest.

David's first night in the woods conjures memories of Frankenstein's Creature stumbling blindly into the forest and gradually becoming aware of the external world, first of birds flitting across his vision (David's earliest memory is of "a bird with big wings," the corporate logo of Cybertronics), then of an immense full moon rising through the trees. In Shelley's novel the moon provides the Creature with his first sensation of pleasure: "I started up, and beheld a radiant form rise from among the trees. I gazed with a kind of wonder" (*F* 1818, ii iii 68). In *A.I.* the moon David gazes at in wonder turns out to be a hot-air balloon, carrying bounty hunters in pursuit of cast-off Mechas to sell to a horrific entertainment called the Flesh Fair. David's experience at the Flesh Fair plays on the recurrent slavery theme, heightened here in a gruesome scene that features the killing of a Mecha in black-face. Yet, on the whole, the Flesh Fair episode seems under-imagined, too derivative of gladiator fights in post-apocalyptic movies such as *Mad Max: Beyond Thunderdome* (1985) or *The Running Man* (1987). More effective is the supplanting of humanity by robots (and later by aliens, with whom robots are metaphorically equated). David's robot companion Gigolo Joe (Jude Law) expresses the theme most directly: "They hate us, you know,

Figure 14 Jude Law as Gigolo Joe, *A.I.: Artificial Intelligence*, dir. Steven Spielberg (2001)

the humans . . . They made us too smart, too quick, and too many. We are suffering for the mistakes they made, because when the end comes, all that will be left is us" (figure 14).

Joe grows angry and defiant under persecution, like Frankenstein's Creature, but the film's prevailing tone is elegiac. The movie ends, as it began, with melancholy for all that has been lost. There are hints of this valedictory tone in the farewell words Frankenstein's Creature utters, just as there were in Roy's death speech, but *A.I.* extends the lament to encompass a multitude of losses: Professor Hobby mourns the loss of his son; David, of his mother; the aliens mourn a vanished humanity. (Knowing that Spielberg was asked to take on this project, originally conceived by Stanley Kubrick, shortly after that director's death, one suspects that this film also mourns Spielberg's cinematic predecessor.) The aliens tell David that they revived him because of his memories: "there is nothing too small that you didn't store for us to remember." The irony is that this artificial creature has become the last bearer of the human legacy: "David, you are the enduring memory of the human race." When the aliens grant David's wish and restore his mother to life for one precious day, the fleetingness of his joy becomes a metaphor for the transitory nature of all human experience. David's mechanical body may be virtually immortal, but he is human in feeling loss as keenly as any of the people who created him.

If, as Professor Hobby maintains, "To create an artificial being has been the dream of man since the birth of science," that dream has ceased to be a nightmare in the work of Spielberg. The robot in *A.I.* is no monster to the aliens who find him but rather "the most lasting proof of [humanity's] genius." This destiny is a far cry from the one Frankenstein envisioned for his Creature. Why is it that our present moment focuses so sympathetically on the fate of the creature? I do not think it means that we have acquired a kind of fatalism about scientific advances. Even if it is only a matter of time before scientists like Moravec and Brooks produce artificial beings with consciousness, the social consequences of these developments are not predetermined. It is up to us to decide how society will respond to the advent of artificial life. The changed attitude toward artificial creatures, it seems to me, stems from the need to redefine personhood in the face of both social and scientific pressures to rethink old boundaries. Perhaps in the final words of Frankenstein's Creature, an unexpected futurity waits: "Soon these burning miseries will be extinct . . . My spirit will sleep in peace; or if it thinks, it will not surely think thus. Farewell" (*F* 1818, III vii 156).

NOTES

1 Mary Wollstonecraft, *A Vindication of the Rights of Woman*, ed. Carol H. Poston (New York: Norton, 1975), p. 151.

2 For an excellent account of the way Frankenstein's Creature has been used to symbolize many of the fears prominent through World War II, see Chris Baldick, *In Frankenstein's Shadow: Myth, Monstrosity, and Nineteenth-Century Writing* (Oxford: Oxford University Press, 1987).

3 See Brian W. Aldiss, *Billion Year Spree: The True History of Science Fiction* (Garden City, NY: Doubleday, 1973), p. 21.

4 Several critics have noted the film's allusions to *Frankenstein*, including David Desser, "The New Eve: the Influence of *Paradise Lost* and *Frankenstein* on *Blade Runner*," in *Retrofitting "Blade Runner": Issues in Ridley Scott's "Blade Runner" and Philip K. Dick's "Do Androids Dream of Electric Sheep?,"* ed. Judith B. Kerman (Bowling Green, OH: Bowling Green State University Popular Press, 1991), pp. 53–65 and Joe Abbott, "The 'Monster' Reconsidered: *Blade Runner's* Replicant as Romantic Hero," *Extrapolation* 34 (1993), 340–50.

5 See Anne K. Mellor, "*Frankenstein*: A Feminist Critique of Science," in *One Culture: Essays in Science and Literature*, ed. George Levine (Madison: University of Wisconsin Press, 1987), pp. 287–312; Alan Rauch, "The Monstrous Body of Knowledge in Mary Shelley's *Frankenstein*," *SiR* 34 (1995), 227–53; and Marilyn Butler, "*Frankenstein* and Radical Science," in *Frankenstein*, ed. J. Paul Hunter (New York: Norton, 1996), pp. 302–13.

6 Among the several critical commentaries on eyes in *Blade Runner*, see especially Kaja Silverman, "Back to the Future," *Camera Obscura: A Journal of Feminism, Culture, and Media Studies* 27 (1991), 109–32; and Elissa Marder, "*Blade*

Runner's Moving Still," *Camera Obscura: A Journal of Feminism, Culture, and Media Studies* 27 (1991), 77–87. Neither connects this motif to *Frankenstein*.

7 All references to this film are drawn from *Blade Runner*, dir. Ridley Scott, director's cut (Warner Brothers, 1992).

8 By personalizing the creator/creature drama and charging Tyrell rather than corporate society with the guilt of betraying his replicant "children," the movie follows Shelley's novel rather than the political critique it elsewhere maintains.

9 See Shelley Jackson, *Patchwork Girl; or, A Modern Monster by Mary/Shelley, and Herself*, CD-ROM (Watertown, MA: Eastgate Systems Inc., 1995). Although Jackson's hypertext is unpaginated, each lexia is identified in the Storyspace maps by an uncapitalized title, which I will cite parenthetically to identify the location of quotations.

10 See Hans Moravec, *Robot: Mere Machine to Transcendent Mind* (New York: Oxford University Press, 1999), pp. 77–78.

11 Rodney A. Brooks, *Flesh and Machines: How Robots Will Change Us* (New York: Pantheon, 2002), p. 174.

12 See William Godwin, *Political Justice* (Harmondsworth: Penguin, 1985), p. 169.

13 Moravec, *Robot*, p. 13.

14 *A.I.: Artificial Intelligence*, dir. Steven Spielberg (DreamWorks Pictures, 2001).

15 Donna J. Haraway makes the same point in her influential article, "A Cyborg Manifesto: Science, Technology and Socialist-Feminism in the Late Twentieth Century," in *Simians, Cyborgs, and Women: The Reinvention of Nature* (New York: Routledge, 1991), pp. 149–81.

2

FICTIONS AND MYTHS

6

STUART CURRAN

Valperga

Valperga: or, The Life and Adventures of Castruccio, Prince of Lucca was a novel surprisingly long in its gestation. Although not published until 1823, its inception actually dates from six years earlier. "I first thought of it in our library in Marlow," Mary Shelley wrote as she was completing it in 1821 (*L* 1 203), thus placing its beginnings at some point in 1817. She does not stipulate what book in the library which she and Percy Bysshe Shelley had assembled in Marlow prompted her to conceive the idea of this new novel, nor is there anything in either's correspondence that would further eluci-date her claim. But among the components of an ideal library P. B. Shelley later enumerated to his cousin Thomas Medwin were the writings of Nicolo Machiavelli,[1] the Italian Renaissance political theorist. Beginning with the first English translations of *The Prince* in the early seventeenth century, it became a common practice to append to that work Machiavelli's admiring biographical account of Castruccio Castracani dei Antelminelli, the warlord of fourteenth-century Lucca, whom Machiavelli, in 1520, looked back on as an exemplary Italian "prince." This is the work that Mary Shelley denigrates in the first sentence of her Preface to the novel as a mere "romance" (*V* 1 5). One might therefore infer that Mary Shelley's original idea for the novel centered on simply setting the record straight about Castruccio; her original title – *The Life and Adventures of Castruccio, Prince of Lucca* – focusing on him alone, would seem to substantiate that inference. The change in title by which *Valperga* became centered was owing to Mary Shelley's father, William Godwin, who reconfigured the novel's balance by emphasizing its female protagonist, the Countess of Valperga, a fictional Tuscan duchy. Mary Shelley readily acceded to this change, as she did to his other emendations to her text; he was, after all, a highly successful novelist with long experience in the London publishing scene. For today's readers, his reconfiguration better conveys the innate dynamics of the novel than the original title, emphasizing the ethical centrality of the fictional Countess who is depicted as falling in love with, then being betrayed by, the medieval warlord Castruccio, who first seizes her duchy in his program of subjugating western Tuscany and afterwards forces her into exile and to her death by shipwreck.

After 1817, it took Mary Shelley some time, and something of a reeducation, to return to the idea of this novel. First, because there was little to rely on in English beyond translations of Machiavelli's brief life, she had to master Italian, which began for her when she, her husband, and her ever-present stepsister, Claire Clairmont, relocated to Italy at the beginning of April 1818. Not until the end of the year, when they all wintered in Naples, did she undertake further research on the project, but she did not resume writing it until early 1820, when she and Percy Shelley attained greater stability by relocating to relative permanence in the area of Pisa.

Pisa lies near the Mediterranean coast of Tuscany only some dozen miles to the southwest of Lucca. Mary Shelley had already come to know Florence, fifty miles further east, from several sojourns there, including the period in the fall of 1819 when she gave birth to her son, Percy Florence, named for the city. Relocating to Pisa provided her with proximity to the other center of her novel's gravity, spurring her imaginative grasp of her subject and allowing her to realize a geographical accuracy in *Valperga* that is uncommon for the age, if scarcely credited as unusual by most readers today. *Valperga*, indeed, reflecting Mary Shelley's acute sensitivity to details of climate, natural phenomena, and topography, is embued with a rare authenticity that quietly presses its authority on the events of the novel, rendering its fictional representations as though they carried the actual weight of history.

On August 12, 1820, a Friday, the Shelleys and Claire Clairmont made an excursion to Lucca to observe first-hand the memorials of the period of her novel. Percy Shelley went on for a two-day hike up Monte San Pellegrino (from which he returned with the beginning stanzas of his poem *The Witch of Atlas*), leaving the two women to conduct their local research according to their own priorities. The vast fortress palace that Castruccio had built in the western quarter of Lucca, said to have occupied a fourth of the medieval city, had been pulled down soon after his own demise in 1328, a sure sign of the relief the citizenry felt to be freed of his martial ambitions. But other monuments of the time remained. The two women climbed to the top of the ancient Palazzo Guinigi, ancestral home of the family who managed, after Castruccio's death, at last to bring peace to Lucca and to promote concord throughout Tuscany. That spirit, so antithetical to Castruccio's desire to rule the province by strength of arms alone, is recreated in the pastoral idyll of Francesco de Guinigi, recounted in the third chapter, in which Castruccio passes his adolescence. The Guinigi tower, then as now, has a landscaped garden on its top with sizable trees, and from this height the two stepsisters looked far out over the plain of Tuscany and north to the mountainous

Garfagnana, where the novel locates the duchy of Valperga. Indeed, from this prospect Mary Shelley must have immediately decided just how to situate the Countess Euthanasia's palace, for a monumental convent, the Convento del Angelo, arrayed in a dazzling white stucco, is the sole structure that stands out in the midst of this rough terrain. In Volume I of *Valperga*, Castruccio looks forth from just such a tower (represented as that of the Antelminelli family) and, studying "the white walls of villages and castles" (V I viii 97) in the hills, he is reminded that the most prominent of these is that retained by his childhood friend Euthanasia. The next morning he renews his acquaintance with Euthanasia in this palace, described as lying six miles due north of the walls of Lucca.

Mary Shelley and Claire Clairmont not only fixed the exact geography of the Lucchese environs during this expedition, but they also visited the site of Castruccio's interment in the church of San Francesco, which in Castruccio's time had been outside the eastern walls of the city. There, Claire dutifully transcribed both a plaque erected in 1749 by Castruccio's descendants and the original fourteenth-century memento mori to him below it. It was surely a sign of an unusual female education that the two young women, reared together in the household of William Godwin, could so easily handle the Latin of these inscriptions. Indeed, Claire notes that the next day, while the two of them awaited Percy Shelley's return from his tour, she entertained herself by reading a fifteenth-century Italian account of Castruccio Castracani, which the two had probably brought with them as a sort of guidebook.[2] The Latin words of this fourteenth-century memorial Mary Shelley uses as the final words of her novel.

Pisa was an important university town, and in its precincts, Mary Shelley at last found the books, some of great antiquity, from which she could retrieve the necessary historical and cultural documentation for her novel. Her principal resource for medieval cultural practices like Euthanasia's three-day "court" (V I xiii–xiv) was Lodovico Muratori's multi-volume *Dissertazioni sopra le antichità italiane* (*Dissertations on Italian Antiquities*), originally published in Latin as *Antiquitates italicae medii aevi* (1742), a work of incomparable learning. This she supplemented with numerous other sources. The one she particularly favored was the extremely rare *Croniche di messer Giovanni Villani cittadino fiorentino* (*Chronicles of Giovanni Villani, Florentine Citizen*), dating from 1537, and about whom she wrote a sprightly essay for the fourth number of *The Liberal* (1823), the periodical started by her husband, Lord Byron, and Leigh Hunt in 1822. If Villani's chronicle history is a fit example, Percy Shelley's remark that Mary Shelley "raked [the novel] out of fifty old books" (*PBSL* II 245) truly testifies to the extensive program of historical research in early Italian texts that supports *Valperga*'s quietly unpretentious but distinctive erudition; few novels of the early nine-teenth century are so meticulously grounded in historical sources. A major exemplar for Mary Shelley in this regard would have been another work she read during the Marlow period, her father's novel *Mandeville*, published in 1817 and set within the scrupulously researched context of the seventeenth-century English civil wars.

It is important, however, for readers two centuries later to realize how comparatively new on the scene was this fictional model. The eighteenth century had certainly witnessed novels set in a distant past – for example, the popular Gothic novel set within the reign of Elizabeth I, *The Old English Baron* by Clara Reeve (1778), which Claire Clairmont was reading just before the expedition of August 1820. But an extensive fictional recasting of actual historical figures and events from the past was first popularized only at the beginning of the second decade of the nineteenth century, in Jane Porter's *Scottish Chiefs* (1810), a novel whose romanticized focus on the struggles of William Wallace and Robert the Bruce had an immediate and far-reaching impact. Its most important consequence, perhaps, was to prompt Walter Scott to recast the abandoned early chapters of *Waverley* (1814) as his initial foray into historical fiction, the genre that he would both shape and dominate over the next two decades. Surely, his unprecedented success was an incitement to the ever-needy William Godwin to reassert his claim as a popular novelist, and *Mandeville* centers on the sort of crucial ideological conflicts in which Scott had begun to invest his historical novels; unlike the conservative Scott, however, Godwin sets his novel within a wholly English and a determinedly republican, anti-monarchical context.

A discriminating analysis of the journals kept jointly by Mary and Percy Shelley suggests that whereas he set the agenda for their reading in earlier poetry and drama, she was an avid reader of contemporary fiction, even after they moved to Italy and it was comparatively difficult to come by.[3] Perhaps that is only to be expected from a woman who took her new career as a writer of novels seriously and who, brought up in a household that doubled as a publishing concern,[4] had been instilled from childhood with a practical sense of the popular market in books. As *Frankenstein* had endeavored to revivify – and revise – the genre of the Gothic novel by divesting it of its stock characters and events and aestheticizing and interiorizing the idea of horror, so *Valperga* seems to have been intended to make a distinctive mark in this new mode of historical fiction. Reverting to the medieval time period with which the form had won its initial fame under Jane Porter, Mary Shelley, uniquely among novelists in English of her day, transports her concerns to the Continent. And, faced with the male-centered, dynastic universe in which Walter Scott characteristically conceptualized the past, Mary Shelley, also uniquely among contemporary novelists, revises that model drastically. She perhaps suggests as much in the dismissive way in which she cites Machiavelli in the first sentence of her preface. She makes her aims explicit, however, only as she begins the concluding chapter, which, in suddenly shifting its mode to invoke Scott's notion of history, almost jolts the reader who has become so deeply accustomed to her own alternate perspective.

> The private chronicles, from which the foregoing relation has been collected, end with the death of Euthanasia. It is therefore *in public histories alone* that we find an account of the last years of the life of Castruccio. We can know nothing of his grief, when he found that she whom he had once tenderly loved, and whom he had ever revered as the best and wisest among his friends, had died. We know however that, during the two years that he survived this event, his glory and power arose not only higher than they had ever before done, but that they surpassed those of any former Italian prince.
>
> (*V* iii Conclusion 438; italics added)

Although the final word here recalls Machiavelli's celebration of Castruccio's successes as a petty prince, the ironic distance of the reportage reminds us that they matter not at all in the scale of values that Mary Shelley has slowly reinforced around her wholly invented figure of the Countess of Valperga. It is Euthanasia and her likewise fictitious counterpart, Beatrice of Ferrara, also in love with Castruccio, who have commanded both our attention and our human allegiances over the course of the novel. Thus, while Castruccio's career as a warlord in fourteenth-century Tuscany can be traced in her Italian sources, the "public histories" to which she refers in this paragraph, those same histories systematically exclude private desires, aspirations, and griefs, the personal and domestic, as they also either simply erase women or at best allow them to function only as appendages of rich and powerful men. Although Mary Shelley had probably worked out the underlying form of *Valperga* before she read Scott's *Ivanhoe* in June 1820, it takes little more than a glance of comparison to realize that, in Mary Shelley's model of "private chronicles," the female protagonists who revolve around Wilfrid of Ivanhoe – Rebecca of York, a Jew identified (like Beatrice) by her religious devotion and community, and Lady Rowena, similar to Euthanasia in her regal bearing – belong at the center, not the periphery, of our historical consciousness.[5] As Deidre Lynch argues in chapter 8, the inability of Euthanasia and Beatrice to survive the fratricidal struggles of warring masculinity in the Middle Ages is the true index of its history. And in Mary Shelley's revisionary assessment, that medieval history, far from deserving Machiavelli's (or Scott's) celebration of it as lurching through unavoidable strife toward a civilized stability, is life-denying in its energies and therefore essentially tragic in its cast.

Yet, at the same time, the political factionalism in which *Valperga* by necessity is immersed, with ideological demarcations from many centuries past that may seem to today's reader simply academic, bears surprisingly relevant import for Mary Shelley's day. We can best approach this nineteenth-century context, however, after a closer look at the medieval milieu of the novel. Although Charlemagne's inclusion of northern Italy within the Holy Roman Empire he founded in 800 CE lasted for only a generation after his death, the reassertion of the claim by his powerful successor Frederick Barbarossa after 1160 CE ignited a state of war throughout the Italian peninsula that continued on and off for well over two centuries. On the surface it might look as if the Ghibellines, aligned with the Holy Roman Emperor against the Guelf supporters of the temporal power of the Papacy, were merely pawns of a foreign usurper of Italian territory, but the political terrain was much more complicated than such an explanation suggests. After all, the Papacy was also international in its aims and structure, and for much of the fourteenth century was based not in Rome but Avignon, in southern France. Nor does the division between these factions easily narrow into a competition between equally authoritarian entities, nor even one between squarely secular and theocratic allegiances. Moreover, although the Ghibellines did manifest their united allegiance to the Empire, however much individual princes or political entities might strive for predominance within it, the Guelfs were often split between adherents of the Church per se and those who used that adherence as a cover for preserving local civic institutions. When at the beginning of the fourteenth century the Papacy attempted to reassert its authority over such nominal autonomy in Florence, the result was a major schism among the Guelfs between the Papal party, now called the Black Guelfs, and those, the White Guelfs, who like the Ghibellines saw the only buffer against the authoritarian temporal power of the Church to be the Holy Roman Empire. Dante Alighieri was a leader of this latter faction, and in 1302 he and his party were exiled from Florence on pain of death. Dante never returned to his native city, spending his last twenty years under the protection of Ghibelline princes in northern Italy.

Although we might wish to exclaim with Shakespeare's Mercutio, destroyed through this kind of deadly factionalism, "A plague o' both your houses" (*Romeo and Juliet* III i 105), to Mary Shelley (as to many readers today), the Ghibellines represented an oppressive centralized authority exerted over all of Europe and embodied in a single man. When Mary Shelley was writing, one such figure had just been overthrown and sent into exile – Napoleon Bonaparte – and another, the Hapsburg Emperor of Austria, had succeeded to Napoleon's dominion over Italy, imposing an even stricter authoritarianism.[6] However the policies of the dictator altered, the general effect for those living under his hegemony was still tyranny. The alternative, from Mary Shelley's perspective, was hardly an embrace of theocracy. Rather, it was to see in those local medieval city-states such as Florence the beginnings of an essentially republican vision of civic polity that pointed the way for a new political order in post-Napoleonic Europe. This is how Euthanasia articulates her ideals to Castruccio:

> "Florence was free, and Dante was a Florentine; none but a freeman could have poured forth the poetry and eloquence to which I listened: what though he were banished from his native city, and had espoused a party that seemed to support tyranny; the essence of freedom is that clash and struggle which awaken the energies of our nature, and that operation of the elements of our mind, which as it were gives us the force and power that hinder us from degenerating as they say all things earthly do when not regenerated by change.
>
> "What is man without wisdom? And what would this world become, if every man might learn from its institutions the true principles of life, and become as the few which have shone as stars amidst the night of ages? If time had not shaken the light of poetry and of genius from its wings, all the past would be dark and trackless: now we have a track – the glorious foot-marks of the children of liberty; let us imitate them, and like them we may serve as marks in the desert, to attract future passengers to the fountains of life. Already we have begun to do so; and Dante is the pledge of a glorious race, which tells us that, in clinging to the freedom which gave birth to his genius, we may awake the fallen hopes of the world."   (*V* I x 109–10)

To verify that such sweeping enthusiasm for early Italian republicanism is not limited to Mary Shelley's indulgent affection for the country that had become her second home, we might turn to the exactly contemporary perspective of Sydney Owenson, Lady Morgan, the other important woman novelist of this period to offer a female-oriented, liberal alternative to Scott's conservative model of the historical novel. But in this case, the context is provided by the second of her highly politicized travel writings, the multi-volume *Italy* of 1821, where she, too, explicitly pays tribute to its medieval heritage (see chapter 15). Italy, she declares, "has thrice given to Europe letters, arts, and sciences, under the Etruscans, under the Romans, and under her republics."[7] Unlike the bulk of travel writings devoted to Italy, Lady Morgan's *Italy* is unique in emphasizing both the contemporary scene and the monuments to freedom that survive from the medieval republics. Arriving in Bologna, site of the western world's first university, Lady Morgan succinctly characterizes its history: "This ancient republic struck us to be one of the States of Italy, which best deserved a free government, and to be the most determined to obtain it." As she surveys the art collections of Bologna's renowned Pinacoteca, Lady Morgan pauses before a Guido Reni portrait of Simone da Pesaro and launches a paean very like that of Mary Shelley's Euthanasia: "What a race did the free States of Italy leave behind them! What noble countenances! What splendid forms! . . . Energies developed, passions awakened, views ennobled by their objects, imaginations heated and exercised – these are the true sources of beauty; sources soon dried up under the influence of unlimited power."[8] In the resonances of Lady Morgan's deeply politicized reconstruction of Italy, that last phrase – "unlimited power" – could apply equally to the medieval Holy Roman Empire, supported by the Ghibellines, and to its nineteenth-century descendant, the Austrian Empire, with its stranglehold over most of the Italian peninsula.

In *Valperga* Mary Shelley, too, places her novel firmly within a political framework that sees the future through the perspective of this medieval past, one that offers a democratic and feminist alternative to a modern Europe that, by the 1820s, had been thrown back two generations to the dynastic autocracies against which a previous generation had unleashed ferocious, revolutionary energies. But it is not by mere coincidence, or because of like-minded liberal values tested by life under heavy-handed Austrian authority in Italy, that Mary Shelley and Lady Morgan come to share such a view of Italian history. Their valorization of the heritage of the medieval republics owes its conception (and not a few of its examples) to a monumental historical undertaking that was finally available to Europe as a whole in 1818: J. C. L. Simonde de Sismondi's *Histoire des républiques italiennes du moyen âge* (*History of the Italian Republics of the Middle Ages*). The sixteen richly documented volumes of this work gave it the kind of authority claimed by Edward Gibbon's *Decline and Fall of the Roman Empire* (1776), but it carried a democratic ideological burden that made it both unique and controversial. Here, for instance – couched very much in the timbre of Euthanasia – is Sismondi's summary of the achievement of fourteenth-century Florence:

> For the citizen who has once known it, it is the sweetest of pleasures to influence the destiny of the country, to take part in its sovereignty, above all to place oneself directly under its law, and to recognize the authority of those one has oneself created . . . In the midst of the convulsions of civil war, Florence renewed architecture, sculpture, and painting; it produced the greatest poet that Italy still today can boast; it set philosophy once again in honor; it gave an impulse to the sciences, which was followed by all the free states of Italy; and from barbarity it caused to ensue centuries of the fine arts and good taste.[9]

Nor was the contemporary historical application of *Valperga* lost on its readers. John Gibson Lockhart, who wrote the most detailed review of the novel, for *Blackwood's*, preferred Machiavelli's "glowing and energetic sketch" of the heroic Castruccio to Mary Shelley's "modern and feminine" conception of him as a man of innate sensibility perverted by the power politics of his age. What Lockhart discerned in this portrait, moreover, was an essentially allegorical and pointedly contemporary perspective. He complained particularly about "this perpetual drumming of poor Buonaparte," a modernizing practice in which he asserted Mary Shelley, like too many other authors of contemporary historical fiction, was participating.[10]

Lockhart also saw an ulterior purpose behind Mary Shelley's conception of Beatrice of Ferrara, though here he complains not on historical but on moral grounds. Citing Beatrice's long account of her travails, and particularly her renunciation of her once-fervent Christianity in volume III, chapter iii, Lockhart voices his decidedly mixed feelings:

> It is impossible to read it without admiration of the eloquence with which it is written, or without sorrow, that any English lady, should be capable of clothing such thoughts in such words . . . [A]las! What is here put into the mouth of this frantic girl, mad with love and misery, has been of late put forth so frequently, and in so many different forms, by the writers of that school, with which this gifted person has the misfortune to be associated.[11]

Although Mary Shelley expressed her "utter surprise" that the novel was "not pounced upon" (*L* I 374) by the conservative establishment, it is clear that Lockhart was capable of pouncing, rather than merely scolding, if he had wished to engage in polemics. In any case, he certainly saw her novel as partaking in the subversive dynamics of what Robert Southey had labeled the "Satanic School," a liberal coterie formed by Percy Bysshe Shelley and Lord Byron. We later readers would make a mistake not to be as conscious of the novel's skeptical thrust as Mary Shelley's contemporary reviewer.

Yet, what is truly subversive of the piety Lockhart seeks to protect may be less Beatrice's open renunciation of her faith than the highly religious circumstances in which Beatrice was herself born and reared. Here, Mary Shelley points us to another way in which her historical researches may be seen to impact with radical force upon her own culture. In the novel, Beatrice is the illegitimate daughter of a woman called Wilhelmina of Bohemia. The historical Wilhelmina settled with a companion named Magfreda in Milan late in the thirteenth century, becoming superficially a model of devout piety, but at the same time creating a secret heretical sect with striking feminist overtones. Her followers believed that she was the daughter of the Holy Ghost sent in place of Jesus to redeem humanity and that her principal follower, Magfreda, should replace the Pope and reorient the entire Church to their matriarchal creed. Since Beatrice is Wilhelmina's daughter, conceived (according to Magfreda) while she was still a virgin, this phenomenon, at least as represented by Magfreda's confession to the priest who rescued the child, would place Beatrice on a par with Jesus as the product of a virgin birth. That without knowing anything of her parentage, the devout Beatrice later calls herself an *ancilla dei* (handmaiden of God), inherently vindicates her powers of prophecy. In *Valperga*, this entire account (*V* II ii) is presented by the Bishop of Ferrara from the point of view of orthodox revulsion, though he does confess himself humanely moved by Magfreda's saintly deportment before the Inquisition. Yet, the bishop's firm adherence to the strictures of his faith does not for a moment change the character of the feminist heresy Mary Shelley uncovered in Muratori's *Italian Antiquities* and prominently inserts into her novel. That history had left this heresy behind only to be resuscitated by two dedicated scholars in separate centuries hardly diminishes its assault on the underpinnings of traditional Christian faith, whether Catholic or Anglican. A proper "English lady," to revert to Lockhart's formulation, however exemplary a scholar, should not be engaged in spreading heresies – especially those that spring from women living lives radically independent from men.[12]

And this point might, then, lead us to rethink Mary Shelley's own place in the two radical cultures that she uniquely bridged: first, that of the group who assembled in Italy and founded *The Liberal* to confront the English establishment from a liberated continental perspective; and second, that other culture, rooted in the previous generation and embodied by the parents whom Mary Shelley read incessantly and whom she deeply revered. Lockhart's placing of her among the so-called Satanic School interestingly echoes John Wilson Croker's hostile representation of the heritage claimed by *Frankenstein*:

> It is piously dedicated to Mr. Godwin, and is written in the spirit of his school. The dreams of insanity are embodied in the strong and striking language of the insane, and the author, notwithstanding the rationality of his preface, often leaves us in doubt whether he is not as mad as his hero. Mr. Godwin is the patriarch of a literary family, whose chief skill is in delineating the wanderings of the intellect, and which strangely delights in the most afflicting and humiliating of human miseries.[13]

The fact that the inception of her historical novel coincides with the writing of *Frankenstein* in 1817, which at first sight could seem strangely incongruous, might suggest that, from the beginning, Mary Shelley was still thinking of herself within the Godwinian terms discernible both in the dedication of her first novel to her father and in the exposition of *Frankenstein*. Although there is, famously, no female character in her first novel to rival the prominence, personal authority, and passion with which she endows both Euthanasia dei Adimari and Beatrice of Ferrara in *Valperga*, even a cursory comparison of Mary Shelley's first two novels might identify in Castruccio Castracani many of the traits – both good and bad – that her readers have long recognized in Victor Frankenstein. Highly intelligent but willful, shrewd in penetrating the motives of others, Castruccio is almost blind to his own weaknesses. He is well educated, but all his breadth of training is ultimately of no value to the city-state he plunges into continual strife. He requires affection, even devotion, from his associates but is always self-contained and finally self-serving in his relations with them. He can seem generous to those under his authority, but anyone brought within his influence risks destruction. He is a dominant, at times a domineering figure, but when he leaves the scene, his dynamic force departs with him, leaving less a memory to be treasured than a vacuum to be wondered over. He is a driven masculine figure, of a kind with Robert Walton, Victor Frankenstein, and even the creature, and, like them, he owes not a little of his conception to the like-minded protagonists of Godwin's novels.[14] In dedicating *Frankenstein* to her father, then, Mary Shelley not only demonstrated her filial affection; she also thus sought immediately to suggest the contemporary fictional mode within which to read her first novel critically.

And if *Frankenstein* gave her little room, or even interest, in developing powerful female characters, in *Valperga* she certainly sought to balance that earlier lack. Indeed, this urge to offer strong women characters may likewise have a deep family impulse behind it, one balancing the Godwinian delineation of Castruccio Castracani. On the profoundest level, Euthanasia dei Adimari represents the ideal to which Mary Wollstonecraft subscribed throughout her writings, and particularly in the *Vindication of the Rights of Woman*. Euthanasia is devoted to liberty, believes that she has a public duty to foster it, and, inheriting a feudal office, seeks to nurture the well-being and individual development of those she presides over as Countess. Deprived of her mother at an early age, she is educated, like Mary Shelley, by a learned father who imbues her both with the classics and the literature of her own culture so that she can, in turn, become a force for enlightenment within it. Thus, like Mary Wollstonecraft, she actively participates in promulgating that culture: Euthanasia's three-day "court" at the end of the first volume is an open celebration of its variety, richness, and humane potentiality.

And if Euthanasia represents the Wollstonecraft ideal on a public plane, she also subscribes to it on a personal level as well. She refuses to sacrifice her noble ideals for a conventional marriage that would compromise them. Faced with the wreck of all she desires, she stoically endures and finds the strength to help Beatrice recover a sense of purpose and some measure of integrated identity. Moreover, in Beatrice herself, we encounter, in a remarkably non-judgmental and psychologically penetrating form, the attribute that Mary Wollstonecraft had both principally inveighed against and tragically embodied, a passionate sensibility unsusceptible to rational control. As much as any of Wollstonecraft's polemics on the subject of what happens when women allow themselves to be identified solely by their emotions, Beatrice of Ferrara constitutes a powerful object lesson to young female readers, particularly in a culture that, raised on Germain de Staël's *Corinne* (1807), had become obsessed with the transports of female genius. But then, of course, Euthanasia is equally an object lesson, and her refusal to condemn the confused, lovelorn Beatrice; her recognition that Castruccio has a moral obligation to this bereft young woman; and her attempt, against the dictates of her own heart, to make him fulfill it, all testify to the generous, life-sustaining humanity through which she filters her own rational decisions. In making Euthanasia the moral center of her novel, then, Mary Shelley, in tone if not explicitly, dedicates her second novel to her mother, in symmetrical balance with the formal dedication of *Frankenstein* to her father. Godwin's recasting of her original title, rather than constituting officious interference with her intentions, might thus be read as a judicious paternal (rather than patriarchal) understanding of his daughter's intellectual devotion to the mother she never knew.

Valperga did not have the impact in its time that *Frankenstein* had: several reviews, indeed, compare it unfavorably with that novel. A later time, however, need not fall back indulgently on such invidious comparisons between two works conceived within very different generic modes. What modern readers can do, however, is at once recognize the significant continuities between the two novels and mark the ways in which *Valperga*, originally conceived during the composition of *Frankenstein*, shows Mary Shelley already moving forward to embrace a larger conception of her role as novelist and thinker. In reaching out to assimilate history and political analysis to the acute psychological portraiture of her first novel, she greatly enlarges the arena in which she is willing to engage a public. Moreover, subscribing herself on the title page as "the Author of 'Frankenstein,'" she makes clear that she will do so on her own terms, conspicuously refusing to accept the implicit gender limits that barred women from focusing upon public issues in their writing. For its time, *Valperga* was an audacious novel, a direct challenge to the "Author of 'Waverley,'" a historical recreation of distinctive learning and artistry, and, above all, an embodiment of a feminist aspiration to equality that boldly reclaims Mary Wollstonecraft's legacy for a new generation. It retains all of these attributes today.

NOTES

1 See Newman Ivey White, *Shelley*, 2 vols. (New York: Knopf, 1940), II 234.
2 For their separate accounts of the expedition, see *The Journals of Claire Clairmont*, ed. Marion Kingston Stocking, with the assistance of David Mackenzie

Stocking (Cambridge, MA: Harvard University Press, 1968), pp. 169–71, and *J* 1 328–29.

3 The Shelleys' reading list can be found, with the individual reader usefully designated, where known, in *J* 11 631–84. That list may be supplemented by the similar compilation for Mary's stepsister, Claire Clairmont, in her *Journals*, pp. 501–17.

4 The Juvenile Library, though nominally under the guidance of Mary Jane Clairmont, Claire's mother and Godwin's second wife, published numerous children's histories by one Edward Baldwin, a pseudonym used by Godwin.

5 I have expounded at length on the specific ways in which Mary Shelley effects a reversal of Scott's priorities in the "Introduction" to my edition of *Valperga* (New York: Oxford University Press, 1997), pp. xiv–xviii.

6 For the late medieval context, see Harry Hearder, *Italy: A Short History* (Cambridge: Cambridge University Press, 1990), pp. 72–88; for the nineteenth-century context, *ibid.*, pp. 153–77 and Denis Mack Smith, *The Making of Italy 1796–1866* (New York: Holmes and Meier, 1988), pp. 37–55.

7 Lady Morgan, *Italy* (Paris: A. and W. Galignani, 1821; 3 vols. [London: Colburn, 1821; 2 vols.]), 1 23. Lady Morgan's first such venture in the genre was *France* (1816), which, published immediately after the restoration of the Bourbon monarchy, celebrated the achievements of the Napoleonic regime while satirizing the new and precariously unpopular monarchy.

8 Lady Morgan, *Italy*, 11 29.

9 J. C. L. Simonde de Sismondi, *Histoire des républiques italiennes du moyen âge*, 16 vols. (Paris: Treuttel et Würtz, 1818), IV 169–70 (translation by the author). In a notebook she used for reference, Mary Shelley drew up a chronology of the events surrounding her novel, from 1269 to 1328, derived, with page references carefully noted, from the early volumes of Sismondi's *Histoire*; it is reproduced as Appendix 1 of the edition edited by Michael Rossington (Oxford: Oxford World Classics, 2000), pp. 382–84.

10 *Blackwood's Edinburgh Magazine* 13 (March 1823), 283, 284.

11 *Ibid.*, 290. The passage in question can be found in V 111 iii 328–31.

12 Wilhelmina of Bohemia has virtually disappeared from accounts of the medieval Church written in English. But her feminist heresy has in recent years attracted Italian scholars who have attempted to place it within the context of Church politics at the turn of the thirteenth century. See Luisa Muraro, *Gulielma e Maifreda: storia di un'eresia feminista* (Milano: La Tartaruga, 1985), and Marina Benedetti, *Io non sono Dio: Guglielma di Milano e i figli dello spirito santo* (Milano: Edizioni Biblioteca Francescana, 1998). The latter contains an extensive bibliography, including several sources in English.

13 *Quarterly Review* 36 (January 1818), 382.

14 The best account of Godwin's obsessed and self-destructive male protagonists is that supplied by Marilyn Butler in the introduction to *The Collected Novels and Memoirs of William Godwin*, 8 vols. (London: William Pickering, 1992), 1 7–46. See also Pamela Clemit, *The Godwinian Novel: The Rational Fictions of Godwin, Brockden Brown, Mary Shelley* (New York: Oxford University Press, 1993).

7

KARI E. LOKKE

The Last Man

When Mary Shelley's *The Last Man* was published in 1826, her Lionel Verney entered a literary scene already peopled by a significant number of last men, such that reviewers could not resist jokes at the expense of this crowd of solitary survivors.[1] Cousin de Grainville's prose epic *Le Dernier Homme*, posthumously published in 1805, had initiated this post-revolutionary mode. An anonymous English translation entitled *The Last Man, or, Omegarus and Syderia, a Romance of Futurity* appeared in 1806. Byron's poem "Darkness," one of his best-known works among his contemporaries, was written in 1816 at Lake Geneva, where Shelley also began *Frankenstein*. And the most popular variation on this theme, Thomas Campbell's lyric "The Last Man," appeared in 1823 and was followed, in the next decades, by a wealth of imitations and parodies as well as by John Martin's remarkable, apocalyptic paintings of the subject from 1826, 1833, and 1850.

Shelley thus joins her contemporaries in her apocalyptic response to the horrors of the French Revolution, the subsequent carnage of the Napoleonic wars, and the metaphysical and cultural uncertainties attendant upon Romantic-era attacks on religious and political authority. Yet the extremity of her particular form of apocalypse bears comparison with twentieth-century existentialist, absurdist, and nihilist reactions to two World Wars, the Holocaust, and the atomic bomb, such as Camus's *La Peste* or Ionesco's *Les Chaises*, thus revealing *The Last Man*, like *Frankenstein*, as an uncannily prescient novel. In its refusal to place humanity at the center of the universe, its questioning of our privileged position in relation to nature, then, *The Last Man* constitutes a profound and prophetic challenge to Western humanism.

Shelley's *The Last Man*, drawing a contrast between the sickness of humanity and the health of nature, stands out as unique against its literary precursors that depict the demise not only of humanity but also of nature – or even of the entire universe. Whereas most nineteenth-century versions of the "last man" theme represent the end of the human race at the hands of transcendent cosmic or divine forces that also destroy the earth itself, Shelley's humanity succumbs to the plague in the face of a vigorous and blooming nature utterly indifferent to its fate. Thus the opening of volume III, following the declaration of inevitable universal extinction that concludes volume II, offers a particularly trenchant critique of Judeo-Christian or humanist notions of man as the "lord of the creation," as the measure of all things:

> Hear you not the rushing sound of the coming tempest? Do you not behold the clouds open, and destruction lurid and dire pour down on the blasted earth? See you not the thunderbolt fall, and are deafened by the shout of heaven that follows its descent? Feel you not the earth quake and open with agonizing groans, while the air is pregnant with shrieks and wailings, – all announcing the last days of man?
>
> No! none of these things accompanied our fall! The balmy air of spring, breathed from nature's ambrosial home, invested the lovely earth, which wakened as a young mother about to lead forth in pride her beauteous offspring to meet their sire who had been long absent . . . Where was pain and evil? Not in the calm air or weltering ocean; not in the woods or fertile fields . . .
>
> (*LM* III i 229)

Mother Nature in *The Last Man* is utterly oblivious to her human progeny and their tragic fate. Despite its exquisite beauty, then, Shelley's nature does not serve a Wordsworthian function as "the nurse, / The guide, the guardian of [man's] heart, and soul / Of all [his] moral being" ("Lines Written a Few Miles above Tintern Abbey," lines 110–12). Nor can the end of humankind be rationalized as divine retribution against the disobedient "favourite of the Creator" (*LM* III i 229).[2]

In this challenge to humanism, *The Last Man* also renders a devastatingly modern critique of the political, scientific, spiritual, and artistic aspirations of the post-revolutionary, Romantic era. *The Last Man* demands as well to be read as a *roman-à-clef*, an act of mourning for Percy Bysshe Shelley and for the three children they had lost, for Byron, and for the collective life they had led.[3] The affinities between Percy Shelley and the character Adrian, Earl of Windsor; Byron and Lord Raymond; Perdita, Lionel Verney and Mary Shelley herself are unmistakable. Yet because the objects of Shelley's mourning are among the central literary and intellectual figures of her age – figures in conversation with an earlier generation of writers and thinkers – her *roman-à-clef* inevitably entails representations, both elegiac and profoundly bitter, of Percy Bysshe Shelley's idealism, Byron's titanism, Wordsworth's naturalism, Coleridge's aestheticism, and the progressive political commitments of her parents, Mary Wollstonecraft and William Godwin (see chapter 2).

Shelley's complex and deeply ambivalent critique of these Romantic ideologies also demands a recognition of her identification of "pain and evil," of the plague itself, with human nature. At the same time, then, that Shelley denies humanity the consolations of a benevolent nature or a redemptive relation to Divinity, she also charges humankind with the responsibility for its own downfall. To the question, "Where was pain and evil?" her narrator Lionel Verney responds that it is inseparable from human nature:

> Look at [man] – ha! I see plague! She has invested his form, is incarnate in his flesh, has entwined herself with his being, and blinds his heaven-seeking eyes. Lie down, O man, on the flower-strown earth; give up all claim to your inheritance, all you can ever possess of it is the small cell which the dead require.
>
> (*LM* III i 229–30)

Shelley, thus, firmly rejects both the biblical claim that human beings are the inheritors of the earth and the Romantic, secular cult of the titanic human imagination.

"Love and ruin": plague as will to power

Significantly, the plague does not enter this novel until the beginning of volume II. Rather than causing the end of the Windsor idyll in volume I, the plague in fact merely manifests forces already "incarnate in," "entwined with" the beings whom Verney so lovingly portrays in the retrospective romance of volume I. This romance depicts the youth, friendships, and betrothals of the novel's central characters, leading to an idealized community, a "happy circle" (*LM* I vi 64) founded upon the marriages of Lionel Verney and Lady Idris, and Lord Raymond and Lionel's sister, Perdita. Based upon passionate love rather than political, economic, or conventional considerations, these marriages at the locus of British power hold out the hope of revivification or rejuvenation of English society as a whole. In fact, none of the central players in the Windsor idyll dies of the plague. Even before the menace of the plague threatens, Lord Raymond's imperialist campaigns against the Turks and his adulterous love affair with the Greek princess Evadne Zaimi have shattered irrevocably the hopes and happiness of the central characters of this novel. Thus Lionel opens the final chapter of volume I with the assertion that "A moral tempest had wrecked our richly freighted vessel, and we, remnants of the diminished crew, were aghast at the losses and changes which we had undergone" (*LM* I x 111). The metaphors of sea and vessel that describe English life and culture from the first to the last paragraphs of this novel reveal that the tragic devastation of this Windsor microcosm of English society precedes the advent of the plague. As a result of his unrequited love for the seductive Evadne, Adrian has already suffered a descent into despair and madness akin to that of the maniac in Percy Bysshe Shelley's *Julian and Maddalo*. The members of the love triangle of Raymond, Evadne and Perdita seem doomed to future sorrow. Perhaps most poignantly, Shelley reveals the victimization of Clara by her parents Raymond and Perdita, who abandon her both literally and figuratively. Raymond leaves her first as he descends into dissipation and then again when he embarks on his second Turkish campaign. And Perdita, in her despair, "sought solitude" and "neglected even her child; shutting her heart against all tenderness" (*LM* I x 111). Cruelly, she forbids even the merest mention of Clara's father. Ultimately, the idyll that opens *The Last Man* reveals a vision of human nature as ruled by a will to power that overwhelms all other human impulses of love, compassion, generosity, and justice. This will to power is inseparable from a death drive against which Eros, however attractive, never really stands a chance. Indeed, as the distraught Adrian writes, Eros and Thanatos are an inseparable pair: "O wherefore are love and ruin for ever joined in this our mortal dream? So that when we make our hearts a lair for that gently seeming beast, its companion enters with it, and pitilessly lays waste what might have been an home and a shelter" (*LM* I iii 32).

The plot line of *The Last Man* in fact mirrors this conflict between Eros and Thanatos, a conflict resolved by the ultimate and complete absorption of love into death and destruction. The novel opens under the sign of Eros, as couples pair off to form the nucleus of elite families who will rule the island republic of Britain from their idyllic and isolated seat of Windsor. Lionel Verney, the Wordsworthian and antisocial child of nature is tamed, falls in love with the humanistic and progressive ideals of the Shelleyan Adrian, heir to the British throne, and marries his sister Idris. Perdita, Verney's wild and reclusive sister, a figure associated with Wordsworth's Lucy poems, is paired off with the Byronic Raymond, who takes on the rulership of England when Adrian's unworldliness and self-destructive love for the mysterious, eastern Evadne make him unfit to do so. Evadne's creativity and sexuality remain uncontained by marriage and ultimately seduce Raymond, who embarks on his conquest of the East once his betrayal has been discovered by Perdita. Raymond's attack on Constantinople disseminates the plague and initiates a narrative of death that will not end until the entire human race, save the narrator, Lionel, is gone. The final two volumes of the novel are inimitably dark as they tell the tales, one by one, of the death of each member of Lionel's beloved circle, set against the backdrop of plague, natural disasters, and human conflagrations. Having left England for the more salubrious climate of Italy with a small band of survivors, Lionel is alone in Rome at the conclusion of *The Last Man*, preparing to set out for sea in search of other lone survivors.

Both Evadne and Raymond incarnate a death drive, a will to power, in its most explicit and destructive form – limitless ambition, untamed pride, and uncontrollable passion. When the novel opens, Raymond is a Lord Byron who, instead of dying at Missolonghi, has led Greece in its successful war of independence against the Ottoman empire. His youth had been characterized by pride and "presumptuous ambition" (*LM* I viii 85): "Power . . . was the aim of all his endeavors; aggrandizement the mark at which he for ever shot. In open ambition or close intrigue, his end was the same – to attain the first station in his own country" (*LM* I iii 27). Beyond his desire to rule an England that he hopes will revert from republic to monarchy, his goals are unequivocally and brutally imperial: "[M]y first act when I become King of England, will be to unite with the Greeks, take Constantinople, and subdue all Asia. I intend to be a warrior, a conqueror; Napoleon's name shall vail to mine; and enthusiasts . . . shall adore my majesty, and magnify my illustrious achievements" (*LM* I iv 40). Desire for power rules his erotic relations as well. Irresistibly seductive to women by virtue of his great personal beauty and charm, he "tyranniz[es] over them according to his mood, but in every change a despot" (*LM* I iv 33). Yet for all his power over others, he is helpless in the face of his own passions, as he himself acknowledges: "I cannot rule myself. My passions are my masters; my smallest impulse my tyrant" (*LM* I ix 109).

Similarly, Evadne is a female version of the Byronic hero, characterized by her "restless energy of character" (*LM* I vii 81), the "too great energy of her passions" (*LM* I vii 83), her tameless pride, great ambition, and "concentrated self-will" (*LM* I vii 83). Contemptuous of Adrian's benevolent humanitarianism and his republican politics, she is drawn to Raymond's desire for mastery and his will to dominate the East; her love for him is explicitly described in terms of a master/slave dynamic: "Overpowered by her new sensations, she did not pause to examine them, or to regulate her conduct by any sentiments except the tyrannical one which suddenly usurped the empire of her heart" (*LM* I iii 31). Thwarted in her love for Raymond, she turns her thoughts to political ambition, returns to Greece, marries, and plots with Russia to install her husband as ruler of Wallachia (Romania) so that she can then be Princess of this realm. When this plot fails, her husband commits suicide and Evadne is torn by just the kind of guilt that afflicts the Byronic heroes of *Manfred* or *The Giaour*. Having betrayed her country's emancipatory struggles, she becomes a political and social pariah in her homeland; finally, she returns to England: "[R]epulse and denial, as to a criminal convicted of the worst of crimes, that of bringing the scythe of foreign despotism to cut away the new springing liberties of her country, would have followed her application to any among the Greeks" (*LM* I vii 82). Through the character of Evadne, termed a Sultana of the East, and whose upbringing is associated with "oriental magnificence" (*LM* I viii 92), Shelley asserts her belief that a destructive drive to power is not limited to men or to the West, but is ubiquitous in human nature.

The characters of Raymond and Evadne are crucial to the symbolic significance of the plague in *The Last Man*, for in their mutual drive to rid Constantinople of Islamic, Turkish influence and to claim dominion for Christianity and Europe over the East, they ultimately unleash the plague on the entire world. Metaphorically, however, Raymond is already sick before he leaves England. Shelley makes clear that his sexual union with Evadne is not the cause of his infection, portraying their relations most sympathetically as an expression of Raymond's admiration for Evadne's genius and compassion for her self-abasement. No, Shelley will not condemn Eros even in its adulterous forms. Rather it is Raymond's denial of his love affair to his wife Perdita – deceit rooted in his pride – that draws infection to him:

> [H]is spirit was as a pure fire, which fades and shrinks from every contagion of foul atmosphere: but now the contagion had become incorporated with its essence, and the change was the more painful. Truth and falsehood, love and hate lost their eternal boundaries, heaven rushed in to mingle with hell . . . His passions, always his masters, acquired fresh strength . . . the clinging weight of destiny bent him down; he was goaded, tortured, fiercely impatient of that worst of miseries, the sense of remorse.   (*LM* I viii 91)

This contagion is communicated, in turn, to Perdita, who in "the concentrated pride of her nature" (*LM* I ix 98), cannot forgive Raymond. Like Raymond and Evadne, Perdita has a history of "unsubdued self-will" (*LM* I viii 86) that, like her pride, links her to the power struggles that for Shelley doom humanity. Her response to proof of Raymond's perfidy underscores the breach between nature and humanity so central to this novel even as it highlights the human longing for union with insensate nature:

> [Perdita's] faculties were palsied. She gazed on some flowers that stood near in a carved vase . . . "Divine infoliations of the spirit of beauty," she exclaimed, "Ye droop not, neither do ye mourn; the despair that clasps my heart, has not spread contagion over you! – Why am I not a partner of your insensibility, a sharer in your calm!"   (*LM* I viii 96)

Perdita now shares Raymond's metaphorical sickness as well, for she perceives their marriage henceforth as a "masquerade," that "keeps up a perpetual fever in [her] veins" and "frets [her] immedicable wound" (*LM* I ix 104). Flight from guilt over his shattered marriage impels Raymond to abdicate his position as Lord Protector of England and embark on his fatal conquest of Constantinople. Fittingly, the death wish wrung from Perdita in this passage is fulfilled when she jumps overboard from the ship carrying her back to England. Ultimately, Perdita chooses death over abandoning Raymond's Athenian tomb.

In Raymond's Turkish campaign, Shelley offers a devastating critique of Western imperialism, showing how political power struggles mirror the psychic forces that engender them. For Shelley, as for contemporary feminists of a later era, the personal *is* political and vice versa. At the outset, Lionel depicts Raymond's hopes for his conquest of Constantinople for Greece in exaggeratedly grandiose and ethnocentric terms; they are hopes that Lionel seems to share:

> Raymond . . . counted on an event which would be a landmark in the waste of ages, an exploit unequalled in the annals of man; when a city of grand historic association . . . which for many hundred years had been the strong hold of the Moslems, should be rescued from slavery and barbarism, and restored to a people illustrious for genius, civilization, and a spirit of liberty.
>
> (*LM* II i 128)

In one of *The Last Man*'s countless bitter ironies, Raymond's exploits are indeed "unequalled in the annals of man," constituting "a landmark in the waste of ages" – the letting loose of a plague that will destroy the entire human race.

Adrian, who in many ways represents the novel's moral heart, clearly recognizes the realities behind Raymond's "ideal of war" (*LM* I x 116) and refuses to "sympathize in [his] dreams of massacre and glory" (*LM* I x 117), despite his commitment to the Greek cause. Having joined Raymond's campaign, Adrian is gravely wounded in his efforts to protect a Muslim woman from rape by two Christian soldiers. By highlighting such atrocities on the part of the Greeks and Europeans, Shelley calls into question the civilizing nature of Raymond's mission, conducted as it is by men with impulses equally as barbaric as those attributed to the Turks. In the end, we are left with little doubt that Shelley herself shares Adrian's eloquently expressed anti-war sentiments when, wounded, he has returned to England:

> It is well . . . to prate of war in these pleasant shades, and with much ill-spent oil make a show of joy, because many thousand of our fellow-creatures leave with pain this sweet air and natal earth . . . The Turks are men; each fibre, each limb is as feeling as our own, and every spasm, be it mental or bodily, is as truly felt in a Turk's heart or brain, as in a Greek's.   (*LM* I x 116)

Participation in the destruction of an entire Turkish city, the action that concludes Adrian's military career, calls forth compassion for the entire human race regardless of nation, race, or creed:

Every breathing creature within the walls was massacred. Think you, amidst the shrieks of violated innocence and helpless infancy, I did not feel in every nerve the cry of a fellow being? They were men and women, the sufferers, before they were Mahometans, and when they rise turbanless from the grave, in what except their good or evil actions will they be the better or worse than we? (*LM* I x 116)

Similarly, Lionel is horrified when he takes up arms in Raymond's campaign and witnesses the resultant slaughter in the name of the Christian West. Identifying himself as "one of the murderers," he surveys a battlefield at sunset and sorrowfully concludes that pursuit of this war has alienated him from his "higher powers" and represents anything but human freedom. Shelley's rhetoric emphasizes the struggles among sources of psychic power that lead to master/slave relations of dominion and submission:

During the busy day, my mind had yielded itself a willing slave to the state of things presented to it by its fellow-beings; historical association, hatred of the foe, and military enthusiasm had held dominion over me. Now, I looked on the evening star, as softly and calmly it hung pendulous in the orange hues of sunset. I turned to the corse-strewn earth; and felt ashamed of my species. (*LM* II i 130–31)

Lionel had once been blind to the ubiquity of human brutality and ignorant of the horrors of war, but his harsh military exploits expand his sympathies and deepen his understanding of human motivation, transforming him into a spokesman for Shelley's trenchant moral vision. This hard-earned wisdom and that of Adrian, however, go unheeded and seem powerless against the violation of humanity that will ultimately take the form of pestilence.

The significance of the plague, both psychic and political, is mysteriously revealed in its association with the deaths of Raymond and Evadne, who has joined his campaign disguised as a soldier. Evadne's dying curse, delivered to the horrified Lionel, defines the power imbalances between West and East, man and woman, self and other, that call forth the scourge of the plague:

This is the end of love! . . . Many living deaths have I borne for thee, O Raymond, and now I expire, thy victim! . . . [T]he instruments of war, fire, the plague are my servitors. I dared, I conquered them all, till now! I have sold myself to death, with the sole condition that thou shouldst follow me – Fire, and war, and plague, unite for thy destruction . . . (*LM* II i 131)

Power struggles between man and woman, West and East, self and other create inseparable and mutually destructive master/slave, persecutor/victim pairs, mimetic doubles that ultimately doom the entire human race. Raymond himself seems to understand this when he unquestioningly accepts the truth of Evadne's curse as confirming his own inner sense of his inevitable fate.

Thus, Shelley holds Raymond accountable, if not for the Egyptian-born plague, then for the imperialistic urge to have "the title of Victor of Constantinople" (*LM* II ii 141) inscribed upon his tomb, to plant the Christian cross on the mosques of that symbolic border between East and West. As Raymond advances alone on his coal-black charger beyond the gates of the city already decimated by the plague, he looses an apocalyptic explosion that seems to send fragments of his body into the fatal air:

> Thunderlike [the crash] reverberated through the sky, while the air was darkened. A moment more and the old walls again met my sight, while over them hovered a murky cloud, fragments of buildings whirled above . . . while flames burst out beneath, and continued explosions filled the air with terrific thunders . . . I conjured [the men] to turn back and save their General, the conqueror of Stamboul, the liberator of Greece . . . I would not believe in his destruction; yet every mass that darkened the air seemed to bear with it a portion of the martyred Raymond.   (*LM* II ii 144)

"A turbid cloud" of smoke and ash hovers over what has now become "a city of fire," an emblem of "burning chaos" (*LM* II ii 145) – an image that inevitably calls to mind the destruction of Hiroshima and, now, suicide bombers and the World Trade Center, to the twenty-first-century reader. That night Lionel dreams of Raymond's form hurling vessels "surcharged with fetid vapour" at him: "[M]y friend's shape, altered by a thousand distortions, expanded into a gigantic phantom, bearing on its brow the sign of pestilence" (*LM* II ii 146). It is difficult not to see as well in this grim phantom a foreshadowing of the specter of germ warfare that so menaces the twenty-first century.

As Alan Bewell suggests in *Romanticism and Colonial Disease*, Shelley's identification of the plague with Raymond's campaign of conquest reflects her understanding, now proven to be historically accurate, of epidemics as a product of imperial and colonial contact with the East. Terming *The Last Man* "the first and the last history of the British Empire," Bewell suggests that the novel "articulates Britain's darkest fears, that colonialism has unleashed forces that dwarf European medical, technological, and social know-how."[4] At the same time, Shelley is merciless in exposing her characters' arrogant refusal to acknowledge such fears until the plague forces them to do so. Their blindness stems from a conviction of the invulnerability of the "cultivated" and "civilized" world of Europe by comparison to America and Asia. Recording the thoughts of his countrymen as the epidemic approaches, Lionel documents this sense of racial and cultural distinction: "It drinks the dark blood of the inhabitant of the south, but it never feasts on the pale-faced Celt" (*LM* II v 169). As Audrey A. Fisch has so convincingly shown, this fiction of English invulnerability bears comparison with white, heterosexual America's projection of the AIDS epidemic onto the racial and sexual Other – the Haitian, the African, the homosexual.[5] Indeed, the novel opens with Lionel's smug assertion of tiny England's vast superiority to other countries of much greater size and population, a superiority rooted in "mental power." "So true it is," Lionel continues, "that man's mind alone was the creator of all that was good or great to man, and that Nature herself was only his first minister" (*LM* I i 5). The agonizing course of the novel, in fact, demonstrates that the human mind is above all the source of the evil that is universally suffered. And the relentless progress of the plague shows uncontrollable and inscrutable nature to be anything but the minister of man.

"The mysteries of our nature": art as antidote

Since Lionel is writing this retrospectively, one wonders if he has learned anything at all from witnessing the destruction of the entire human race, if he is simply recording a pre-pestilential state of consciousness, or if perhaps he himself is taking a perverse and masochistic pleasure in the deep irony of his words. Oddly, Lionel himself does fall victim to the plague, but he alone, of the central characters, recovers from it. He contracts the plague from "a Negro half-clad" whom he encounters in London in a gruesome and troubling scene: "[H]e held me with a convulsive grasp. With mixed horror and impatience I strove to disengage myself, and fell on the sufferer; he wound his naked festering arms round me, his face was close to mine, and his breath, death-laden, entered my vitals" (*LM* III ii 245). Throwing "the wretch" from himself, he returns to the arms of his family and soon falls ill. Yet he makes a miraculous recovery such that his body enjoys almost superhuman health and vitality. Critics have read this disturbing sequence of events in diametrically opposed ways. Alan Richardson finds here proof of Shelley's complicity with her character/narrator's racism.[6] Anne K. Mellor, on the other hand, reads in this "unwilling but powerful embrace of the racial other" a possible alternative to the relentless forces of destruction that overtake human society in *The Last Man*: "Can we see in this episode a suggestion that if one were forced to embrace the Other rather than permitted to define it exclusively as 'foreign' and 'diseased,' one might escape this socially constructed plague?"[7] What is clear from these disparate readings of the same pivotal incident is that Mary Shelley, as a cosmopolitan female author, in focalizing her tale through the voice of a lone British male narrator, creates a vehicle for a powerful and complex textual indeterminacy.[8] Furthermore, whatever one's reading of this scene, it indisputably highlights the power struggles between Europe and its non-European Others, struggles charged with both erotic and destructive energy, that hold the key to the significance of this novel.

The central question, then, for contemporary readers of *The Last Man* is whether the plague it portrays is, as Mellor suggests, socially constructed or whether it is a manifestation of an ultimately uncontrollable and uncontainable impulse – death-drive? will-to-power? – at the heart of human nature. Approaching this perhaps unanswerable question requires examination of the political, religious, and aesthetic responses to the plague depicted in *The Last Man*. And Shelley's depictions of these cultural responses reflect her own highly ambivalent reactions to the liberal ideologies of her parents, and the Romantic ideologies of her husband and dearest friends. Despite the seemingly relentless progress of the plague, a purely nihilistic reading of *The Last Man*, however tempting, is clearly insufficient, given the strong element of social criticism that underscores nearly every central crisis depicted in the novel and that holds out the possibility that things could be otherwise, if human beings would only will them so. Set in the twenty-first century, the heart of this novel is indeed appropriately framed as an ancient prophecy of the Cumaean Sybil, recovered and pieced together by an anonymous and fictionalized author/editor in 1818.

Thus, if one examines Shelley's treatment of gender in the novel, for example, a clear pattern emerges from Lionel's narrative. Whereas his initial depictions of the female characters in the novel place them in culturally sanctioned stereotypes, Shelley demonstrates that these roles simply cannot contain their energies. At first glance, the female characters seem drearily conventional, particularly by comparison with the remarkable women of Shelley's previous novel, *Valperga* (see chapter 6). Idris is the saintly, nurturing mother and devoted spouse, "the admired type of feminine perfection" (*LM* III iii 262). Evadne, on the other hand, is the femme fatale, the seductress, or as Lionel writes, a "monument of human passion" (*LM* II i 132). Perdita moves between self-sacrificing wife and proud mistress. And the Countess is the treacherous, devious, and power-hungry female aristocrat. Women, it seems, are praised by Lionel to the extent that they are submissive, self-sacrificing, and nurturing but condemned for striving beyond the limitations of the domestic. Lionel's masculinist depictions of the women close to him reveal his significance as conscious artistic creation rather than mere authorial alter-ego. As previously suggested, this gap between author and first-person narrator opens the door to fascinating and troubling textual indeterminacies.

Yet the novel provides ample evidence of the destructiveness of these limitations, revealing in Shelley the unmistakable legacy of Mary Wollstonecraft. Thus Lionel regrets compelling Idris to cease her tireless efforts to care for the entire Windsor community, demanding that she withdraw into the protected sphere of her family when her anxiety becomes all-consuming:

> If Idris became thin and pale, it was anxiety that occasioned the change; an anxiety I could in no way alleviate. She never complained, but sleep and appetite fled from her, a slow fever preyed on her veins . . . gloomy prognostications, care, and agonizing dread, ate up the principle of life within her . . . I often wished that I had permitted her to take her own course, and engage herself in such labours for the welfare of others as might have distracted her thoughts. But it was too late now. (*LM* III i 231)

Thus, the consumption that kills her is explicitly metaphorical, embodying the self-destructive effect of contained and repressed psychic and physical energies. Lionel's expanding consciousness of Idris's need for and right to a field of endeavor beyond the private and familial parallels his earlier development of a pacifist and humanitarian critique of Raymond's imperialist and ethnocentric campaign. In phrases echoing both Wollstonecraft and Byron, Perdita expresses intense frustration with her passive feminine role when she contemplates the adventure and freedom of Raymond's Greek campaign: "Would that I also had a career! Would that I could freight some untried bark with all my hopes, energies, and desires, and launch it forth into the ocean of life – bound for some attainable point, with ambition or pleasure at the helm!" (*LM* I x 117). Evadne is clearly also drawn to Raymond because he enables her vicariously to assert her passionate and ambitious nature, also expressed in her striking design for the national art gallery, which reunites them with such disastrous consequences. As she expires, part witch, part Amazon, cursing Raymond, Evadne leaves the reader wondering what would have been her fate had her passion and ambition found expression in artistic or architectural endeavor. Similarly, the cruel and manipulative behavior of the Countess of Windsor can be read as frustrated ambition, a "love of power" (*LM* I i 13) that must be displaced onto her son and daughter because its direct expression is not socially sanctioned. And because it is unacceptable for her to express her "energetic feeling," Shelley portrays her as a model of female repression whose manner is a mask for her "fiery passions" (*LM* I iv 51).

By and large, feminist critics have read the plague in *The Last Man* as symbolizing "the eruption of pent-up female discontents, no longer affecting only the interior psychological balance of the individual, but exteriorized, on a vast scale, to threaten the continuity of the human race as a whole."[9]

The plague is thus repeatedly personified as female, as the "Queen of the World" (*LM* III iii 252), or as an unvanquishable female foe. When it vanishes from the earth, Lionel clearly allegorizes the plague as a ruthless and archetypal female power only finally subdued by the sublimity of the Alps: "Her barbarous tyranny came to its close here in the rocky vale of Chamounix . . . From this moment I saw plague no more. She abdicated her throne, and despoiled herself of her imperial sceptre among the ice rocks that surrounded us" (*LM* III viii 310). In this context of gender relations, then, Shelley's plague is indeed socially constructed and *The Last Man* points to the possibility that cultural institutions and practices fostering direct and freer expression of female psychic, libidinal, and physical energy might very well restore health to a sick European society.

If, however, one examines Shelley's treatment of existing institutions or theories as possible solutions for inequities among genders, social classes, ethnic or national groups, hope fades. *The Last Man* represents a full spectrum of political positions and possibilities for governance, none of which can maintain its integrity in the face of the onslaught of human fear, greed, and ambition. Monarchists, republicans, democrats, imperialists, theocrats, idealists, and utopian visionaries all prove ineffectual in the face of universal pestilence. As Lee Sterrenburg has observed, Shelley writes in the tradition of fictional anatomies that typically analyze a wide range of "diseases of the intellect" through the vehicles of debate, dialogue, and colloquy. In the juxtaposition between these debates and the relentless plot of the novel, all ideas for reform are eventually "canceled out by the advent of the plague."[10] Thus the radical discourses of Godwin and Wollstonecraft's generation that figure the French Revolution as a purgative disease of the body politic are exposed as fictions. Likewise, the conservative discourse of Edmund Burke, who asserts the regenerative power of the body politic to fight off the plague of revolution, anarchy, and chaos, is also proven false.

The centrality of French Revolutionary events to the conception of *The Last Man* cannot be overemphasized, for as Doris Kadish suggests, Shelley's plague arises in 2092, exactly 300 years after the Revolutionary Terror, and serves as an allegory for that period in French history.[11] Furthermore, Paris in particular becomes "a scene of shame" (*LM* III vi 287) in the novel, a site of violent and irrational contentions. Most significantly, *The Last Man* attacks Enlightenment faith in the inevitability of progress through collective efforts, a faith that allowed thinkers from Condorcet and Kant to Wollstonecraft and Staël to retain confidence in the triumph of French Revolutionary ideals even after the debacle of the Terror: "[W]e call ourselves lords of the creation, wielders of the elements, masters of life and death, and we allege in excuse of this arrogance, that though the individual is destroyed, man continues for ever . . . [We] glory in the continuity of our species, and learn to regard death without terror" (*LM* II v 167), Lionel sardonically asserts. Shelley thus obliterates the keystone of Enlightenment ideology in her symbolic annihilation of the human race.

In the aftermath of the failed French Revolution and the grim Restoration of the *ancien régime* all over Europe after the fall of Napoleon, Shelley surveys the political theories and practices of her day and finds them all inadequate. We have already seen the disastrous consequences of Raymond's titanic and Promethean politics as his allegiances shift from monarchy, to republic, to empire, all in the service of his own ego. And from the outset of the novel, monarchist tendencies are embodied in the deplorable Countess of Windsor, who is willing to drug, kidnap, and force her daughter Idris into an arranged marriage rather than witness her union with a husband of a lower social class. The democratic, egalitarian principles of the populist Ryland prove hollow as well, when, in the face of pestilence, he hoards food and isolates himself from his community in a futile and contemptible effort to escape the plague. And the theocrat, the so-called impostor who promises immunity from the plague and universal salvation to his elect followers, is condemned in the harshest terms as an emissary of "the enemy of mankind" (*LM* III vi 292), an incarnation of "the principle of evil" (*LM* III vi 293) for exploiting the fears of his followers: "Men love a prop so well, that they will lean on a pointed poisoned spear; and such was he, the impostor, who, with fear of hell for his scourge, most ravenous wolf, played the driver to a credulous flock" (*LM* III vi 295). Shelley's various portraits of the self-destructive and irrational tendencies of human nature foreclose any possibility of effective social or political action.

Even Adrian's republicanism, clearly the most sympathetically portrayed political position, can do little more than smooth the road to death. Still, Shelley's strongly positive portrait of the period of Adrian's rule of England in volumes II and III suggests that his egalitarian and humanitarian efforts are unquestionably worthwhile, even if they do little more than veil the horrific truth:

> Adrian's chief endeavor, after the immediate succour of the sick, had been to disguise the symptoms and progress of the plague from the inhabitants of London. He knew that fear and melancholy forebodings were powerful assistants to disease; that desponding and brooding care rendered the physical nature of man peculiarly susceptible of infection . . . I could read the influence of my friend in [the Londoners'] quickened motions and cheerful faces . . . Order, comfort, and even health, rose under his influence, as from the touch of a magician's wand. (*LM* II vi 181–82)

Similarly, when England's imperial policy turns back upon itself in the form of an Irish invasion even after the plague has already devastated much of both countries, Adrian's peacemaking efforts are represented as clearly heroic. And likewise, his love of humankind and concern for the "general welfare" (*LM* III iv 277) of the multitude under his leadership – qualities linked to his republican values – enable him to quell the destructive conflicts between rival camps of British emigrants, once they reach Paris. Thus Shelley endorses humanitarian practices and republican policies as essential to human dignity and worth pursuing even in the face of the irrational, inscrutable, and indomitable forces represented by the plague. In the character of Adrian, Mary Shelley's republican sympathies clearly reveal themselves, as does her insistence that these beliefs manifest themselves in concrete practical actions rather than in utopian theorizing.

Thus, if Shelley explicitly endorses Adrian's political praxis, once he has become Lord Protector of the doomed nation, she subjects his idealistic theorizing to an irony laced with contempt. On the eve of the world's destruction by pestilence, Adrian holds forth on the advent of the millennium and the eradication of disease:

> [E]arth will become a Paradise. The energies of man were before directed to the destruction of his species: they now aim at its liberation and preservation. Man cannot repose, and his restless aspirations will now bring forth good instead of evil. The favoured countries of the south will throw off the iron yoke of servitude; poverty will quit us, and with that, sickness. What may not the forces, never before united, of liberty and peace achieve in this dwelling of man? (*LM* II iv 159)

Here Adrian mirrors both the Godwin of *Political Justice* who foresees a future humanity devoid of disease and Percy Bysshe Shelley's idealistic and ungrounded alter ego in *Julian and Maddalo*, who lauds the infinite capacities of human will. The subsequent course of the novel will undermine every one of Adrian's assertions, proving the cynical retort of the realist Ryland to be much closer to the truth:

> Be assured that earth is not, nor ever can be heaven, while the seeds of hell are natives of her soil . . . when the air breeds no disorders, when its surface is no longer liable to blights and droughts, then sickness will cease; when men's passions are dead, poverty will depart. When love is no longer akin to hate, then brotherhood will exist . . . (*LM* I iv 159)

In fact, Ryland's pessimism provides a precise and succinct summary of the forces, both natural and human, that doom the human race in *The Last*

Man. In particular, the dark mysteries of human irrationality and passion, the inseparability of love and hate, pleasure and pain, Eros and Thanatos, life and death instincts, seem intractable and by definition out of reach of any political movement or transformative process.

It is precisely in this realm of the mysterious and the irrational, however, that Mary Shelley makes room for art and even for art's potential as an agent of political change and progress through its heightening of human consciousness. In the interactions of the wild and savage young Lionel and the cultivated Adrian, Shelley makes it clear that the world of literature partakes of the struggle for power so central to all worldly battles at the same time that it transcends them. Thus Lionel speaks of Adrian's "conquest" of him through intelligence, active benevolence, and "the spirit of high philosophy" (*LM* 1 ii 18):

> We sat in his library, and he spoke of the old Greek sages, and of the power which they had acquired over the minds of men, through the force of love and wisdom only . . . As he spoke, I felt subject to him; and all my boasted pride and strength were subdued by the honeyed accents of this blue-eyed boy.
>
> (*LM* 1 ii 18)

Here, art and philosophy do indeed have the power to contend with the (self-) destructive impulses of humanity as they are embodied in the young (and not so noble) savage, Lionel.

Lionel, then, eventually chooses literature as his vocation and becomes the central figure for the artist in the novel, as it is of course he who transmits the tale of the devastation of humankind to the world and time beyond. Shelley treats Lionel's naive enthusiasm for authorship with the same combination of sympathy and sharp critique that she accords Adrian's idealism. "I turned author myself," he explains: "As my authorship increased, I . . . found another and a valuable link to enchain me to my fellow-creatures . . . Suddenly I became as it were the father of all mankind. Posterity became my heirs" (*LM* 1 x 113). Since, of course, posterity will not exist, is indeed a fiction in the context of this novel, the reader cringes at Lionel's self-designation as the intellectual father of mankind, "a candidate for immortal honors" (*LM* 1 x 113). And his depositing of his historical romance – the skeleton of a fallen race – in the immortal city of Rome, now deserted and barren, constitutes both a tribute to Western humanism – and a slap in its face. Similarly, the rich web of quotations from classical and Romantic sources in this novel both honors those works and insistently turns them against themselves.[12] Finally, the rich, sensuous beauty of Lionel's depictions of an impassioned and indifferent nature both charms and disconcerts the reader of this deeply troubling novel.

At the same time, however, Lionel's narrative does indeed survive him, as does humanity itself. In contemplating this paradox, the reader recalls the Introduction that frames the novel and identifies the Cumaean Sybil as the original author of this prophetic narrative that was then deciphered and transcribed by the early nineteenth-century editor/author. Strangely, this profoundly historical novel is thus imputed to a sacred source beyond history. The nameless editor, neither woman nor man, who gives voice to the "divine intuition of the Cumaean damsel" (*LM* 1 4), source of repressed archetypal female energy, provides as well a clue to the cultural and even political significance of art.[13] Readers who have suffered through the deaths of all but one of the novel's characters can only vigorously assent when the editor asks, "Will my readers ask how I could find solace from the narration of misery and woeful change?" (*LM* 1 4). Shelley responds with what she terms "one of the mysteries of our nature": "that the excitement of mind was dear to me, and that the imagination, painter of tempest and earthquake, or, worse, the stormy and ruin-fraught passions of man, softened my real sorrows and endless regrets, by clothing these fictitious ones in that ideality, which takes the mortal sting from pain" (*LM* 1 4).

This conception of art clearly identifies Mary Shelley as progenitor of and participant in the aestheticist philsophical tradition that extends from Schiller's *Naive and Sentimental Poetry* (1795–96) through Schopenhauer's *The World as Will and Representation* (1818) and Nietzsche's *The Birth of Tragedy* (1886) to Freud's *Beyond the Pleasure Principle* (1920). Art sheds a comforting light on the dark world of the irrational and the Dionysian; its dreamlike Apollonian quality gives form to the painful struggles of that abysmal and seemingly unfathomable realm. Or in Freud's terms, art embodies the tension between Eros and Thanatos, the life and death instincts, change and repetition compulsion. Lionel himself defines his own art in precisely this fashion in the opening chapter of volume II, at exactly the moment when the plague enters the narrative:

> In early youth, the living drama acted around me, drew me heart and soul into its vortex. I was now conscious of a change . . . I was inquisitive as to the internal principles of action of those around me . . . and for ever occupied in devining their inmost mind. All events, at the same time that they deeply interested me, arranged themselves in pictures before me . . . This undercurrent of thought, often soothed me admidst distress, and even agony. It gave ideality to that, from which, taken in naked truth, the soul would have revolted: it bestowed pictorial colours on misery and disease, and not unfrequently relieved me from despair in deplorable changes. (*LM* II i 126)

In addition to its soothing ideality and formal beauty, Lionel also attributes to art the function of interrogating "the internal principles" of human action and exploring the inmost reaches of the human mind. Aesthetic detachment allows the author an understanding of human nature, an awareness of what we now term the unconscious, an awareness otherwise difficult to attain.

Shelley herself, bereft of her loved ones, and disillusioned with contemporary politics and Enlightenment ideals, illuminates, in *The Last Man*, a will to power and a death drive at the heart of unconscious human nature. Yet she also accords the artist the potential power to understand and to transform these unconscious urges through awareness. She furthermore suggests the possibility, if not the certainty, that these psychic conflicts are indeed culturally determined by social injustices, by inequities between man and woman, wealthy and poor, West and East, self and other. Her insistent political analysis resists essentializing these imbalances as unchangeable at the same time that it asserts the urgent necessity of collective psychic transformation. Thus, in *The Last Man*, Shelley's sibylline invocation of the vortex created by the human passion for power as it cuts a path of universal destruction becomes the voice of a Cassandra that we ignore at our peril.

NOTES

1 For discussions of "the last man" theme, see Henry F. Majewski, "Grainville's *Le Dernier Homme*," *Symposium* 17.2 (1963), 114–22; A. J. Sambrook, "A Romantic Theme: The Last Man," *Forum for Modern Language Studies* 2 (1966), 25–33; Jean de Palacio, "Mary Shelley, *The Last Man*: A Minor Romantic Theme," *Revue de Littérature Comparée* 42 (1968), 37–49; and Morton Paley, "*The Last Man*: Apocalypse without Millennium," *OMS* 107–23. Palacio and Paley provide surveys of contemporary reviewer response to *The Last Man*.

2 See Paley, "The Last Man," *OMS* 114–21, for an excellent discussion of Shelley's secularization of the biblical, millennial tradition.

3 For the auto/biographical significance of *The Last Man*, see Walter E. Peck, "The Biographical Element in the Novels of Mary Shelley," *PMLA* 38 (1923), 196–219; and Mellor, Introduction, *LM* vii–x.

4 Alan Bewell, *Romanticism and Colonial Disease* (Baltimore: Johns Hopkins University Press, 1999), pp. 307, 301.

5 Audrey A. Fisch, "Plaguing Politics: AIDS, Deconstruction, and *The Last Man*," *OMS* 267–86.

6 Alan Richardson, "*The Last Man* and the Plague of Empire," *Romantic Circles* MOO Conference, September 13, 1997. http://www.rc.umd.edu/villa/vc97/richardson.html.

7 Anne K. Mellor, Introduction, *LM* xxiv.

8 For a discussion of the role of indeterminacy in *The Last Man*, see Robert Lance Snyder, "Apocalypse and Indeterminacy in Mary Shelley's *The Last Man*," *SiR* 17 (1978), 435–52.

9 Jane Aaron, "The Return of the Repressed: Reading Mary Shelley's *The Last Man*," in *Feminist Criticism: Theory and Practice*, ed. Susan Sellers (New York: Harvester Wheatsheaf, 1991), p. 17.
10 Lee Sterrenburg, "*The Last Man*: Anatomy of Failed Revolutions," *Nineteenth-Century Fiction* 33 (1978), 343.
11 See Doris Y. Kadish, *Politicizing Gender: Narrative Strategies in the Aftermath of the French Revolution* (Piscataway, NJ: Rutgers University Press, 1991), p. 33.
12 For an eloquent discussion of intertextuality in *The Last Man*, see Anne McWhir, Introduction to *The Last Man*, ed. Anne McWhir (Peterborough, Ontario: Broadview Press, 1996), xxxii–xxxvi. McWhir also offers a subtle analysis of Raymond and Evadne as embodiments of the will to power.
13 For related analyses of the crucial role of art in *The Last Man*, see Hartley S. Spatt, "Mary Shelley's Last Men: The Truth of Dreams," *Studies in the Novel* 7 (1975), 534–36 and Snyder, "Apocalypse and Indeterminacy," 448–52.

8

DEIDRE LYNCH

Historical novelist

Shelley and the Scottish magician

Early in 1820 the Shelleys, then living in Italy, received a crate packed with various household articles and a selection of the new novels that had become the talk of the nation. In one, *Ivanhoe*, the "Dedicatory Epistle" – a letter purportedly sent by one Laurence Templeton to his antiquarian colleague, the Reverend Dr. Dryasdust – mentions a "Scottish magician, [who], you say, was . . . at liberty to walk over the recent field of battle, and to select for the subject of resuscitation by his sorceries a body whose limbs had recently quivered with existence, and whose throat had but just uttered the last note of agony."[1] Templeton's necromancer, who must have reminded Mary Shelley of the "unhallowed arts" of her own Victor Frankenstein, was none other than Templeton's own creator, Sir Walter Scott. In the opinion of numerous reviewers, such necromancy, resuscitating bygone figures from historical fields as varied as Norman England and eighteenth-century Scotland, had endowed the novel form itself with a new dignity. Typical is one review, which advises that Scott's *Waverley* should not be "consider[ed] . . . in the light of a common novel, whose fate it is to be devoured with rapidity for the day, and to be afterwards forgotten for ever"; it should rather be, this critic wrote, lauded as a "vehicle of curious accurate information upon a subject which must at all times demand our attention – the history and manners of . . . the inhabitants of these islands."[2] This claim for historical novels' pedagogic and national significance was to become a refrain over the next decade and a half, repeated on the appearance of each new entry in what Scott was to call the "Waverley Series," after his immensely popular novel of 1814.

Mary Shelley also paid tribute to the powers of the "Scottish magician." The three novels occupying her in the decade after she read (and reread) *Ivanhoe* – *Valperga; or, The Life and Adventures of Castruccio, Prince of Lucca* (1823), *The Last Man* (1826), and *The Fortunes of Perkin Warbeck:*

A Romance (1830) – all in varying ways lay claim to the territory of public history. Each shares the Waverley Series' defining concerns with individual and collective memory, with the work of time, and with the intersection between those events that seem to make or to alter history and the continuities of everyday life. Each novel interrogates the contrast – one that Scott had made central to his Waverley novels and one whose revamping by Shelley this chapter will explore – between the comprehensive views of a neutral narrator, who can discern the deep-rooted and impersonal economic and social forces that produce historical change, and the narrow views that are the lot of individuals living *in* history, trapped inside their time.

This chapter will take issue with a conventional characterization of Shelley's career that finds her, after 1820, forsaking the imaginary horrors of *Frankenstein* in favor of historical materials. On this view, Shelley realized, in the wake of Scott's success, that history had become fiction's chief selling point; she undertook *her* historical turn so as to ease her re-entry into the respectable sector of the literary field, from which the extravagance of her debut work – and, some would add, its politics – had exiled her. Admittedly, this way of accounting for Shelley's career contains some truth. The novel's new linkage to the nonfictional genre of the historians seemed to many to have made novel-writing a more respectable profession. Those who had been vexed by women writers' dominance of the literary field in the late eighteenth century found in Scott's success reassuring proof that the novel had assumed a more manly form.[3] Not surprisingly, the now familiar argument about the development of the British novel – the one that maintains that the novel "rises" when it realizes that its future lies not with the emotional excesses and Gothic fancies of such works as *Frankenstein*, but, rather, with realism – was first marshaled in exactly this context.[4] Not coincidentally, Shelley's *Valperga* and *Perkin Warbeck* advertise the sober studiousness that has led their author to pore over the annals of, respectively, late medieval Tuscany (see chapter 6) and early Tudor England. By this means Shelley confirms that the scene of novel-reading might justifiably be relocated from the sofa (that troublingly feminized site) to the study.[5] And Shelley's decision to be known in her historical novels as "The Author of 'Frankenstein,'" though probably occasioned by her promise not to use the Shelley name, links her all the more closely with Scott, "The Author of 'Waverley.'"[6]

At the same time, however, that persona also aligns her with the "anonymity game" – the vanishing acts, disinformation campaigns, and outright hoaxes – in which the "Great Unknown" indulged when, following his publicly avowed career as a poet, he took his authorship under cover.[7] Her likeness to the figure who had brought fiction closer to history and its facts also likens her to a figure who in his interactions with the public played games with fictions, often fancifully and exuberantly – as when the imagined characters Laurence Templeton and Dr. Dryasdust review the accomplishments of their real author. Indeed, fiction itself, arguably in its purest, most primitive form, is flaunted in that Dedicatory Epistle to *Ivanhoe*. It was supposed to be the romance, the archaic form of fiction that predated both the modern respect for facts and probabilities and the modern rise of the novel, which made supernatural enchantment its stock in trade.[8]

Fictionality is similarly flaunted when Shelley turns to history. In works such as *Valperga* and *Perkin Warbeck* she surreptitiously contests the notion that fiction *needed* history; instead, she reveals this relationship to be a two-way street. As this chapter will suggest, when Shelley performs the balancing act between history and fiction that is the task of the historical novelist, she identifies fiction as the form better suited to the task of reopening the closed book of the past.[9] *The Fortunes of Perkin Warbeck*, to which we will turn shortly, may be Shelley's most crucial novel in this effort to "read" the past.

Both Shelley and Scott might have agreed with the German philosopher Novalis's claim that the novel as a form might make up for the shortcomings of history. For both novelists, the past was a moment when a plurality of future worlds was possible; a moment when, accordingly, things might have been otherwise. And both concur with the paradoxical proposition that the irresolution and contingency of the past could be made available to modern audiences only through fiction.[10] But the Authors of "Waverley" and of "Frankenstein" nonetheless held different views of fiction's compensations – of what such pasts might either explain about the present, or accomplish for it.

To elaborate on these points, we need to consider more closely the cultural context that gave rise to the novelists' turn to history. Specifically, we will examine the historical novel as a British response to the remaking of national consensus in the era that followed the French Revolution, an era in which the relations between domestic intimacies and the affairs of state were reconsidered and sometimes renegotiated. The coda that follows our discussion of *Perkin Warbeck* will return to the proposition, hinted at throughout Shelley's works, that the only *true* response would be one assuming fictionalized form.

Historical novels and national narratives

The historical novel came into being, according to many scholars of Romanticism, when a generation woke up to discover that it had survived the failed French Revolution, the end of the liberal hopes it represented, and the close of more than two decades of warfare. Between the fall of the Bastille in 1789 and the Battle of Waterloo in 1815, politics and war had become mass experiences, impacting the everyday lives of virtually all Britons. By 1815, people had become conscious of being the products of the history that had preceded them; at the same time, they had become conscious, too, of being placed at an irrevocable, estranging distance from the past of their own culture. Customs, domestic practices, and modes of social organization that their parents and grandparents had taken for granted now appeared quaint and foreign. The first readers and writers of historical fiction belong, in short, to a generation very aware of how history sets the conditions on the individual's actions, of how one's character is derived from the character of one's age. In this context, the traditional protocols for depicting individual agency – the emphasis on the statecraft of kings and popes, and even the emphasis on events that had formerly characterized historiography – seemed outdated. Accordingly, the ground of history shifted decisively from "action" to "experience and perception."[11]

To explain this shift, contemporary scholars have often ascribed to those early nineteenth-century readers and writers a longing for identifiable principles of historical motion – laws of social development and institutional change. Such laws, conservatives felt, would explain (away) the French Revolution, revealing it as an aberration in history. Liberals, on the other hand, hoped that such laws would reveal the aberration to be, instead, the Restoration of myriad principalities following Waterloo. Beneath William Godwin's interest in seventeenth-century English republicanism and Shelley's friend Sismondi's research on Italy's medieval city-states lay the belief that, by studying the past, one would not only discover the inner mechanism of historical change, but would by that means demonstrate that the forward progress of liberty was only temporarily halted.

Such investigations of the past were, with a new insistence, defined as investigations of a particular *period* – a word that only then began to designate a span of time possessed of its own distinctive character. Contemporary scholars have often observed that the periodizing strategies of the new historical novel supplied readers with the means to define *as* a period, the era we now know as the Revolutionary–Napoleonic period (1789–1815). The retrospective view that defines the genre of historical fiction and the particular emotional charge of historical recall in Scott's novels reinforced the British public's sense that an era of epochal modernization had come to a close, that theirs was a time of aftermath. The power of Scott's example populates much historical fiction with characters whose own sense of belatedness mirrors that of their readers. In "Ferdinand Eboli," for instance, a tale published in the *Keepsake* for 1829, Shelley's narrator regrets that wartime has given way to "this quiet time of peace" in which "the very names of Europe's conquerors are becoming antiquated to the ears of our children."[12] The narrator continues with a statement whose (Romantic) period flavor is unmistakable: "Those were more romantic days than these." The ceremonies of closure performed by Scott's fictionalized histories orchestrate readers' recognition of a shared contemporaneity. Hence, the modus operandi of the "Scottish magician" is to summon the ancient dead from their sepulchres, only to have them die a second, more conclusive death that puts the past in its place.

Waverley first taught readers how to reclose the book on the bygone past. Edward Waverley believes that in becoming embroiled in the Jacobite cause and enlisting in Prince Charles's army, he is binding his personal fate to public history. In fact, Scott's plotting works to privatize this protagonist's story. Removing Edward from the aristocratic field of military glory, Scott ensconces him in a middle-class marriage plot, which, in joining this representative Englishman to a Scottish woman, allegorizes the conciliatory, cross-cultural union of the two peoples who had recently faced each other on the battlefield. And over the course of the novel, Scott reinvents history: once a glamorous past of bold insurrection and individual daring, history comes to be identified with the invisible, impersonal, quasi-mechanical processes of economic modernization described by thinkers of the Scottish Enlightenment. In modernity, when the extension of commerce can palliate old national prejudices by integrating former enemies into the same circuits of imperial exchange, history is not a series of violent conquests and drastic upheavals. Instead, history designates a holding pattern, "normal change."[13]

Recast in such terms, history offers few opportunities for individual agency; it therefore gravely disappoints the dreams of Waverley. To live in history now is rather to share the passivity of the travelers described in the Postscript to *Waverley*, "who drift down the stream of a deep and smooth river [and] . . . are not aware of the progress [they] have made until [they] fix [their] eye on the now-distant point from which [they] set out."[14] One notes the political quietism implicit in this image for historical process; a river flows in one direction only. Scott's determinism closes down the political possibilities that republican historiographers such as Godwin and Sismondi were attempting to keep open: that is, the possibility of resurrecting the democratic potential of bygone social formations and seeing "the buried form of Liberty" (to quote *Valperga*) exhumed as the occasion for something more than nostalgic retrospection (V I vi 71).

As we have seen in chapter 7, Shelley challenges such closure in *The Last Man* (1826) by running the tape of history backward. The unidentified editor whom we encounter in her Author's Introduction has assembled a narrative from scattered pages discovered in the cave of the Cumaean Sibyl. We soon discover that this prophetic text, enabling us to read our future, doubles as a retrospective history narrated by Lionel Verney, the sole survivor of the epidemic that has destroyed human society in the late twenty-first century. Midway through Lionel Verney's narrative, he wraps up his account of his era's wars against the Turks (cast as a people who stood still "while every other nation advanced in civilization" [*LM* II i 27]) and recounts how the plague arrives in England on a ship that has voyaged east across the Atlantic from Philadelphia. Shelley's plague un-makes history precisely by undoing the historiographic convention on which Lionel draws for his characterization of Turkey's ahistorical stasis: the convention that diagrams time's linear, progressive advance as a westward migration of civilization from Greece to Rome to England to America. An earlier chapter depicting the effects of rumors about the epidemic's progress has similar effects. The process whereby the army in Constantinople "disbanded itself," so that "[e]ach individual, before a part of a great whole moving only in unison with others, now became resolved into the unit nature made him" (*LM* II i 127, III ii 142), finds Shelley disassembling social contract theories of the Enlightenment, whereby nations grow out of communities and empires out of nations. Lionel Verney's words put that historiography into reverse.

This dismantling of Enlightenment discourse on the evolving states of society dismantles, as well, the narrative of modernization and national unification that organizes the historical novel, including the Waverley novels and Shelley's later *Fortunes of Perkin Warbeck*. The Waverley Series, for instance, reconstructs a series of local skirmishes whose stories are preserved only in unfamiliar, out-of-the-way corners of the nation's archives: this mode of micro-history enables Scott to put a human face on history, expose the historicity of private life, and in the meantime cater to antiquarian curiosity about the forgotten idiosyncrasies of the past. But in one novel after another, Scott sets those skirmishes against a broader backdrop. He zigzags between local and national perspectives, the latter of which unfailingly discloses long-term progress toward modernity. Regardless of whether Scott is treating the eighteenth century or the thirteenth, the Waverley novels' perennial topic is the transition, which had focused Enlightenment historiography, from a world of princes and edicts to a "bourgeois milieu of contracts and conversation."[15]

Moreover, a closer look reveals the peculiarity in Scott's handling of this passage from "then" to "now." The skirmishes on which his novels focus are merely that, skirmishes. The heroic acts they involve ultimately prove beside the point, for, as one Scott protagonist after another learns, the course of history was already decided; "then" was already "now." The Waverley novels open in the aftermath of the turning points identified by established, official historiography. One side in the clash of cultures that the historical novel stages must therefore figure as an anachronism and as the casualty of the civilizing process – but even so, a casualty for which Scott's novels mourn. Whether Jacobite rebels (as in *Waverley*) or an older, embattled generation of Saxon thanes (as in *Ivanhoe*), Scott's representatives of the past (of "then") begin their stories already doomed, already lost to history.[16]

Perkin Warbeck, the pretender hero, and the lost cause

With *Perkin Warbeck*, Shelley both exemplifies and questions this generic pattern in an almost ruthless manner. The novel's action unfolds mainly in the last decade of the fifteenth century, a time marked, as Scott's *Quentin Durward* (1823) had shown, by the consolidation of centralized governments. This era's alliances between absolute monarchs and an emergent middle class brought into being a world in which kings' pursuits of political expediency and burghers' needs for financial security left little room for the gallant deeds of chivalric heroes. The first piece of dialogue in *Perkin Warbeck* – which opens on the fateful day of August 22, 1485 – signals that it is this time frame the novel engages. "Am I then too late?" the Yorkist knight plangently asks, after Henry Tudor's decisive victory on Bosworth Field (*NSW* v 210).

That Shelley's subject matter overlaps with both Shakespeare's *Richard III* and Jacobean dramatist John Ford's *Chronicle History of Perkin Warbeck, A Strange Truth* (1634; republished in 1811), suggests that she was working in cramped territory.[17] Any story of the lost heir of Edward IV and his efforts to gain the throne necessarily unfolds under the pressure of the known fate of the murdered boy princes. The premise of *Perkin Warbeck* is that Perkin is not Perkin (the Pretender) but Richard, ostensibly the one prince who survived that imprisonment. Shelley casts her hero – a "phantom duke," a "ghost" (*NSW* v 144) – as someone who is deemed by his contemporaries to have died long since. She makes him a hybrid character: a historical personage who, despite his historicity, is close kin to the spectral mothers who populate the ruined castles of eighteenth-century Gothic romance. Moreover, insofar as he is known to his countrymen, as to his country's historians, not as Richard IV but by the alias Perkin Warbeck, his true identity is overshadowed by that of another one of the dead children who haunt this novel. For in an early chapter, we learn that the prince's protectors had him assume the identity of the dead son of a Flemish money-lender.

Entrapping him inside his time, this relationship to a buried past bars Richard/Perkin from resembling a Waverley hero. We hear an allusion to the "Author of 'Waverley'" when Shelley's narrator observes, regretfully, that Richard/Perkin possessed in his ever-plotting "secretary Frion" a "counseller . . . admirably calculated to prevent all wavering" (*NSW* v 196).

That allusion, however, represents Shelley's calculated means of marking the difference between her hero and Scott's "middling," ambivalent protagonists.[18] Scott's heroes embody the long-term continuities in national life because, collectively, they have been endowed with a gift for temporizing; in fact, they sometimes represent a third or middle way in the clash between chivalric and commercial cultures. By arranging for their not-quite-intentional defection from lost causes, Scott almost always permits them to turn the loss of the past into private profit. As Katie Trumpener observes, in the ending of *Waverley* "a private happiness . . . sublates the historical dislocation of Highland culture" and thereby gives "the violence of history a retroactive meaning, purpose, and alibi."[19] But Shelley's hero, who embodies the lost cause from which the novel's bearers of historical progress can defect, cannot deviate from the course that leads to his ultimately futile martyrdom.

In his study of "pretender" heroes and heroines, Richard Maxwell remarks how often it appears that these characters would have been happier had they been permitted to remain in peaceful, private anonymity. The premise underwriting this subgenre of historical fiction is that those with royal blood will invariably attempt to compel the world to recognize their existence, but these books appear ambivalent about delivering their protagonists over to the tumultuous public world of recorded history. As Maxwell notes, "Pretender protagonists have basically middle-class instincts, seeking, more often than not, domestic security [and] quiet romantic fulfillment."[20] With increasing frequency in the second half of *Perkin Warbeck*, which traces the few years that intervene between the hero's marriage to Lady Katherine Gordon and his execution in 1499, Richard/Perkin acknowledges the attractions of a *Waverley* plot that would see him exchange public ambition for a private domesticity; he names Katherine as "his sole subject" and himself, "monarch" of her "soft heart" (*NSW* v 394). But even though his convictions are shaken by the defection of Yorkist noblemen who abjure the horrors of civil war; and even though Shelley grants him the insight that chivalry makes the "right appertaining to one man, the excuse for the misery of thousands" (*NSW* v 252), Richard/Perkin represents a character who cannot change. He remains trapped by the elegiac framework the novel uses to establish his belatedness.

In one chilling episode, Richard/Perkin breaks *into* the Tower of London, his prison during childhood. When he suddenly recognizes the chamber in which he has sought sanctuary, he wonders whether time has not gone backward: "Was he alone changed? had he sprung up into manhood, thought, experienced, suffered; and had the material universe stood still the while?" (*NSW* v 179). The reader of this passage glimpses a view of history that foregoes the notions of linear advance and modernization usually stressed by the novel's narrator. For a Gothic moment, time moves in circles.

In *The Last Man*, the novel in which Shelley unsettles chronology in even more thoroughgoing ways, Lionel Verney reflects self-consciously on the power the writer of history wields in arranging events, which will form "a picture in whose very darkness," Lionel says, "there will be harmony"(*LM* II viii 193). In this same paragraph, though, Lionel refers to the history-writing he has used to wile away his solitary hours at the end of time as his "opiate" (*LM* II vii 192). This paragraph might be read as Shelley's critique of the historical novel: a critique not only of how the genre's long views of historical process accommodate the audience to what Godwin memorably called "things as they are," but also of how the genre's bitter-sweet mourning for the ruined past makes the present seem worth the high price paid by history's victims. Unwittingly, Lionel Verney queries the aestheticizing that converts the harshness of history's verdicts into something picturesque.

In some respects, *Perkin Warbeck* continues such self-reflexive criticisms. The novel's memorializing of a doomed prince feels politically suspect every time readers are reminded of how much bloodshed Richard/Perkin's commitment to his role as king occasions.[21] And if, in the Waverley Series, progress alibis the violence that accompanies national unification, *Perkin Warbeck* by contrast refuses one aspect of the definition of historical truth that such a notion of progress entails. For the miscellanea from the past that this novel assembles thwart efforts to order them into a larger, harmonious whole. Casting that past as the prelude to Shelley's own day pointedly does not exhaust the meanings of the era that the novel reconstructs. Instead, through the character of Hernan de Faro, the Flemish money-lender's son-in-law (and once the foster-father of Richard/Perkin), the novel gestures toward an alternative, republican futurity that will unfold elsewhere. De Faro serves as navigator on Columbus's voyages, which are contemporaneous with Richard/Perkin's adventures. In *Perkin Warbeck*, the idea of America – a future state in "the golden isles beyond" (*NSW* v 63) – supplies a counterpoint to Shelley's portrait of fifteenth-century England, a place haunted by a heritage of violence.

There is one other way in which *Perkin Warbeck* contests the historical novel's vision of national history as a smooth synthesis of differences. The attention the novel devotes to Monina de Faro's aggressive role in advancing her foster-brother Richard's public ambitions queries the construction of femininity evoked when Richard/Perkin calls his wife, Katherine, his "single subject." The attention the novel devotes to the relationships among its female characters (arguably more important than the relationships they have with the hero) works to the same end. Writing women into the historical novel, Shelley writes against the grain of official historiography's definitions of the truth about the past.

Shelley's challenge to her hero's "middle-class" wish to see Katherine as a symbol of the domestic pleasures denied him by his royal blood, her reminder that "home" signifies something other than a haven to the sex usually confined to it, are most apparent in the final chapter of *Perkin Warbeck*. Here, Shelley traces Katherine's life in the court of Henry VII in the years following her husband's execution. This inclusion of the survivor's story (which Katherine recounts in her own person) gives a jagged feeling to *Perkin Warbeck* at the precise moment when the narrative, according to the conventions of its genre, should join up seamlessly with official history. Shelley's footnote, in which she names this character her "favourite" and wonders whether the chapter will be deemed "superfluous," compounds the effect (*NSW* v 395). Granting women stories beyond those that can be subsumed within the marriage plot undermines the very alignments of private and public, domestic and national, accomplished in the marriage plots of the Waverley novels. For Scott, such marriages both end the hero's flirtation with history and symbolize national reconciliation. His marriageable heroines (with some notable exceptions) provide the solution to the formal problem posed by harmonizing public and private views of events and squaring a protagonist's personal "romance" with collective history.

Shelley is less ready than Scott to engage in a merely instrumental use of her female characters. Monina and Katherine, like Beatrice and Euthanasia in the earlier novel, form a duo that would have reminded readers of *Ivanhoe*'s Rebecca and Rowena and *Waverley*'s Flora and Rose. But since Shelley foregrounds the relationships between women, rather than the hero's prudential choice between fair and dark heroines, her novels gesture toward stories falling outside the purview of his narratives of national progress. By refusing Scott's solution, *Perkin Warbeck* directs attention back to what Scott's national historiography deems "superfluous." In her earlier *Valperga*, Shelley also set out to displace that dominant model of historical understanding. Even as it recuperates the legacy of Mary Wollstonecraft (see chapter 6), *Valperga* construes the history of how local governments were overtaken by centralized states during the late Middle Ages, as the story of how women were forced to "descend to the rank of . . . private individual[s]" (*V* II ix 267) – how women were forced, in other words, to become a people both without and outside history.

The resurrection of romance

There is likely a hint of asperity, therefore, in the passage near the end of *Perkin Warbeck* in which Richard/Perkin reflects "with some wonder that, in every adversity, women had been his resource and support" (*NSW* v 352).

"Wonder," a word nudging readers toward a recognition of this princely hero's failings, returns us to the fictionality (the "romance" in the generic sense of that term) which historical novelists graft onto the historical record. Shelley frequently associates that fictionality with her female characters who, in secret or unrecorded acts, make history happen or, alternatively, stand for counter-factual possibilities that tragically never achieved realization in the past. Monina, whose support for Richard IV involves her in a series of daring escapades, is a character Shelley invents, as are the two imagined heroines – Euthanasia and Beatrice – who share *Valperga* with the historical figure Castruccio Castracani. The women of *Valperga* each figure an ideal of a distinctively female historical agency: Beatrice starts her story as a prophetess; Euthanasia, as the anachronistically liberal ruler of the imaginary principality of Valperga. Both, however, end up the victims of Castruccio's quest for the military glory that will secure *his* place in the historical record. When the ship that carries Euthanasia, exiled by Castruccio, disappears in a storm (a fate later suffered by Hernan de Faro), and the reader is told that Euthanasia "was never heard of more; even her name perished" (*V* III xii 436), *Valperga* goes on to complicate further our sense of the relation between history's reality and the novel's realism. In the final chapter, the narrator notes that "the private chronicles" drawn on for Euthanasia's story end with her death; that in the "public histories" drawn on for Castruccio's story there is no account "of his grief when he found that she whom he had once tenderly loved . . . had died" (*V* Conclusion 438).

By adjusting and readjusting her historical novel's ontological status in this unsettling way, Shelley shows how gender figures in the question of what will count as historical and what will not. Clearly, this represents a different use of the historical novel's powers to resurrect the perished than those envisaged by the "Author of 'Waverley.'" At the same time, Shelley's emphasis on what is not in "public histories" – on the ethical-pedagogical work that fiction can do *as* fiction – allies her to Scott. Specifically, it recalls how Scott's gamesome prefaces and postscripts emphasize the romancer's transmutation of real facts of a real historical sociology; emphasize, that is, the fictionality of historical narratives.

While she positions Euthanasia and Beatrice outside time and makes them represent ideals not achievable *in* time, Shelley also evokes the legacy of Gothic romance. The Gothic novels of Ann Radcliffe, for instance, spin their narratives out of just those aspects of the past that were not passed down in history. In works such as *A Sicilian Romance* and *The Mysteries of Udolpho*, servants' gossip, not written documents, keeps alive the memory of the wrongs done to the narratives' dispossessed, spectral mothers. Radcliffe thereby makes the truth of the past the charge of the group conventionally associated with illiteracy, superstition, and delusion. Montoni's downfall and Udolpho's capture, the narrator pointedly tells us at the end of *Udolpho*, never "obtain[ed] a place in any of the public records of that time."[22] The most audacious move Shelley makes in *Perkin Warbeck* builds on these Gothic antecedents: to dissociate the "truth" of Tudor history from all the official modes of collective memory. Impudently bringing her novel closer to Gothic romancers' modes of memorializing than to those favored by historians proper, Shelley uses fiction not to flesh out a national story already outlined by the historians, but rather to render her hero's life as if the subsequent generations had gotten it all wrong. They remember Perkin as a pretender; Shelley remembers him as a prince.[23]

At the same time, however, *Perkin Warbeck* exemplifies what Maxwell calls the "process of semantic drift" through which "pretender" ceases to designate "one who makes a royal claim" and instead identifies "one who makes things up."[24] Richard/Perkin's last days, when he is Henry VII's captive in the Tower, are described as "mimes." There is the "mime" of his last escape attempt, which amounts to nothing but an empty show because his jailers were forewarned (*NSW* v 384). Earlier, there is the bizarre way in which he almost slips out of the view of the narrator (as if he really were a counterfeit, rather than the genuine article) into the "tawdry masque and mime" (*NSW* v 343) that mark his route through London:

> It was suddenly proclaimed, that Perkin would go in procession from Westminster to Saint Pauls . . . A troop of horse at the appointed hour left the Palace: in the midst of them rode a fair young gentleman, whose noble mien and gallant bearing gave lustre to his escort . . . "He is unarmed – is that Perkin? No, the Earl of Warwick – he is a prince sure – yet that is he!" Such murmurs sped around; at some little distance followed another burlesque procession; a poor fellow, a Cornishman, was tied to an ass, his face to the tail; and the beast now proceeding lazily, now driven by sticks . . . made an ill-fashioned mirth for the multitude. (*NSW* v 343)

The closing pages of this historical novel thus render history the occasion for an exploration of fictionality. Such self-reflexive moments go against the grain of the contemporary reviews that acclaimed historical novels for their commitment to external sources, for didactically purveying the historical "facts." Yet such moments within *Perkin Warbeck*, I have been suggesting, are anticipated in the work of Scott, who had his own line in mock-Tudor "masque and mime." As the correspondence of Dr. Dryasdust and Laurence Templeton suggest, and as a pageant-filled novel like *Kenilworth* does too, Scott was as inclined as Shelley to put fictions on parade.[25] Granted a holiday from fact, Scott's reader is, in exchange, required to recommit to living in the present as though recorded history were true. Having learned from Scott, Shelley also makes fiction conspicuous when she writes history – but so as to call attention, not to what is deemed true, but to what, though counter-factual, was possible.

History-writing and hoaxing

And yet, as I close, I want to stress that Shelley's use of historical knowledge to foreground fiction is presaged by additional precedents than those provided by the "Author of 'Waverley.'" Consider the fact that in telling Perkin Warbeck's story as that of the would-be Richard the Fourth, Shelley pays tribute to Horace Walpole's 1768 *Historic Doubts on the Life and Reign of King Richard the Third.* Walpole explicitly set out to vindicate Richard III from the murder charges that had been laid at his door; but a second agenda involved an attack on the unacknowledged fictionalizing of the historians of Ricardian England who had shaped this consensus of condemnation. His motive, Walpole claims, is to redeem scholarship by banishing the passages of improbability found even in "our best historians," passages which placed the annals of "that reign on a level with the story of Jack-the-killer." Walpole's close study of the historians does not restore their discipline's authority; to the contrary, it creates a legitimacy crisis. Observing how historians contradict one another, Walpole declares himself unable to determine which historian he should treat as the "lawful monarch" and so resolves to "treat one of them *at least* as a *pretender.*"[26] These sly hints about the pretending that mingles with historians' "facts" make *Historic Doubts* a fitting sequel to that germinal text of the Gothic tradition, *The Castle of Otranto*, in which Walpole had first evinced his gadfly attitude toward the truth claims of the historians. In 1765, before *Otranto* was a Gothic "novel" – before, that is, Walpole prefaced it with an account placing his ghost story within a tradition of British fictions – it was presented to the reading public as an antiquarian windfall, the translation of a twelfth-century document that illuminated the beliefs of a medieval world whose benighted, priest-ridden inhabitants saw specters.

Shelley, it appears, construes the lineage of the historical novel differently than did those reviewers who acclaimed Scott for saving the novel from the illusions of romance. For her, that lineage leads back past Scott, past his redaction of the Enlightenment "human sciences," and joins up with the line of Gothic romance. Evidently, Shelley thought hard about how Walpole's Gothic story initially appeared as history, was subsequently revealed as an exercise in counterfeiting, and only after that was read as fiction.[27] If we regard *Perkin Warbeck* against the Gothic backdrop of Walpole's iconoclastic anti-historicism and anti-realism, then Shelley's interest in imposture, in a hero whose name became a byword for "forgery," insists that hoaxing and history-writing are intertwined.

For Shelley, a two-way traffic links the discourses of fact and of fiction. *Perkin Warbeck* appears richer, I would hazard, once we acknowledge that this is how Shelley's historical novel might self-reflexively recount its own generic prehistory. Despite the grim way in which it outlines the plight of a hero trapped in his time, *Perkin Warbeck* begins, then, to make sense as Shelley's companion piece to the merry historiographic shenanigans of "Roger Dodsworth: The Reanimated Englishman" (1826). "Roger Dodsworth" is the magazine piece that Shelley wrote in response to a series of evidently spurious newspaper articles reporting that an eponymous seventeenth-century antiquarian had lately been exhumed alive from an Alpine glacier. Shelley's contribution to the hoax is a story about suspended animation. The action of the frost, her narrator says, had allowed the re-animated Englishman to outlast his time. Furthermore, the news that this eye-witness of past times has been born again has prompted "Mr. Godwin" to "[suspend] for the sake of such authentic information the history of the Commonwealth he had just begun"(*CTS* 43). The suspense continues for, as of the time of this narrator's writing, Mr. Dodsworth inconsiderately has yet to return to his native land.

"Roger Dodsworth" is Shelley's sly retort to Scott's work as the "national resurrection-man" who summoned the British dead from their graves to renew life and community in the modern nation.[28] "Roger Dodsworth" pointedly prolongs the antiquary's expatriate state. And, obliquely arguing with the way that, by 1826, the critical validation of the novel had come to depend on fictions' new alignment with fact, it reaffirms the fictionalist's power to keep the historian in suspense.

NOTES

1 Sir Walter Scott, *Ivanhoe*, ed. Ian Duncan (Oxford: Oxford University Press, 1996), p. 15. Mary Shelley read the novel twice in the next two years.

2 Review in the *British Critic*, August 1814, reprinted in *Scott: The Critical Heritage*, ed. John O. Hayden (New York: Barnes and Noble, 1970), p. 69.

3 Ina Ferris, *The Achievement of Literary Authority: Gender, History, and the Waverley Novels* (Ithaca, NY: Cornell University Press, 1991), pp. 74–94.

4 Fiona Robertson, *Legitimate Histories: Scott, Gothic, and the Authorities of Fiction* (Oxford: Clarendon, 1994), p. 32.

5 I owe this description of the early nineteenth-century relocation of the scene of novel-reading to Ferris, "Transformations of the Novel," in *The New Cambridge History of English Literature: The Romantic Period*, ed. James Chandler (Cambridge: Cambridge University Press, forthcoming).

6 Stuart Curran remarks on the allusion to Scott embedded in Mary Shelley's choice of a public persona: see his Introduction to *Valperga* (*V* xv).

7 On Scott's anonymity game, see Jane Millgate, *Walter Scott: The Making of the Novelist* (Toronto: University of Toronto Press, 1984), p. 67.

8 Ian Duncan argues that Scott's success also depended on late eighteenth-century antiquarian and literary-historical efforts, which had both recovered the contours of the romance and asserted this genre's historical obsolescence; see *Modern Romance and Transformations of the Novel: The Gothic, Scott, Dickens* (Cambridge: Cambridge University Press, 1992), p. 5.

9 In an unpublished essay entitled "History and Romance," William Godwin (rumored in 1814 to be the "Author of 'Waverley'") declares history "little better than a romance under a graver name"; see Appendix IV to Godwin, *Caleb Williams*, ed. Maurice Hindle (London: Penguin, 1988), p. 372.

10 In *Redgauntlet* (1824), Scott followed up his earlier accounts of the Jacobite rebellions of 1715 and 1745 in *Rob Roy* and *Waverley* with a historical novel whose focusing event, the return to Scotland of Bonnie Prince Charlie for a third Jacobite rebellion in the summer of 1765, never took place. See Tilottama Rajan in "Between Romance and History: Possibility and Contingency in Godwin, Leibniz, and Mary Shelley's *Valperga*," *MST* 88–102.

11 Mark Salber Phillips, *Society and Sentiment: Genres of Historical Writing in Britain, 1740–1820* (Princeton: Princeton University Press, 2000), p. 51. See also pp. 19–63; and James Chandler, *England in 1819: The Politics of Literary Culture and the Case of Romantic Historicism* (Chicago: University of Chicago Press, 1998), especially Chandler's account of the historical novel's relationship to the historiographic as well as anthropological endeavors of the Edinburgh Enlightenment, pp. 94–151.

12 "Ferdinando Eboli: A Tale," *CTS* 65.

13 On history as "normal change" see Jerome Christensen, *Romanticism at the End of History* (Baltimore: Johns Hopkins University Press, 2000), p. 169.

14 Sir Walter Scott, *Waverley*, ed. Claire Lamont (Oxford: Oxford University Press, 1986), p. 340.

15 Christensen, *Romanticism at the End of History*, p. 160.

16 See Diane Elam, *Romancing the Postmodern* (New York: Routledge, 1992), p. 64; and Homer Obed Brown, *Institutions of the English Novel* (Philadelphia: University of Pennsylvania Press, 1997), pp. 138–70.

17 Another important source is Horace Walpole's revisionist account of Richard III, which I discuss below.

18 The most influential discussion of their "middling" nature is provided by Georg Lukács in *The Historical Novel*, trans. Hannah and Stanley Mitchell (1937; rept. Lincoln: University of Nebraska Press, 1986), pp. 33–42.

19 Katie Trumpener, *Bardic Nationalism: The Romantic Novel and the British Empire* (Princeton: Princeton University Press, 1997), p. 148.

20 Richard Maxwell, "Pretenders in Sanctuary," *Modern Language Quarterly* 61.2 (June 2000), 304.

21 See Betty T. Bennett, "The Political Philosophy of Mary Shelley's Historical Novels: *Valperga* and *Perkin Warbeck*," in *The Evidence of the Imagination*, ed. Donald H. Reiman, Michael C. Jaye, and Betty T. Bennett (New York: New York University Press, 1978), pp. 363–69.

22 Ann Radcliffe, *The Mysteries of Udolpho*, ed. Bonamy Dobrée (Oxford: Oxford University Press, 1966), p. 522.

23 See Lisa Hopkins, "Memory at the End of History: Mary Shelley's *The Last Man*," *Romanticism on the Net* 6 (May 1997). http://users.ox.ac.uk/~scat0385/lastman.html.

24 Maxwell, "Pretenders in Sanctuary," p. 347.

25 Stephen Arata, "Scott's Pageants: The Example of *Kenilworth*," *SiR* 40.1 (Spring 2001), 99–108.

26 Horace Walpole, "Supplement," *Historic Doubts on the Life and Reign of King Richard the Third*, introd. P. W. Hammond (Gloucester: Alan Sutton, 1987), pp. 127, 131; emphasis added.

27 E. J. Clery, *The Rise of Supernatural Fiction 1762–1800* (Cambridge: Cambridge University Press, 1995), pp. 53–67.

28 Ian Duncan, "The Upright Corpse: Hogg, National Literature and the Uncanny," *Studies in Hogg and his World* 5 (1994), 48.

9

KATE FERGUSON ELLIS

Falkner and other fictions

The trouble with "men as they are"

"I am now writing 'Falkner,'" writes Mary Shelley in her journal for June 7, 1836. "My best it will be – I believe" (*J* II 548). What could she have been thinking, a modern reader might well ask. The identifying moral qualities of her characters appear immediately, and the "roundness" that Forster praised as being "capable of surprising in a convincing way" and which the novel as a genre has cultivated, is nowhere to be found.[1] Yet Shelley was optimistic during the conception and execution of this, her last long work of fiction. Writing to her publisher, Charles Ollier, in January 1836, she told him she had had

> no intention of writing another – but in consequence of what you said, I began to reflect of the subject – and a story presented itself so vividly to my mind that I began to write almost directly – and have finished one volume . . . It is in the style of Lodore, but the story more interesting & even, I should think, more popular.
> (*L* II 263)

Not only did she write the book "with a rapidity [she] had never done before" (*L* II 267), but in a letter to her fellow novelist Edward Bulwer-Lytton, she remarked that "it is not always the most studied & (consequently) the favourite works of an author that are his best titles {to} fame . . . but the flower that springs to bloom most swiftly is the loveliest" (*L* II 296).

In *Lodore*, Shelley had turned in a new direction as a novelist in that she revisited the terrain of intense father–daughter relationships that lead to a tragic end for the heroines of *Matilda* and *Valperga*; in *Lodore*, however, Ethel marries the young man she loves and reconciles with her now-enlightened mother. But the sweet, dependent Ethel has no control over the recklessly passionate side of her father that had led first to his leaving England for the wilds of America with his daughter, then to his death in a duel in New York. Like other Shelleyan heroines, Ethel is either too young or, when older, too "pliant to [her father's] will"(*NSW* VI 18) to extinguish his hypersensitivity to the demands of honor that draw him into the duel and deprive her of a parent. This masculine obsession with honor, which Shelley explores repeatedly in her fiction, constitutes a thematic legacy she inherited from her own novel-writing father.[2]

In *Falkner*, however, Shelley names her heroine after Elizabeth Lavenza of *Frankenstein*, the first of her female progeny, but gives her story a very different outcome. The contrast is made more overt, in fact, by the traits that the two heroines share. At the outset of each narrative, they are both children who have been abandoned by family members of a higher social rank than the families taking care of them. Elizabeth Lavenza is the casualty of her father's exertion "to obtain the liberty of his country," whereas her counterpart in *Falkner*, Elizabeth Raby, is first orphaned by the deaths of doting parents and then rejected by her father's family because he had married a penniless woman who did not embrace their Catholicism. In addition, the little girls share a beauty that sharply contrasts to their bleak surroundings. Finally, both possess, at least initially, an irresistible power "to soften and attract," as Victor Frankenstein says of his childhood companion in the 1831 edition, and to "subdue" the destructive and self-destructive impulses of the male protagonists "to a semblance of her own gentleness." So Victor does not become "sullen in [his] study, or rough through the ardor of [his] nature" (*F* 1831, ii 37), and Falkner does not kill himself, as he was intending to do when he saw *his* angelic little girl at the grave of her parents.

Victor's Elizabeth loses her ability to influence him when, impatient with being "cooped up in one place" (*F* 1818, I ii 26), he sets out for Ingolstadt. In her role as comforter, Elizabeth "veiled her grief" (*F* 1831, iii 92) and remained thereafter in what her community considered "her place." Her one endeavor in the public sphere, her attempt to defend Justine Moritz against the accusation of murder, ends in failure, and Victor never considers sharing his secret with her. What distinguishes the Elizabeth of *Falkner* not only from her predecessor but from *all* of Shelley's earlier heroines, is that her point of view prevails. Elizabeth Raby travels everywhere with her adopted guardian, and ultimately manages to subdue Falkner's extreme pessimism and hopelessness. Moreover, Shelley allows her heroine to subdue not only this powerful male figure her father's age, but also the desire to avenge his mother's death that drives her lover, Gerard Neville, to try to destroy the other man in Elizabeth's life.

That Elizabeth Raby's point of view prevails over the agendas of the novel's two male protagonists suggests that Shelley was working out an explanation of human suffering that was imbued with her father's opposition to the injustice of class privilege. However, the solution she arrives at in her final novel goes beyond her father's rational individualism to posit female empowerment as the only lasting solution to injustice of every sort, since it alone could rein in the desire for unlimited power and social approval that drives her male characters. In each of her novels, we see women who espouse a set of values that counters these destructive scenarios and offers in their place a demonstration of "the amiableness of domestic affection."[3] In each novel prior to *Falkner*, the women characters are powerless when disaster strikes. But though Elizabeth Raby cannot obliterate the death that gives rise to the agendas of the two men, since it happened when she was a child, she does derail those agendas by imposing her own in their stead.

I will return to the merits of Elizabeth's agenda. But a brief examination of the gendered struggles in Shelley's fiction will help clarify the feminist vision that she achieves, I am arguing, in her last novel. These struggles occur because "men as they are," beginning with Victor Frankenstein, refuse to acknowledge the rightfully dominant role of love in human affairs. Love as the arena for female power is a staple of the romance tradition that Shelley is continuing.[4] But only in *Falkner* does the heroine's point of view prevail. This view sees *Falkner* as a participant in two genres that shape Shelley's fictional world: the "women's Gothic,"[5] exemplified preeminently in the writing of Ann Radcliffe, and the politically radical fiction inspired and written by her father.

Failed heroines

No aspect of Shelley's 1831 revision of *Frankenstein* is more dramatic than her reworking of the women characters to contrast more fully with the men. Walton, in his second letter to his sister, tells her about the master of his ship, whose "agreeable nature" is demonstrated in his past willingness to give up his sweetheart, the "Russian lady" who had fallen in love with someone else. In the 1831 version, Walton prefaces this story with a comment about himself: "A youth passed in solitude, my best years spent under your gentle and feminine fosterage, has so refined the groundwork of my character, that I cannot overcome an intense distaste to the usual brutality exercised on board ship" (*F* 1831, Letter II 68). In his fourth letter, Shelley adds an exchange between Walton and Victor that underlines the egomania common to their different enterprises. "I was easily led," Walton says,

> to use the language of my heart, to give utterance to the burning ardour of my soul; and to say, with all the fervour that warmed me, how gladly I would sacrifice *my* fortune, *my* existence, *my* every hope, to the furtherance of *my* enterprize. *One man's life or death* were but a small price to pay for the

acquirement, or the knowledge which I sought, for the dominion I should acquire and transmit over the elemental foes of our race.

(F 1831, Letter IV 77, my italics)

To emphasize the point, Victor adds, "Unhappy man! Do you share my madness?" and proposes to "dash" from Walton's lips "the intoxicating draught" (*F* 1831, Letter IV 77). Yet in both versions, Victor begins with a grandiose dream of a new species that "would bless me as its creator and source" (*F* 1818, I iii 32; *F* 1831, iv 101). And in both, he shows how little he has been changed by his encounters with the monster when he urges Walton's crew to remain faithful to a vision he assumes to be theirs, of being "hailed as the benefactors of your species; your names adored, as belonging to brave men who encountered death for honour and the benefit of mankind" (*F* 1818, III vii 149; *F* 1831, vii 257).

Against Victor's unchanging motive, which he justifies to the end of his life, Elizabeth's transformation from a cousin to an orphan is all the more pointed. Once in the "peaceful home" of her adoptive family, Elizabeth imitates her new mother, "the guardian angel to the afflicted" (*F* 1831, i 83), while the "brightest living gold" of her hair that had set "a crown of distinction on her head" (*F* 1831, i 83) becomes "a shrine-dedicated lamp" that she uses, not for "following the aerial creations of the poets" (*F* 1818, I i 20), but to deliver her own kind of "feminine fosterage" to Victor and Clerval. No longer does Victor "love to tend on her, as I should on a favorite animal" (*F* 1818, I i 20). She is now an essential source of "harmony" for the household's younger generation. In chapter 1, Anne K. Mellor has pointed out the places in the 1831 version in which Shelley construes nature "as a mighty and amoral machine" and reshapes Victor in the image she now has of herself, "as a victim of destiny." By the 1830s, Shelley had also focused her interest in "men as they are" on the question of whether, in such a world, "feminine fosterage" is always doomed to failure.

Begun in childhood, "feminine fosterage" seems to work better, in *Frankenstein* at least, when it is administered from a distance. Walton does finally decide that more than "one man's life or death" is at stake in his "enterprize," and turns back. Safely ensconced in England with her husband and children, Margaret Saville can be the "shrine-dedicated lamp" to which Walton returns, however reluctantly. Had her circumstances been different, she might have joined him, as Austen's Mrs. Croft joins her husband in *Persuasion*, but by 1831, Walton sees her "tutored and refined by books and retirement from the world," as "somewhat fastidious" and thus the source of his "intense distaste to the usual brutality exercised on board ship" (*F* 1831, Letter II 68). Similar views in place in the world of the Frankenstein family must have played a role in keeping Elizabeth from accompanying Clerval on his visit to his friend and her future husband. But the role of the women in that family is to suppress their concern for themselves, and Elizabeth plays it to the hilt.

But this is not the situation of Euthanasia, the heroine of Shelley's second novel. *Valperga* (1823), represents Shelley's boldest use of female characters as moral expositors. Yet both of the novel's heroines, Euthanasia and Beatrice, die young, suggesting the ultimate impotence of "domestic affection" – women's specialty – and the concomitant danger to women of romantic thralldom. That masculine ambition and feminine impotence are two sides of the same coin is brought home when Euthanasia, whose hereditary wealth has given her some power in the faction-ridden world of fourteenth-century Italy, joins a conspiracy against her former lover Castruccio out of the still-common female delusion that she knows who her lover really is, mistakenly believing that military defeat will bring back her beloved, but essentially imaginary, man.

Readers from Godwin on have been drawn to Beatrice, whose delusions about God's role in bringing Castruccio into her life and her bed make her the object of the Inquisition's persecution. Yet though Euthanasia resists these particular delusions, befriending Beatrice as she loses whatever slim hold rationality ever had on her, she is doomed from the start as well. As a Guelf, she is a member of "the papal party" responsible for banishing Castruccio's Ghibelline family from Lucca. Thus, although "[s]he is attached to the cause of the freedom of Florence, and not to the power of her Popes" (*V* I viii 99), her actions cannot transcend the power struggle between imperial and papal authority that was still raging in Italy in Shelley's day. She wants "peace" and "liberty," but so, in his way, does Castruccio:

> "Triumph, my sweet girl," he said; "all my laurels are spoils for you. Nay, turn not away as if you disdained them; they are the assurances of the peace that you desire . . . This sword has made me master of peace and war; and need I say that my wise and gentle Euthanasia shall direct my counsels, her love and honour being the aim and purpose of my life?" (*V* I xi 118)

Shelley's point, of course, is that power invested in one person is not the means to peace, but the novel does not suggest any viable alternative.

There are a number of reasons for this, some having to do with the historical material on which Shelley drew for *Valperga*. But mostly they are rooted in Shelley's Godwinian suspicion of institutions for curtailing individual autonomy. Like Valperga, the castle that is a stand-in for its owner's public being, Euthanasia is isolated except when her father, Castruccio, or finally Beatrice, is in her life. The only model for liberty that the novel offers is Guinigi, the "military peasant" to whom Castruccio's father has sent his son, a man who "had turned his sword to a ploughshare" (*V* I iii 31), and who

> hoped, how futilely! to lay a foundation-stone for the temple of peace among the Euganean hills. He had an overflowing affection of soul, that could not confine itself to the person of his son, or the aggrandizement of his country, or be spiritualized into a metaphysical adoration of ideal beauty. It bestowed itself on his fellow-creatures, and to see them happy, warmed his heart with a pleasure experienced by few. (*V* I iii 33)

Guinigi has more in common with Euthanasia than with his orphaned male charge, yet as a Virgilian figure of agrarian contentment, he calls up a past that was peaceful, Joseph Lew reminds us, only because of a colonial expansion that provides Euthanasia with her hero.[6]

Rather, Euthanasia, like Adrian and Perdita of Shelley's next novel, *The Last Man* (1826), shares Percy Shelley's fate of being simply too good to live, a resemblance underlined, as Shelley herself was aware, by the similarity of their deaths.[7] In *Clarissa* (1748), Samuel Richardson brought this vision of a female virtue too pure to survive into the purview of popular fiction. But Richardson also knew that a fictional world that will not reward female virtue cannot long sustain its didactic edge, at least for a female reading public. In her reading of *Valperga*, Barbara Jane O'Sullivan argues that, "[B]y domesticating female power" (in her later novels), "Shelley finally finds an acceptable way to write about it."[8] But this shift does not fit comfortably with a feminist, as opposed to a conservative, reading of Shelley's later work. Power domesticated would seem to be just what a patriarchal social order would insist on, and O'Sullivan does view Elizabeth in *Falkner* as "a model Victorian heroine, emerging intact from a Gothic melodrama."

The empowered Gothic heroine

Today the phrase "Gothic melodrama" usually carries negative connotations. Yet as E. J. Clery has argued, women Gothicists were engaged, in continuing a disavowed tradition of romance, "in a polemical revision of literary practice involving the transgression of gender expectations."[9] So if Elizabeth Raby is Victorian in her ability to "foster" gentleness in two difficult men, her triumphant reconciliation of their differences makes her Shelley's heroine par excellence. One way to define the romance is as a struggle between the competing imperatives of adventure and domestic security, with men desiring the former and women the latter. Up until the nineteenth century, the pull toward domesticity is no match for the imperative of adventure which seduces Shelley's Castruccio in *Valperga*, and which requires of a hero that he not linger in one place.

But the balance of power begins to shift in the late eighteenth century with the rise of the Gothic as a popular genre, and particularly with the popularity of its most celebrated practitioner, Ann Radcliffe. We see this shift fully achieved, of course, in Charlotte Brontë's *Jane Eyre* (1847), in the marriage of the heroine and Rochester that disturbs many feminists, this one included. For there is nothing egalitarian about Jane's marriage. After hearing her master described as "a fixture" by a loyal innkeeper in the neighborhood, Jane literally reanimates him; her income and her care for him return him to a life over which she now has complete control. This subversion of usurped male control over family assets is standard fare, however, in the Gothic novel, where heroines regularly foil attempts to usurp property and other forms of wealth that are rightfully theirs.[10]

In *Falkner*, Elizabeth Raby is also disowned by, and finally reunited with, her father's wealthy family. Published only a decade before *Jane Eyre*, the novel opens at a remote graveyard in Cornwall where Elizabeth, as a small child, has come to sit by the tombstones of her parents: "Her dress, in some of its parts, betokened that she belonged to the better classes of society," and she has the "angelic" expression and "perfect loveliness" of all of Shelley's heroines (*NSW* VII 7–8). Before Elizabeth's mother died, she wrote to her friend Alithea asking that she adopt her soon-to-be-orphaned daughter, but the letter is unaddressed. When Falkner appears, bent on suicide, his haggard appearance suggests not just that "many singular, perhaps tragical, incidents were connected to his history," but also the possibility "that he had been the active machinator of his fate, not the passive recipient of disappointment and sorrow" (*NSW* VII 16).

It is this look of anguish, the visible signifier of a sense of guilt that he is unable to hide, that Elizabeth's entrance into his life will ultimately change. For two thirds of the novel, the reader wonders if his body is revealing a truth or a distorted perception of himself. Shelley drops many hints, and Falkner's reaction to the letter to Alithea gives the reader the distinct impression that she is his victim. But it is not until the middle of the second volume, after he and his "adopted" daughter have traveled all over Europe and after Elizabeth has fallen in love with the son of the unfortunate Alithea, that Falkner tells the young man: "I am your mother's destroyer" (*NSW* VII 151). This son has been obsessed for most of his life with the imperative of avenging his mother's death and clearing her name of the charge that she deserted him and his father by running off with another man. Naturally, Falkner's confession leads to his arrest and prosecution by this injured father and son, and it is up to Elizabeth, who refuses to believe that a man who has been "more than a father" to her could have cold-bloodedly committed murder, to clear his name and change her beloved's mind.

She is pitted against an idea of masculine honor that, in various guises, dooms not only the male protagonists of Shelley's previous novels but her father's creations as well, especially Falkland, the aristocratic protagonist of *Caleb Williams* (1794) and the eponymous hero of *St. Leon* (1799). For Falkner *has* run off with Alithea, the love of his life from an early age, after hearing from her about her unhappy marriage. Using a convention of the early novel, he writes his story down for Elizabeth – and the reader: "'Surely there is no greater enemy to virtue and good intentions, than that want of self-command,'" he writes. "'I was the same slave of passion I had ever been . . . I lifted her light figure into the carriage; I jumped in after her; I bade her boy follow. It was too late . . . I called to Osborne to stop; he gave no heed to my cries'" (*NSW* VII 186). Reaching their destination, however, Falkner regrets his rash action and goes out to tell the coachman to prepare to bring Alithea back to her husband and abandoned child, only to see, on his return, Alithea's dead body swept up in the rising tide.

This story clears Alithea of the wrong of which she was accused. "'She knew not of my relenting,'" Falkner says, "'she feared my violence, she resolved to escape'" (*NSW* VII 190). But it is Elizabeth who fills in the details that supply a motive for Alithea's impetuous action: "She fancied her awakening on the fatal morning, her wild look around." Then, setting out toward home along "the well-known shore . . . she thought only of her child, from whom she had been torn." Elizabeth puts herself in Alithea's shoes and imagines

> her fears of being, through the deed of violence which had carried her off, excluded from her home for ever . . . The last word murmured in her last sleep – the last word human ears heard her utter, was her son's name. To the last she was all mother; her heart filled with that deep yearning, which a young mother feels to be the very essence of her life, for the presence of her child.
>
> (*NSW* VII 194–95)

How does Elizabeth know this? She was not there and has not been "a young mother." We must conclude, I think, that Shelley herself is intervening here to express, through the medium of Elizabeth, her own remembered pain.

> There is something so beautiful in a young mother's feelings. Usually a creature to be fostered and protected – taught to look to another for aid and safety; yet a woman is the undaunted guardian of her little child. She will expose herself to a thousand dangers to shield his fragile being from harm. If sickness or injury

approach him, her heart is transfixed by terror: readily, joyfully, she would give her own blood to sustain him . . . Such a mother was Alithea . . . What wonder that, reviving from death, her first and only thought was to escape – to get back to him – to clasp him to her heart – never to be severed more?

(*NSW* VII 195)

In this scenario, Alithea is "innocent" because it drains her of any "warm" feelings, or even ambivalent ones, for Falkner.

Elizabeth's creation of an innocent Falkner is no less an act of the imagination. While it is clear that he did not literally murder his beloved, his earlier acknowledged "want of self-command" that left him "the same slave of passion [he] had ever been," led, at a minimum, to Gerard being left behind. Yet Falkner's version of the masculine code of honor requires that he torture himself to the point where his will to live can be sustained only by the constant presence of Elizabeth. *Cui bono?* Elizabeth asks, in effect, and she substitutes for the masculine code of honor that demands Falkner's death, either by his own hand or by the hand of Gerard, a higher and more natural one of her own. "'If it be heroism,'" she tells Gerard, "'to find our chief good in serving others; if compassion, sympathy, and generosity, be greater virtues, as I believe, than cold self-absorbed severity, then is your feeling [for your mother] founded on the purest portion of our nature'" (*NSW* VII 150). This ethic is of a piece with Alithea's maternal selflessness. Men as well as women have this quality as part of our common "nature," Shelley seems to say, but in men it is effaced by ambition, pride in hereditary status, and other components of their false code of honor. When these false pieces of armor are torn away, as Euthanasia thought they would be when Castruccio was defeated by the conspiracy, men's true nature can emerge.

"Feminine fosterage" and men as they might be

Elizabeth's alternative definition of heroism places universal love, expressed as "compassion, sympathy, generosity" toward all, on a higher plane than the love of particular others, or the love of self. In this she takes sides, in a long-lived and still vigorous argument about women's nature, allying with those who assert its moral superiority by virtue of its greater concern with the welfare of others. In her earlier work, Shelley assigned ambition primarily to men and love to women, but here she elevates love to the plane of disinterested benevolence in order to trump both Gerard and Falkner, whose idea of honor is an expression of their differing but equally intense attachments to Alithea. The "men as they are" in *Falkner*, as in the rest of Shelley's fiction, claim to be concerned with lofty values such as peace, justice, and the welfare of others. But left to their own devices, they remain mired in an egocentricity reinforced by their culture's definitions of masculinity.

It is quite clear to Elizabeth that, without her constant presence, Falkner will slip back into the suicidal mentality of their first meeting. It is equally clear that she does not want to surrender her heterosexual future to a father figure. Shelley thus revisits the theme of filial relations that she took to its toxic limits in *Matilda*. Disobeying one's father may send Walton, Victor, and Castruccio into the mouth of danger, but for women it is an unthinkable act, though daughterly obedience is no guarantee of happiness. Thus the "principles" Euthanasia's father taught her become the compass that guides all of her actions after he dies, while the intense devotion of Ethel and Mathilda to their fathers is debilitating for one and deadly for the other. The relationship between Falkner and Elizabeth could have moved in any of these directions, but instead Shelley allows Elizabeth to gain a husband without relinquishing a father, and retain a father without forfeiting a husband. And she does so not by surrendering, but by "subduing" them both to an ethical standard that privileges forgiveness over punishment.

Contrasting *Falkner* with *Matilda*, too controversial for publication in Shelley's lifetime, sheds light on what Shelley may have had in mind in her return to the charged subject of father–daughter incest. First of all, as Mellor and others have pointed out, in these, as in all of Mary Shelley's fictional families, the mother is absent.[11] Mathilda's father was raised by an overindulgent mother, but corrective "feminine fosterage" was supplied, though briefly, by his adored wife, Diana. His response to her early death was to separate himself from his daughter for sixteen years. Falkner lost his mother before he could remember her, and was rescued from an abusive father and uncle by Mrs. Rivers, a former school friend of his mother's who "could subdue the stoniest heart by a look" (*NSW* VII 162). Here he encountered her daughter Alithea as a child, and the bond with a female childhood playmate that so profoundly influenced both Victor and Castruccio provided the only light in Falkner's otherwise miserable life at boarding school.

Alithea's mother died, however, and her father, returned from the navy, banished Falkner from their house. He spent ten years in India where his "'only object was to prove [himself] worthy of her; and [his] only dream for the future was to make her [his] for ever'" (*NSW* VII 172). Needless to say, when he returned she was married and the mother of little Gerard. So Elizabeth Raby, like her predecessor in *Frankenstein*, takes on the role played by Alithea's mother (and later by Alithea herself) of supplying the "feminine fosterage" that will subdue the violent, impulsive side of this man "to a semblance of her own gentleness." The word "subdue," from Shelley's 1831 revision of *Frankenstein*, is an apt one, I want to suggest, because only by living in permanent subjection to the "fosterage" of women can the men "as they are" in Shelley's fiction be directed away from destructive behavior.

This is the state to which Euthanasia imagines bringing Castruccio once he is defeated by the conspiracy.

Yet excessive devotion to the source of this restraint can backfire, as it does for Mathilda's father when a candidate for his daughter's hand appears, or in Falkner when he sees "his" Alithea married and a mother. Then "the hot hell that always in him burns" breaks forth, as it does in Milton's Satan at his first sight of Eve, in the face of "pleasures not for him ordain'd" (*Paradise Lost* IX 467–70). Nevertheless the fires of that "hot hell" in Falkner are extinguished by Elizabeth, while those in Mathilda's father are transferred from father to daughter. In her reading of *Matilda*, Mellor notes that "a culture in which women can play no role but that of daughter, even in their marriages,"[12] blurs the line between filial and erotic love. That Mathilda fails where Elizabeth Raby succeeds, suggests that Shelley strove to show, in her earlier treatment of incestuous feelings, that those fires are more dangerous to the daughter, not less, when her dependent entanglement with her father ignites them in her as well.

Shelley's later fiction is not usually considered particularly feminist, though Mellor's reading is an exception to this assessment. Mellor posits, as the ground for her argument, a celebration of "the egalitarian bourgeois family" even as Shelley "acknowledges that it has never existed." If Shelley's novels "reveal the limitations of that ideology,"[13] as I would agree that they do, some better model of gender and familial relations must be present, if only in her mind, against which the dysfunction being pointed out can be measured. But is this model egalitarian? Or does Shelley's pessimism about all social institutions, combined with her belief in the socially produced superiority of the gender that mothers, give us a feminism in which women must be always in charge? It is a feminism that might reasonably be held by someone who believed, as Godwin surely did when he published his memoir about his wife, that her vilifiers were wrong and that she, with her complex relationships not only to Godwin but also to Henry Fuseli and Gilbert Imlay, exemplified a virtue higher than that of her critics.

Judged by a standard that values artistic control over one's materials, *Falkner* is certainly not Mary Shelley's best novel. But as I have argued here, her goals as a serious writer are not those that the genre embraced. Jane Austen's "3 or 4 families in a Country Village"[14] points the novel in a direction that takes up the lives not of exceptional people but of ordinary ones, and reveals their actions and feelings not *in extremis* but in the realm of "common life." Clearly Shelley had no interest in doing this. She was the daughter of a famous mother, the wife of a great poet, and the child of an admired philosophical thinker; a woman who placed herself on the same plane and saw herself carrying on their great work, to translate their highest visions and most devastating social critiques onto the page. She wrote romances, which do not deal in "common life," and, like her mother, she was consumed with the problem of "men as they are" and how even the best of them fall away from their own higher natures. I have argued that *Falkner* is her final word on this subject, presenting her vision with a clarity that took seven novels to achieve, and that its radical vision is what she had in mind when she wrote, "My best it will be – I believe."

NOTES

1 E. M. Forster, *Aspects of the Novel*, ed. Oliver Stallybrass (London: Edward Arnold, 1974), p. 54.

2 See Pamela Clemit, *The Godwinian Novel: The Rational Fictions of Godwin, Brockden Brown, Mary Shelley* (New York: Oxford University Press, 1993, rpt. 2001); and Katherine Richardson Powers, *The Influence of William Godwin on the Novels of Mary Shelley* (New York: Arno Press, 1980).

3 Writing in his wife's voice, Percy Bysshe Shelley states in the preface to the 1818 edition of *Frankenstein*, "my chief concern in this respect has been limited to the avoiding the enervating effects of the novels of the present day, and to the exhibition of the amiableness of domestic affection, and the excellence of universal virtue" (*F* 1818, 5–6).

4 See for instance "The French Romance," in Ros Ballaster, *Seductive Forms: Women's Amatory Fiction from 1684–1740* (Oxford: Oxford University Press, 1992), pp. 42–49.

5 See Ellen Moers, "Female Gothic," *EF* 77–87; E. J. Clery, *Women's Gothic: From Clara Reeve to Mary Shelley* (Plymouth: Northcote House, 2000).

6 Joseph Lew, "God's Sister: History and Ideology in *Valperga*," *OMS* 177.

7 See Mary Shelley to Jane Williams, January 12, 1823 (*L* 1 304–07); to Maria Gisborne, May 3, 1823 (*L* 1 333–36). Susan Wolfson comments that Shelley "makes her husband's death less a loss than a translation along the proper path of one too refined for this world" in "Editorial Privilege: Mary Shelley and Percy's Audience," *OMS* 48.

8 Barbara Jane O'Sullivan, "Beatrice in *Valperga*: A New Cassandra," *OMS* 154.

9 Clery, *Women's Gothic*, p. 7.

10 For examples, see Kate Ferguson Ellis, *The Contested Castle: Gothic Novels and the Subversion of Domestic Ideology* (Urbana: University of Illinois Press, 1989), esp. pp. 99–128.

11 Anne K. Mellor, *Mary Shelley: Her Life, Her Fiction, Her Monsters* (New York: Methuen, 1998), pp. 189, 200, 217.

12 *Ibid.*, p. 200.

13 *Ibid.*, pp. 216, 217, 216.

14 Jane Austen to Anna Austen, September 9, 1814, *Jane Austen's Letters*, collected and edited by Deirdre Le Faye, 3rd edn. (Oxford: Oxford University Press, 1995).

10

CHARLOTTE SUSSMAN

Stories for the *Keepsake*

Mary Shelley's decision to start writing short stories for the literary annuals in the 1820s and 1830s is usually represented as discontinuous with her earlier career, part of the fall into commercialism and conservatism occasioned by Percy Shelley's death. Even those who have paid critical attention to the stories often denigrate them. Gregory O'Dea, for instance, writes: "For much of her later literary career, Mary Shelley was a hack writer . . . [She] filled the spaces between her increasingly disregarded novels by turning her pen to essays, reviews, bits of history and travelogue, and, what certainly marks her reduced circumstances, tales for *The Keepsake*."[1] One recent biographer calls these "insipid tales for ladies' annuals" "wordy and pedestrian."[2]

Yet it is important to remember that Mary Shelley always wrote for money. Any sharp distinction between what Shelley wrote for profit, and what she wrote inspired by a creative urge above Mammon would be false, although we may be able to distinguish the degree of financial pressure exerted on her various compositions. Indeed, her first short story, "Mounseer Nong-tongpaw," written when she was ten and a half, made a good profit for her father's publishing company. Until her father-in-law's death in 1844, Mary Shelley's financial situation, throughout her early life, marriage, and most of her widowhood, was never comfortable. Even during her union with Percy Bysshe Shelley, she was caught between her father's demands for money and her husband's lack of ready cash. Before their elopement, Percy Bysshe Shelley had raised money for Godwin on a post-obit loan (a loan secured by the inheritance the poet expected to receive after his father's death), but this was only the first of Godwin's demands for money from his son-in-law. The profit from Mary Shelley's own works might have helped to ease this tension and she tried on several occasions to direct her artistic production toward that end. While her husband was still alive, Mary Shelley attempted to defuse her father's demands for money by offering him the advance she tried to raise on her first novel after *Frankenstein*, *Valperga*. When she failed to raise enough money in this way, she simply sent the manuscript to Godwin to sell to a publisher, so that he could have the profit from it. After Percy Bysshe Shelley's death, her financial situation became even more difficult; she needed the proceeds from her work to help her family, especially her father, since her son was to some degree provided for by Sir Timothy Shelley. Although many of the letters Mary Shelley exchanged with the editors of the *Keepsake* and other annuals concern money, that fact does not distinguish them from the letters she wrote to the publishers of her novels. Thus, Mary Shelley's numerous publications for the annuals, from which she was assured an income, were less discontinuous from her earlier career, in this respect at least, than they are usually taken to be.

Shelley herself did not regard writing for the annuals as degrading, nor should she have:[3] the annuals were a major mode of literary production in the 1820s and 1830s, bringing together in their pages writers from formerly opposing artistic camps.[4] Publishing in them put Shelley in the company of the other leading writers of her day, including Wordsworth, Scott, Coleridge, and Southey. In addition, the annuals gave her a way of participating actively in polite society, which often otherwise shunned her due to her scandalous past. As much as she was able, she used the annuals to rehabilitate her husband's reputation, giving three of his previously unpublished poems and his fragment, "On Love," to the *Keepsake*.

The annuals

Mary Shelley wrote twenty-one stories for gift-books or periodicals between 1823 and 1839; of these, sixteen were published in the *Keepsake*. Owing to the constraints of the annuals, most stories are relatively brief, a fact about which Shelley complained to Maria Gisborne: "When I write for them, I am worried to death to make my things shorter and shorter – till I fancy people think ideas can be conveyed by intuition – and that it is a superstition to consider words necessary for their expression."[5] Some of these stories relate exciting events in faraway places – for example, "Euphrasia: A Tale of Modern Greece," published in the *Keepsake* for 1839, or "The Evil Eye," a tale of Albania, published in the *Keepsake* for 1830; others treat faraway times – for instance, "The Dream," which takes place during the reign of Henry IV of France and was published in the *Keepsake* for 1832. Shelley's mix of the domestic and the exotic, and of heterogeneous settings in place and time, was a hallmark of the gift-book genre.

The rise of gift-books and literary annuals brought new developments in the way poetry, essays, and short fiction were produced and consumed. These books, starting with the *Forget Me Not* in 1822, collected stories, poems, and essays by various authors, along with handsome engravings, in lavishly produced volumes. They were explicitly marketed not only as books, but also as tasteful gifts, objects to be coveted and admired. By 1831, sixty-two annuals and gift-books were in circulation. The *Keepsake*, first published in 1828, was owned by Charles Heath and edited by Frederick Mansel Reynolds. They planned their marketing strategies very carefully, embarking on a kind of tour to solicit well-known authors for contributions to the 1829 volume. Figures such as Scott, Wordsworth, and Southey were offered high fees to overcome their reluctance to publish in such a popular form; they agreed to contribute, but after 1829, the editors decided that paying such sums to well-known male authors was not worth the trouble. The *Keepsake*, the most successful of the annuals, was a particularly attractive object, bound in crimson watered silk, with gilt-edged pages. The volumes were published in two sizes, the smaller priced at thirteen shillings, the larger at two pounds, twelve shillings and sixpence. In tribute to their importance, the steel-plate engravings could be purchased separately. Indeed, authors, including Shelley, would be asked to compose stories or poems to accompany pre-existing illustrations. Several of the major artists of the day, including J.M.W. Turner and Edwin Landseer, published in the *Keepsake*.

The aesthetic attributes of the *Keepsake* are usually assumed to have appealed to middle-class female readers, who could display these tasteful objects in their parlors, as well as read them. Indeed, the association between the annuals and a kind of frivolous and feminine consumerism is responsible for much of the abuse heaped upon them, both now and in their own day. Wordsworth, despite his own involvement with them, lambasted the annuals as "those greedy receptacles of trash, those Bladders upon which the Boys of Poetry try to swim";[6] Thackeray characterized them as "a little sham sentiment . . . employed to illustrate a little sham art."[7] Such statements work to divide the popular annuals, associated with women, from high art, associated with masculinity. One contemporary review, for instance, explicitly links the annuals with femininity and ornament:

> There they are, the pretty things! Criticise them? We might as well think of criticising the colours of a bed of tulips in full bloom . . . A critique of them should only be written in a lady's boudoir; by her own taper and jeweled fingers; with finest crow-quill, the gilt and silver tassels hanging from its top, and quivering at every movement of its jetty plumage . . .[8]

The comparison to flowers not only evokes the ornamental quality of the annuals, but also underscores their impermanence; like flowers, they fade quickly and constantly need to be replaced. Christian Isobel Johnstone, the editor of *Tait's Edinburgh Magazine*, reiterates the point: "The writing of the Annuals, taken as a whole, is certainly not flattering to the national vanity . . . Still, independently of art, these ephemeral productions have excellent uses."[9] The uses Johnstone has in mind are primarily commercial, the hope that "the English Annuals are becoming a new branch of exportable manufacture." Thus, the very success of the annuals – the need to produce a new version every year – associates them with the passing forms of female fashion.

As objects, then, the *Keepsake* and other annuals appealed to middle-class women; the handsome volumes served as a sign both of good taste and of consumer power. Their contents, too, were attractive to such readers, inculcating middle-class ideas of propriety and, as we will see later, financial responsibility, while at the same time offering readers a chance to explore foreign settings such as Italy or Greece, and Gothic situations in which heroes and heroines overcame great danger or suffering. These stories and poems allowed their readers to explore exotic, even supernatural, events, while maintaining values and language that conformed to bourgeois ideals of propriety. Thus, the annuals question the routines of domesticity without directly challenging them; moreover, they use exotic settings to investigate the ways in which women's lives were susceptible to sudden changes in health or status. Surveying the themes of the *Keepsake*, Terence Hoagwood and Kathryn Ledbetter conclude that

> tales about unhappy or arranged marriages, the lack of opportunities for women to support their own families, the damage wrought by society's double standard, the self-destructive effects of jealousy caused by competition in the marriage market, the fate of fallen women, society's neglect of laboring women, the depressing status of orphans and single women, mental and emotional abuse of women by men, and the sickness of a class-bound society regulated by a hierarchy that enclosed women in the home appear in most *Keepsake* volumes.[10]

Thus, there was a certain tension between form and content in the *Keepsake* – between the volatile situations often explored in the stories, and the stable material qualities that guaranteed the books' value as commodities. The production values of the *Keepsake* seem to stabilize this exploration of female experience within a framework of aesthetic beauty and permanence by focusing the reader's attention on the striking engravings and beautiful bindings with which the stories are surrounded.[11] Yet the stories themselves often juxtapose the value of the commodity form, as it is determined by the market, with the fluctuating value of the female form, particularly as it is valued in the marriage market. In this way, the annuals offer two aspects of femininity for their readers' consideration: an ideal of permanent and static beauty, and an acknowledgment of the built-in obsolescence and fragility of feminine attractions. One might say that the cultural capital proffered by the annuals as static, visible markers of both social and aesthetic propriety promised to protect their purchasers against the threats of physical, psychological, and financial decline described in their pages. The stability of the book is meant to compensate for the instability of experience. Even so, the question of evanescence is also raised by the material object, since the mode of production for the annuals demanded that representations of women, by women, and for women have a kind of built-in obsolescence. Mary Shelley's stories for the annuals often take up this gendered intersection of the human form and the commodity form, suggesting that the problem of valuing women's lives can be linked to the difficulty of creating lasting representations of women.

Many of Shelley's stories highlight the fragility of individual identity by showing the way a person's role in the world can be cataclysmically altered either by an internal emotional upheaval, or by some supernatural occurrence that mirrors an internal schism. One variation on this theme, which Shelley explored in "Roger Dodsworth: The Reanimated Englishman" (submitted to the *The New Monthly Magazine* in 1826) and returned to in "Valerius: The Reanimated Roman" (unpublished during Shelley's lifetime, but probably written in 1819), concerns an individual brought alive into the wrong time. In all her tales of the mutability of identity, a radical external discontinuity renders the character unrecognizable, or invisible, to others, while internal continuity conserves the individual's knowledge of him or herself. This interest in the discontinuity of identity can be read autobiographically, through the dislocations of place and status that dominated Shelley's own life. But Shelley's gift-book and annual stories persistently emphasize the mechanisms of economic expenditure and exchange that both stabilize and destabilize the self. In her stories, Shelley often literalizes what Andrea Henderson calls "a relational, changeable identity associated with superficiality, contingency, and indeterminacy of market values":[12] characters find their clothes, social standing, family ties, even their bodies, literally exchanged for another's, with or without their volition.

For Shelley, such shifts in identity are particularly catastrophic when they happen to women. She represents female identity as almost always linked to female value in the marriage market – a value derived from a combination of physical beauty and moral virtue. Therefore any change in a woman's status, whether voluntary or involuntary, that alters her relationship to the marriage contract, undermines her physical and psychic identity. Shelley's male characters, in contrast, are able to reverse, and even profit by, such transformations: male bodies and minds are not corroded by exchanges in the markets for marriage and goods. In this chapter, I focus on stories that exemplify this frequent and important theme in Shelley's stories: "Transformation," probably one of the most widely read of Shelley's tales; and "The Mourner," and "The Parvenue," two of the most autobiographical.

Exchange

Mary Shelley wrote several stories about the exchange of identity through exchanged clothing, such as "Fernando Eboli," and "The Sisters of Albano," and several others about women cross-dressing to save their male beloveds, such as "A Tale of the Passions," and "The False Rhyme." These stories, in spite of their conventional romance settings, have been read as undermining traditional gender roles.[13] (Shelley's interest in cross-dressing and the assumption of new identities had a real-life corollary in her involvement with Mary Diana Dods, who transformed herself into Walter "Sholto" Douglas in order to live as the husband of Isabel Robinson.[14]) These stories investigate the importance of outward markers, such as clothes, in determining selfhood. Such outward transformations often prove effective and galvanizing, leading the characters who attempt them in and out of life and death situations.

By far the most elaborate of these tales of identity exchange is "Transformation." In this story, bodies are exchanged, rather than simply clothing, and the exchange is carried out through supernatural power, not mere human will. Here, too, the relationship between the exchange of human identities and the exchanges of the economic marketplace is cast into sharp relief. "Transformation" tells the story of Guido, a well-born youth of Renaissance Genoa, betrothed to marry Juliet, the daughter of his father's best friend, Torella. Unfortunately, before the marriage can take place, Guido exhausts his inheritance in a dissipated visit to Paris. When he returns to Genoa, he finds the marriage contract void, since he can no longer fulfill its financial obligations. "Irritat[ed] to madness" by this turn of events, Guido attempts to kidnap Juliet and her father (*CTS* 129). Banished from the city for his crimes, he wanders along the seashore, where he meets a demonic dwarf with a chest of gold and jewels. The dwarf offers to exchange the treasure for the use of Guido's handsome young body for three days, and Guido, driven by "a mad desire to possess this treasure," gives in to the dwarf's demands (*CTS* 129). Demonic and untrustworthy, the dwarf breaks his promise, and never returns to give back Guido's body. Realizing that the dwarf intends to apologize to Torella and marry Juliet in his place, Guido, in the dwarf's body, returns to Genoa, and tries to kill the dwarf who usurped his body. Waking, he finds himself restored to his own body, married to Juliet, and the dwarf nowhere to be seen; he gives up on the riches of the chest.

There are striking similarities between this story and Byron's dramatic fragment, *The Deformed Transformed*, which Shelley transcribed in 1822–23. In Byron's text, Arnold, born a hideous hunchback and rejected by all who know him (including his own mother), is about to commit suicide, when he is given the chance to transfer himself into another body by the Devil. He chooses the body of Achilles, while the devil takes up his discarded, deformed body. Shadowed by the Devil as a reminder of his deformed past, Arnold participates in a Renaissance siege of Rome and attempts to court the beautiful Olimpia. As Paul Cantor notes, while Byron's protagonist gives up a deformed body for a beautiful one, Shelley's exchanges a handsome body for a grotesque one. "Only by destroying part of himself – his masculine pride – can Guido be freed to experience true love with Juliet," Cantor argues; "Shelley thus tells the story of the taming and domestication of the Byronic hero."[15] Shelley's story can thus be read as a feminine revision of Romantic ideology, a revision that assimilates the Faust myth to the values of the annuals.

Yet there is another dimension to Shelley's version that is missing from Byron's. While Byron's Arnold gives in to the Devil's temptation out of a desire for love and power, Shelley's Guido, ruined by his own extravagance, takes on a new body for a chest of jewels. Hence, all exchange is a kind of economic transformation: all substances – lands, goods, money, and bodies – fungible. As Guido says about his dissolute life in Paris:

> Who could control me? not the letters and advice of Torella – only strong necessity visiting me in the abhorred shape of an empty purse. But there were means to refill this void. Acre after acre, estate after estate, I sold. My dress, my jewels, my horses and their caparisons, were almost unrivalled in gorgeous Paris, while the lands of my inheritance passed into the possession of others.
>
> (*CTS* 123)

Here, the liquidity of ancestral possessions is amply illustrated; land is transformed into personal adornments. The image of the neutral space of economic equivalence through which these transactions pass is Guido's empty purse, its "abhorred shape" prefiguring the tale's embodied agent of transformation, the dwarf. When Guido finds that his "comely face and well-made limbs" are as fungible as his lands, he reconciles himself to the exchange in much the same way: "I felt myself changed to a shape of horror, and cursed my easy faith and blind credulity. The chest was there – and the gold and precious stones for which I had sold the frame of flesh which nature had given me. The sight a little stilled my emotions: three days would soon be gone" (*CTS* 130). Since Guido firmly believes that the chest will allow him to "command the world" (*CTS* 129), he is able to accept what he believes is the transitory loss of his "frame of flesh," itself a gift of nature. He himself has become that "abhorred" "shape of horror" that signifies the universal equivalence of goods.

Guido's "strong necessity" (*CTS* 123) is, of course, not necessity, but its opposite: extravagance. The figuring of that conventionally feminine vice as an empty purse underlines the sexual connotations of the image. The "abhorred shape" of the empty purse can be seen not only as a figure for the site of exchange, but also as a figure for feminine sexuality – a "nothing" that can never be filled or defined. Were Guido to marry Juliet, her body would become the empty space through which more goods and money would arrive at his disposal. The "abhorred shape" thus suggests both female anatomy and the infernal transformations of the marketplace. When Guido himself is reduced, as women often are, to a value based on his attractive body in the dwarf's bargain, the story's crucial doubling of marriage and economic exchange is exposed. Significantly, the marriage contract between Guido and Juliet's father, Torella, is doubled by the spoken contract between Guido and the dwarf; both contracts balance bodies (Juliet's, Guido's) against goods (Guido's estates, the dwarf's chest of gold). And both contracts are broken by avarice (Guido's, the dwarf's), the motor of the story until Guido's knife, thrust at the dwarf, returns both money and bride to the man for whom they were initially intended.

This violent blow seems to end the series of exchanges, establishing the stable values of the domestic sphere in place of the inhuman equivalence of the markets. Yet the transformation of all Guido's assets – lands, goods, and body – into marital domesticity haunts that stability, suggesting that a beautiful wife is as fungible as anything else. Still, in "Transformation," that exchangeability is no tragedy, but rather supplies the groundwork for a happy ending. Only through such transformations of materials of equivalent value can Guido regain the happiness he thought lost. The male body, furthermore, retains its coherence through these exchanges – even after Guido trades it away, he can get it back.

Expenditure

If "Transformation" tells the story of the domestication of an aggressive and extravagant masculinity, it also posits a certain stability to masculine identity, for Guido eventually ends up with the body with which he was born, only "a little bent" (*CTS* 135). In Shelley's stories about female suffering, however, the female body is usually not recuperable in the same way, but is instead subject to a kind of physical and economic entropy. In these stories, we see a radical questioning of the economic value of female beauty. There seems to be something about femininity that cannot be exchanged, something that can only be wasted in an expenditure without return. Here, the "emptiness" of femininity is not neutral, but a corrosive force, breaking apart the very social connections it is supposed to cement. In a number of stories, including "The Invisible Girl," "The Mortal Immortal," "The Mourner," and "The Parvenue," as in "Transformation," Shelley also considers the problem of marriage, examining how the female body endures economic exchange. In these stories, however, the central object of economic exchange – the marriageable body of a woman – wastes away, through grief and hardship, becoming lifeless or invisible. This economic and physical transformation is usually accompanied by emotional collapse; these stories all involve melancholia and suicidal urges.

Only in "The Invisible Girl" (*Keepsake* for 1833), the most optimistic of these stories, can that body be restored. The heroine, Rosina, is cruelly dismissed from her adoptive family's house when the eldest son transgresses class boundaries and falls in love with her. Without resources, she takes refuge in a deserted seaside tower, and becomes known in the neighborhood as the invisible girl. Her invisibility is both social and, increasingly, physical; her "slender, wasted form" is "the living shadow" of her former "Hebe beauty" (*CTS* 200). When chance drives her lost beloved, Henry Vernon, onto the very shore she inhabits, he restores her both to social and to physical visibility, so that she "resemble[s] once more the picture drawn of her in her days of bliss, before any visitation of sorrow" (*CTS* 201); this "picture" is the same as the engraving that illustrates the story in the *Keepsake*. Rosina's physical ability once again to match the unchanging beauty of the picture provides an unusual instance among Shelley's stories in which femininity is recuperable and can regain its lost value. The woman in the story is the same as the woman in the annual illustration; feminine beauty is captured in a stable representation, in which a living body becomes identical to an exchangeable object. Like Guido in "The Transformation," Rosina is able to recover the body she almost loses and to regain her social visibility through a happy marriage.

Yet, if Rosina's joyful acceptance of the marriage contract enables her reinsertion into an economy of visibility, another paradigm, in which resistance to the terms of marriage erases female value, occurs more often in Shelley's stories, including "The Mourner," published in the *Keepsake* for 1830. This story of a supposed parricide is one of the more autobiographically resonant of Shelley's annual stories, as it poignantly describes the overwhelming depression following a loved one's drowning. Yet "The Mourner" also conforms to the tone of "self-perpetuating sorrow" and "continuously memorialized loss" that Pascoe considers "is the most consistent register of gift book aesthetics."[16] Furthermore, the story reveals that the annuals' emphasis on commemoration is shadowed by the specter of forgetting, the possibility that female beauty and worth are too evanescent to be remembered. This anxiety is also articulated in L[etitia] E[lizabeth] L[andon]'s poem for the 1831 *Keepsake*, "The Forgotten One":

> Thou art forgotten! – thou, whose feet
>   Were listened for like song!
> They used to call thy voice so sweet; –
>   It did not haunt them long.
> Thou, with thy fond and fairy mirth –
> How could they bear their lonely hearth!
>
> There is no picture to recall
>   Thy glad and open brow;
> No profiled outline on the wall
>   Seems like thy shadow now;
> They have not even kept to wear
> One ringlet of thy golden hair.[17]

Here, all the conventional "keepsakes" of visual memory – miniatures, silhouettes, hair ornaments – have not been realized and the beautiful woman, like Rosina before her restoration, has become invisible to those who once claimed to love her. Unlike Rosina, however, no representation of her exists that might return her to memory, except the words of the female poet.

"The Mourner" opens with the hero, Horace Neville, remembering a woman who has disappeared. Neville takes his new fiancée, Juliet, to visit the grave of a woman he loved in his youth:

> No stone was there to commemorate the being who reposed beneath – it was thickly grown with rich grass, starred by a luxuriant growth of humble daisies: a few dead leaves, a broken bramble twig, defaced its neatness; Neville removed these, and then said, "Juliet, I commit this sacred spot to your keeping while I am away. –
>
> "There is no monument," he continued: "for her commands were implicitly obeyed by the two beings to whom she addressed them. One day another may lie near, and his name will be her epitaph . . . promise me, Juliet, to preserve this grave from every violation."   (*CTS* 85)

As in L.E.L.'s poem, the responsibility of saving the grave from complete invisibility and oblivion devolves upon another woman. Here, however, we learn that the lack of commemoration has been self-imposed.

Neville then relates the story of his involvement with the woman in the grave. Running away from cruel treatment at Eton as a schoolboy, he encounters a girl, Ellen, living alone in Windsor Forest. Although she seems to be already verging on invisibility, her beauty in suffering deeply impresses Neville; "'she was pale even to marmoreal whiteness; her chestnut-coloured hair was parted in plain tresses across a brow which wore traces of extreme suffering; her eyes were blue, full, large, melancholy, often even suffused with tears'" (*CTS* 87). Although the attraction to female beauty in suffering is conventional during the period, this story is remarkable for

[confusing] the boundary between physical and mental sensation . . . [E]very pulsation of her heart was a throb of pain . . . The idea that chiefly haunted her, though she earnestly endeavoured to put it aside, was self-destruction – to snap the silver cord that bound together so much grace, wisdom, and sweetness – to rob the world of a creation made to be its ornament. (*CTS* 89)

The words used to describe these suicidal urges resonate with the aesthetics of the annuals. If women are meant to be beautiful, visible ornaments, suitable for commodified exchange in the pages of the gift-books, the desire for invisibility through withdrawal, or even suicide, is a form of thievery.

Indeed, Ellen has "robbed" someone of her beauty, by disappearing instead of going through with a previous marriage agreement, after a devastating emotional event. Born Clarice, daughter of Lord Eversham, and betrothed to marry Lewis Elmore, she accompanies her beloved father when he visits his properties in Barbados. On the return journey, their ship catches fire mid-ocean, and Ellen refuses to leave her father until only one of them can be saved. The loss of her parent, combined with her fellow passengers' accusations of parricide, triggers a psychic upheaval: "[H]er own servants had perished, few people remembered who she was; but they talked together with careful voices as they passed her, and a hundred times she must have heard herself accused of having destroyed her parent. She spoke to no one, or only in brief reply when addressed" (*CTS* 94). This silence is the beginning of Ellen's disappearance. She never contacts Elmore, although he searches for her; she changes her name and disappears into Windsor Forest. Eventually, the physical effects of her depression lead to Ellen's death, which she attempts to explain in a letter to Neville: "'I have vowed never to mention certain beloved names, never to communicate with beings who cherished me once, to whom my deepest gratitude is due; and, as well as poor bankrupt can, is paid . . . Describe your poor Ellen to [Ellmore], and he will speedily see that *she* died on the waves of the murderous Atlantic'" (*CTS* 98). Unlike the economic exchanges of "Transformation," Ellen's emotional transformation has been permanent, an expenditure without return – the debilitating double of masculine extravagance – leaving her metaphorically "bankrupt," the psychic equivalent to an empty purse. Significantly, she uses the vocabulary of finance to describe her lack of psychological resources, emphasizing that marriage, and its refusal, are economic structures. Ellen's excessive devotion to her father and her consuming melancholy after his death have led her to refuse a seemingly happy marriage with a man who loves her. This resistance has drained her physically and emotionally, leaving her without affective "funds" to pay her debts of gratitude. The wasted body of the melancholic suicide undermines the stability of the marriage contract by emptying out one of its terms of value: the physical and emotional plenitude of a virtuous woman. Furthermore, as we see from the beginning of the story, Ellen's resistance to this economy also makes remembering her difficult, for herself, as well as others.

"The Parvenue," another story of female disappearance, again has obvious autobiographical significance for Shelley. A bitter account of a young woman persecuted by her family's demands on her wealthy husband for money, the story ends on a note of despair. The husband's refusal to lend money to his wife's family echoes Percy Bysshe Shelley's rebuke of Godwin in 1820, when he forbade his wife's father from trying to borrow any more funds through her: "she has not, nor ought she to have the disposal of money, if she had poor thing, she would give it all to you . . . I cannot consent to disturb her quiet & my own by placing an apple of discord in her hand."[18] As does Percy Bysshe Shelley, "The Parvenue" depicts money as the "apple of discord" that shatters the "Eden" of marriage. Yet the story is also interesting for its descriptions of charity and extravagance, and the toll they take on female happiness and health.

After a happy childhood, the narrator, Fanny, the daughter of a land steward, is courted by an aristocratic land-owner, Sir Reginald Desborough. Initially content, husband and wife soon clash over her spending habits:

> My charities, they were called – they seemed to me the payment of my debts to my fellow-creatures – were abundant. Lord Reginald peremptorily checked them; but as I had a large allowance for my own expenses, I denied myself a thousand luxuries to which it appeared to me I had no right, for the sake of feeding the hungry. Nor was it only charity that impelled me, but that I could not acquire a taste for spending money on myself – I disliked the apparatus of wealth. My husband called my ideas sordid, and reproved me severely, when, instead of outshining all competitors at a fête, I appeared dowdily dressed, and declared warmly that I could not, I would not, spend twenty guineas on a gown, while I could dress so many sad faces in smiles, and bring so much joy to so many drooping hearts, by the same sum. (CTS 269)

Here, two forms of excess expenditure conflict: charity and female ornamentation. Both signify a particular kind of feminine virtue or duty. Again, Shelley stresses the universal equivalence of goods and bodies: twenty guineas buy one dress, or so many smiles. The narrator actively opposes the gendered norms of her husband's class, refusing the "apparatus of wealth" that would make her a social ornament. Characteristically, Shelley has her describe this marital struggle in terms of the gradual physical erasure of the female body. Fanny compares her commitment to charity to religious martyrdom: "Do not think me presumptuous in this simile," she says, "for many years I have wasted in the slow fire of knowing that I lost my husband's affections because I performed what I believed to be a duty" (*CTS* 270). Thus, the economic "waste" of charity (in her husband's eyes an expenditure without return) leads, in this case, to the psychic "wasting away" of emotional alienation.

This conflict is exacerbated by the narrator's relatives' demands on her husband's money. Her brother-in-law is typical of the family in being "rendered absolutely insane by the idea of having a lord for a brother-in-law": he "launch[es] into a system of extravagance, incredible as it was wicked" (*CTS* 273). Although Fanny agrees with her husband that his wealth should not be used to raise her family's station, she is still forced to solicit funds from him on numerous occasions. Finally, when Fanny must ask for money to support her dying mother, Lord Reginald demands that she choose between him and an allowance sufficient to her family's needs. Fanny chooses to support her family. Lord Reginald's cruelty reinforces the suggestion made in many of Shelley's stories that marriage is an all-or-nothing choice: remaining inside the institution ensures visibility for the wife, if she is willing to forget all other ties; resistance to that stricture erodes her visibility and value.

"The Parvenue" can be read as a conservative story about the difficulties of raising one's social status through marriage. It can also be read as upholding middle-class values by criticizing Lord Reginald's support of aristocratic extravagance and opposition to charity.[19] Fanny finally condemns him as selfish and cruel. What is most striking about the tale, however, is its description of the physical and psychological toll this economic conflict exacts on the narrator, and her gradual disappearance under the strain. After her mother's death, Fanny chooses to emigrate to America to join her sister:

> Let me seek a strange land, a land where a grave will soon be opened for me. I feel I cannot live long – I desire to die. I am told that Lord Reginald loves another, a highborn girl; that he openly curses our union as the obstacle to his happiness. The memory of this will poison the oblivion I go to seek in a distant land. – He will be free. Soon will the hand he once so fondly took in his and made his own, which, now flung away, trembles with misery as it traces these lines, moulder in its last decay. (*CTS* 274)

Here again, Shelley emphasizes the physical destruction wrought by economic conflict. Fanny begins to disappear, both geographically, into America, and corporeally, into the grave. The narrative itself comes under strain, as the hand that writes it trembles. Once she refuses the position of ornament, Fanny's capacity to represent her own experience becomes more tenuous.

Markets

Whereas Guido survives through his capacity to transform himself and his wealth from one thing into another and back again, the female protagonists of "The Mourner" and "The Parvenue" waste away rather than conform to the demands of the marriage market, which require them to transform themselves to fit the "apparatus of wealth." In these stories of marriages refused or destroyed, Shelley posits that femininity might not have the stable exchange value asked of it by both the literary and the marriage market. In her stories for the *Keepsake*, then, Shelley offers two contrasting representations of the marriage market: one in which economic value and the male body are conserved through a chain of exchanges; and another one in which economic value and the female body waste away through a similar chain. If "Transformation" eventually celebrates the triumph of domestic life, Shelley's stories about young women can be read as critiques of the strictures of marriage. Her heroines resist the edict that the marriage vow supersedes all other affective ties, particularly those to family. Yet the only way such female resistance to the socio-economic demands of marriage can manifest itself is negative.

These descriptions of female suffering undermine the ideal of femininity seemingly offered by the engravings in the annuals – static, lasting images of virtue and beauty. Instead, such wasting away threatens to erase women from memory, making any permanent memorial or representation of them difficult to maintain. Through such narratives, Shelley's stories criticize the dominant conception of female value. They posit that the value accrued through marriage stabilizes identity for men, like Guido, and women, like Rosina, who consent to its terms and the conventional "apparatus" of class status. Yet the dominance of this form of value drains visibility and vitality from women who dissent from it, by refusing marriage or its terms. In Shelley's day, even women who evaded the economic pitfalls of refusing marriage were thought to be subject to this evacuation of psychic energy (and we should remember that Shelley herself never remarried). Shelley herself never took up the plight of the female artist in her stories, but her fellow contributor, L.E.L., did. Her "Stanzas on the Death of Mrs. Hemans" (1835) imagines the female writer as a diminishing commodity, wasted through her contributions to the literary marketplace.

> Ah! Dearly purchased is the gift,
>   The gift of song like thine;
> A fated doom is hers who stands
>   The priestess of the shrine.
> The crowd – they only see the crown,
>   They only hear the hymn; –
> They mark not that the cheek is pale,
>   And that the eye is dim.
>
>   . . .
>
> The charm that dwelt in songs of thine
>   My inmost spirit moved;
> And yet I feel as thou hadst been
>   Not half enough beloved.
> They say that thou wert faint, and worn
>   With suffering and with care;
> What music must have filled the soul
>   That had so much to spare![20]

Here, the aesthetic of mourning and the economics of artistic production are combined. The woman writer gives her spare energy to the literary market-place, draining herself in the process. In this context, "the abhorred shape of an empty purse" seems more than ever a figure for femininity. Its emptiness is both economic uselessness and a representational void.

By turning these representations of the tragedy of female commodification into commodities, the annuals both reinforce dominant ideas about female value and offer a tantalizing alternative to them. On the one hand, it is the very ephemerality of representations of women that made them profitable for the annuals, allowing them to offer up a new batch of images every year. Indeed, we might say Shelley herself, in writing stories for the annuals, was complicit in manufacturing the very obsolescence of femininity that she laments within the stories. On the other hand, the annuals offered some women the satisfaction and independence of writing for profit, the literary market creating an alternative form of value to the marriage market. Rather than disappearing, L.E.L., Felicia Hemans, and Mary Shelley herself all managed to support themselves as professional writers; moreover, a series of aristocratic women edited the *Keepsake*, while L.E.L. edited her own annual, *Fisher's Drawing-Room Scrapbook*, from 1832 until her death. In this context, women found a way to profit by obsolescence, rather than letting it bankrupt them. Thus Shelley's critiques of the way women's economic value is controlled by the marriage market arrive in a medium that helped construct another form of value within the domestic sphere: a medium that construed women not merely as marriageable bodies, but as readers and writers. If the images in the annuals offer a piece of femininity preserved in amber, the stories and poems within them undermine both that ideal of femininity, and that structure of economic value.

NOTES

1 Gregory O'Dea, "'Perhaps a Tale You'll Make it': Mary Shelley's Tales for *The Keepsake*," *ID* 62. There are also several excellent readings of the stories, most of which are cited below.
2 Miranda Seymour, *Mary Shelley* (London: John Murray, 2000), pp. 402, 338.
3 Judith Pascoe warns against equating Shelley's financial need with "aesthetic indifference," citing "a letter Betty T. Bennett dated to 1835, [in which] Mary Shelley copies her poem published in the 1831 *Keepsake* for Maria Gisborne, calling it 'the best thing [she] ever wrote'"; see "Poetry as Souvenir: Mary Shelley in the Annuals," *MST* 180.
4 Peter Manning, "Wordsworth in the *Keepsake*, 1829," in *Literature in the Marketplace: Nineteenth-Century British Publishing and Reading Practices*, eds. John O. Jordan and Robert L. Patten (Cambridge: Cambridge University Press, 1995), pp. 44–74, 55.
5 Mary Shelley to Maria Gisborne, June 11, 1835; quoted in Charles E. Robinson, "Introduction" to *CTS*, xiii–xiv.
6 Quoted in Manning, "Wordsworth in the *Keepsake*, 1829," p. 68.
7 Quoted in Glennis Stephenson, *Letitia Landon: The Woman Behind L.E.L.* (Manchester: Manchester University Press, 1995), p. 128.
8 *Monthly Repository*, n.s., 2 (1828), 845. Quoted in Manning, "Wordsworth in the *Keepsake*, 1829," p. 59.
9 Quoted in Stephenson, *Letitia Landon*, pp. 129, 129.
10 Terence Hoagwood and Kathryn Ledbetter, "L.E.L.'s Verses and the *Keepsake* for 1829," *Romantic Circles*. http://www.rc.umd.edu/editions/contemps/lel/toc.htm, p. 10.
11 On the objectification of women in the engravings, see Sonia Hofkosh, "Disfiguring Economies: Mary Shelley's Short Stories," *OMS* 206.
12 Andrea K. Henderson, *Romantic Identities: Varieties of Subjectivity, 1774–1830* (Cambridge: Cambridge University Press, 1996), p. 49.
13 A. A. Markley, "'The Truth in Masquerade': Cross-Dressing and Disguise in Mary Shelley's Short Stories," in *Mary Shelley's Fictions: From "Frankenstein" to "Falkner,"* ed. Michael Eberle-Sinatra (New York: St. Martin's Press, 2000), p. 119.
14 Betty T. Bennett brought this relationship to light in *Mary Diana Dods, A Gentleman and a Scholar* (New York: William Morrow, 1991; rev. edn., Baltimore: Johns Hopkins University Press, 1994).
15 Paul Cantor, "Mary Shelley and the Taming of the Byronic Hero: 'Transformation' and *The Deformed Transformed*," *OMS* 103.
16 Pascoe, "Poetry as Souvenir," *MST* 183.
17 *The Keepsake* (London: Hurst, Chance and Co., 1831), p. 205.

18 August 7, 1820. Quoted in Emily Sunstein, *Mary Shelley: Romance and Reality* (Boston: Little, Brown, 1989), p. 183.

19 Both Manning ("Wordsworth in the *Keepsake*, 1829," pp. 67–68) and Stephenson (*Letitia Landon*, p. 135) discuss the tension between aristocratic and bourgeois values in the annuals.

20 L.E.L., "Stanzas on the Death of Mrs. Hemans," first printed in the *New Monthly Magazine* 44 (May–August 1835), 286–88; see *Letitia Elizabeth Landon: Selected Writings*, eds. Jerome McGann and Daniel Reiss (Peterborough: Broadview Press, 1997), pp. 171, 172.

JUDITH PASCOE

Proserpine and *Midas*

When Mary Shelley set out in 1820 to transform Ovid's tale of an overreaching king into "A drama in two acts," she took liberties with Ovid's narrative, inverting the two main plot lines so that the story of Midas's disastrous wish (in Shelley's version: "Let all I touch be gold, most glorious gold!") follows the less well-known story of Midas's inopportune intervention in a competition between Apollo and Pan (*NSW* II 102). In Ovid's tale, Midas gets his wish to be a walking alchemist, learns the sad error of his ways, petitions Bacchus to be freed of his golden touch, and finally, after bungling across the piping competition of Apollo and Pan, acquires donkey ears as punishment for favoring the music of Pan. In Mary Shelley's drama, Midas earns his oversized ears early in Act I, and then makes his fateful wish as the act ends so that its dramatic realization must await Act II's curtain rise.

Mary Shelley meddles with Ovid's tale to excellent theatrical effect. The interlude between the two acts provides an opportunity for the stage to be transformed, for the quotidian earth tones of Midas's world to be transformed into a glittering spectacular tableau. When the actor playing Midas enters, a gold rose in his hand, his first soliloquy, with twenty declarations of the word "gold" in forty-four lines, creates a verbal simulacrum of the stage set's golden excess. Midas invokes, "a golden palace, / Surrounded by a wood of golden trees, / Which will bear golden fruits. – The very ground / My naked foot treads on is yellow gold, / Invaluable gold! my dress is gold! / Now I am great!" (*NSW* II 103–04). The reward for Shelley's manipulation of Ovid's story line is this transformation scene, a spectacle capable of drawing an audience's attention back to the stage.

In actual fact the gilded stage, the actor playing Midas, and the audience are all theoretical constructs since neither *Midas* nor its companion play *Proserpine* were ever staged. Nor is there evidence to show that Shelley made a serious attempt to attract the interest of a theater manager. Mary Shelley's surviving correspondence records two attempts to see *Midas* published in gift-book annuals. In December 1820, she offered the editor of the *Forget Me*

Not "a short mythological comic drama in verse" on the subject of Midas, and sixteen months later she sent the same play to Alaric Watts, editor of the *Literary Souvenir*, suggesting that it might also be of interest to his wife, who edited the *New Year's Gift and Juvenile Souvenir* (L II 161). "I may mention that this drama has been seen & liked by two or three good judges whose opinion emboldens me to send it to you," Shelley wrote to Watts (L II 161). A version of *Proserpine* was ultimately published in another annual, the 1832 *Winter's Wreath*.

Critics generally agree that *Midas* and *Proserpine* were never intended for a public stage. "Certainly written for the closet, not the stage," Julie Carlson asserts of these plays, a view seconded by Alan Richardson, who writes, "[L]yrical drama, or 'mental theater,' with its emphasis on character over plot, on reaction over action, and its turn away from the theater is the genre to which *Proserpine* and *Midas* certainly belong."[1] Vincent F. Petronella similarly suggests that the two verse dramas, "more accurately dramatic poetry, do not move beyond the confines of the closet."[2] Closet drama or mental theater are the terms critics use to describe the unstageable plays that proliferated during the Romantic period, seemingly as expressions of Romantic writers' vexed relationship to the actual theater.[3] To explain this oblique genre, theater historians contrast Romantic literary interest in the exploration of human emotion with the spectacular special effects favored by theater managers charged with filling newly enlarged theaters. After being destroyed by fires in the first decade of the nineteenth century, both the Drury Lane and the Covent Garden theater were rebuilt on a scale that considerably decreased theatrical intimacy. Mary Shelley wrote *Midas* and *Proserpine* at a moment when theater managers routinely resorted to theatrical gimmicks in order to lure large audiences. Actual horses stormed the stage in combat scenes, and a live elephant memorably trod the boards in at least one Christmas pantomime.[4] Shelley's contemporaries, however, did not all assume that an enlarged stage automatically undermined their dramatic projects. Joanna Baillie, in the 1812 address "To the Reader" in *A Series of Plays: In Which It Is Attempted to Delineate the Stronger Passions of the Mind. Each Passion Being the Subject of a Tragedy and a Comedy* (1798–1812), was careful to deny any automatic opposition between her plays' portrayal of heightened emotional states and the special effects employed in the theaters of her day:

> Did our ears and our eyes permit us to hear and see distinctly in a Theatre so large as to admit of chariots and horsemen, and all the "pomp and circumstance of war," I see no reason why we should reject them. They would give variety and an appearance of truth to the scenes of heroic Tragedy, that would very much heighten its effect.

Although Baillie discussed the ways in which a big theater conspired against the success of "legitimate Drama" – she noted the audience's inability to hear the actors' words and worries about the loss of "the finer and more pleasing traits of the acting" – she also acknowledged the legitimate appeal of even the more extravagant flourishes of stagecraft, and she was intent on seeing her own plays performed. Baillie accurately inventoried the ways in which changes in theater size and management decreased the likelihood that plays like hers would be staged, but she also appreciated the allure of "active, varied movements in the objects before us," of "striking contrasts of light and shadow," of "splendid decorations and magnificent scenery."

Baillie set out to inventory the entire range of human emotions, an ambition she believed was best realized in drama enacted on an actual stage. She writes, "A play but of small poetical merit, that is suited to strike and interest the spectator, to catch the attention of him who will not, and of him who cannot read, is a more valuable and useful production than one whose elegant and harmonious pages are admired in the libraries of the tasteful and refined."[5] Mary Shelley's sense of kinship with Baillie's project is demonstrated in her rewriting of Ovid's tales in ways that heighten the emotional content of the stories, that prolong suspense, and that allow for the theatrical realization of human transformation. Whether Shelley, inspired by Baillie's example, imagined her plays being performed on a public, as opposed to a closet or mental, stage, we cannot know with certainty. We should, however, respect these verse dramas' textual representation *as* plays, and, in so doing, recall Shelley's keen awareness of and engagement with dramatic practice.[6] Far from standing as anomalous works at the margins of Shelley's literary oeuvre, these verse dramas bring into focus her larger investment in Romantic theater. This chapter sets out to discuss *Midas* and *Proserpine* as stage adaptations of Ovid's tales, first recalling Shelley's preparation for writing the plays, and then proceeding to demonstrate the theatrical impetus behind her several acts of revision. Mary Shelley found in Proserpine's tortuous equilibrium, especially, a situation ripe for theatrical invention. Seized by Hades and carried off to the underworld, Proserpine eats of the fruit of the pomegranate and, by this action, ensures that she can never be fully restored to her frantic mother Ceres. Proserpine's story – along with that of Midas – allowed Mary Shelley to attempt the theatrical evocation of transformation and loss.

Mary Shelley, aspiring playwright

Shelley's plays have benefited from astute and appreciative editors and commentators, beginning with A. Koszul, who reprinted a short essay on "The

Necessity of a Belief in the Heathen Mythology" from Mary Shelley's journal as part of his 1922 edition of *Proserpine* and *Midas*, arguing in his introduction that they signaled a Romantic revival of interest in classical mythology. Subsequent critics have similarly focused on Shelley's transformations of classical mythology, reading the verse dramas as feminist interventions fueled by her fraught experience of motherhood. Susan Gubar, in "Mother, Maiden and the Marriage of Death," emphasizes Shelley's retelling of the Proserpine myth from a mother's point of view, while in Julie Carlson's reading of the plays, *Proserpine* and *Midas* share "a depiction of the mother as absent-presence that generates lives, stories, texts, but not tragedy." Marjean Purinton links Midas's greed, in Shelley's depiction, to that of Gilbert Imlay, whose business affairs motivated Mary Wollstonecraft's travels in Sweden; Purinton associates *Proserpine* with Wollstonecraft's feminism and gender-bending.[7] Given the events leading up to Shelley's writing of the verse dramas – the death of her infant Clara in 1819, swiftly followed by the death of the three-year-old William and the birth of Percy Florence in November of that year – the biographical and feminist bent of most of the critical literature on *Proserpine* and *Midas* is entirely reasonable, but it tends to slight the theatrical apprenticeship Shelley served in that same period.

Mary Shelley's absorption in drama, as both printed text and theatrical performance, is a constant of the peripatetic years leading up to the creation of *Proserpine* and *Midas*. The Shelleys' reading list, compiled by Paula Feldman and Diana Scott-Kilvert as part of their edition of Mary Shelley's journals, shows her immersed in a private Shakespeare tutorial in the years 1818 to 1819; she read nearly all of Shakespeare's plays, sometimes on her own, sometimes in tandem with her husband.[8] Her 1818 reading includes: *Richard III* from August 6 to 8, *Henry VIII* from August 10 to 11, *Troilus and Cressida* from August 17 to 18, *Measure for Measure* from September 2 to 14, *Cymbeline* from October 5 to 7, *The Tempest* on October 6, *Two Gentlemen of Verona* also on October 6, *A Winter's Tale* from October 8 to 10, *Timon of Athens* from October 10 to 11, *All's Well That Ends Well* on 12 October, and *Macbeth* on October 23 (*J* II 631–84). The Shelleys were avid theatergoers, attending operas, ballets, and plays both in London and in the Italian cities where they touched down during their travels. Biographer Emily Sunstein points to a broader immersion in drama and dramatic theory, describing how Shelley, at the urging of a husband who was convinced by *Frankenstein* that his wife had a gift for drama, carried out a two-year-course of reading that included essays on drama, along with the great English, French, Latin, and Italian plays.[9] Percy Shelley originally conceived of his drama *The Cenci* as a project for his wife. Mary Shelley recalled, "[H]e urged the subject to me as one fitted for a tragedy . . . This tragedy is the only one of his works that he communicated to me during its progress. We talked over the arrangement of the scenes together."[10] That Shelley would seek out his wife's advice for a work he specifically intended for the stage further testifies to his view of her as a promising playwright.

Charles E. Robinson's facsimile edition of the workbook in which Shelley inscribes her plays allows us to see the way she inscribed her theatrical intentions in her fair copies of the verse dramas.[11] On the first title page for the small exercise book, Shelley wrote "Mythological Dramas" on an otherwise blank page followed by the title page for *Proserpine*, which contains only this play's title followed by the phrase, "A Drama in Two Acts." The next page lists "Dramatis Personae." These three references, in the manuscript notebook's first three pages, to the dramatic nature of what follows, point to Shelley's textual positioning of these works as playscripts. If she conceived of the play primarily as a piece to be read, she would not have so exactly replicated the textual conventions of a playscript. Although she did not specify actual actors in her page devoted to the list of "Dramatis Personae," the segregated listing constructs the characters delineated as roles to be enacted. The plays' status as vehicles for embodied performance is reinforced by stage directions like the one Shelley provides for the scene in which Ceres and Proserpine are first reunited. Shelley writes parenthetically: "Ceres and her companions are ranged on one side in eager expectation; from the cave on the other, enter Proserpine, attended by various dark & gloomy shapes bearing torches; among which Ascalaphus. Ceres & Proserpine embrace; – her nymphs surround her" (*NSW* II 86). The directive positions characters at either side of a stage, describing aspects of a set (the cave), the characters' appearance (dark and gloomy shapes), and the props (torches), as well as providing acting cues. Shelley imagines actors performing the "eager expectation" of Ceres and her companions, as well as the embrace shared by Proserpine and Ceres.

Strikingly, Shelley rejects several opportunities for dazzling an audience inherent in Ovid's tale; one of the more striking of these bits of potential, but neglected, stage business involves Ascalaphus. In a passage of Ovid's tale excised from Shelley's *Proserpine*, Ceres is outraged to learn that Ascalaphus detected Proserpine's sampling of the pomegranate in Hades's underworld, and, by his broadcasting of this event, ensured that Proserpine would not be able to return to her mother. In Jacob Tonson's 1717 edition of *The Metamorphoses*, translated "by the most Eminent Hands," Ceres's reaction is described as follows:

> But now a Queen, She with Resentment heard,
> And chang'd the vile Informer to a Bird.
> In *Phlegeton's* black stream her Hand she dips

Sprinkles his Head, and wets his babbling Lips.
Soon on his Face, bedropt with Magick Dew,
A change appear'd, and gawdy Feathers grew.
A crooked Beak the Place of Nose supplies,
Rounder his Head, and larger are his Eyes.
His Arms and Body waste, but are supply'd
With yellow Pinions flagging on each Side.
His Nails go crooked, and are turn'd to Claws
And lazily along his heavy Wings he draws.
Ill-omen'd in his Form, th' unlucky Fowl,
Abhorr'd by Men, and call'd a Scrieching Owl.[12]

One might well ask why Shelley overlooked or consciously refused this the-atrical opportunity (and one might ask a similar question of other flashy scenes in Ovid's tale, such as Cyane's dissolve into a fountain, also left out of *Proserpine*). Baillie's dramatic practice provides an answer. Shelley, like Baillie, may have been more interested in drama's capacity to express human emotion than in its ability to dazzle an audience with startling visual effects.

The reference to Ascalaphus in Shelley's directive can help to explain how Shelley, like Baillie, could write with a stage in mind without feeling com-pelled to reproduce the visual extravagance of the contemporary theater. While Shelley eschews the showy transformation of Ascalaphus into a screech owl, she stages other scenes of transformation in which set design could serve to reflect visually a character's frame of mind. I began by noting how Shelley rewrites Midas's story so that its most spectacular twist – Midas's acquisition of a golden touch – occurs during the break between the two acts, so that the stage in Act II can be gilded to reflect Midas's brief but giddy realization of greedy desire. Similarly, in *Proserpine*, Shelley breaks her version of Ovid's tale between the two acts so that the curtain of Act II rises on Ceres's grief, visually echoed in a brown, wintry scene. As Ino reports:

How all is changed since that unhappy eve!
Ceres forever weeps, seeking her child,
And in her rage has struck the land with blight;
Trinacria mourns with her; – its fertile fields
Are dry and barren, and all little brooks
Struggling scarce creep within their altered banks;
The flowers that erst were wont with bended heads,
To gaze within the clear and glassy wave
Have died, unwatered by the failing stream. –
And yet their hue but mocks the deeper grief
Which is the fountain of these bitter tears.

(*NSW* II 83)

What distinguishes this scene from the rejected account of Ascalaphus's transformation is that the emphasis is on the portrayal of emotional extremity, rather than on shocking visual effects. A sere and desolate stage set, acting as a visual realization of Ceres's mental anguish, could rivet an audience's attention, but it would do so in the service of the play's emotional trajectory rather than as a means to startle, dazzle, or surprise for no thematic end.

In addition to using transformation scenes to convey dramatically the charged emotional status of her characters, Shelley also revises and expands upon Ovid's tales in order to compound suspense. Ovid's story of Proserpine straightforwardly portrays Hades's violent act of seizure. Shelley's play, by contrast, leaves both Proserpine's companions and the play's reader or spectator in a state of anxious uncertainty as to why Proserpine cannot be found. The opening scene of the play anticipates this ambiguous turn of events and heightens its tension in a number of ways. First, Ceres's departing words cast a pall over Proserpine and her attendant nymphs, warning:

> Depart not from each other; be thou circled
> By that fair guard, and then no earth-born Power
> Would tempt my wrath, and steal thee from their sight
> But wandering alone, by feint or force,
> You might be lost, and I might never know
> Thy hapless fate.   (NSW II 74)

Foreshadowed by these cautionary words, the tale Ino proceeds to narrate (in a lyric poem penned by Percy Bysshe Shelley) of Arethusa's abduction by Alpheus compounds the sense of foreboding. Arethusa, in Ino's tale, chillingly cries: "Oh, save me! oh, guide me! / And bid the deep hide me, / For he grasps me now by the hair!" (NSW II 77). Shelley's Proserpine is remarkably obtuse, thanking Ino for having "beguiled an hour" and referring to this storytelling session as a period of "ease and idleness" (NSW II 79), but anyone reading or watching the play is put in the position of an uneasy prognosticator, dreading the result of Proserpine's wandering. Just before Mary Shelley marks her exit, Proserpine plans to "pass that yawning cave and seek the spring / of Arethuse," an intention that only adds to the building sense of dread (NSW II 79).

The rest of Act I is dedicated to anxious speculations about Proserpine's disappearance. "I dread she may be lost," cries Ino, her anxiety multiplied by Eunoe's reminder of Ceres's imminent arrival (NSW II 80): "Why does my heart misgive? & scalding tears, / That should but mourn, now prophecy her loss?" cries Ino, just before Eunoe, who has exited the stage long enough to ask the Naiad of the brook for news of Proserpine, re-enters only to wail, "Alas, all hope is vanished!" (*NSW* II 81). As Act I closes, a frantic Ceres sets out to look for her daughter, with the audience or reader knowing little more than the pining mother does.

In Shelley's rewriting of Ovid's Midas tale there is a similar amplification of theatrical suspense, but this time for comic effect. In the conclusion of Ovid's tale, Midas's "Barber-Slave" whispers news of the king's embarrassing ears into a hole in the ground and, from this hole, a crop of trembling reeds arises to whisper this secret to the winds. Shelley turns a matter of a few concluding lines in Ovid's tale into a prolonged piece of comic business that heightens the audience's anxious anticipation of exactly when Midas's ears will be revealed. In Shelley's version, Midas's Prime Minister Zopyrion is the reluctant keeper of the king's secret, and he communicates in a soliloquy just how likely he is to burst into laughter and inadvertently reveal what he knows. Once Zopyrion's vulnerability is established, Shelley stages an extended dialogue in which Zopyrion, conversing with the courier Asphalion, repeatedly teeters on the edge of revelation. Asphalion enters just after Midas has sworn Zopyrion to silence; his first line – "Know you, Zopyrion – ?" – is interrupted by Zopyrion, eager to assume that Asphalion already knows the king's secret. "What you know it too?" Zopyrion blurts out, before realizing that Asphalion is referring to old Silenus rather than the king. By the time Zopyrion becomes aware of his mistake, he has given enough away to make Asphalion eager to know more, and this allows Shelley to tantalize the audience with Zopyrion's comic inability to stay mute: "I am choked!" Zopyrion declares, "I'd give full ten years of my life / To tell, to laugh – & yet I dare not speak" (*NSW* II 99). The barber on whom Zopyrion's character is based figures fleetingly in Ovid's tale, but Shelley dramatically exploits his comic flaw in her rewriting.

Despite the several ways in which Mary Shelley used theatrical strategies to convey her characters' emotions and to communicate dramatic suspense, one might look on the ultimate publication of *Proserpine* in a literary annual as a final severing of play from stage. But even as Shelley pared down that play (cutting 120 lines or one fifth of the play) in advance of its publication in the *Winter's Wreath*, she seems to have done so with a theatrical imperative still in mind. She eliminated some of the storytelling in the first act and rewrote lines in ways that enhance their dramatic intensity. In the most overt instance, she rewrites her earlier version of Ceres's departure scene. Whereas in the manuscript version, Proserpine bids her mother farewell and then immediately turns to her companions and bids them tell stories, in the *Winter's Wreath* version, Proserpine speaks these new lines:

. . . What unknown pain is this –
This heavy fear that weighs upon my heart?
Were I a mortal peasant girl, who ne'er
Had wandered from her natal cot, without
A parent's watchful eye to guard her step,
I could not feel more desolate and lone. . . [13]

This speech is far more self-dramatizing than the call for stories that it re-places. Even as Shelley was editing the play for a literary annual, she still focused on theatrical effect.

Mary Shelley, theatrical novelist

The verse dramas *Proserpine* and *Midas* may stand as Mary Shelley's closest approach to the stage, but her novels provide an additional demonstration of her dramatic gifts and her affinity for theatrical conventions. The characters in her novels often seem to be self-consciously performing even at their considerable remove from actual theaters. The long monologues of Victor and the creature in *Frankenstein*, and of Castruccio Castracani in *Valperga*, resemble the soliloquies that punctuate drama, in general, but especially the plays of Joanna Baillie. In Baillie's effort to communicate the emotional tor-ment of her tragic character De Monfort, for example, in the play of that same name, she periodically halts forward action in order to allow her hero to discourse at length on his febrile state of mind. Similarly, the shocking plot turns of *Frankenstein* – the murder of William, the conviction of Justine, the destruction of the female creature, the murder of Elizabeth – are interwoven with long talky passages in which Victor or the creature assay and explain their states of mind. And the frequent visual outlining of the creature, in window frames, for example, mimics the proscenium of a stage.

Vincent Petronella has explored features of Shelley's novels derived from Shakespeare's plays as well as from the "sometimes transmogrified Shake-speare found in the Romantic drama."[14] He claims that Shelley's novels, more so than her verse drama, exhibit a dramatic energy that is a direct re-sponse to the dramatic creations of others. The scene from *The Last Man*, in which the narrator Lionel Verney happens upon a performance of *Macbeth* by "the first actor of the age" while wandering the streets of a twenty-first century, plague-ridden London, creates a futuristic echo of Edmund Kean, the pre-eminent Romantic actor whom Mary Shelley saw perform in May of 1817.[15]

Besides borrowing from and alluding to the Shakespearean productions of her day, however, Mary Shelley peoples her novels with self-dramatizing characters, best demonstrated by the novella she wrote in the period of sustained theatrical absorption from which *Midas* and *Proserpine* emerged. Shelley wrote *Matilda* between November 9, 1819 and February 1820, making it the immediate precursor to the two verse dramas. The narrator Mathilda fashions a self from enacted versions of literary heroines, explaining, "I brought Rosalind and Miranda and the lady of [Milton's] Comus to life to be my Companions, or on my isle acted over their parts imagining myself to be in their situations" (*NSW* II 13). She consistently turns a spectator's eye on her own performances, noting, for example, "the fanciful nun-like dress" she dons for her escape from her guardian's house, as well as how the demeanor of a "youthful Hermitess dedicated to seclusion and whose bosom she must strive to keep free from all tumult" allows her to conceal "the wild, raving & most miserable Mathilda" (*NSW* II 44). Disappointed by her relationship with the poet Woodville, Mathilda describes herself as "a tragedy; a character that he comes to see act." "[N]ow and then," she continues, "he gives me my cue that I may make a speech more to his purpose . . . I am a farce and play to him; but to me this is all dreary reality" (*NSW* II 56).

That Mary Shelley's most self-consciously theatrical fictional heroine was created in the months leading up to her engagement in the writing of "verse dramas" provides further evidence that we should attend at least as carefully to these works' status as drama as we do to their working through of Shelley's fraught biography or to their feminist response to classical mythology. Shelley makes this connection explicit when Mathilda, describing the aftermath of her painful break with her father, recalls, "Often, when my wandering fancy brought by its various images now consolation and now aggravation of grief to my heart, I have compared myself to Proserpine who was gaily and heedlessly gathering flowers on the sweet plain of Enna, when the King of Hell snatched her away to the abodes of death and misery" (*NSW* II 19–20).

When Percy Bysshe Shelley, the advocate for Mary Shelley's playwriting efforts, penned the preface to *Frankenstein*, he suggested that his wife's choice of supernatural situations allowed for the "delineation of human passions more comprehensive and commanding than any which the ordinary relations of existing events can yield" (*F* Preface 5). In his reference to the delineation of human passions, he recalled, whether consciously or not, Joanna Baillie's *Plays on the Passions*, but he also anticipated Mary Shelley's next several creative projects, the self-dramatizing heroine of *Matilda* and the emotional drama of *Midas* and *Proserpine*. With these singular plays, Mary Shelley, the serious student of stagecraft, fulfilled a theatrical imperative that fuels most of her literary work, and she moved as close as she allowed herself to come to an actual stage.

NOTES

1 Julie Carlson, "Coming After: Shelley's *Proserpine*," *Texas Studies in Literature and Language* 41.4 (1999), 367; Alan Richardson, "*Proserpine* and *Midas*: Gender, Genre, and Mythic Revisionism in Mary Shelley's Dramas," *OMS* 125.

2 Vincent F. Petronella, "Mary Shelley, Shakespeare, and the Romantic Theatre," in *Jane Austen and Mary Shelley and Their Sisters*, ed. Laura Dabundo (Lanham, MD: University Press of America, 2000), p. 132.

3 Catherine B. Burroughs examines Romantic women writers' theater practice as a means to counter the too-automatic association of closet drama with antitheatricality; see *Closet Stages: Joanna Baillie and the Theater Theory of British Romantic Women Writers* (Philadelphia: University of Pennsylvania Press, 1997). For an overview of the Romantic theater, see Marilyn Gaull, *English Romanticism: The Human Context* (New York: Norton, 1988), pp. 81–105.

4 Frederick and Lise-Lone Marker, "Actors and Their Repertory," in *The Revels History of Drama in English*, eds. Clifford Leech and T.W. Craik, 8 vols. (London: Methuen, 1975), VI 110.

5 Joanna Baillie, *A Series of Plays: In Which It Is Attempted to Delineate the Stronger Passions of the Mind*, 3 vols. (1798–1812; reprint with an introduction by Donald H. Reiman, New York: Garland, 1977), III xvii, III xvi, I 65.

6 Jeffrey N. Cox credits Shelley with crafting "a mythological diptych that indites on stage the forces of oppression"; see "Staging Hope: Genre, Myth, and Ideology in the Dramas of the Hunt Circle," *Texas Studies in Language and Literature* 38 (Fall/Winter 1996), 256.

7 Susan Gubar, "Mother, Maiden and the Marriage of Death: Woman Writers and an Ancient Myth," *Women's Studies* 6 (1979), 301–15; Carlson, "Coming After: Shelley's *Proserpine*," p. 354; Marjean D. Purinton, "Polysexualities and Romantic Generations in Mary Shelley's Mythological Dramas *Midas* and *Proserpine*," *Women's Writing* 6.3 (1999), 385–411. See also Melanie Margaret Austin's "An Integral Relationship; Mary Shelley's Use of the Persephone Myth" (Ph. D. diss., Washington State University, 1996).

8 Stuart Curran surveys the thespian pursuits of the Shelleys' Pisan circle in "Shelleyan Drama," in *The Romantic Theatre: An International Symposium*, ed. Richard Allen Cave (Gerrards Cross: C. Smythe, 1986), pp. 62–66.

9 Emily W. Sunstein, *Mary Shelley: Romance and Reality* (Boston: Little, Brown, 1989), p. 138.

10 [Percy Bysshe] *Shelley: Poetical Works*, ed. Thomas Hutchinson (Oxford: Oxford University Press, 1968), p. 332.

11 Mary Shelley, *Mythological Dramas: "Proserpine" and "Midas,"* ed. Charles E. Robinson, vol. X, *The Bodleian Shelley Manuscripts*, gen. ed. Donald H. Reiman (New York: Garland, 1992).

12 *Ovid's Metamorphoses in Fifteen Books* (London: Jacob Tonson, 1717; rpt. AMS Press, 1980), pp. 167–68.

13 *Proserpine, The Winter's Wreath for 1832* (London: Whittaker, Treacher, and Arnot, n.d.), pp. 1–20.

14 Petronella, "Mary Shelley, Shakespeare, and the Romantic Theatre," p. 122.

15 *Ibid.*, p. 132.

3

PROFESSIONAL PERSONAE

12

SUSAN J. WOLFSON

Mary Shelley, editor

Readers "divided into two classes"

"I am to justify his ways; I am to make him beloved to all posterity," pledged Mary Shelley as her late husband's editor, aware that many thought her an unworthy mate.[1] She proved herself with considerable labor: *Posthumous Poems* in 1824; two editions of *Poetical Works* in 1839; a volume of essays, letters, translations, and fragments the next year; and across the 1830s, the development of a mainstream audience with the literary remains she placed in the *Keepsake*, one of the gift-book annuals. The 1839 *Works* was the canonizing event, the "first stone of a monument due to Shelley's genius, his sufferings, and his virtues" (*PW* I Preface xvi). This monument was, in no small part, a reconstruction: a plan to rationalize and mediate a poetry of "mystic subtlety" or "huntings after the obscure" (xiii), and a plea of "extenuation" for "whatever faults" the poet had (viii), especially atheism and sedition. In giving "the productions of a sublime genius to the world, with all the correctness possible" (vii), more was involved than redemptive service to the poet: justifying the poet's ways to man, the editor also meant to redeem her worth to him. Across her volumes, she emerges as a uniquely privileged mediator, the intimate who is the poet's ideal, best reader. For this office, she had ready resources: her intimacy with the poet from 1814 on, her literate sympathy for his poetry and, not the least, her possession of much of his unpublished work.

Shelley's self-fashioning into the poet's best reader is honed on a refinement of reading per se. The 1839 Preface parses the canon "into two classes." One, "purely imaginative," admits the "curious and metaphysical anatomy" of "passion and perception" in poems such as *The Witch of Atlas*, *Adonais* and *The Triumph of Life*; the second is more accessible, its appeal based on emotions "common to us all": "love"; "grief and despondency"; or "the sentiments inspired by natural objects" (*PW* I x).[2] To unfold this appeal, the editor deploys a series of afterwords, part commentary, part biography.[3]

One challenge for these narratives, on the cusp of the volatile 1840s, was to conjure the poet's warm sympathies without the heat of radical politics that, during his own lifetime, burned his reception to a crisp. The editor's chief tack is to write the political passions into sentimental narrative. In the winter that produced *The Revolt of Islam* (a lightning rod in its day for political attack), the poet "had a severe attack of ophthalmia, caught while visiting the poor cottages." "This minute and active sympathy with his fellow-creatures," she suggests, "gives a thousand-fold interest to his speculations, and stamps with reality his pleadings for the human race" (1 377). She calls readers to meet "Shelley" on these terms: "Those who have never experienced the workings of passion on general and unselfish subjects," advises her Preface, will not grasp his devotion to "political freedom"; nor will "the younger generation," who "cannot remember the scorn and hatred with which the partizans of reform were regarded some few years ago, nor the persecutions to which they were exposed" (1 viii–ix).

The rare purity of the political passions, proposes the inaugural *Note* of 1839 (on a poem admired by radicals, *Queen Mab*), is to be distinguished from mere worldly politicking:

> Shelley possessed a quality of mind which experience has shown me no other human being as participating, in more than a very slight degree: this was his *unworldliness*. The usual motives that rule men, prospects of present or future advantage, the rank and fortune of those around, the taunts and censures, or the praise of those who were hostile to him, had no influence whatever over his actions, and apparently none over his thoughts . . . His sympathy was excited by the misery with which the world is bursting. He witnessed the sufferings of the poor, and was aware of the evils of ignorance. He desired to induce every rich man to despoil himself of superfluity, and to create a brotherhood of property and service, and was ready to be the first to lay down the advantages of his birth. (*PW* 1 99, 100)

So, too, *The Cenci*, a controversial drama of patriarchal tyranny, incest-rape, and parricide: this was "urged on by intense sympathy with the sufferings of the human beings whose passions, so long cold in the tomb, he revived" (*PW* 11 274). "Shelley," as this kind of reviver of life from the tomb, is the ethical twin of Mary Shelley's tomb-raider, Victor Frankenstein.

In the perspective of these passions and compassions, the visionary poet and the political advocate are one. The poet who demurs on collaboration with Leigh Hunt and Lord Byron on *The Liberal* (a journal of politics and art) was acting "partly from pride, not wishing to have the air of acquiring readers for his poetry by associating it with the compositions of more popular writers," and partly from fear of being "shackled in the free expression of his opinions, if any friends were to be compromised" (*PW* IV 154). The nicety neatly dodges the taint of *The Liberal* without detracting from the poet's courage or faith to his friends. Shackle-shy Shelley is politically detoxified, a poet of ideas rather than incitement. The *Note on Queen Mab* likens him to "a spirit from another sphere, too delicately organised" for worldly contention (*PW* I 97), and the preface to *Essays* concludes with an image of the poet radically "unshackled," released by death from all that "hedged him in on earth" (*EL* I 19) – a narrative seeded in the 1824 Preface, which renders his death as a fated translation for one too refined for this world: "his unearthly and elevated nature is a pledge of the continuation of his being, although in an altered form. Rome received his ashes" (*PP* vii).

A more difficult task was to represent – to depict and to answer for – a poet willing to frustrate, even disdain, his readers. Admitting that "Shelley did not expect sympathy and approbation from the public" (*PW* IV 51), the editor spins a style resistant to popular favor into a sign of integrity: a writer is "always shackled" when he "endeavours to write down to the comprehension of those who could not understand or feel a highly imaginative style" (*PW* III 207). To both Shelleys, shackle-shyness not only entails but justifies elitist poetics. Some poems, Mary Shelley advises in the 1839 Preface, will serve "a taste shared by few," perhaps only "minds who have resemblance to his own" (*PW* I xii–xiii). Her preface to *Essays* elaborates this requirement in introducing *A Defence of Poetry*. Here is "a work whence a young poet, and one suffering from wrong or neglect, may learn to regard his pursuit and himself" under the aspect of "genius," cleansed of "the mire of the earth: It will elevate him into those pure regions" of "the holy brotherhood, whose vocation it is to divest life of its material grossness" (*PW* I 6). And even in this select company, the poet Shelley's superiority "in intellectual endowments and moral worth" will be apparent (*PW* III 163). If his editor stoops to explicate the allegory of *Prometheus Unbound*, she will not apologize for its "abstruse and imaginative theories": "[I]t requires a mind as subtle and penetrating as [Shelley's] own to understand the mystic meanings scattered throughout the poem. They elude the ordinary reader by their abstraction and delicacy of distinction" (*PW* II 135).

The production of the volumes, early and late, enforces this elite appeal. Printed on fine ribbed paper with wide margins and priced at 15 shillings, *Posthumous Poems* was not for the working classes who had enjoyed the cheap pirated editions of *Queen Mab*. Nor would they feel welcomed by foreign languages in the poet's titles, epigraphs, and notes (all untranslated).[4] The editor follows suit, quoting Greek in her 1839 Preface (*PW* I xii) and *Note on The Prometheus Unbound* (*PW* II 136–37), and Petrarch's *Rime sparse* in the prefaces of 1824 and 1839 and *Note on Poems of 1818* (*PW* III

164). That her quotation at the close of the 1839 Preface does not even cite Petrarch has the effect, and intention, of designating readers as cognoscenti:

Se al seguir son tarda,
Forse avverrà che'l bel nome gentile
Consacrerò con questa stanca penna.[5]

Petrarch's name at least is tagged to the tercet that appears on the title page of each of the four volumes of the first 1839 edition:

Lui non trov' io, ma suoi santi vestigi
Tutti rivolti alla superna strada
Veggio, lunge da'laghi averni e stigi – PETRARCA.

This is from *Rime* 306 ("Him I do not find, but his sacred footsteps / All turned to the highest road / I see, far from the avernian and stigian lakes"; Avernus, near Naples, was thought to lead to the underworld lakes). To bind the cognoscenti into a ritual consecration of the poet's divinity and his widow's devotion, Shelley follows her final *Note* of 1839 with a reprint of her 1824 Preface (*PW* IV 237–40), headed by the epigraph from Petrarch on the 1824 volume's title page:

In nobil sangue vita umile e queta,
Ed in alto intelletto un puró core;
Frutto senile in sul giovenil fiore,
E in aspetto pensoso anima lieta. – PETRARCA.

This is from *Rime* 215 ("In noble blood, humble and quiet life, / And in lofty intellect a pure heart; / The fruit of age in a youthful flower, / And in aspect thoughtful, soul light").[6]

If Mary Shelley's designations of elite readership contradict the narrative of a generous poet advanced in her prefaces and several notes, the effect is subtly purposeful, and it involves her regendering of the rhetorical positions and pronouns in her quotations of Petrarch's passionate addresses to his lost Laura. Speaking as the devoted mortal survivor of her lost love, the editor arrays a myth of spiritual devotion that is also an editorial allegory. Even as Petrarch authorizes himself in creating the poetic text of his "Laura," so editor Shelley authorizes herself as the textual producer/recreator of poet Shelley.

Constructing "Shelley"

The Petrarchan epigraphs hint at the material work of editorial devotion: gathering Percy Bysshe Shelley's *rime sparse* (scattered rimes) into a poetic corpus. Of the many designated "fragments" in the 1824 *Poems, Edinburgh Magazine* complained of a "very unfinished state": to gain access to "the workshop of Genius" is to see only "materials confused and heaped together, before they have received their last touches from the hand of the poet, and been arranged in their proper order."[7] As editor, Shelley took the risk of presenting the nascent stage as viable creative work. She introduced some fragments as principal poems (*The Triumph of Life*) and grouped others in a subsection titled "Fragments," convinced (she said later) that "broken and vague" as these are, such verses will be valued by "those who love Shelley's mind, and desire to trace its workings" (*PW* III 68–69).[8] "A mind so original, so delicately and beautifully moulded, as Shelley's," she contends, "would never be shattered and dispersed by the Creator"; "the qualities and consciousness that formed him, are . . . indestructible" (*EL* I 12). Yet the textual dispersion posed no small challenge. There were poems "scattered in periodical works" (1824 *PP* Preface vii) and then a chaos of manuscripts: "so confused a mass, interlined and broken into fragments," the editor later commented, "that the sense could only be deciphered and joined by guesses" (*PW* IV 226n). And other than *A Defence*, all the essays she put in shape for publication were "fragments of Shelley" (*EL* I 9–13).

When Matthew Arnold praised "Mrs. Shelley's representation" of 1839 for producing a "rare spirit – so mere a monster unto many,"[9] his terms evoke her other signature representation, also a tale of creation from fragments: *Frankenstein*. The "Author's Introduction" for the 1831 version might well be a description of her editorial labor: "perhaps the component parts of a creature might be manufactured, brought together, and endued with vital warmth." With Percy Shelley's living encouragement, this Author overcame the "mortifying negative" of "blank incapability" (*F* 1831, Intro 58–60) to create a tale in which another "author" of sorts, Frankenstein, "bestow[s] animation" at the climax of a studious "collecting and arranging" of his "materials," scraps and fragments of the dead (*F* 1831, iv 52).[10] These allied productions haunt about the shape of the 1839 Preface, which tells the story of creating a posthumous literary corpus.

By fragments and wholes, Mary Shelley produced "Percy Bysshe Shelley." She was the first to publish *Julian and Maddalo, The Triumph of Life, Letter to* [Maria Gisborne], *The Witch of Atlas, Swellfoot the Tyrant, Peter Bell the Third*, and "The Pine Forest" (later divided into "To Jane. The Invitation" and "To Jane. The Recollection"); the first to give *Queen Mab* a reputable imprint; the first to gather the essays, to publish *A Defence* and the fragments *On Life* and *On Love*. She designated a canon of principal works to precede the chronological ordering of the rest.[11] Her writing framed a life, her own "liveliest recollection" (*PW* I xvi) supplying to the poetry "the history of those productions, as they sprung, living and warm, from his heart and brain" (*PW* I vii) and enlivening the poet himself with tales of his "animated" social relations and "warm affection," of his "mind keenly alive" (*PW* I viii, xi). "These characteristics breathe throughout his poetry" (*PW* I ix), she insists, and grants them an afterlife: "his influence over mankind, though slow in growth, is fast augmenting" (*PW* I xv).

Shelley's work had such important consequences that Jack Stillinger, esteemed editor and critic, cites her editions as an instance of "multiple authorship."[12] Scholar Sylva Norman contends that any edition lacking Shelley's notes would look "truncated and outrage our sense of unity."[13] Shelley's integration of her work with her husband's effected a new and compelling composite. In her notes she represents her role as practical muse to the living poet. Convinced by the "surpassing excellence" of *The Cenci*, she urged her husband to try for greater "popularity, by adopting subjects that would more suit the popular taste" (*PW* IV 51):

> It was not only that I wished him to acquire popularity as redounding to his fame; but I believed that he would obtain a greater mastery over his own powers, and greater happiness in his mind, if public applause crowned his endeavours ... Even now I believe that I was in the right ... I had not the most distant wish that he should truckle in opinion, or submit his lofty aspirations for the human race to the low ambition and pride of the many, but, I felt sure, that if his poems were more addressed to the common feelings of men, his proper rank among the writers of the day would be acknowledged.
>
> (*PW* IV 51–52)

Here the editor shapes the unrealized poet; elsewhere she draws credit as the muse of realization. *Rosalind and Helen* and *Lines written among the Euganean Hills*, she reports in the Preface of 1839, "I found among his papers by chance; and with some difficulty urged him to complete" (*PW* I xi). The former first was "thrown aside – till I found it; and, at my request, it was completed," her note elaborates (*PW* III 159). "We talked over the arrangement of the scenes together," reports the *Note on the Cenci*; "I ... triumphed in the discovery of the new talent brought to light" (*PW* II 274). And she does not hesitate to congratulate the result: "The Fifth Act is a masterpiece. It is the finest thing he ever wrote, and may claim proud comparison not only with any contemporary, but preceding poet" (*PW* II 279). In this service, the wife may claim a comparison, too: the ideal partner of the sort the poet created for his hero Laon, "a woman such as he delighted to imagine – full of enthusiasm for the same objects" (*PW* I 376).

A crux for the widow was how to manage enthusiasm for those textual objects that might vex enthusiasm for the poet. Planning a volume of prose, she was bedeviled by *On the Devil and Devils*: "I have scratched out a few lines which might be <u>too shocking</u>," she reports to Leigh Hunt, then sighs, "yet I hate to <u>mutilate</u>" (October 6, 1839; *L* II 326). This is not personal caution, but a matter of reception:

> [C]onsider the fate of the book only – if this Essay is to preclude a number of readers who else would snatch at it – for so many of the religious particularly like Shelley – had I better defer the publication . . . Remember <u>I</u> do not enter into the question at all. It is <u>my</u> duty to publish everything of Shelley – but I want these two volumes to be popular – & would it be as well to <u>defer</u> this Essay?
> (October 6 and [?]9, 1839; *L* II 326)

She had decided as much the day before, telling publisher Edward Moxon to save it for a later edition, so as not to "excite a violent party spirit against the volumes which otherwise I believe will prove generally attractive" (October 8, 1839; *L* II 327); she never did publish it. A ghost from an earlier time (1813) was more of a problem: "<u>I</u> have a great love for Queen Mab," she assured Hunt, recalling that Shelley "was proud of it when I first knew him & it is associated with the bright young days of both of us" (December 14, 1838; *L* II 305); but she knew sparks would fly. Denounced by the Tory press and pirated by its radical champions, *Queen Mab* was a canonized favorite with radical workers' groups by the 1830s. The *Mab*-less *Posthumous Poems* (1824) had been issued by the Hunts, willing provokers of state prosecution. But it was now 1839 and Moxon was establishment, his list including a decidedly Tory Wordsworth. Moxon would allow *Mab* but only with the "too shocking & atheistical" sections cut. Shelley was torn. Insisting to an old friend, "I dont like mutilations – & would not leave out a word in favour of <u>liberty</u>," she wondered if the passages of "irreligion" and "disputing the existence of the Creator" were themselves a mutilation of the poem's merits (December 11, 1838; *L* II 301). She rehearsed her plight to Leigh Hunt the next day (*L* II 304), then wrote him two days later to argue that the poet himself would not have reprinted the problem passages (*L* II 305), even as she tested Moxon on printing "the whole <u>poem</u>" less the run of incendiary notes (December 12; *L* II 303), hoping that his prestige would deflect legal action. When Moxon refused, she set her *Note* (the first in the edition) to spin a logic: *Mab* was juvenile work that the poet had meant for coterie circulation only and "never intended to publish as it stands"; in a letter of June 1821 to *The Examiner* (which she prints), he reported taking legal action against the piracies, feeling these would misserve political aims with speculations that now seemed "crude" and "immature" (*PW* I 103–06).[14]

When her cuts were protested anyway, Shelley ably harnessed the heat.[15] "I have heard much praise" but also "regrets <u>from all parties</u> on account of the omissions in Q.M." she tells Moxon in March 1839, prodding him to do *Mab* whole for the new edition on the argument that "it would improve the sale" (*L* II 311).[16] The editor's postscript to the Preface was happy to advertise the "restored" text and thus "a complete collection of my husband's poetical works," the good news repeated in the first paragraph of her note to the poem (*PW* 2nd edn. xi 37). About the restorations, she had been vigilant. Noticing some of the poet's words dropped in proofs, she protested the "imperfect & mutilated" result (September 8, 1839; *L* II 324). No matter how controversial, she writes of another dicey piece, "the world has a right to the entire compositions of such a man" (*PW* 2nd edn. 191).[17]

These restorations, too, have an uncanny precedent in *Frankenstein*: "Since you have preserved my narration," Frankenstein says to Walton, "I would not that a mutilated one should go down to posterity"; he then "correct[s] and augment[s] [Walton's] notes," especially to give "life and spirit" to the record (*F* 1831, xxii 253). Shaping the text of P. B. Shelley for lively posterity, Mary Shelley felt a similar sense of proprietorship. In December 1838, she insists to Moxon that her production of *Posthumous Poems* gave her exclusive "copy right":

> The M.S. from which it was printed consisted of fragments of paper which in the hands of an indifferent person would never have been decyphered – the labour of putting it together was immense – the papers were in my possession & in no other person's (for the most part) the volume might be all my writing (except that I could not write it).

Thus editor M. S. claims "The M.S." as her creative and legal property: "a Posthumous publication must belong entirely to the editor, if the editor had a legal right to <poss> make use of the MS" (*L* II 300).[18] When Hunt offered some annotation, she thanked him but insisted that the labor "must rest on myself alone . . . The edition will be mine" (*L* II 305).

Reconstructing "Shelley"

When Hunt received *The Mask of Anarchy* in 1819 to publish in the wake of the Peterloo massacre, he backed off (indeed, waited until the Reform Bill year of 1832). A posthumous volume of Shelley was no easier sell in the England of 1823. The heat after *Mab* was fanned anew by polemical obituaries following the poet's drowning in July 1822. So it was with relief that Mary Shelley could report to Hunt in September 1823 that three "great admirers of our S—" had come forth to "risk" a venture (*L* I 384; 386n). Thus subvened, *Posthumous Poems* was issued the next June in a run of 500; by August over 300 had sold, with about a dozen reviews. Then the poet's father, Sir Timothy Shelley, with a care for the family name and honor, bought up and suppressed the remainder and required the widow not to bring Percy Bysshe Shelley's name before the public again during his lifetime (*L* I 444), lest he rescind his annuity for her and her son. No wonder that her penultimate note of 1839, with an echo of *Adonais*, anticipates a time when the poet's "calumniators" and "the poison breath of critics" will have "vanished into emptiness" and his "fame" be confirmed (*PW* IV 150). It was this poison, she suggests, that impelled the poetry into those abstruse idioms: "An exile, and strongly impressed with the feeling that the majority of his countrymen regarded him with sentiments of aversion, such as his own heart could experience towards none, he sheltered himself from such disgusting and painful thoughts in the calm retreats of poetry, and built up a world of his own" (*PW* II 139).

Her Preface of 1824 had begun this story, glossing the poet's retreats as a philosophical and ethical reorientation: "His life was spent in the contemplation of nature, in arduous study, or in acts of kindness and affection. He was an elegant scholar and a profound metaphysician" (*PP* iv). The poet's inspirations, especially for all those "purely imaginative" poems, get located not in abstruse, unorthodox ideas but in the embrace of nature:

> "Prometheus Unbound" was written among the deserted and flower-grown ruins of Rome, and when he made his home under the Pisan hills, their roofless recesses harboured him as he composed "The Witch of Atlas," "Adonais" and "Hellas" . . . At night, when the unclouded moon shone on the calm sea, he often went alone in his little shallop to the rocky caves that bordered it, and sitting beneath their shelter wrote "The Triumph of Life" . . . The beauty but strangeness of this lonely place, the refined pleasure which he felt in the companionship of a few selected friends, our entire sequestration from the rest of the world, all contributed. (*PP* v–vi)

These places, though remote, come bearing a familiar aesthetic genre – the picturesque. By this romance of description, the editor preempts charges of poetic obscurity by implying aesthetic truth: Shelley's poems keep faith with these strange and lonely places.

By these same lights, Percy Bysshe Shelley is returned to the kindness and affection of readers willing to count themselves among the "selected friends" to his rare values. The Editor's Preface celebrates his idealism over and against a hostile, uncaring world:

> his fearless enthusiasm in the cause, which he considered the most sacred upon earth, the improvement of the moral and physical state of mankind, was the chief reason why he, like other illustrious reformers, was pursued by hatred and calumny. No man was ever more devoted . . . The ungrateful world did not

feel his loss, and the gap it made seemed to close as quickly over his memory
as the murderous sea above his living frame.   (*PP* iii–iv)

With the double senses of "devoted" (dedicated, doomed), the editor sets an
unfeeling, ungrateful hegemony, no less murderous than the sea, over and
against a cult of visionary dedication: "To his friends his loss is irremediable:
the wise, the brave, the gentle, is gone for ever! He is to them as a bright
vision, whose radiant track, left behind in the memory, is worth all the
realities that society can afford" (*PP* iv). Mary Shelley's last volume, the
prose, grants Percy Bysshe Shelley the benefit of his own ideals: "'Gentle,
brave, and generous,' he describes the Poet in Alastor: such he was himself"
(*EL* I 19). The 1824 Preface gave a blueprint to the poet's champions. Hunt
quoted it liberally in *Lord Byron and Some of His Contemporaries* (1828),
and G. H. Lewes's influential review of the 1839 poems canonized its story:
against "another dark instance of the world's ingratitude," the poet displayed
"the obduracy and strength of a martyr; an angel-martyr, however, not a
fanatic."[19]

Meanwhile the first hagiographer was working in other ways to refurbish
angel Shelley for any house. She placed three of his poems (under the title
Fragments) and the essay *On Love* in the *Keepsake for MDCCCXXIX* – such
a coup for this already popular annual that it was bruited in the preface,
the editor happily "indebted to the kindness of the Author of Frankenstein"
for the event.[20] Readers warmly embraced *On Love*.[21] In this growing hos-
pitality, Shelley shaped her 1839 notes to add the appeal of the Victorian
sage: here is a poet with "two remarkable qualities of intellect – a brilliant
imagination and a logical exactness of reason" (*PW* III 374), "clear, logical,
and earnest, in supporting his own views; attentive, patient, and impartial,
while listening to those on the adverse side" (*PW* III 163). In the contours
of this mature character, the poet's radical politics could be assigned to the
century's passionate childhood and absorbed into an elegiac, or at least for-
giving, reading of that generation. The *Note on Poems of 1819* tactically
runs the political questions into a romance of the spirit of the age. With a republican's love of democracy and intense hatred of despotism, the poet was
roused to "indignation and compassion" by the "Manchester Massacre"
(Peterloo) at a peaceful demonstration of mill-workers:

> Inspired by these feelings, he wrote the Masque of Anarchy . . . for the people,
> and is therefore in a more popular tone than usual: portions strike as abrupt
> and unpolished . . . But the most touching passage is that which describes the
> blessed effects of liberty; they might make a patriot of any man whose heart
> was not wholly closed against his humbler fellow-creatures.

Shelley loved the People . . . He believed that a clash between the two classes of society was inevitable, and he eagerly ranged himself on the people's side. He had an idea of publishing a series of poems adapted expressly to commemorate their circumstances and wrongs – he wrote a few, but in those days of prosecution for libel they could not be printed. (*PW* III 205–07)

The time, in other words, was out of joint.[22] That the 1830s have "seen the rise and progress of reform" (*PW* II 344) allows a reform, even, of hostility to that problem child, *Queen Mab*:

[H]e loved truth with a martyr's love: he was ready to sacrifice station and fortune, and his dearest affections . . . he was too enthusiastic, and too full of hatred of all the ills he witnessed, not to scorn danger . . . He did not in his youth look forward to gradual improvement: nay, in those days of intolerance, now almost forgotten, it seemed as easy to look forward to the sort of millennium of freedom and brotherhood, which he thought the proper state of mankind, as to the present reign of moderation and improvement . . . In this spirit he composed QUEEN MAB. (*Note on Queen Mab, PW* I 99, 100, 101)

Here, politics are subsumed to rash, youthful romance and polished to a gleam of Christlike idealistic martyrdom first glanced in the Preface of 1824.

In other ways, the notes of 1839 play out the romance of that first influential preface. The editor recounts the poet's generosity to friends and family; domesticates him in the pleasures and pains, the anxieties and griefs of fatherhood; puts the visionary poet amid homes, haunts, jaunts, and the inspirations of the natural world: "It was on a beautiful summer evening, while wandering among the lanes, whose myrtle hedges were the bowers of the fire-flies, that we heard the carolling of the sky-lark, which inspired one of the most beautiful of his poems" (*PW* IV 50). Hunt was so charmed by this story that he published it verbatim (with credit to Mary Shelley) in his own note on the poem in *Imagination and Fancy* in 1844.[23] Such familiarizing frames particularly mattered to the poems that readers found too fanciful, abstract, incomprehensible, such as *Alastor* and *Prometheus Unbound*:

He visited some of the more magnificent scenes of Switzerland, and returned to England from Lucerne, by the Reuss and the Rhine. The river navigation enchanted him . . . he visited the source of the Thames, making the voyage in a wherry from Windsor to Crichlade. His beautiful stanzas in the churchyard of Lechlade were written on that occasion. "Alastor" was composed on his return. He spent his days under the oak shades of Windsor Great Park; and the magnificent woodland was a fitting study to inspire the various descriptions we find in the poem. (*Note on Alastor, PW* I 140–41)

> The house was cheerful and pleasant; a vine-trellised walk, a Pergola, as it is
> called in Italian, led from the hall door to a summer-house at the end of the
> garden, which Shelley made his study, and in which he began the Prometheus.
>
> (*Note on Poems Written in 1818, PW* III 160)

Humanizing the poet and domesticating some of his more extravagant or
transgressive works, these scenes also serve a Victorian taste for travelogue.
The poet's study in Italy

> looked out on wide prospect of fertile country, and commanded a view of
> the near sea. The storms that sometimes varied our day showed themselves
> most picturesquely as they were driven across the ocean; sometimes the
> dark lurid clouds dipped towards the waves, and became water-spouts,
> that churned up the waters beneath, as they were chased onward and scat-
> tered by the tempest . . . In this airy cell he wrote the principal part of the Cenci.
>
> (*PW* II 275–76)

This accumulating narrative shaped a reception for both poet and editor. Lewes praised the notes as "most interesting, sympathising, and
affectionate"[24] and was so impressed by the one on *Alastor* that he gave
it entire; where the editor designates the poem for "individual interest only"
(*PW* I 139), Lewes asserts "the generality" of its appeal. Even Arnold, who
viewed the poet as an "ineffectual angel," was charmed by the notes for
giving "the very picture of Shelley to be desired," the "soul of affection, of
'gentle and cordial goodness,' of eagerness and ardour for human happiness." Arnold not only excused the idealizing effect of memory and regret,
but proposed that the editor's intimacy with her subject licensed defenses
which otherwise could breed only "impatience and revolt."[25] W. M. Rossetti
declared the notes an authoritative source for any interest in the poet's life.

Reconstructing "Mary Shelley"

Even so, the sum of reaction was divided, the welter of conflicting voices
leaving Shelley with a sense of the radical privacy of her recollections and
their incommensurability with any coherent public reception, either of the
poet or his editor. Several of their friends berated the cuts and suppressions,
and some reviews were not as supportive as she had hoped, contradicting
one another in their complaints, grudging in praise.[26] In still other reviews,
she lamented to Hunt, her labors "met with no remark," and "like all else I
do, attracted no attention" (July 20, 1839; *L* II 318). Restoring the poet
was taking a toll on the editor: "publishing the book writing the notes
& receiving disagreable [*sic*] letters had so violent an effect on my health
that I really felt in danger of losing my senses," she tells Hunt (*L* II 318).

At work "editing Shelley's Poems, and writing notes for them," she wrote in her journal, "I am torn to pieces by memory. Would that all were mute in the grave!" (February 12, 1839; *J* II 559) – a self-fragmentation that not only belies her efforts to unify and revivify the poet's works but also returns her to an era of grief when her powers as author were tied utterly to Shelley's presence as her audience: "I write – at times that pleases me – tho' double sorrow comes when I feel that Shelley no longer reads & approves of what I write" (September 3, 1824; *J* II 482–83).

Yet it is as a reader and writer that Mary Shelley would recover a relationship. In the thrall of grief, the only correspondence she can imagine is a compatible death-in-life, her life entombed with his: "Now I am alone! Oh, how alone! . . . my thoughts are a sealed treasure, which I can confide to none" (October 2, 1822; *J* II 429). Or enacting forever the scene of his death: "I am a wreck – by [what] do the fragments cling together – why do they not part & be borne away by the tide to the boundless ocean where those are whom day & night I pray that I may rejoin" (September 3, 1824; *J* II 483). In her first editorial effort, she composes herself, the fragmented wreck of a life, by composing Shelley's remains. Her desire is "to live where I am now in the same house, in the same state" and to regenerate him, "collecting His manuscripts – writing his life," so as to join him before "joining him"; "Without that hope I could not study or write" (August 27, 1822; *L* I 252–53). When, just after his death she closes a letter to Maria Gisborne with a sigh, "Well here is my story – the last story I shall have to tell," she is already intuiting the Petrarchan scheme that will sustain her labor as his editor: she means to become "worthy to join him. Soon my weary pilgrimage will begin" (August 15, 1822; *L* I 250). She recovers her life in devotion to his: "I shall write his life – & thus occupy myself in the only manner from which I can derive consolation" (November 17, 1822; *L* I 444–45). Resuming her journal after his death, she animates him in writing: "Oh my beloved Shelley – It is not true that this heart was cold to thee. Tell me, for now you know all things – did I not in the deepest solitude of thought repeat [to] myself my good fortune in possessing you?" (October 2, 1822; *L* I 429–30).

By 1838 Mary Shelley was convinced that "the greatest happiness of woman was to be the wife or mother of a distinguished man" (*L* II 306), and her editions announce this office: "*The Poetical Works of Percy Bysshe Shelley. Edited by Mrs. Shelley*" reads the title page of each of the four volumes of 1839. In this linking of names, the affinity of privilege and privacy subtends a qualified editorial authority. "You know how I shrink from all <u>private</u> detail for the public," she reminds Maria Gisborne early in 1835, adding, "Shelley's letters are beautifully written, & every thing <u>private</u> could be omitted" (*L* II 221). Moreover, unspeakable privacy may double as a display of privileged privacy: "I abstain from any remark on the occurrences of his private life," the editor says of the poet in the Preface of 1839, hinting at a "truth" of which "no account . . . has even been given at all approaching reality in their details" (*PW* I vii).

This shimmer of what the public may witness second-hand but never know is the subtext of her final notes, which bend editorial commentary into the editor's autobiography of her premonitions and her lasting grief: "My task becomes inexpressibly painful as the year draws near that which sealed our earthly fate; and each poem and each event it records, has a real or mysterious connexion with the fatal catastrophe," she begins this finale in the *Note on Poems of 1821* (*PW* IV 149).[27] Here, inexpressible privacy is framed by a new textual event: bookending her *Note on Poems Written in 1822*, her last and longest note, are twin-themed poems by both Shelleys. The *Note* closes with a question cast to all readers of the uncanny: "who but will regard as a prophecy the last stanza of the 'Adonais?'" (*PW* IV 236). She then prints it. At the top of this farewell *Note*, untitled, unattributed, and inserted into the record of Shelley's *Poetical Works*, is a poem known from the *Keepsake for MDCCCXXXI*, there titled *A Dirge* and signed, "By the Author of 'Frankenstein.'" It is her own version of the last stanza of *Adonais*, its prophecy fulfilled:

> This morn thy gallant bark
>   Sailed on a sunny sea,
> 'Tis noon, and tempests dark
>   Have wrecked it on the lee.
>   Ah woe! Ah woe!
> By spirits of the deep
> Thou'rt cradled on the billow,
> To thy unwaking sleep.
>
> Thou sleep'st upon the shore
>   Beside the knelling surge,
> And sea-nymphs evermore
>   Shall sadly chant thy dirge.
>   They come! they come,
> The spirits of the deep,
> While near thy sea-weed pillow
> My lonely watch I keep.
>
> From far across the sea
>   I hear a loud lament,
> By echo's voice for thee,
>   From ocean's caverns sent.
>   O list! O list,

The spirits of the deep;
They raise a wail of sorrow,
While I for ever weep.
(*PW* IV 225)

Part of the rhetorical drama is the reader's tacit recognition of Mary Shelley as its author, indeed as a poet enacting Percy Shelley's most fundamental poetics: a call to a spirit not of this world. In her address to him, all along her muse, editor joins poet by speaking his part. Another part of the drama, however, is the voicing of a radically private grief, within which "the spirits of the deep" seem less a mythologized community of sympathy out there than figurings of Mary Shelley's own deep isolation. In this circuit, "O list!" tells readers of their exclusion, of having to recognize her privilege as Shelley's sole spiritual audience.

The arrangement of the final editorial project, the prose, replays this symbolic drama. The second volume opens with a reissue of the couple's youthful collaboration, *History of a Six Weeks' Tour*. While the editor says she includes it to recover its extraordinarily "beautiful descriptions" (Preface *EL* 1 15), she also recovers the couple's history in its high romantic phase, their legendary elopement to the Continent, now inscribed in the Percy Shelley canon.[28] Then follow sixty-seven *Letters from Italy*, the last one to "My dearest Mary." It closes with his promise to write to her, "my best Mary," again by the next post, and signs off,

Ever, dearest Mary,
Yours affectionately,
S.

By closing with this scriptive embrace, and not with the actual last letter "S." wrote (to Jane Williams), Mary Shelley exercises editorial privilege to claim her status, for herself and to the world, as the poet's most enabling and loving reader, his best, and last, audience while he lived.[29] She must have been pleased to read in *The Monthly Chronicle* (February 5, 1840) that these letters testified to her place in her husband's affections. George Gilfillan's 1847 essay on her for *Tait's Edinburgh* concludes with a confirmation that also credits her authorial importance: "Of one promised and anticipated task we must, ere we close, respectfully remind Mrs. Shelley; it is the life of her husband . . . No hand but hers can write it well . . . she alone, we believe, after all, fully understands him; she alone fully knows the particulars of his outer and inner history."[30] Shaping Shelley for public justification, Mary Shelley had redeemed herself, as the uniquely privileged authority of the poet's outer, and most especially, inner history.

NOTES

1 Thomas Jefferson Hogg, *The Life of Shelley*, ed. Humbert Wolfe, 2 vols. (London: Dent, 1933), I 5.
2 *Note on Alastor* proposes "individual interest only" (*PW* I 139), and only confirmed Shelleyans may embrace the satiric, "peculiar views" of *Peter Bell* and *Swellfoot the Tyrant*, both withheld from the first 1839 edition.
3 The 1839 *Poetical Works* had fourteen such notes in the first edition, fifteen in the second. Shelley innovated the practice of notes "mingled" with poems, or so she describes her plan to Leigh Hunt, hoping he would contribute some to the 1824 *Poems* (*L* I 393). Her practice was followed in the 1840s by both Wordsworth (in the "Fenwick" notes) and R. M. Milnes, in Keats's *Life, Letters and Literary Remains*.
4 Some of the foreign languages were dropped in the first 1839 edition; all were restored in the second.
5 *PW* I xvi; Petrarch *Rime sparse* 297: "if I am slow to follow, / Perhaps it will happen that her lovely noble name / I shall consecrate with this weary pen."
6 Mary Shelley recalls Petrarch's *Rime* 307 and 309 when she writes to an admirer of *Posthumous Poems*,

> I wish that the preface had (in the absence of Hunt's notice) been longer and better, but
>
> > Trovaimi all' opra via piu lento a frale
> > D'un picciol ramo cui gran fascio piega
> > Adunque
> > Beati gli occhi che lo vider vivo.
> > (*L* I 430)

7 *Edinburgh Magazine*, 2nd ser. 15 (July 1824), 15.
8 The second 1839 edition presents eighty-five pieces either titled "Fragment" or implying this status ("Cancelled Passage," "Cancelled Stanza," "Original Draft," "Variation," "Another Version").
9 Matthew Arnold, "Shelley," in *The Complete Prose Works*, ed. R. H. Super, 11 vols. (Ann Arbor: University of Michigan Press, 1960–77), 306.
10 All references are to the 1831 text of *Frankenstein*, the most proximate to Shelley's editorial labors; for Victor Frankenstein as "author," see *F* 1831, ix 137; x 147; xxiv 262. For further discussion linking Mary Shelley's editing to *Frankenstein*, see Mary Favret, "Mary Shelley's Sympathy and Irony: The Editor and Her Corpus," *OMS* 17–38, and P. D. Fleck, "Mary Shelley's Notes to Shelley's Poems and *Frankenstein*," *SiR* 6 (1967), 252.
11 The first section of *Posthumous Poems* introduced *Julian and Maddalo, The Witch of Atlas, Letter to* [Maria Gisborne], *The Triumph of Life, Fragments from an Unfinished Drama, Prince Athanase, Ode to Naples, Marianne's Dream; Mont Blanc* and *Alastor* were republished to win new readers (Preface vii). In the first 1839 edition the principal poems were *Queen Mab* (sanitized), *Alastor, The Revolt of Islam* (vol. I); *Prometheus Unbound, The Cenci, Hellas* (vol. II), with *Swellfoot* added to the second edition.
12 See Jack Stillinger, *Multiple Authorship and the Myth of Solitary Genius* (New York: Oxford University Press, 1991), p. 205. Although her emendations and

non-chronological ordering were criticized by later nineteenth-century editors, notably H. B. Forman, and although like most nineteenth-century efforts, hers have been superseded, her editions were a turning point in the reception of Percy Shelley and profoundly influential for later editors. W. M. Rossetti was the first of many editors to reprint her notes and prefaces; Thomas Hutchinson used her notes in his 1904 Oxford edition, reprinted several times, most recently, 1971. Acclaimed editor Donald H. Reiman cites her editions for "authoritative variant readings" and ascribes the faults to a "Golden Age of Editing" when the aim was not to establish texts with scholarly rigor but to present a record of a career for the general reader; see *Romantic Texts and Contexts* (Columbia: University of Missouri Press, 1987), p. 35. Newman Ivey White and Emily W. Sunstein both regard the notes as a critical event in redeeming the poet's reputation. See White, *Shelley*, 2 vols. (New York: Knopf, 1940), II 394; and Sunstein, *Mary Shelley: Romance and Reality* (Boston: Little, Brown, 1989), p. 345.

13 Cited in Kenneth Neill Cameron, *The Young Shelley: Genesis of a Radical* (New York: Macmillan, 1950), pp. 82–83.

14 Mary Shelley also cut the dedicatory verses to his first wife Harriet, who eloped with the poet, bore him two children, and committed suicide after he jilted her. The verses cut were the radical favorites from sections IV, VI, and VII, all denunciations of the tyranny and hypocrisy of Church and State.

15 *The Examiner* (February 3, 1839) cried "emasculation" and Friedrich Engels's contempt was plain: "the middle classes" read only "ruthlessly expurgated 'family' editions" catering to "the hypocritical moral standards of the bourgeoisie"; see *The Condition of the Working Class in England* (1845), trans. and eds. W. O. Henderson and W. H. Chaloner (Stanford, CA: Stanford University Press, 1958), p. 273.

16 Moxon's initial cautions were more prudent than prudish: prosecution was not impossible and a judgment of blasphemy could cost him his copyright (see *L* II 302 n3). When the second edition appeared, some radical publishers, eager to use him as a stalking horse for legal reform, forced his indictment and trial for blasphemous libel. He was convicted but not punished; see White, *Shelley*, II 167, 407–08; for an account of *Queen v. Moxon*, see Sylva Norman, *Flight of the Skylark: The Development of Shelley's Reputation* (Norman: Oklahoma University Press, 1954), pp. 149–53.

17 This is *Swellfoot*, a satire on the trial of Queen Caroline which, she notes, was "published anonymously; but stifled at the very dawn of its existence by the Society for the 'Suppression of Vice,' who threatened to prosecute it, if not immediately withdrawn" (*PW* 2nd edn., 191).

18 Responding to Moxon's offer of £200 for an edition of 2,000, Shelley offered the copyright for £500. Moxon agreed, paying installments as each of the four volumes of the first edition appeared in early 1839 (*L* II 300, 311, 313, 316).

19 See G. H. L[ewes], *The Westminster Review* 35 (1841), 304 and 307.

20 [Frederic Mansel Reynolds, ed.], *The Keepsake* (London: Hurst, Chance and Co., and Robert Jennings, 1829), p. iv.

21 *New Moral World*, the Owenite standard, reprinted *On Love* as admirable socialist doctrine (4.188 [June 2, 1838], 256; 5.27 [April 27, 1839], 423–24; 3rd ser. 3.3 [September 25, 1841], 99), as more mainstream journals such as *London Magazine*, *Monthly Review* and the *Athenæum* added their praise.

22 What is not said in this romance of a people's poet, thwarted only by state suppression and booksellers' fears, is that Regency England had an active libelous press, including the Hunts' *Examiner*, and that P. B. Shelley was averse to associating with anyone lower than Hunt. As elsewhere, Mary Shelley fronts an argument on poetic quality: these works are "not among the best" and Shelley "had meant to adorn the cause he loved with loftier poetry" (*PW* III 207).

23 Leigh Hunt, *Imagination and Fancy* (London: Smith, Elder, 1844), p. 273.

24 L[ewes], *Westminster Review*, 310, 324.

25 Arnold, "Shelley," 306.

26 She was stung by the notices in the *Examiner* (no longer edited by Hunt) and the *Spectator*. The *Examiner* not only hated the "emasculation" of *Mab* but found her notes affected, "cold and laboured," inadequate to the poetry; the *Spectator* accused her of partiality and then of crass trading on Shelley's name, publishing everything without discrimination, "the circumstance of her taste harmonizing with the weakest and most defective parts of his mind"; 12.252 (January 26, 1839), 88–89. See Norman, *Flight of the Skylark*, pp. 146–48; Betty T. Bennett, *L* II 333n; and Karsten Klejs Engelberg, *The Making of the Shelley Myth: An Annotated Bibliography of Criticism of Percy Bysshe Shelley, 1822–1860* (London: Mansell; Westport, CT: Meckler, 1988), pp. 251–69.

27 For a sharp reading of the narrative dimensions of these last two notes, and the semiotic of Shelley's dirge, see Favret, "Mary Shelley's Sympathy and Irony," pp. 32–34.

28 It also represents, once again, Mary Shelley as author: its opening pages refer to its characters as "the author, with her husband and friend" (*EL* II 11).

29 See *EL* II 356–60.

30 George Gilfillan, "Female Authors. – No. III. – Mrs. Shelley," *Tait's Edinburgh Magazine* ns 14 (1847), 854.

13

BETTY T. BENNETT

Mary Shelley's letters:
the public/private self

To date, some 1,307 of Mary Wollstonecraft Shelley's letters have been published, spanning the years from September 1814 until shortly before her death on February 1, 1851.[1] The letters are wide-ranging in subject – family, friends, politics, travel, literature, culture, publishing, finances, and issues of daily life – as would be expected of a cosmopolitan figure in a world in which letters provided a major means of communication. So, too, do Mary Shelley's correspondents vary, ranging from the remarkable Godwin–Shelley inner circle through friends and acquaintances, among whom were many eminent figures who influenced the history of the era, to strangers attracted to her family by their prominence.[2] But for Mary Shelley, the letter genre took on a purpose beyond the exchange of information. She, along with the other English Romantics, interpreted the political ideology of individual rights into a metaphoric literary ideology: so, too, whatever their differences, the Romantics depicted the world around them based on their perceptions of, and responses to, an era of political, scientific, and social revolution. As a result, through their choice of themes, diction, structure, and point of view, they matched their advocacy of political and social reform with an assault on what they viewed as entrenched literary conventions. Not surprisingly, Mary Shelley disrupted a number of conventions in her works, not the least making politics and power a central focus for a woman's writing. Stylistically, she redefined the notion of "mixed genres" from an amalgam of verse and prose to a prose style infused by lengthy poetic reflections, for which she was variously praised and faulted.[3] And in ways different from any other English Romantic author, Mary Shelley used the letter genre not only to bridge public and private concerns, but to link them in bold, original ways in her fiction, travelogues, memoirs, and editions.

Mary Shelley's antipathy to the separation of individual interests and public interests came naturally to the daughter of William Godwin and Mary Wollstonecraft. Their social status – Godwin excluded from public office as a Dissenter; Wollstonecraft, as a woman; and both, as writers, socially marginalized – had made "public" concerns very much personal.[4] Following her mother's example and contrary even to most Enlightenment philosophers, Mary Shelley includes women in the revolutionary concepts of individual worth and the capacity for self-determination. Going beyond rejecting gender barriers, she rejects the usual polarized positions the social code assigned to genders. In fictions as varied as *Frankenstein*, *Valperga*, and *The Last Man*, she advocates a more flexible model of gender, one that rescues women from being exclusively assigned to "domestic" roles. In these, and other works, Mary Shelley was among a relatively small number of women writers who published visions of women actively engaged in the public sphere.

Apprenticeship in the letter genre

Mary Shelley's tutorial in the personal letter began at an unusually early age. In the summer of 1800, Godwin left his daughter, almost three, and her half-sister, Fanny Imlay Godwin, six, to make a six-week visit to Ireland. In part, he went to discuss the custody of the little girls with Wollstonecraft's sisters, Everina Wollstonecraft and Eliza Bishop, who had expressed their wish to have both girls with them.[5] He left the children in the care of his ever-reliable friend, James Marshall. Godwin's letters to Marshall reported the progress of his journey, but also included direct and affectionate messages to his two daughters. Along with kisses, Godwin sent his daughters assignments that closely associated reading and writing skills with letter-writing.[6]

For example, on July 11 he wrote to Marshall, "I hope you have got Fanny a proper spelling-book. Have you examined her at all, and discovered what improvement she has made in her reading?" That same letter sent an apparently worried Mary (perhaps she had heard some talk of the Wollstonecraft sisters wanting the little girls) assurances that he "would never give her away, and she shall be nobody's little girl but papa's." On August 2, he sent a message for Marshall to read to Fanny: "I hope next summer, if I should ever again be obliged to leave them for a week or two, that I shall write long letters to Fanny in a fine print hand, and that Fanny will be able to read them to herself from one end to the other. That will be the summer 1801." On August 14, he wrote, "Perhaps I shall be on the sea in a ship, the very moment Marshall is reading this letter to you,"[7] pointing out that there were passages in Mrs. Barbauld's book, one he particularly recommended for children, about travel by ship. Though the children learned to read at home, in 1799 Godwin sent Fanny to a local day school, and two years later, he also sent Mary.[8] Beyond reading what others wrote, the children were expected to learn to write by writing letters. As Mary Shelley would note years later, William Godwin believed "any aspirant to authorship" should write much but publish little. From these exercises, the author could develop the "energy and force and eloquence" necessary for a subject "worthy of the author's genius."[9]

Much changed in the lives of the Godwin girls on December 21, 1801, when William Godwin married Mary Jane Clairmont, herself an author and translator of children's books, and the mother of Charles and Claire Clairmont, ages six and three.[10] To this variegated family, the couple added their only child together, William Godwin, Jr., born on March 28, 1803. But William Godwin's emphasis on education remained constant, pervading the lives of all the children in the household. When away from home, both parents used letters to communicate with the children, either directly or via separate messages within letters to each other. A July 9, 1805 letter from Ann Godwin, William Godwin's mother, provides some record of the Godwin girls' progress in letter writing. She marked "great improvement" in the latest letters she received from the eight-year-old Mary and eleven-year-old Fanny. In May 1808, when William Godwin was away, he reminded Mary Jane Godwin, "I shall be very happy to receive the children's letters,"[11] indicating that by then, letter-writing had become the family norm.

Mary Shelley's childhood letters, along with those of most of her siblings, remain unlocated.[12] But Godwin's letters and journals make clear that when his daughter was at Miss Petman's school for the children of Dissenters at Ramsgate between May 17 and December 19, 1811 for health as well as for education, the family correspondence continued. During the months Mary Jane Godwin and William Jr. remained with Mary at Ramsgate, her health and family finances were the main topics of the Godwins' letters. Though William Godwin sent Mary a message that he would not write directly to her while her stepmother was with her, his letters expressed his affection for her and for William, and his charming despair at the children's "criminal omission" of messages to their father.[13] Once Mary Jane Godwin returned home, William Godwin did write directly to his daughter, as indicated by journal entries of July 20, August 28, September 13, and October 2, 1811.

Family letters to Mary Godwin are more difficult to track between 1812 and 1814, when she was sent to live with the William Baxter family in Dundee, Scotland, for health reasons; during this period, Godwin corresponded directly with Baxter, a family friend, and also directly to Mary Godwin on August 31, 1812, December 11, 1813, and March 16, 1814. Though no record exists to confirm it, letters written in 1816 suggest that Mary Godwin maintained direct correspondence with Fanny Godwin.[14] And the earlier Godwin family pattern makes clear that while none of Mary Shelley's letters from this era have been located, she certainly corresponded with her family.

Since letters were a major source of otherwise unavailable news, adults often shared them with each other. The education of the Godwin–Clairmont children included sharing germane letters with the children as well. Family members often read letters aloud like stories, just as William Godwin had expected Marshall to read passages from his 1801 letters aloud to his daughters. In the same vein, William Godwin probably read aloud passages from Coleridge's letters in which the poet sent admiring comments from himself and from his young son Hartley to Mary Godwin in 1800–01.[15] As the Godwin–Clairmont children matured, they would be given letters from friends and family to read on their own. Among those were Percy Bysshe Shelley's 1812 letters of self-introduction to William Godwin, and those he sent subsequently, introducing the aspiring author and reformer to the entire Godwin family.[16] Following this pattern, Mary Shelley developed a lifelong habit of sharing letters within her circle, as well as a cautious awareness that letters that one did not want shared, might well be.

Godwin, with one eye to posterity, routinely copied his letters (or had family members copy them), filing them in what would become a vast family archive, along with letters from the wide spectrum of his correspondents.[17] Godwin's letters cover a range of philosophic and literary subjects, but he also wrote countless business letters, which include attempts to raise money for the Godwins' ever-faltering publishing firm of M. J. Godwin & Co.; arrangements with book-dealers; or requests to friends, among them Wordsworth, Mary and Charles Lamb, and Coleridge, to contribute to the firm's list of children's books.[18] Mary Shelley observed, and most likely performed (in a hand that strongly resembled her father's), this copying practice, which taught her to value the personal letter as a component of public history.[19]

Mary Shelley also learned in the Godwin household that letters, depending on their author, were in themselves historical artifacts. This view was in keeping with Godwin's belief that to understand the potential of "social man," one must gain knowledge of the "human heart" by understanding history through biography. One gathered knowledge of illustrious models from the details of family life, professional writing, letters, and journals.[20] Discussing "men of genius," Mary Shelley would voice a similar view: "As a help to the science of self-knowledge, and also as a continuance of it, they wish to study the minds of others, and particularly of those of the greatest merit."[21] So, too, would Mary Shelley follow William Godwin's lead in her appreciation for that paradigm of historical study through individual lives, Plutarch's *Parallel Lives*, which she drew on in *Frankenstein* and *The Last Man*, and on which she modeled her own biographical *Lives* (see chapter 15). Mary Shelley also read and often referred to collections of published letters. Among her early reading were the letters of Lady Mary Wortley Montagu (which she cited in *History of a Six Weeks' Tour* and in her story "Giovanni Villani"), as well as the letters of Gibbon and Burke.[22]

Mary Shelley also believed in using letters to tell the story of a writer's works and philosophy. Indeed, her own letters tell us a great deal about her professional career. For example, in letters that refer to *Frankenstein*, she asserts herself rather than Percy Bysshe Shelley as the novel's author to no less a reader than Walter Scott; she declares to Leigh Hunt that she has "written a book in <favor> defence of Polypheme – have I not?"; and in an 1823 letter, she speculates: "I own I have great respect for that faculty we carry about us called Mind – and I fear that no Frankenstein can so arrange the gases as to be able to make any combination of them produce thought or even life – However happy conjectures must always instruct even if they fail from entirely attaining their object."[23] But Mary Shelley had a far more unusual style of incorporating passages from her letters directly into her own works. Cultural and geographic descriptions, travel routes, her occasional outspoken political commentary, and most tellingly her letters of 1822 narrating Percy Bysshe Shelley's death, would obviously lend themselves to public use (*L* I 15: Aug. 1822). But a less obvious and significant source for her public writing resulted from her general style of letter-writing, which quite often reveals a historian's or literary researcher's habit of "note-taking." Just as for the most part she left clues to, rather than extended exposition of, remembered events in her journals (see chapter 15), she left herself and history similar clues in her letters through relatively brief allusions to important experiences. Still, she abhorred the idea of using letters or memories in the service of writing sensationalized posthumous biographies about famous friends or biographies that would cast shadows on the living. As she wrote on Thomas Medwin's biography of Byron, "Years ago 'When a man died the worms ate him.['] – Now a new set of worms feed on the carcase of the scandal that he leaves behind him & grow fat upon the world's love of tittle tattle – I will not be numbered among them."[24] In the 1840s, her own fear of scandal would prompt her to ask that letters pertaining to an attempted blackmail be burned (*L* III 312 and following; see chapter 16).

Unlike Percy Bysshe Shelley, who at times used letters as paper boats, Mary Shelley's view of the letter as valued artifact made her the Shelleys' archivist, as the vast Abinger Collection demonstrates.[25] Her sense of Percy Bysshe Shelley's literary significance inspired her, when she could, to make copies of his letters and, on some occasions, she, Claire Clairmont, or others also made copies of her own letters. Her fiction, travel works, and her 1839 editions of Percy Bysshe Shelley's works, demonstrate the great historical use she would make of family correspondence. Just as she asked correspondents of her husband (as she would later ask correspondents of her father and sometimes of her own) to return their letters, she also sent back letters Godwin received to the authors or their families (*L* II 274–77). But letters had become a commodity, sold on the open market and in defiance of property rights. It is no surprise that Mary Shelley and her son, Percy Florence Shelley, purchased family letters that came up for auction; on at least two occasions, several men used Percy Bysshe Shelley's and her own letters, legally her property, in attempts to extort money from her (*L* III 85–86, 245).

Among Mary Shelley's correspondence, she saved letters not only from the already famous but from lesser-known figures who at times have proven to be intriguing in themselves; two brief notes from Mary Diana Dods (alias David Lyndsay) and Walter Sholto Douglas stimulated the search that revealed a hidden transvestite charade and Mary Shelley's part in it.[26] These and her other letters to the famous and near-famous unfold the history of her era and her place in it, otherwise not found in traditional accounts. Incrementally, they give perspective on her advocacy of human rights, including her often discounted agenda for women's rights and equal rights. They offer contemporary data on expectations of women's use of language, women's networking, and women's insistence on their strong interest in the social and political issues of the day. Above all, the letters allow us unmediated access to her through her own words and actions, instead of confining us to the assessments of political and cultural historians, past and present.

Reshaping the personal/professional letter

By the nineteenth century, the epistolary novel was a well-established genre. Epistolary novels such as Samuel Richardson's *Pamela* and *Clarissa* certainly would have influenced Mary Shelley's appreciation and use of the literary letter.[27] But the epistolary works that most influenced Mary Shelley were those by her parents, who were among the first authors to modify the genre to reflect their reformist agendas. Godwin's *Caleb Williams* reshaped the epistolary novel into his protagonist's desperate testimony denouncing aristocratic tyranny.[28] Wollstonecraft's *Letters from Norway, Sweden, and Denmark* transposed the traditional travelogue into a proto-Romantic confession, exploring issues of gender, class, and politics as well as voicing private griefs. Furthermore, Wollstonecraft's use of the epistolary form in her novels, *Mary* and *Maria: or, The Wrongs of Woman*, also drew close together the predicaments of women and the disenfranchised. Raised within a family in which the political and the private were neither separate nor abstract spheres, Mary Shelley's professional writing would change the epistolary form as materially in her way as her parents had in theirs, for she would draw as confidently on letters and journals as she did on literature, history, biography, and other genres.

Like the other Romantics, Mary Shelley refracted the world through the prism of her own personal experience. She publicly advocated the Romantic author's "intrusion of self in a work of art," which through the "habit of self-analysation and display" resulted in books in which "the human heart" becomes "the undiscovered country."[29] As an extreme example of the individual perspective, Mary Shelley pointed out that Lord Byron, in *Beppo* and in his "private and familiar letters," relied only "on his own experiences" without offering "elaborate explanations." Nevertheless, he provided a remarkable view of the age because he was "one of the few strangers who was admitted, or would choose to be admitted, behind the scenes of that singular stage."[30] Mary Shelley advocated the same "intrusion of self" for historians, citing the model provided by Gibbon, "who, while he left the pages of his Decline and Fall unstained by any thing that is not applicable to the times of which he treated, has yet, through the medium of his Life and Letters, given a double interest to his history and opinions."[31] And as Mary Shelley noted in her review of Godwin's novel *Cloudesley*, letters, like personal experience, required selection and reshaping to transform their raw material into art: "Merely copying from our own hearts will no more form a first-rate work of art, than will the most exquisite representation of mountains, water, wood, and glorious clouds, form a good painting, if none of the rules of grouping or colouring are followed."[32]

Mary Shelley's own "intrusion of self in a work of art" is readily apparent in her first published work, *History of a Six Weeks' Tour*, in her use both of personal experience and political and social commentary drawn from the joint journal that mostly she, and to a lesser degree, Percy Bysshe Shelley, had kept of their 1814 elopement journey. Mary Shelley's epistolary format for a travel memoir was commonplace in the era; what was not common, however, was a narrative sidestepping sights and cities to explore instead the feelings, adventures, and misadventures of three young people as they wandered, seemingly without a careful itinerary, through war-torn Europe. In its completed form, *History of a Six Weeks' Tour* was truly a collaborative effort (see chapter 16). Mary Shelley wrote it and Percy Bysshe Shelley edited it, appending two of his own 1816 letters as well as his poem, *Mont Blanc*, and two 1816 letters by Mary Shelley (L 1 19). Into one of Mary Shelley's letters to Fanny Godwin, one of the Shelleys interpolated some passages from a letter by Percy Bysshe Shelley to Peacock.[33] Despite the fact that both Shelleys recognized the work as Mary Shelley's, she incorporated it into her 1839 edition of Percy Bysshe Shelley's works.

Though published earlier, *History of a Six Weeks' Tour* was written after Mary Shelley had completed *Frankenstein*, in which she first established the pattern of linking private and public letters that would characterize her professional writing. In *Frankenstein*, her use of letters as framing devices, interpolated documents, and testimony of questionable reliability suggests the unwitting interdependence, even the complicity, of her characters. Equally importantly, she modified the epistolary Gothic novel genre by linking scientific ambition and achievement to the contemporary social and political structures based on privilege and power, both personal and public, to illustrate metaphorically systemic irresponsibility. In *Frankenstein*, Mary Shelley incorporated not only her own political views but also observations from her own travels to the Continent and to Scotland; these observations provide the first instance in which she drew on the Shelleys' journal and letters as resources, a pattern she would continue throughout her career. But to multiply perspectives was not the only use she made of letters in her fiction. While *Frankenstein* and the 1819 novella *Matilda* are both epistolary novels, the latter uses the epistolary form to dramatize the heroine's desperate melancholy after surviving her father's incestuous passion and his suicidal death. In *The Last Man*, Mary Shelley complicates the idea of letters in a chiastic structure: while the Sibyl's scattered leaves represent prophetic, multilingual messages from the past to the present and the future, these leaves contain the testament to posterity of Lionel Verney, who, far in the future, unknowingly relates to us his ordeals (see chapter 7). For the last man, of course, there will *be* no posterity. In all these narratives, Mary Shelley also uses public and private exchanges of correspondence for plot and exposition. In her other novels, *Valperga*, *Perkin Warbeck*, *Lodore*, and *Falkner*, she dispensed with the single narrative perspective, instead building her stories from various points of view. As in *The Last Man*, her characters' letters about politics and love reveal, both in confession and in deception, how ultimately alike were public and private letters in their effect on society.

Immediately after Percy Bysshe Shelley's death, Mary Shelley began to gather his letters, prose, and poetry with the intention of publishing them as part of a biography of his life (*L* 1 252). Her decision to include the letters was not unusual by the standards of her day. But Percy Bysshe Shelley's controversial literary reputation and relatively small audience would have made such a publication quite unusual, and not of interest to most publishers. Thus, as Mary Shelley prepared the 1824 edition of *Posthumous Poems*, she decided to hold back Percy Bysshe Shelley's essays and letters, which she had been transcribing for inclusion. Her strategy was to attract the larger audience that had eluded him and that he so patently wanted during his lifetime by first publishing a selection of his poetry, and then following up with the essays and letters (see chapter 12). That plan was to be delayed for some fifteen years after 1824, when Mary Shelley acceded to her father-in-law's demand to suppress the remaining copies of the *Posthumous Poems* and not bring the Shelley name into the public arena during his lifetime. In exchange, she received a repayable allowance for her son's and her own support.[34] Given Sir Timothy Shelley's poor health, Mary Shelley believed the delay would be of short duration. But in 1835, with Sir Timothy Shelley still very much alive, Mary Shelley was once more engaged in the project of arranging Percy Bysshe Shelley's letters and works for publication. The publisher Edward Moxon offered her £600 for an edition of Percy Bysshe Shelley's works, presumably with an introductory memoir. Though Mary Shelley understood that her father-in-law would never agree to anything approaching an extended biographical notice, she intended to compensate for that absence in part by including Percy Bysshe Shelley's letters. In anticipation, she again began the process of collecting letters to copy, beginning with those to Maria and John Gisborne (*L* II 220). When Sir Timothy Shelley granted permission in 1838 to publish the edition without a biography, she also contacted Hunt for six of Percy Bysshe Shelley's letters that he had included, with "a few asterisks & omissions," in his 1828 *Lord Byron and Some of His Contemporaries*. She was anxious to include the entirety of those letters; Hunt responded that he could no longer locate them.[35]

During this same period, Mary Shelley was also engaged in editing another set of family letters. Following William Godwin's death in April 1836, Mary Jane Godwin, his widow, signed a contract with the publisher Henry Colburn. She was to receive 350 guineas for the publication of 1,000 copies of Godwin's "Personal Memoirs and Correspondence," but the contract stipulated that Mary Shelley would be the editor of the two-volume edition, with sole discretion as to the contents.[36] Though the Godwin biography was left incomplete, Mary Shelley's letters indicate how actively she corresponded with Godwin's friends in her effort to collect his letters, at times in return for his correspondents' letters (see chapter 15).[37]

Mary Shelley's commitment to publish Percy Bysshe Shelley's and Godwin's letters reflect her awareness that in addition to facts they reveal about lives, letters also were significant in dramatizing interactions between correspondents and in detailing their reflections on their own – and one another's – lives. The letters of Godwin and Percy Bysshe Shelley also often serve as an exterior gauge of progress on a project, efforts to publish, joys, ambitions, and frustrations, about individual works and the writing life in general. At the same time, Mary Shelley was aware that letters offer insights into the mind of an author, both conscious and unconscious, an idea she

spelled out in an introductory "Note on the Revolt of Islam" in her 1839
edition of Percy Bysshe Shelley's *Poetical Works:*

> I extract a portion of a letter written in answer to one of these friends; it best
> details the impulses of Shelley's mind and his motives; it was written with
> entire unreserve; and is therefore a precious monument of his own opinion of
> his powers, of the purity of his designs, and the ardour with which he clung, in
> adversity and through the valley of the shadow of death, to views from which
> he believed the permanent happiness of mankind must eventually spring.[38]

Mary Shelley's final book, *Rambles in Germany and Italy in 1840, 1842,
and 1843* (1844), based on her travels with Percy Florence Shelley and his
friends, like the *History of a Six Weeks' Tour*, was written in the epistolary
mode. For *Rambles*, she gathered and drew on letters written to a number
of correspondents during those travels, along with some written by her son
and his friends (*L* III 100); though she kept no journal, she did maintain
records reflecting costs of travel, hotels, and miscellaneous items. *Rambles*
clearly demonstrates how readily she adapted those private letters into her
"public letters." The letters in *Rambles* include her political convictions and
her philosophical reflections on her experiences of the world around her in
historic context.

Mary Shelley also treats brief phrases in her personal travel letters, as
she had done with letters and journals while writing the *History of a Six
Weeks' Tour*, as reminders for her public letters. For example, her letters
only fleetingly commented that Venice had made her "Melancholy," and
that Rome, "a place full of melancholy at once & delight to me," was made
more difficult when at Percy Florence Shelley's wish they took rooms at 64
Via Sistina, in the same house her friend, the artist Amelia Curran, occupied
in 1819 and next door to where William Shelley died at 65 Via Sistina.[39] For
publication in *Rambles*, Mary Shelley considerably expands these reflections,
beginning with "Letter One," in which she openly invokes her personal life
with Percy Bysshe Shelley, establishing a continuum between that past and
the present:

> Can it, indeed, be true, that I am about to revisit Italy? How many years are
> gone since I quitted that country! There I left the mortal remains of those
> beloved – my husband and my children, whose loss changed my whole exis-
> tence, substituting, for happy peace and the interchange of deep-rooted affec-
> tions, years of desolate solitude, and a hard struggle with the world; which
> only now, as my son is growing up, is brightening into a better day. (*NSW* VIII
> 75–76)

In the same way, the 1843 journey on the Brenta to Venice recalls the Shelleys' harrowing 1818 journey from Este to Venice in their futile effort to save the life of their dying one-year-old daughter, Clara:

> Death hovered over the scene. Gathered into myself, with my "mind's eye" I saw those before me long departed; and I was agitated again by emotions – by passions – and those the deepest a woman's heart can harbour – a dread to see her child even at that instant expire – which then occupied me. It is a strange, but to any person who has suffered, a familiar circumstance, that those who are enduring mental or corporeal agony are strangely alive to immediate external objects, and their imagination even exercises its wild power over them . . . the peculiar flickering of trees – the exact succession of objects on a journey – have been indelibly engraved in my memory, as marked in, and associated with, hours and minutes when the nerves were strung to their utmost tension by the endurance of pain, or the far severer infliction of mental anguish. Thus the banks of the Brenta presented to me a moving scene; not a palace, not a tree of which I did not recognise, as marked and recorded, at a moment when life and death hung upon our speedy arrival at Venice. (*NSW* VIII 269–70)

Mary Shelley's gleanings from her letters, in which traumatic events were "marked and recorded" for her professional writing, illustrates a pattern through which she translated personally significant experiences into life-long literary symbols. An arresting example of this intertextuality occurs in Mary Shelley's many references to the *assiolo*, the small, downy owl that the Shelleys became familiar with in Italy, and which most readers of the Romantics associate with Percy Bysshe Shelley's poem "The Aziola." This poem was first published in the *Keepsake* for 1829, contributed by Mary Shelley, represented in the poem as hearing the bird first and pointing it out to Percy Bysshe Shelley. He assumes it is "some tedious woman," whose distant cry directly threatens him with derision. Mary Shelley's laughing response, perhaps itself tinged with a hint of the very mockery he suspected in the distant voice, rescues Percy Bysshe Shelley from fear, but not from his self-absorption. In the second stanza, he transforms the bird's cry into something unearthly, "nor voice, nor lute, nor wind, nor bird, / The soul ever stirr'd." The cry that first frightened him he now describes as "far sweeter" than earthly sounds. Rather than the sound of ridicule, he now attributes to it a sadness, and it is that sadness that leads him to love it, along with its "sad cry." Rather than objectify the bird, Percy Bysshe Shelley uses it, as he does his other subjects, to symbolize his own feelings.

For Mary Shelley, however, the *assiolo* brings not threats, but assurances of natural continuities. In "The Sisters of Albano," also published in the *Keepsake*, she celebrates the owl and its place in nature:

The spring had nearly grown into summer, the trees were all in full but fresh green foliage, the vine-dresser was singing, perched among them, training his vines; the cicala had not yet begun her song, the heats therefore had not commenced; but at evening the fireflies gleamed among the hills, and the cooing aziola assured us of what in that country needs no assurance, fine weather for the morrow.   (*CTS* 51)

Similarly, in the "Note on the Poems of 1821" in her 1839 edition of the *Poems of Percy Bysshe Shelley*, the bird "cooed in the quiet evening." In fact, a letter written fifteen years earlier (July 29 [1824]) from England to Leigh Hunt in Italy prefigures this note: "I wish we could change places – I should not wish for better than the chestnut covered hills & olive groves of Maiano – glowing sunsets, fire flies – the cry of the aziolo" (*L* I 441). On June 27, 1825, again to Hunt, she wrote: "So you are about to bid adieu to fireflies – azioli – the Tuscan peasantry & Tuscan vines!" (*L* I 492).

Mary Shelley also used the *assiolo* as a symbol of the beauties of nature and Italy in a number of her "public" writings. In her poem *The Choice* (July 1823), memorializing Percy Bysshe Shelley, she writes:

> The Serchio's stream upon whose banks he stood –
> The pools reflecting Pisa's old pine wood,
> The fire:flies['] beam – the aziolo's cry –
> All breath[e] his spirit, which shall never die. –
> Such memories have linked these hills & caves,
> These woodland paths, & streams – & knelling waves
> Fast to each sad pulsation of my breast
> And made their melancholy arms the haven of my rest[.]
>   (*LL* IV 126–27)

A talisman of her pleasure in the Italian landscape, the *assiolo* is mentioned twice in her 1823 novel *Valperga*, again in *The Last Man* (1826), and in her last novel, *Falkner*, where she once again places the owl in an idyllic, sensuous landscape: "It is night; the cooing aziolo, the hooting owl, the flashing fire-fly – the murmur of time-honoured streams; the moonlit foliage of the grey olive woods – dark crags and rugged mountains, throwing awful shadows – and the light of the eternal stars; such are the objects around me" (*NSW* II ix 154). Thus, while the *assiolo* serves as an example of the couple's mutual influence, their particular contextualizations of the owl more importantly suggest the profound differences in their philosophic perspectives. Where Percy Bysshe Shelley translates the owl's voice into something "sweeter" than "voice . . . lute . . . wind . . . bird" but inexorably sad, Mary Shelley embraces the owl's existence together with its voice as illuminations of the wonder and the potential of the world.

In recent years, a number of critics have been reviewing and analyzing women's "private" letters, seeking in those letters authentic women's voices of their era.[40] Mary Shelley's letters, in their assertiveness, practicalities, human insights, and confessional directness, leave no doubt of their writer's authentic voice. But more than this, Mary Shelley's remarkable intersection of private letters with professional writing provides a unique synthesis of political ideals, personal experience, and literary gifts.

NOTES

1 Some 1,276 letters are collected in the three volumes of *L*. Twenty-four more letters appear in Betty T. Bennett, "Newly Uncovered Letters and Poems by Mary Wollstonecraft Shelley," *KSJ* 46 (1997), 51–74; six more in Betty T. Bennett, "The Science of Letters," *KSJ* 50 (2001), 27–34; and one in Nicholas A. Joukovsky, "Mary Shelley's Last Letter?" *Notes & Queries* 242 (September 1997), 338.

2 See Introductions in *L* and *Selected Letters of Mary Wollstonecraft Shelley*, ed. Betty T. Bennett (Baltimore: Johns Hopkins University Press, 1995).

3 See, for example, *The Panoramic Miscellany; or, Monthly Magazine and Review of Literature*, March 31, 1826, 386, which complains that in *The Last Man*, Mary Shelley's writing is not imaginative enough for poetry but too "fanciful for prose"; in contrast, in its review of *Lodore*, the *Athenaeum*, March 28, 1835, 239, praises Mary Shelley for throwing "the poetry of her own spirit over her story."

4 William Godwin's religious heritage barred Dissenters from participating in government and in attending the elite public schools and universities, where education at times played a secondary role to networking.

5 [C.] Kegan Paul, *William Godwin: His Friends and Contemporaries*, 2 vols. (London: Henry S. King, 1876), I 363–74.

6 His tour included visiting Mary Wollstonecraft's sisters, Everina Wollstonecraft and Elizabeth Bishop. See *ibid.*, I 364, 373.

7 *Ibid.*, I 370, I 373.

8 On February 28 and March 3, a "school-dame" called at the Polygon, the first time with William Godwin's sister, Hannah Godwin, who may have introduced the teacher to her brother as she had introduced him to Louisa Jones. Dates established by William Godwin's journal. Lady Mountcashel to William Godwin: Abinger Collection Dep. C. 507, August 6, 1801: William Godwin sends his "little girl of four years old to school." The Abinger Collection is in the Bodleian Library, Oxford.

9 *Collected Novels and Memoirs of William Godwin*, ed. Pamela Clemit, 2 vols. (London: William Pickering, 1992), II ix.

10 Charles Clairmont, born June 4, 1795; Claire Clairmont, born April 27, 1798.

11 Paul, *William Godwin*, II 136, II 172: May 8, 1808.

12 A few letters from Charles Clairmont and William Godwin, Jr. are extant, and are in the Abinger Collection.

13 Paul, *William Godwin*, II 184.

14 For her first visit to Dundee, Mary Godwin left London on June 7, 1812 and returned on November 10, 1812. She left for her second visit on June 3, 1813 and returned on March 30, 1814.

15 See, for example, *Collected Letters of Samuel Taylor Coleridge*, ed. Earl Leslie Griggs, 6 vols. (Oxford: Oxford University Press, 1956), I 580, 588.

16 William Godwin to Percy Bysshe Shelley, March 14, 1812: Abinger Collection Dep. C. 524.

17 In addition to hand-copied letters, many of Godwin's letters were duplicated as he wrote them onto translucent paper by a letter-press machine, which his friend Thomas Wedgwood gave him in 1795. See *LL* IV 58, 98.

18 See William St. Clair, *The Godwins and the Shelleys* (New York: Norton, 1989), pp. 279–314.

19 An example of her knowledge of William Godwin's copies occurs in 1843, after Mary Jane Godwin's death. In an effort to retrieve some of Godwin's letters from Claire Clairmont that Mary Jane Godwin had held back from Mary Shelley, she told Claire Clairmont that though Mary Jane Godwin had given her "early letters of Shelleys," she had kept Percy Bysshe Shelley's and her "fathers (& I know he kept copies)" written in the summer of 1814; see *L* III 102–03.

20 William Godwin, "Essay of History and Romance," in *Political and Philosophical Writings of William Godwin*, gen. ed. Mark Philp (London: Pickering, 1993); vol. V, *Educational and Literary Writings*, ed. Pamela Clemit, 293–94; see also "Account of the Seminary," V 18.

21 Mary Shelley, "Giovanni Villani," *NSW* II 128–29.

22 Mary Shelley apparently read an edition of *The Complete Letters of Lady Mary Wortley Montagu* prior to 1814, as there is no record of it in her journal reading. See *NSW* VIII 38; *NSW* II 131.

23 TO [SIR WALTER SCOTT], Bagni di Lucca June 14, 1818; TO LEIGH HUNT, Rome, Tuesday – April 6, 1819; TO SIR RICHARD PHILLIPS, Friday November 14 [1823].

24 *L* I 453: October 10, 1824. *As You Like It* IV i 110: "Men have died from time to time, and worms have eaten them." Mary Shelley quotes this line in the same context in her letter of November 10, 1824 to John Cam Hobhouse, *L* I 455–56.

25 Kenneth Neill Cameron and Donald H. Reiman, eds. *Shelley and his Circle, 1773–1822*, 6 vols. (Cambridge, MA: Harvard University Press, 1961–71), IV 558; Thomas Love Peacock, *Memoirs of Shelley*, in *The Life of Percy Bysshe Shelley* (London: J. M. Dent, 1933), II 339.

26 See Betty T. Bennett, *Mary Diana Dods: A Gentleman and a Scholar* (New York: William Morrow, 1991; reprint, Baltimore: Johns Hopkins University Press, 1994).

27 Mary Shelley read Richardson's *Pamela* in 1814 and again in 1819; Richardson's *Clarissa* in 1814 and again in 1819 (*J*).

28 William Godwin's 1784 epistolary novel, *Italian Letters: or, The History of the Count de St. Julian*, according to Mary Shelley,

> was a traditional romance; a novel in two small volumes written in three weeks & find no story – no development of character & situation – scarcely any of that anatomy of heart for which the imaginative writings of Mr. Godwin is conspicuous. Occasional energy/of style – and a strong admiration of the higher & more stoical virtues, are the only characteristics.
>
> (Abinger Collection Dep. C. 606/1, fos. 98–99)

29 Mary Shelley, "Giovanni Villani," *NSW* II 129–39.

30 In Mary Shelley's review of James Fenimore Cooper, *The Bravo, NSW* II 220.
31 Mary Shelley, "Giovanni Villani," *NSW* II 131.
32 *NSW* II 203.
33 For a discussion of the original letter and the passages interpolated, see Cameron and Reiman, *Shelley and his Circle*, VII 38–41.
34 *L* I 438, 444.
35 *L* II 330. Hunt informed Mary Shelley that he was unable to find the letters; see July 26?, 1839 and December 22, 1839 to Leigh Hunt. Three of the letters, dated March 22, 1818, August 15, 1819, and August 26, 1821, are republished in *EL* II 110–11, 220–23, 325–27, as Hunt gave them; the letter of September 27, 1819 has passages added to it in *EL* II 226–29; the letters of December 2 and December 23, 1819 are not included.
36 On July 19, 1836 (Bodleian Library, Ms. Eng. Lett. C461).
37 See, for example *L* II 270 to Mary Hays; *L* II 272 to Henry Crabb Robinson; *L* II 275–76 to Josiah Wedgwood; *L* II 277 to William Hazlitt, Jr., for Godwin's letters to his father.
38 *PW* I 377–78.
39 *L* III 42, 62.
40 See, for example, Amanda Gilroy and W. M. Verhoeven, eds., *Epistolary Histories* (Charlottesville: University Press of Virginia, 2000).

14

GREG KUCICH

Biographer

Social isolation, financial stress, and haunting grief over deceased loved ones put Mary Shelley in "deep sorrows" throughout much of the 1830s, yet she found one alleviating source of "pleasure" in the research and writing of biographical essays (*L* II 257, 209). "[T]here is," she declared, "no more delightful task" (*LL* I 116). Biographical writing fascinated Shelley throughout her literary career. At seventeen, she started a life of Jean Baptiste Louvet de Couvrai, himself a memoir writer and man of letters as well as a Girondist leader during the French Revolution. The core narrative of *Frankenstein*, the creature's account of his own history and the life of Safie, functions as both autobiography and biography. Much of Shelley's later fiction, such as *Valperga* and *The Fortunes of Perkin Warbeck*, draws on biographical sources and assumes the shape of fictional life writing. In 1823, Shelley contributed a biographical essay on Rousseau's beloved Madame d'Houdetôt to *The Liberal*, the radical journal established in Italy by Leigh Hunt and Lord Byron. Several years later, Shelley proposed to the publisher John Murray an ambitious range of biographical ventures, including lives of Madame de Staël, Empress Josephine, Columbus, Mahomet, the "English Philosophers," and "Celebrated women" (*L* II 113–15). As Susan J. Wolfson shows in chapter 12, Mary Shelley's 1824 edition of Percy Shelley's *Posthumous Poems* and her larger 1839 edition of his works feature extensive biographical comments on his life. Shelley also wrote a "Memoir" of her father, William Godwin, for the 1831 reissue of his novel *Caleb Williams*, and she later composed an advanced draft of his biography, a work she never completed. Shelley joined in many other biographical projects during these years, including her memoir of Lord Byron, now lost, and manuscript notes for a planned life of Percy Shelley, which Thomas Jefferson Hogg later used, or rather distorted, for his life of Percy Shelley (1858). She also produced biographical sketches for Thomas Moore's life of Byron (1830), and Cyrus Redding's portrayal of Percy Shelley in the 1829 Galignani edition of his poetry.

From 1834 to 1839, Shelley worked almost continuously on the majority of biographical essays for two large collections of lives in Dionysius Lardner's popular *Cabinet Cyclopaedia*, the three-volume *Lives of the Most Eminent Literary and Scientific Men of Italy, Spain and Portugal* (1835–37) and the two-volume *Lives of the Most Eminent Literary and Scientific Men of France* (1838–39).[1] Lardner's *Cabinet Cyclopaedia* was published in 133 moderately priced and widely distributed volumes between 1829 and 1846; it contained works on world history, biography, natural history, science, arts and manufactures, and other subjects, or "cabinets," composed by some of the most distinguished writers of the early nineteenth century, including Sir Walter Scott, Thomas Moore, Robert Southey, J. C. L. de Sismondi, and John Herschel. Shelley contributed numerous short and extended biographical essays to *LISP* and *LF*, amounting to upwards of three-quarters of the 1,756 total pages for both collections. Her investment in these two collections alone distinguishes her as a prolific, accomplished biographer, who looked to biographical reading as well as writing for a valuable source of emotional refreshment, creative stimulation, and political action.

Although critics have probed her use of biography for expressing divided sentiments about Godwin and Percy Shelley, only a few critical studies have directly addressed her broader aims and strategies as a biographer, pre-eminently manifested in the *Lives*.[2] This lack of attention to her greatest biographical achievement, which remains virtually unknown in the undergraduate classroom, derives in part from long-standing critical tendencies to dismiss the *Lives* as hack work churned out rapidly in order to pay off debts. Moreover, scholarship on the nonfictional writings of her later years has remained somewhat undeveloped until just recently. W. H. Lyles's Shelley bibliography has compounded the problem by under-representing the large volume of her contributions to the *Lives*.[3] Precise attribution of all the biographical essays in *LISP* and *LF* is very difficult. Lardner employed several contributors for *LISP* and at least one author besides Shelley for *LF*, leaving specific attributions indefinite in contents pages and advertisements. Shelley's letters and Lardner's advertisements do confirm, however, that she was at least the major author of *LISP* and produced considerably more essays in these volumes than Lyles assigns to her. Still the greatest obstacle has been the lack of ready access to her *Lives*, which have never been reproduced from the now obscure *Cabinet Cyclopaedia*.

Happily, new advances in Shelley scholarship have dynamically altered these critical and editorial conditions. With the expansion of the Pickering and Chatto Mary Shelley edition to include the four volumes of *Mary Shelley's Lives and Other Writings*, Shelley's *Lives* are now easily available in their first edited format, with informational notes and critical commentary.

The Pickering editors also present a strong case for attributing many more of the *Lives* to Shelley's hand than have been previously thought hers, virtually all the essays in the French volumes of the *Lives*. Modern scholars and students now have the opportunity to explore hundreds of pages of Shelley's writing that have received little previous scrutiny.

Many new insights and areas of discussion will emerge: the impressive range of Shelley's literary, historical, and linguistic knowledge, manifested in her prodigious research across several centuries and in multiple languages; her narrative skill and psychological insight in dramatizing the inner lives of her subjects, which ranks her among the important biographical writers of her time; her literary professionalism and public presence during her later years; the politics of her particular approach to women's lives; and, still more complex, her experiments with emerging forms of feminist historiography that intervene substantially in national politics, especially regarding gender. Close attention to this political dimension in Shelley's *Lives* affords us a more nuanced understanding of the complex mixture of personal withdrawal and social engagement in her later career, one of the more controversial issues in current Shelley studies.[4] I will focus my comments on the historiographical innovations Shelley deploys throughout the *Lives* to enact a significant, if somewhat muted, argument for what she calls "Improvement" (*LL* III 337) in national government and, particularly, in the politics of gender.

Biography and women's historical writing

Shelley saw great potential in the merging of biography and history as interrelated modes of applying the life of the past to the politics of the present. Reflecting on the nature and function of her own *Lives*, she claims that a successful sketch of a life entails not only "the biography of an individual" but also the political history of an era (*LL* III 241). As she notes elsewhere, biographical writing should "form as it were a school in which to study the philosophy of history" (*LL* I 172). The search for "lessons" from this school (*LL* I 143) consistently drew her to historical examples of good and bad government, international political relations, and different forms of domestic economy. For Johanna Smith, Shelley's historical "lessons" pointedly forward critiques of what feminist historians today call "sex-gender systems" that are "injurious to women."[5] Shelley's recognition of the suitability of biographical and historical writing for such political purposes stemmed from her alertness to the ways in which many of her female contemporaries were reconstructing the past in order to redress the social and gender inequalities of the present.

Historical modes of thought emerged in the later eighteenth century as "the paradigmatic form of knowledge to which all others aspired,"[6] becoming a crucial discursive site where Romantic-era ideologies of class, nation, empire, and gender clashed. Moreover, pronounced shifts toward sentimentality and mental portraiture in the Enlightenment historiography of Hume, Smith, Robertson, and others gave historical discourse a new appeal for women readers and writers. The increasing sway of middle-class commercialism in eighteenth-century British society inspired Hume's generation of historians, dissatisfied with the exclusive plots of military conquest and monarchial power in conventional historiography, to place a new emphasis on mercantile growth, industry, the arts, social relations, domestic life and its affective components. This realignment, intensified by the rise of sentimentality across later eighteenth-century narrative genres, produced an unprecedented historical interest in the social, the inward, and particularly the realm of affect. As Mark Salber Phillips summarizes, Hume features many "sentimental scenes of suffering and farewell" in his famous *History of England* (1754–63) while generating sympathy for historical sufferers like "poor King Charles."[7] The makers of this new history, particularly Hume, targeted women readers and addressed women's experience as part of their concentration on the social fabric of the past.[8] They also created a sentimental field in mainstream historiography open to the affective qualities of generic forms – the sonnet, novels of feeling, the drama – practiced by rapidly increasing numbers of women writers throughout the later eighteenth century. When Catherine Moreland complains in Jane Austen's *Northanger Abbey* about the "tiresome" quality of mainstream or "solemn history," particularly its exclusion of women, she does not convey female resistance to *all* current historiography. Rather she touches upon a growing desire among women readers and writers for the new history of social and affective life. So Eleanor Tilney responds, "I am fond of history," especially "the production of Mr. Hume or Mr. Robertson . . ."[9]

Phillips concludes that numerous women writers, such as Helen Maria Williams in her *Letters from France* (1790–96), now embraced the "affective possibilities" of historical narration.[10] Yet Catherine Moreland's complaint also represents an underlying discontent, which surfaces throughout Austen's own parodic *History of England*[11] and in the charge of her later heroine from *Persuasion*, Anne Eliot, that histories remain suspect because men have always told "their own story . . . the pen has been in their hands."[12] Such dissatisfaction with that phallic story echoes throughout the historical ventures of contemporary women writers. Lucy Aikin aims to wrest the historical "pencil" from man's grasp, for instance, in her revisionary *Epistles* on the untold "Fate of Woman" (1810), and Anna Jameson begins her *Characteristics of Women* (1832) with a protest that "history . . . disdains to speak of [women]."[13] Why these objections persist in spite of history's growing appeal to women stems from the failure of mainstream historians, in the eyes of many female critics, to go far enough in opening the landscapes of the past to affect and social life inclusive of women's experience.

For all of Hume's interest in the sentimental and the social, his sections on character and domestic economy come rather briefly at the end of long disquisitions on political and military history, to which they remain subordinate. His pathos, though evocative, functions mainly for entertainment value in oases of private sentiment cut off from the sprawling and ultimately more important terrain of public action. Moreover, the new Enlightenment historiography often embraces but sequesters private life and subordinates it to abstract teleologies of human progress, such as the progressive stages of human civilization theorized by the Scottish philosophers Smith, Ferguson, and Robertson; the alternating cycles of progress and retrogression in the philosophical histories of Volney and Condorcet; or the brutal oscillations of supply and dearth in Malthus's population theory. However much this new history opened doors for women writers, it also relegated many of their social priorities and discursive practices to a private, feminized zone separated from the main stuff of public and philosophical history.

Many of those women who seized the historical pen thus assumed the challenge with strategic adjustments in mind. These entailed not simply inserting more women into the historical record, urgent as that effort became. An even more important step altered the basic epistemological structures of mainstream history, not so much by repudiating its philosophical and public concerns but rather by escalating its sentimental and private elements into the center of historical consciousness. Catherine Macaulay declares in her prestigious eight-volume *History of England* (1763–83) that "sympathising tenderness" for "the particular sufferings of . . . individuals," especially within the sphere of the family, makes up the essence of historical knowledge.[14] Joanna Baillie, criticizing the abstract inclinations of what she calls "real history," argues instead for an unprecedented kind of "sentimental" history grounded in sympathetic evocations of inner life, particularly "misfortunes . . . of the more familiar and domestick kind."[15] To position sentiment and domesticity at this higher level did not mean restricting historical discourse to a conventionally feminine realm of private feeling. Quite the opposite, Macaulay tilts rationally throughout her work with the major political historians of her time and simultaneously infuses her mode of "sympathising tenderness" into the core of national debate. Baillie seeks through her affective type of historical drama to inspire new sympathies in social makers and shakers – judges, magistrates, advocates – resulting in a more compassionate, "better" society.[16]

Such a new form of sympathetic history was crucial to the way women helped to shape national politics and values during the Romantic era: its affirmation of the subjectivities of historically marginalized groups of sufferers – such as women, the poor, and African slaves – argued for their political rights in the present; its infusion of domestic sympathies into public debate addressed the political and moral consciousness of the nation; and its critique of abstract teleologies of human progress countered the visionary and universalizing tendencies in literary Romanticism that often promoted masculine codes of knowledge antagonistic toward women. As an early form of what we now call "feminist historiography,"[17] this new, more sympathetic story of the past thus entered into the centers of political discourse and challenged the masculine gender ideologies that infiltrate much of Romanticism's writing practices.

Shelley would not have found this paradigm in all women's historicism of her time, and she could have noted that some historical writing by men inclined more in its direction than others – most notably for her, Godwin in "Of History and Romance" and *Essay on Sepulchres*.[18] Nevertheless, she devoted considerable time to the study of its various formulations and political imperatives in such women writers as Mary Wollstonecraft, Macaulay, Jameson, Joanna Baillie and others. Her interest in adapting its general patterns surfaces throughout her fiction, such as the episode in *Frankenstein* when Safie and the creature weep together over the ruins of history, or the various scenes of domestic affection and suffering in historical novels like *Valperga* and the futuristic *The Last Man*. One of Shelley's most influential models for this sympathetic investment in the past emerged in the ways various female contemporaries – such as Mary Hays, Jameson, Elizabeth Hamilton, and Elizabeth Benger – were adapting biography for the political functions of the new interiorized history.

The general rise of biography as a major historical genre in the late eighteenth and early nineteenth centuries offered unique opportunities for women writers interested in deepening the affective structures of mainstream historiography. Where the classical training often required of male historians could present obstacles to women writers – Hamilton feared that historical writing "may be deemed too classical for a female pen"[19] – biography's accommodation of memoirs, reminiscences, and narratives of friends and loved ones opened its historicism to a wider range of authors and encouraged more vivid and sustained outpourings of sentiment. Goldsmith, in his *Life of Richard Nash* (1762), argues that "none can properly be said to write history, but he who understands the human heart, and its whole train of affections and follies."[20] Johnson defends the social importance of biography over history precisely because of its lessons about "private life."[21] Not only did this interiorized approach to the past welcome affective experiments, but such claims for its cultural significance also legitimated biography as a prominent historical genre in which women writers could stand on equal footing with classically trained male historians. This explains why so many women writers of the Romantic era took up biographical writing as experiments in sympathetic historiography, many of them focused particularly on female subjects, such as Aikin's *Memoirs of the Court of Queen Elizabeth*; Hays's *Female Biography*; Jameson's *Memoirs of Female Sovereigns*; Benger's various *Memoirs*; and Hamilton's *Memoirs of the Life of Agrippina*.

Yet even here, revision of the biographical practices established by Johnson's generation and later continued by such distinguished figures as Godwin, Southey, and Hazlitt, proved necessary. For the interior movement of standard biography often swerves outward onto the large stage of public events in order to demonstrate how personal character or choice both shapes and becomes conditioned by the grand flow of political and military history, still central to most biographical as well as historical writing. Godwin thus presents his 1803 life of Chaucer as a history of the poet's "mind" but affirms that the fundamental "subject of this book" is "the state of England."[22] Although this macro level of interest attracted those women writers seeking a place in national debate through historical narration, it also reinforced the biases they found in mainstream historiography. Benger complains, for instance, that most biography concentrates too heavily on the "facts and dates" associated with "warriors and adventurers," while failing to engage with the essence of biography and history: "the history of the individual" in "domestic life" whose "secret chagrins and anxieties" compose a "record . . . of suffering and feeling" that speaks most powerfully "to our sympathies."[23] The fact that Benger, Hays, Hamilton, and Aikin all produced specialized lives of women indicates the gendered preoccupations of this corrective response. Their adjustments brought increased numbers of women into the recorded history of private life. Even more significant, their new records of feeling extended the affective possibilities and the political import of that overall process of deepening historical sympathy. This kind of biographical history transformed the past, as Benger declares, into a "school of suffering" whose poignant lessons of injury and exclusion particularly encourage, in Hays's memorable phrase, "the advancement . . . of my sex . . . [in] the generous contention between the sexes for intellectual equality."[24]

These early developments of what we now call "feminist biography"[25] intrigued Shelley, who conceptualized biographical writing herself as a politically charged investment in "private history" capable of producing a new "philosophy of history" (*LL* 1 90, 172). In her 1823 essay on Madame d'Houdetôt, she emphasizes both her subject's "sympathizing compassion" and the "disgust[ing]" social practice of disposing "the person of woman" in marriage for material profit.[26] When a pragmatic Shelley recognized that biography of this sort could also provide fresh income, she proposed that ambitious range of biographical projects to Murray in 1829–30. Her opportunity finally came with Lardner's invitation to produce the *Lives*, which manifest her most comprehensive adaptation of the feminist historiographical procedures she had been cultivating throughout her literary career.

Shelley's biography and the politics of interior history

Comparing Shelley's source material with her own strategic interjections demonstrates how she put the new interiorized history to work in biographical narrative. She recurrently characterizes her essays, for instance, as histories of the inner lives of her subjects, presenting her life of Petrarch as a "history of his heart" (*LL* I 32), her sketch of Bernardo Pulci as a "private history" (*LL* I 90). Although Shelley acknowledged Johnson's biographical emphasis on "character" as a formative influence on this inward history (*LL* I 226), her own method concentrates more intensively on the emotional ties of friendship, romantic love, and especially family connections. She devotes a considerable portion of her Petrarch essay to the "family concord" that graced his upbringing and the generosity of his interactions "with many dear friends" (*LL* I 37). In the life of Vittoria Colonna, she dwells extensively on the "utmost tenderness" exchanged between Vittoria and her spouse (*LL* I 176). Her life of Vincenzo Monti stresses the "tenderness of feeling" he inherited from his parents, which "caused him to be idolised in his domestic circle" (*LL* I 296). Such ties of domestic affection, foregrounded within the broad scope of public events, stand out as what counts in the history documented by Shelley's *Lives*.

This record of the heart's domestic affections gains special resonance from Shelley's highly personal applications of "sympathising tenderness" for her biographical subjects. Blocked by Sir Timothy Shelley's restrictions from publishing any details of her life with Percy Shelley,[27] she circumvented that gag order by locating poignant versions of her own traumatic family experience of loss and betrayal in the domestic histories of her subjects, such as her special emphasis on mothers dying in childbirth in the lives of Rousseau and Luis de León (*LL* III 320; *LL* II 72); her poignant treatment of the "distress" brought to the "warm heart" of Cervantes by "the falling off of . . . [old] friends" (*LL* II 148); and, perhaps the most anguished of all these episodes considering Shelley's grief-stricken isolation in the 1830s, her vivid portrayal of Vittoria Colonna mourning the early death of her husband for years afterward, giving "herself up entirely to sorrow . . . liv[ing] in re-tirement . . . Dedicating herself wholly to memory" (*LL* I 177–78).

Immersing herself in the personal calamities of others gave Shelley some relief from her own harrowing memories, which she called "the medicine of mind" issuing from the "quieter work" of biography (*L* III 92; *J* II 532, 539). To sink behind her subjects in this "quieter work" could thus indulge her avowed wish to retreat from public life and politics in later years. Yet the task also enabled her, through the mediation of biographical distance, to pull herself and her sorrows forward in ways she was otherwise reluctant to attempt. Moreover, her use of allegory to counter Sir Timothy's strictures illuminated her own personal grievances in a way that subtly intensified her display of the history of domestic sorrows. If Macaulay shed many tears over historical sufferers, Shelley's habit of grieving *with* them brought the pangs of domestic history, particularly her own, into the literary marketplace with unusual force.

The gender politics of that emphasis became evident to Shelley as soon as she joined the *Cyclopaedia* project in 1834, halfway through its completion, as the sole female contributor (a role prominently noted in advertised lists of the several dozen contributors). Tensions accrued from that situation im-mediately, with Shelley complaining that a gluttonous James Montgomery – the "Omnipresent Mr Montgomery" – swallowed up some of the best Italian lives (Dante and Ariosto) and botched the job through his masculine dis-tortions (*L* II 219, 222, 260). Montgomery's life of Dante does betray a smirking tone of masculine condescension, introducing the sublime Beatrice as "the little lady" (*LISP* I 6). Moreover, its general emphasis on Dante's public achievement and indifference to his personal or domestic situations suggests the biases of masculine historiography, which are ubiquitous in the historical and biographical contributions to the *Cyclopaedia* that pre-ceded Shelley's involvement. James Mackintosh characterizes his *History of England*, for instance, as a broad delineation of national motions of progress; E. E. Crowe, in his *History of France*, loftily claims that the historian should "cast away . . . prejudices and passions" in the objective pursuit of fact and truth.[28] Shelley's curt reaction to such a historical outlook may be judged from her verdict on Montgomery's life of Tasso: "I should have written it better" (*L* II 257). She remained sensitive to the gender implications of thus "bettering" the outlook on history in the *Cyclopaedia* project, expressing at one point her discomfort with the dominant male presence where she con-ducted research in the British Library (*L* II 260). She also included several women's biographies in the *Cyclopaedia Lives of Eminent . . . Men* (my emphasis).

The gender politics at stake here mounted considerably with the cultural work enacted by the *Cyclopaedia* project. Growing out of the educational reform movements of the 1820s, Lardner's *Cyclopaedia* joined other ventures in diffusing knowledge to provide an ascendant population of middle-class readers with cultural refinement. Lardner and his publishers, Longman and the firm of John Taylor, specifically marketed their volumes to the *"general reader,"* to those nonspecialists who, according to one of their advertisements, "seek that portion of information respecting [professional subjects] . . . which is generally expected from well-educated readers . . . The present work will claim a place in the drawing-room and the boudoir."[29] The type of upwardly-mobile purchasers whom Lardner and his publishers expected to inhabit these book-filled drawing-rooms and boudoirs emerges in the product advertisements that pepper the *Cyclopaedia*: from table cutlery for "merchants, captains, families, [and] new-married couples" to treatises on female "accomplishments" for "young lad[ies]."[30] Part of the process of marketing cultural refinement to this rising class of male and female consumers also involved disseminating conservative British values and customs. Reviewers of the series found it teaching "gratitude" for the "blessings" of British government,[31] and the editors specifically directed such lessons at those new social groups and institutions acquiring prominence both at home and abroad: "Families resident in the Country . . . Emigrants . . . Libraries of Mechanics' Institutions, Literary and Philosophical Societies, The Army and the Navy, and of Colonial Institutions."

Lardner's series became one of the most successful purveyors of this conservative cultural schooling, thanks to its prestigious list of contributors and its clever marketing strategy of offering "Cabinet" subjects to the new purchasers of culture for separate sale at only six shillings a volume. Although Lardner's disgrace following a scandalous liaison coincided with a downturn in sales around 1840, the *Cyclopaedia* remained profitable enough to vaunt itself upon completion by 1845 with a reviewer's blurb proclaiming it to be "One of the most valuable contributions that has ever been made to the cause of general knowledge and national education."[32] However conservative that education, the *Cyclopaedia*'s mass appeal to a rising group of general readers, many of them female, also created unique opportunities for a more liberal contributor like Shelley to address a female readership's desire for "advancement" while shaping the social values of a large class of new readers. Given that the print run of the *Lives* ran to several thousand copies per volume – a number considerably higher than the average for Shelley's novels – her use of biography to forward the social agenda of women's historiography became one of her most influential political interventions.[33]

The gender priorities of that plan surface clearly in Shelley's remarks on patriarchal hierarchies and irresponsibility. She ironically criticizes the actions of Goldoni's father, for instance, when professional openings prompted his move to a new city: "Thus fortunately situated," Shelley observes, "he resolved to have his son with him. He does not appear to have thought of inviting his wife also" (*LL* 1 231). In her life of Alfieri, Shelley addresses historical sex-gender systems more analytically, condemning the laws of primogeniture for "degrading" women and expressing "utmost abhorrence" at the moral degeneracy of the *cavaliere servente* system, which gave tacit approval to lovers for well-born married women (*LL* 1 284). In contrast to her strictures against such examples of individual and institutional misogyny, Shelley also commends societies noteworthy for their progressive gender relations: "No slur was cast by the [Renaissance era] Italians on feminine accomplishments," she points out; "Where abstruse learning was a fashion among men, they were glad to find in their friends of the other sex, minds educated to share their pursuits" (*LL* 1 174).

Shelley's most intensive social criticism in the *Lives*, however, entails her direct use of sympathetic historiography to critique the gender ideologies of her own time. In charting the "secret chagrins and anxieties" of her biographical subjects, she often contrasts forms of masculine egotism related to contemporary social biases with the sympathetic exchanges she had always promoted as the model of healthy personal relations and good government. She particularly faults masculine egotism – in comments applicable to a fictional character like Victor Frankenstein as well as to the man he sometimes resembles, Percy Shelley – for injuring women and children. Thus she deplores Ugo Foscolo's "worship of self," which leads to violent passions for women and makes "his own individuality the mirror in which the world was reflected" (*LL* 1 130).

Shelley's life of Rousseau repays close analysis in this regard. She finds his philosophical self-absorption egregiously culpable for spreading a masculine ideology of selfhood that infects her age. As Pamela Clemit documents in chapter 2, Shelley's qualms about Rousseau date back at least to *Frankenstein*. There she indirectly expresses ambivalence, supportive of Rousseau's revolutionary ideals but critical of his domestic irresponsibility exemplified in Frankenstein's parental neglect of the Creature. By the late 1830s, however, following the tragic outcome of Percy Shelley's neglectful treatment of their own children, Sir Timothy's ongoing cruelty, and Godwin's protracted emotional disconnection, Mary Shelley caustically focuses all her attention on Rousseau's catastrophic misbehavior to his family. Impugning his selfish irresponsibility to his lover, Thérèse Levasseur, and their five children, whom he abandons to a foundling hospital, Shelley lashes out,

"[H]e took her as a sort of convenience, and when inconveniences arose from the connection, he was disposed to get rid of them on the easiest possible terms" (*LL* III 334). Rousseau's insidious attempt to rationalize his behavior through a philosophy of natural sublimity provokes Shelley's most embittered condemnation:

> [I]n point of fact, nothing can be more unnatural than his natural man. The most characteristic part of man's nature is his affections. The protection he affords to woman – the cares required by his children; yet Rousseau describes his natural man as satisfying his desires by chance, – leaving the woman on the instant, while she, on her side, goes through child-bearing, child-birth, and child-nurture alone . . . He often dilates on simple pleasures – the charms of unsophisticated affections, and the ecstasy to be derived from virtuous sympathy – he, who never felt the noblest and most devoted passion of the human soul – the love of a parent for his child! (*LL* III 337, 365)

Amid her many expressions of "loathing" for Rousseau's "revolting and criminal . . . system" (*LL* III 335), Shelley also projects an alternative social "system" governed not by abstract political or philosophical ideals but rather by the suffusion of domestic affections throughout social and national life. "Let us advance civilisation to its highest pitch, or retrograde to its origin," she argues, "and let both bring freedom from political and social slavery; but in all let us hold fast by the affections: the cultivation of these ought to be the scope of every teacher of morality, every well-wisher to the improvement of the human race" (*LL* III 337).

Teaching these particular lessons of improvement becomes as central a priority in the *Lives* as exposing the destructiveness of Rousseauvian egotism. As she locates various historical examples of domestic sympathy, Shelley formulates a redemptive model for the improvement of social life and gender relations in the present. Thus she highlights the self-corrective sympathy of Petrarch's father, who had initially scorned his son's literary aspirations, when he recognizes the depth and integrity of young Petrarch's artistic passion (*LL* I 11). She emphasizes the "fraternal kindness" that Metastasio expresses to his siblings upon the death of their father (*LL* I 227). Shelley also stresses Petrarch's abiding concern for his beloved Laura's welfare, which enables him, unlike Rousseau, to control his passions and avert disaster for them both. In the family politics of Shelley's historicism, "improvement" on the national level grows out of emotional sympathies nurtured within domestic circles. She does pitch this alternative social model to both male and female readers, punctuating her *Lives* with numerous male as well as female constructive examples. However, her revisionary historicism centers most provocatively on the private lives and social experience of women, whose conditions stand in particular need of "improvement" and who emerge themselves as the most capable agents of change.

Handed a demanding professional assignment to furnish numerous essays on famous men, Shelley interjected female lives in limited numbers – the sixteenth-century Italian poet Vittoria Colonna, the French revolutionary activist Madame de Roland, and the famous literary personality Germaine de Staël – but with pointed effect. None of these is exceptionally long, yet the lives of Roland and de Staël are comparable in length to those of some of her most important male subjects (roughly fifty pages each on Petrarch, Boccaccio, and de Staël). Her chapters on Roland and de Staël also conclude the French volumes, asserting a strong female intervention at the closure of her *Cyclopaedia* work. Part of the exceptional quality of these female biographies lies in their dedicated attention to women's abilities and the social conditions that either hinder or encourage their potential. Shelley frequently celebrates here the unlimited capacities of female intelligence, but she also insists upon improving female education and calls for the urgent need to correct social systems – such as marital institutions – that limit women's political rights, degrade their humanity, and curb their talents. Her most compelling innovation in the female lives, however, follows up on her claim in the Rousseau essay that women possess a "distinctive virtue" (*LL* II 330) of sympathy for others and should thus assume a leading role in social improvement. Although this claim may seem to promote an essentialist domestic ideology that would confine women's sympathetic influence to the home, Shelley applies such a "virtue" to the fate of the nation. She details, for instance, how Roland learns from her mother's sheltering tutelage to "sympathise . . . with the emotions of others" and grows as an adult role model to extend that "tender sympathy" both to all of her loved ones and to the national causes in France of political justice and gender equality (*LL* III 432, 439).

To trace the growing sophistication of this political theory, from the Italian counter-examples of egotism and sympathy to the French lives specifically addressing women's agency in national improvement, is to recognize how Shelley became increasingly committed to the political potential of revisionary historicism and life writing. That corrective project, worked out in a publishing format distributed to a mass audience on the rise, marks one of her strongest, more progressive engagements with her age's debates about gender, history, and good government. Incorporating the *Lives* into our study of her developing career will thus modify conventional assumptions about the political withdrawal and conservatism of her later years. For if she did grow more reticent as she aged, Shelley's comments on women's maturation in her life of de Staël reveal confidence in her own sustained experiment with the politics of feminist biography and historiography: "When young, [women] are open to such cruel attacks, every step they take in public may bring with it irreparable injury to their private affections, to their delicacy, to their dearest prospects. As years are added they gather courage; they feel the earth grow steadier under their steps; they depend less on others, and their moral worth increases" (*LL* III 492). One of the most important "lessons" we can garner from the *Lives* is to recognize how biographical writing, within the framework of early nineteenth-century women's historiography, gave a maturing Shelley the courage, self-worth, and insight to carry on her own political activism, however mediated the form, throughout even the darkest of times. And that lesson, in turn, can teach us about the later Shelley's special ability to speak across the gap of time to biographers, historians, literary critics, and students today.

NOTES

1 In this chapter, I use the short title *Lives* when referring to both collections. Unless otherwise noted, citations to all lives refer to *Mary Shelley's Literary Lives and Other Writings* (*LL*), gen. ed. Nora Crook, 4 vols. (London: Pickering and Chatto, 2002).

2 See William Walling, *Mary Shelley* (New York: Twayne, 1972), pp. 124–32; Paula Feldman, "Biography and the Literary Executor: The Case of Mary Shelley," *The Papers of the Bibliographical Society of America* 72 (1978), 287–97; Johanna Smith, *Mary Shelley* (New York: Twayne, 1996), pp. 128–44; and Greg Kucich, "Mary Shelley's *Lives* and the Reengendering of History," *MST* 198–213. The present chapter is indebted to this last citation.

3 W. H. Lyles, *Mary Shelley: An Annotated Bibliography* (New York: Garland Publishing, 1975). In sorting out these attribution questions, I am deeply indebted to Nora Crook, general editor of the new Pickering edition of *Mary Shelley's Literary Lives and Other Writings*, which provides a new and thorough analysis of Shelley's contributions to the *Lives*.

4 Syndy M. Conger, Frederick S. Frank, and Gregory O'Dea, editors of *ID*, foreground debates about these split inclinations in their "Introduction," pp. 9–13.

5 Smith, *Mary Shelley*, p. 122. Shelley's reading lists document extensive study of prominent historical and biographical texts, including works by Godwin, Wollstonecraft, Gibbon, Robertson, Plutarch, Louvet de Couvrai, Voltaire, Clarendon, Lady Hamilton, Elizabeth Benger, and Catharine Macaulay, among others (*J* I 85–103, I 346).

6 Stephen Bann, *Romanticism and the Rise of History* (New York: Twayne, 1995), p. 4.

7 Mark Salber Phillips, *Society and Sentiment: Genres of Historical Writing in Britain: 1740–1820* (Princeton: Princeton University Press, 2000), p. 62. Phillips quotes Hume on Charles I (p. 60). My argument here is indebted to Phillips's detailed analysis of sentimental registers in eighteenth-century and Romantic-era historiography.

8 See Hume's "Essay on the Study of History," in *The Philosophical Works of David Hume*, 4 vols. (Boston: Little, Brown and Company, 1854), IV 508–13.

9 Jane Austen, *Northanger Abbey*, ed. Anne Henry Ehrenpreis (London: Penguin, 1985), pp. 123, 123.

10 Phillips, *Society and Sentiment*, p. 93. See also Devoney Looser, *British Women Writers and the Writing of History, 1670–1820* (Baltimore: Johns Hopkins University Press, 2000).

11 Written in 1791 and not published until the twentieth century. See the facsimile edition of Austen's *The History of England*, ed. Deirdre Le Faye (London: The British Library, 1993).

12 Austen, *Persuasion*, ed. D. W. Harding (London: Penguin, 1965), p. 237.

13 Lucy Aikin, *Epistles on Women, Exemplifying Their Character and Condition in Various Ages and Nations*, in *British Literature 1780–1830*, eds. Anne K. Mellor and Richard E. Matlak (New York: Harcourt, 1996), Epistle I, lines 31, 3; Anna Jameson, *Characteristics of Women: Moral, Political, and Historical* (London: Saunders and Otley, 1832), p. xvii.

14 Catharine Macaulay, *The History of England*, 8 vols. (London: Nourse, 1763–83), VI 21, 23, 28, 130.

15 Baillie outlines these points in two of her prefatory essays: *Introductory Discourse to Plays on the Passions* and *Preface to Metrical Legends*, in *The Dramatic and Poetical Works of Joanna Baillie* (London: Longman, 1851), pp. 5, 706, 705, 9.

16 Baillie, *Introductory Discourse*, p. 4.

17 For recent examples of the theory and practice of feminist historiography, see Joan Wallach Scott, ed., *Feminism and History* (Oxford: Oxford University Press, 1996).

18 Although Godwin's "Of History and Romance" remained in manuscript until the late twentieth century (now available in William Godwin, *Things As They Are or The Adventures of Caleb Williams*, ed. Maurice Hindle [London: Penguin, 1988], pp. 362–64), it was composed in 1797 and was probably available to Mary Shelley. Godwin's *Essay on Sepulchres* (1809), turns up on her reading list for 1814 (*J* I 86).

19 Quoted by Elizabeth Benger, *Memoirs of the Late Elizabeth Hamilton*, 2 vols. (London: Longman, 1818), II 41.

20 Quoted by Phillips, *Society and Sentiment*, p. 135.

21 Samuel Johnson, *The Rambler*, eds. W. J. Bate and Albrecht B. Strauss (New Haven: Yale University Press, 1969), vols. III–V of *The Yale Edition of the Works of Samuel Johnson*, gen. ed. John H. Middendorf, 16 vols. (1958–90), III 319.

22 Godwin, *Life of Geoffrey Chaucer . . . with Sketches of the Manners, Opinions, Arts, and Literature of England in the Fourteenth Century*, 2 vols. (London: Richard Phillips, 1803), I viii.

23 Benger, *Memoirs of the Late Mrs. Elizabeth Hamilton*, I 1; *Memoirs of the Life of Mary Queen of Scots*, 2 vols. (London: Longman, 1823), II 52, I 102; *Memoirs of the Life of Anne Boleyn* (Philadelphia: Potter, n.d.), p. 150.

24 Benger, *Memoirs of the Life of Anne Boleyn*, I 34; Mary Hays, *Female Biography*, 6 vols. (London: Richard Phillips, 1803), I iv.

25 See Elizabeth Kamarck Minnich, "Friendship Between Women: The Art of Feminist Biography," *Feminist Studies* 11 (1985), 287–305.

26 Shelley, "Madame d'Houtetôt," *The Liberal* 2.3 (1823), 77, 69. (Mary Shelley uses the idiosyncratic spelling "d'Houtetôt.")

27 For a concise summary of this transaction and Mary Shelley's other efforts to evade Sir Timothy's ban, see Smith, *Mary Shelley*, pp. 147–49.

28 James Mackintosh, *History of England*, 10 vols. (London: Longman, 1830), 1 v; E. E. Crowe, *The History of France*, 3 vols. (London: Longman, 1830), 1 330.

29 "Analytical Catalogue," in *LF* 1 1; quoted by Morse Peckham, "Dr. Lardner's *Cabinet Cyclopaedia*," *The Papers of the Bibliographical Society of America* 45 (1951), 41. The "Analytical Catalogue" is a detailed advertisement for the *Cabinet Cyclopaedia* separately paginated and bound up only in some of the series volumes.

30 "Analytical," in *LF* 1 1; "Advertisement," in *The History of Poland* (London: Longman, 1831), p. 3.

31 Quoted by Smith, *Mary Shelley*, p. 131.

32 "Analytical," in *LF* 1 1.

33 William St. Clair has graciously provided this information on print runs from his research at the Spottiswoode archive in the British Library.

15

JEANNE MOSKAL

Travel writing

Travel writing is both overture and finale to Mary Shelley's career. Her *History of a Six Weeks' Tour* (1817), an account of two continental trips co-authored with Percy Bysshe Shelley, marks an exuberant coming of age: it bursts with young love, defiance of parental control, and a search for political meaning. Her pensive *Rambles in Germany and Italy* (1844) mourns the deaths of her husband and two of her children as well as the loss of her own health, but ultimately comes to terms with those losses, expressing chastened joy at the pleasures that remain: the company of her surviving son, Percy Florence Shelley, and of his friends; the delights of travel; the beauty of mountains and sea, painting and music. *Rambles* also assesses her political losses and those of a generation of English liberals, whose hopes were raised by the French Revolution but dashed by its terroristic and imperialistic results.

History of a Six Weeks' Tour sounds a variation of the customary "Grand Tour," in which young English aristocratic men capped a university education with a two- to three-year journey to France and Italy, accompanied by a tutor. Ostensibly committed to polishing their French and studying Roman antiquities *in situ*, these young men often pursued sexual adventure as well, while their extended absence displayed, at home, the wealth of their families. Thus, by traveling abroad, the son and his family both acquired what sociologist Pierre Bourdieu calls symbolic capital.[1] In the second half of the eighteenth century, the Grand Tour took new, more inclusive, forms: shortened versions affordable by the middle class and continental honeymoons that included women in the ranks of travelers. By Mary Shelley's time, several women had successfully combined the pursuits of traveling and writing, such as her mother Mary Wollstonecraft, Mary Wortley Montagu, Hester Lynch Piozzi, Ann Radcliffe, Germaine de Staël, Charlotte Eaton, and Sydney Owenson, Lady Morgan. The Shelleys' invocation of Montagu and Wollstonecraft in *History of a Six Weeks' Tour* registers their sense that Mary Shelley followed in the footsteps of these trail-blazing females who reshaped the Grand Tour.

In the eighteenth century, travel literature had emerged as a distinct literary genre, with its peculiar conventions and metaphors and a distinct set of audience expectations. These generic conventions complicate our present-day assumption that traveler-writers give an exact, unvarnished account of the lived journey. In fact, earlier readers greeted travel writing skeptically, assuming that travelers were liars, either because they had been duped by their hosts or because they wished to exaggerate their own daring.[2] Thus Mary Shelley worked in a tradition that expected figuration and selection in travel books and in which the boundary between travel and fiction was contested.

Revolutionary tourism

History of a Six Weeks' Tour (1817) is based on two journeys. On the actual first journey, in 1814, Mary Godwin and her married lover, Percy Bysshe Shelley, eloped, accompanied by her stepsister, Claire Clairmont. Their walking tour of France and Switzerland was cut short by lack of funds, so they returned home by boating down the Rhine through Germany and Holland. Two years later, the Shelley party, with baby William, journeyed to meet Lord Byron, visiting Switzerland and the French Alps during the famous summer of the ghost-story contest that produced *Frankenstein*. Their itinerary included tourist sites associated with Jean-Jacques Rousseau as well as Mont Blanc, recently measured as the highest mountain in Western Europe. Mont Blanc was lionized by aestheticians, tourists, and writers as a site of sublimity, an aesthetic term defined by Edmund Burke for natural sites that enraptured its viewers while exciting awed ideas of pain and danger.

The literary form of the first journey is a continuous, undated diary entitled "History of a Six Weeks' Tour," while the literary form of the second journey is epistolary and lyric, comprising four letters, two signed "M" and two signed "S" (for Percy Bysshe Shelley, who almost always went by his surname) and Percy Bysshe Shelley's lyric poem, "Mont Blanc." Building on Donald H. Reiman's observation that the whole travel book was "carefully constructed to culminate" in "Mont Blanc,"[3] I would note that this constructed ascent uses both a traditional hierarchy of genres (her diary, her letters; his letters, his lyric poem) and a conventional hierarchy of gender (writings by a woman superseded by those of a man). Accordingly, Mary Shelley's first "Letter from Geneva" observes:

> From the windows of our hotel we see the lovely lake, blue as the heavens which it reflects, and sparkling with golden beams . . . Gentlemen's seats are scattered over these banks, behind which rise the various ridges of the black

mountains, and towering far above, in the midst of its snowy Alps, the ma-
jestic Mont Blanc, highest and queen of all. Such is the view reflected by the
lake.   (*NSW* VIII 43–44)

The female speaker sees Mont Blanc twice mediated: she looks, through
the window glass, at the mountain's reflection in the lake. The presence of
"Gentlemen's seats" between viewer and view define the gender and class obstacles that prevent her from unmediated apprehension, obstacles overcome
later in the book by her aristocratic male companion, who sees Mont Blanc
directly. By contrast, the Shelleys' use of the traditional gender hierarchies is
counterbalanced by their acknowledgment of Mary Shelley as first author.
Her journal "History of a Six Weeks' Tour," which gives the whole volume
its name,[4] is the longest single item in the book.

The fact that this joint effort closes with a celebration of unshakable natural power contrasts starkly with the view of Napoleon's shattered political power that opens the book. The defeated Napoleon had abdicated and
gone into exile in April 1814, just a few months before the Shelley party's
visit. Mary Shelley worries how the victors will treat Paris (*NSW* VIII 18),
laments the Cossacks' ransacking a small French town (21), and records that
a Frenchwoman warned her of the danger of rape by Napoleon's demobi-
lized soldiers (19). In the interim between the Shelley party's trips, Napoleon
returned to power for the so-called "Hundred Days," a phoenix-like return
that resulted in his defeat at Waterloo in 1815 and a second, permanent,
exile. The writing of the second journey engages this political defeat philosophically and aesthetically, as the Shelleys focus on the forms of sublimity
and power that outlast Napoleon: the literary genius of Rousseau and the
natural sublimity of Lake Geneva and Mont Blanc.

Rousseau anchors the political significance of the *History*. Genevan philosopher, novelist, and key figure of the Enlightenment, Rousseau fueled the
fire of the French Revolution by advocating a simplicity of manners characteristic of republican Rome, opposing these manners to the corruption
and artificiality of the French aristocracy (see chapter 2).[5] His passionate,
confessional style earned him Wollstonecraft's epithet, "the true Prometheus
of Sentiment,"[6] and was welcomed by many as a counterpoint to the cold
rationalism of other Enlightenment thinkers. Mary Shelley's second letter,
written in Geneva, celebrates Rousseau:

> Here a small obelisk is erected to the glory of Rousseau, and here (such is the
> mutability of human life) the magistrates, the successors of those who exiled
> him from his native country, were shot by the populace during that revolution,

which his writings mainly contributed to mature, and which, notwithstanding the temporary bloodshed and injustice with which it was polluted, has produced enduring benefits to mankind. (*NSW* VIII 46)

Significantly, her reaffirmation of faith in the French Revolution – that it produced enduring benefits to mankind – takes place at a site dedicated to Rousseau. Moreover, Percy Bysshe Shelley affirms Rousseau's novelistic skill, writing that his characters "were created indeed by one mind, but a mind so powerfully bright as to cast a shade of falsehood on the records that are called reality."[7] As Gregory Dart observes, both the Shelleys "had been moved to undertake a reassessment of the long history of the French Revolution and of the specific influence of Rousseau upon it."[8] The fact that they did so in a published travel book demonstrates, in my view, the genre's currency in contemporary politics. *Frankenstein*, published soon after the *History of a Six Weeks' Tour*, continues Mary Shelley's reassessment of Rousseau and the French Revolution; for Victor Frankenstein, another Promethean from Geneva, creates an image of humanity that, like the Revolution, begins in benevolence and ends in murder.

Mary Shelley reinforces the liberal politics of *History of a Six Weeks' Tour* by two allusions to Miguel de Cervantes's romance *Don Quixote* (1605, 1615), which her contemporaries would have associated with both Godwinian radicalism and Spanish efforts at reform. Mentioning Cervantes would remind her audience that William Godwin had connected his own ardent support for the utopian reforms of the French Revolution with the miraculous settings of romances such as *Quixote*.[9] Godwin had been further linked with Cervantes when, in 1801, Charles Lucas castigated him as *The Infernal Quixote* in a novel by that name. There Lucas blamed Godwin for undermining the British nation by debauching women and fomenting the Irish Rebellion of 1798. As for Spanish reform, in 1814–17 the Cervantes allusion would have implied support for the beleaguered Spanish constitution of 1812, which limited the powers of the monarchy and the Catholic Church and provided for Spanish colonies to be represented in the Spanish parliament. King Ferdinand VII, restored to the Spanish throne in 1814, ignored the liberal constitution, reinstating the Inquisition, feudal rights, and censorship of the press. Since Britain helped to engineer Ferdinand's restoration, it was complicit, in Mary Shelley's view, in disregarding the constitution. Her support for its reforms seemed like jousting with the transnational windmills of church and state in their reaction against liberalism.

In the first allusion, Mary Shelley writes, "[at Gros Bois] under the shade of the trees, we ate our bread and fruit, and drank our wine, thinking of

Don Quixote and Sancho" (*NSW* VIII 20), evoking not only the questing knight and his squire, who often ate alfresco, but Godwin as well. Traveling through Holland, she makes the second allusion:

> The roads were excellent, but the Dutch have contrived as many inconveniences as possible. In our journey of the day before, we had passed by a windmill, which was so situated with regard to the road, that it was only by keeping close to the opposite side, and passing quickly, that we could avoid the sweep of its sails. (*NSW* VIII 38)

By dodging windmills, the Shelley party recalls Don Quixote's futile joust with a windmill, an incident paradigmatic of the term "quixotic." The placement of these allusions situates Mary Shelley in the tradition of romance and politics. The first allusion, roughly ten pages from the beginning, epitomizes the bohemian freedom from restraint and domesticity in the trope of dining alfresco. Moreover, it serves the purpose of adolescent defiance by suggesting that, in such dining, Mary Shelley is more true to the quixotic model than her little-traveled father. The second allusion, mentioning windmills about ten pages from the end, evokes the sense of futility that permeates a prodigal's trip home because she has run out of money. Parental constraint, in the form of the parents' money, has reared its head again.

The progress of *History of a Six Weeks' Tour*, from surveying Europe's devastation to affirming the natural sublime, draws from a plot shared by a generation of liberal writers. Such progress is also found when Byron's *Childe Harold's Pilgrimage*, Canto III (1816), mourns the carnage of Waterloo and concludes by celebrating the sublimity of the sea, and when the speaker of Wordsworth's *The Prelude* (1850), full of revulsion at post-Terror Paris, finds solace in the sublime on Mount Snowdon. In observing this common move from political to natural sublimity, M. H. Abrams stresses the conservative spin, that writers dismayed by the French Revolution found solace in conservative politics and in private, spiritual concerns. However, the plot has a liberal spin as well, in which nature is troped as the repository of a sublimity, once incarnated in Napoleon, that will re-emerge in politics. It is as if nature were being asked, in Blake's words, to keep "The Divine Vision in time of trouble."[10] Such is the liberal use of the plot in the collaboration of Mary Shelley and Percy Bysshe Shelley in the *History of a Six Weeks' Tour*. It is right to observe Mary Shelley's contribution to this high Romantic pattern, for, as Esther Schor notes, though Mary Shelley has entered the classroom canon through her critique of Romantic egotism in *Frankenstein*, she critiques it from a sympathetic position within the Romantic literary movement.[11]

Rambles and Italian Nationalism

Mary Shelley's last published work, *Rambles in Germany and Italy in 1840, 1842, and 1843* (1844), uses epistolary form to shape two journeys made in the early 1840s with her son, Percy Florence, and his friends. The book draws from Mary Shelley's original correspondence with Claire Clairmont. The journey of 1840 was prompted by her desire to revisit Italy, after seventeen years of absence, where her husband and two of her children, William and Clara, had died. The travelers boated down the Rhine, spent six weeks at Lake Como, and briefly visited Milan. Two years later, Mary Shelley sought a cure for her recurrent headaches at German spas and made "a pious pilgrimage" to Rome, the site of Shelley's grave (*NSW* VIII 348). At the end of her second journey, in Paris, she met Ferdinando Luigi Gatteschi, an Italian aristocrat exiled after his participation in an 1830 revolt against Austrian rule.[12] Imagining him "a hero & an angel & martyr" (*L* III 207), Mary Shelley decided to write a travel book based on her journeys for Gatteschi's financial benefit; she would include in it his memoirs of the revolt. Her attraction to Gatteschi may be explained, in part, by his resemblance to her husband, an aristocratic writer disowned by his parents for espousing liberal causes. In fact, the strength of her devotion overturned her previous resolve not to publish again. But for the hope of helping Gatteschi, she wrote, she would choose to remain silent "that never my name might be mentioned in a world that oppresses me" (*L* III 101).[13]

Rambles comes to terms not only with Mary Shelley's personal losses, but also with the political losses she shared with a generation of English liberals. Their hopes for greater enfranchisement of the middle and working classes had been raised by the French Revolution of 1789 with its cry of "Liberty, Equality, Fraternity," to be dashed by repeated blows: the violence of the Revolutionaries in the Reign of Terror in 1794; the shameless aggression of their successor, Napoleon, in conquering other nations in the name of the revolutionary "liberty"; the harsh repression by the wars' victors, Britain and Austria, of any reforms associated with the French; and the slow pace of liberalism in Britain itself, which led to the Chartist workers' movement in the 1840s. In *Rambles*, Mary Shelley keeps liberal hopes alive by proposing for them a more limited scope (and a more distant one) by directing attention to the nascent nationalist movement in Italy. She speaks for the Risorgimento ("resurgence"), Italy's nationalist movement, and defends the rebellious Carbonari who took their name from the charcoal-pits where they secretly convened. In fact, Mary Shelley's letter to Claire remarking that "I wish I could see a few Carbonari" (*NSW* VIII 137) is probably what prompted the Austrian authorities to intercept her mail in Milan, as part of their ongoing surveillance of nationalist sympathizers.[14]

For centuries, the nation we now know as Italy had been politically divided, a peninsula composed of numerous duchies and city-states, some independent, others ruled by Austria, France, Spain, or the Papacy. The inhabitants accorded their first loyalty to their cities or regions, conceiving themselves as Romans, Venetians, or Sicilians, rather than as Italians. To their minds, they even spoke different languages, for it was only with the Risorgimento that the Tuscan version of Italian was accepted as the national norm, with other local tongues assuming the lesser status of "dialects." Napoleon, after his conquest of the region of Italy in the 1790s, created there several republics as well as a northern "Kingdom of Italy"; the rule of Naples was given first to his brother Joseph and later to his brother-in-law Joachim Murat. Though subjected to the evils of foreign rule, Napoleon's Italian conquests benefited from centralized governments and considerable development of roads and communications. With Napoleon's defeat in 1815, the war's victors returned the various portions of Italy to their pre-war rulers. Hatred of the French under Murat sparked Giuseppe Capo Bianco to found a secret society called the Carbonari, which violently resisted French exploitation and defied the rules of the Roman Catholic Church. Their activities continued after the restoration of Austrian rule, which violently suppressed six Carbonari rebellions in the 1820s and 1830s. Exiled Carbonaro Giuseppe Mazzini then founded a new nationalist organization, "Young Italy," which gained supporters abroad but met defeat in its rebellions in the 1830s and 1840s. Middle-class Italians were initially attracted to nationalism through the less militant "Neo-Guelphs," who advocated a leading role for the Catholic Church. The Risorgimento achieved its aims in 1870, when, due to the military expertise of General Giuseppe Garibaldi and the diplomacy of Count Camillo Benso di Cavour, a politically unified Kingdom of Italy was established.

Mary Shelley's British audience was conflicted about the Risorgimento. Though sympathetic to the Italian expatriates in London who embodied the cause, including Mazzini himself, many maintained the longstanding British prejudice that the "superstitions" of Catholicism rendered its adherents unfit for self-rule. Moreover, many Britons particularly distrusted Italian nationalism because they loathed Napoleon, who, in the judgment of many, had generated the Risorgimento by giving the Italians a taste of loyalties larger than regional ones – a taste with a decidedly French flavor.

Mary Shelley addresses this problem in her Preface, which Bennett and Robinson have made widely available in *The Mary Shelley Reader*.[15] To invite British sympathy for Italian nationalism, Mary Shelley plots Britain, not

Napoleon, as the source of the Italian, American, and even French "aspiration for free institutions":

> Englishmen, in particular, ought to sympathise in their struggles: for the aspiration for free institutions all over the world has its source in England. Our example first taught the French nobility to seek to raise themselves from courtiers into legislators. The American war of independence, it is true, quickened this impulse, by showing the way to a successful resistance to the undue exercise of authority; but the seed was all sown by us. (*NSW* VIII 67)

Here, the undeniable connection between Napoleon and Italian nationalism is cannily refigured: the Risorgimento's ultimate source is Britain ("the seed was all sown by us"). She thus rewrites the historical plot in a way acceptable to her audience. Despite Mary Shelley's removing the Napoleonic sting from the cause of Italian nationalism, she makes her own allegiances clear by challenging the British prejudice against Italians, writing, "no one can mingle much with the Italians without becoming attached to them" (*NSW* VIII 65), an implicit barb at the common practice of British travelers to mix only with other Britons while residing in Italy, and going on to praise Italians' "courtesy, their simplicity of manner, their evident desire to serve, their rare and exceeding intelligence" (*NSW* VIII 65). Moreover, Mary Shelley shuffles the received gender politics of travel, singling out a book by a woman, Lady Morgan, as "dear to the Italians" (*NSW* III 66), despite its notoriety in being banned by the Vatican.[16] More subtly, she critiques the standard charge of the "effeminacy" of Italians that underwrote British prejudices, turning the tables on Britons themselves: "When we visit Italy, we become what the Italians were censured for being, – enjoyers of the beauties of nature, the elegance of art, the delights of climate, the recollections of the past, and the pleasures of society, without a thought beyond" (*NSW* VIII 69). In addition to inviting Britons to consider the arbitrariness of the prejudice by substituting themselves for the Italians in the feminized position, this paragraph implies a link between travel and femininity, a far cry from the usual assumption of travel and sexual adventure as male prerogatives. The hint that femininity characterizes the superior traveler, along with the praise of Lady Morgan, consolidates the sense that Mary Shelley saw herself joining a tradition of women travel writers, including Wollstonecraft and Montagu, mentioned in *History of a Six Weeks' Tour*.

Mary Shelley asserts that Italian literature, as well as Carbonarism, demonstrates Italy's readiness for national autonomy. She summarizes the achievements of poet and novelist Alessandro Manzoni, whose novel, *I Promessi Sposi* (*The Betrothed*), helped make the Tuscan dialect the national language; of playwright Giovanni Battista Niccolini, whose play *Arnaldo da Brescia* called Italians to arms for Garibaldi; and of historians General Pietro Colletta and Michele Amari. And she equates the literary artist's mission with nationalism: "The history of Italian poetry confirms the truth, that the poet follows the real and the sublimest scope of art when he keeps in mind the character *of his country* and of his age" (emphasis added; NSW VIII 329).[17] In advocating such a historically specific involvement on the poet's part, Mary Shelley qualifies her husband's view. While he praised political involvement, declaring that the revolutionary Milton "Stood alone illuminating an age unworthy of him," Percy Bysshe Shelley also emphasized transhistorical values as the essence of poetry, writing that "[t]he distorted notions of invisible things [i.e., historical forms of religion] which Dante and his rival Milton have idealized, are merely the mask and mantle in which these great poets walk through eternity enveloped and disguised" (*SPP* 520, 526).

When treating the Carbonari directly, Mary Shelley faced the problem of justifying their cause, a unified and liberated Italian nation, while disapproving of their violent methods. She elevates the worth of the cause by calling it a *"political religion"* (original emphasis; NSW VIII 318), praising the genius of its founder, Capo Bianco. She argues that, as regrettable as the violence has been, it was necessary in order to overcome the linked tyrannies of church and state. The tyrannies were exemplified in the French government's deceptions in luring Capo Bianco to his death and in the Catholic Church's designating Carbonarism a "sin" that confessors promptly reported to the secular authorities. Her view of the Carbonari stresses their opposition to the French and to Napoleon, making the Risorgimento more palatable to the Napoleon-hating Britons.

Reviews indicate that Mary Shelley found a partial hearing for her cause. *The Morning Chronicle* praises her "spirit of sympathy for the character and prospects of the people" of Italy, while *The Observer* complains, "With her, as with all women, politics is a matter of the heart, and not as with the more robust nature of man, of the head . . . It is an idle and unprofitable theme for a woman."[18] The aftermath of the book's publication included an unexpected sour note: Gatteschi, despite having received the £60 fee for *Rambles*, tried to blackmail Mary Shelley, threatening to expose her letters to him. The contents of the letters are not known: her thoughts of marrying Gatteschi? Indiscreet details of her relations with Shelley? Either would damage the respectability she was trying to forge for her son. In the end, a friend bribed the Paris police to raid Gatteschi's apartment and seize *all* of his papers, which he then destroyed.[19] There is no evidence that Mary Shelley, in her relief, noted the irony that one of her own agents used the same secret, counter-revolutionary police methods that had been inflicted on her earlier by the Milan post office!

Whether or not Mary Shelley's letters discussed her marrying Gatteschi, the topic of a second marriage was a touchy one. Widowed at twenty-four, she understandably sought a companion, but her desires were vexed by her ambiguous social status. She was still, by some lights, unworthy of genteel company, a fallen woman who as a teenager had run away with a married man.[20] By other lights, she had married so high in the poetic pantheon that a worthy successor was unlikely. She herself acknowledged this problem in declining the advances of John Howard Payne, while using him to gain the notice of a worthy possible successor, American novelist Washington Irving.[21] Her 1840s travels were interwoven with the end of her hopes to marry Aubrey Beauclerk, and the writing of *Rambles*, as we have seen, was fired by her admiration of Gatteschi. As if protesting too much against these might-have-beens, *Rambles* forges a key element of the Shelley legend, the image of Mary Shelley as the poet's loyal widow.

Rambles as life writing and as pilgrimage

Mary Shelley sold the idea of *Rambles* to her publisher, Edward Moxon, by describing it as autobiographical, "personal to myself" (*L* III 96). She had long desired to write the life of Shelley (which would also be, in part, her own life), but had been stymied by her father-in-law's threat to cut off her allowance and her son's if she brought the Shelley name into print. For years she evaded the letter of the law by identifying herself as "the author of *Frankenstein*" in her writings. But with Sir Timothy Shelley's death in 1844, she could publish *Rambles* as "By Mrs. Shelley." As autobiographer and travel writer, however, Mary Shelley was constrained by internalized prohibitions as well. As Mary Jean Corbett observes, "most secular women autobiographers . . . can master their anxiety about being circulated, read, and interpreted only by . . . subordinating their histories of themselves to others' histories."[22] Accordingly, Mary Shelley crafted a persona that stressed her roles as widow and mother, though at times she subverts these relational roles by subordinating her husband's memory to her own, still-unfolding drama. Writing in the shadow of Percy Bysshe Shelley's ambiguous reputation, she enhanced her own respectability by suppressing her "fallen woman" status, her husband's multiple infidelities, and her own role in Shelley's desertion of his first wife, Harriet Westbrook, which led to her suicide. Her son, Percy Florence Shelley, appears as a young Cantabridgian, entering upon adulthood among the English gentry.

Rambles juggles several agendas: her need to enhance her reputation (and live down Percy Bysshe Shelley's); her need for healing (possibly the early symptoms of a brain tumor, possibly migraines); and her interest in

Catholicism, despite her very English disdain for its superstitions and her good old Jacobin hatred of the priesthood. Much of the book's power derives, in particular, from Mary Shelley's harnessing the conflict between the impulses to hide the Shelley family dirty laundry and to cleanse her portion of it. Moreover, Mary Shelley had a need to expiate what appears to be "survivor guilt," a contemporary term that came into use in the 1950s and 1960s to characterize the continued suffering of Holocaust survivors.[23] Now generalized to include survivors of military action, terrorist attacks, or life-threatening illnesses, survivor guilt can entail idealization of the dead, remorse that "the wrong person died," with consequent feelings of worthlessness, and the setting of impossible standards to expiate the guilt.

In *Rambles*, Mary Shelley's own expiation of guilt centers on the trope of pilgrimage. In religious practices, pilgrims visit a shrine, often a remote, difficult-to-reach site of saints' bones or other relics, in search of healing or insight; they believe the rigors of the journey will expiate their sins. In the opening letter, Mary Shelley sounds the pilgrim's themes of relics and healing:

> Can it, indeed, be true, that I am about to revisit Italy? How many years are gone since I quitted that country! There I left the mortal remains of those beloved – my husband and my children, whose loss changed my whole existence, substituting, for happy peace and the interchange of deep-rooted affections, years of desolate solitude, and a hard struggle with the world; which only now, as my son is growing up, is brightening into a better day . . . Travelling will cure all . . . (*NSW* VIII 75–76)

Like a pilgrim, Mary Shelley sets out to visit "mortal remains," but those of a secular saint, in hope that the journey "will cure all." At journey's end she specifically names the trip a pilgrimage:

> "What are the pleasures that I enjoy at Rome?" you ask. They are so many, that my mind is brimful of a sort of glowing satisfaction, mingled with tearful associations. Besides all that Rome itself affords of delightful [*sic*] to the eye and imagination, I revisit it as the bourne of a pious pilgrimage. The treasures of my youth lie buried here . . . There is one view from the Coliseum that I am never tired of contemplating. Ascending to the second range of arches, and looking from the verge towards the tomb of Cestius . . . [which], gleaming at a distance, is a resting-place for the eye. (*NSW* VIII 347–48)

The tomb of Gaius Cestius,[24] built at the time of Augustus, overlooks the so-called Protestant cemetery in Rome, where John Keats, Percy Bysshe Shelley, and William Shelley were buried. Her pilgrimage, like a traditional Catholic's, finds its "bourne" or destination in Rome at Holy Week. By mentioning her own attendance at the traditional Holy Week ceremonies – a common tourist activity – Mary Shelley develops a private counterpoint to the Christian belief in the Resurrection, a private religion honoring "myriads of [the] loving spirits" of the dead (*NSW* VIII 123).

Pilgrims have traditionally sought physical healing, from Chaucer's pilgrims seeking the healing intercession of St. Thomas à Becket to the thousands who still travel annually to Lourdes. In Mary Shelley's day, many a secular pilgrim went to the Continent in search of healing. Travel was one of the few treatments in the arsenal of nineteenth-century physicians, along with the narcotic laudanum (opium dissolved in alcohol), to which Samuel Taylor Coleridge and numerous others became addicted. Tuberculosis patients such as John Keats had only travel and "change of air" to treat their symptoms until Sir Alexander Fleming discovered penicillin in 1928. Mary Shelley, hoping that "travelling will cure all," spent three weeks "taking the cure" at the Kissingen spa in Germany. As Beth Dolan Kautz observes, Mary Shelley critiques the spa regimen and its doctors: she chafes at the spa physicians' many prohibitions, choosing her self-directed walks in the picturesque landscape as the more effective cure.[25] This rebelliousness against spa doctors makes local and personal her political advocacy of Italian freedom from Austrian oppression.[26] Kautz notes in particular Mary Shelley's satiric use of military metaphors (e.g., "a regiment of sick people" [*NSW* VIII 169]) to reinforce the likeness. Moreover, the fact that she embeds the spa episode within the book's trajectory toward Rome suggests that she links physical healing less with spas than with the exorcism of her memories of her husband.

For many with survivor guilt, it seems that one's own survival indicates a lack of courage or loyalty to the dead; at the same time, such survivors may focus on unsettled scores with the dead. In Mary Shelley's case, the feelings of worthlessness and guilt bred recurrent suicidal thoughts, expressed in her journals of the 1830s and 1840s (*J* II 521, 548, 571 and n.1), as well as exacerbating painful recollections of her husband's infidelities. To worsen matters, in *Epispsychidion* (1821), Percy Bysshe Shelley blamed his infatuation with Teresa ("Emilia") Viviani on his wife, a "Moon . . . in the sickness of eclipse," "chaste" and "cold" (*SPP* 400, lines 309–10, 281). That Mary Shelley may have internalized her husband's blame is registered in her journal entry: "now I am truly *cold moonshine*" (original emphasis; *L* I 284 [21 Oct 1822]).

After her son purchases a small, unsafe-looking boat at Lake Como (*NSW* VIII 108, 113), Mary Shelley finds an opportunity to expiate her guilt:

> This evening I had the pleasure of finding that I had become not quite a coward, and that I feared for P —— more than for myself. I crossed the lake with Mr. ——; the wind rose, and our little sail was hoisted; but the waves rose with the wind, and our craft is so small that a little breeze seems much. However,

> I had been scolded, and had scolded myself for my timidity, and would not now display even prudence, but went on; and though twenty times I was on the point of proposing to return, I did not, for I was not aware that my companion silently shared my alarm. At length we had nearly reached the opposite side of the lake; the wind and waves had both risen, and if they increased, danger was at hand. I did not feel fear, but I felt the risk. (*NSW* VIII 118)

She plots this experience as a breakthrough, dispelling the self-accusations caused by survivor guilt, namely cowardice ("I had become not quite a coward"; "I did not feel fear, but I felt the risk") and selfishness ("I feared for P —— more than for myself"). Percy Bysshe Shelley, when caught in a storm on Lake Geneva in 1815, had apparently cared more for his boating companion, Byron, than for himself: "I was overcome with humiliation, when I thought that his life might have been risked to preserve mine."[27] Here, Mary Shelley seems to expiate her guilt by miming her husband's terror, if not his drowning. The force of this expiation emerges in a startling moment of enlightenment:

> [L]istening to the ripplet of the calm lake splashing at my feet . . . [m]y heart was elevated, purified, subdued . . . It has seemed to me – and on such an evening, I have felt it, – that this world, endowed as it is outwardly with endless shapes and influences of beauty and enjoyment, is peopled also in its spiritual life by myriads of loving spirits . . . Whether the beloved dead make a portion of this holy company, I dare not guess, but that such exists, I feel. (*NSW* VIII 123)

"Purified" of cowardice and selfishness, Mary Shelley imagines that "the beloved dead" reciprocate the affection of the living as "myriads of loving spirits"; her sense of their presence dispels the sense of unrelieved mourning that opens the book.

Mary Shelley's book participates in the travel-book convention of museum-going.[28] Her interest in sacred art in particular was shared by many English women in the 1830s, 1840s, and 1850s, including her friend, Anna Jameson. Much of this interest focuses on representations of the Madonna, not surprising in a country where the cult of the Madonna reaches such proportions that the Pope officially proclaimed the miracle of the Immaculate Conception in February of 1849, a doctrine consolidated in popular Catholic piety by the apparitions at Lourdes, France, in 1858. Mary Shelley's meditations on Ghirlandaio's *Adoration of the Magi* (1488) spark the expiation of guilt over Harriet Westbrook Shelley's death:

> There is another picture of this age, which to see, is to feel the happiness which the soul receives from objects presented to the eye, that kindle and elevate the imagination. It represents the Adoration of the Magi . . . In the back-ground is represented the Murder of the Innocents, in all its terror; but immediately

in the fore-ground, on each side of the Virgin, kneel two children – the souls of the Innocents who died for Christ, and are redeemed by him. The attitude of these babes, especially of one, has that inexpressible charm of innocence which words cannot convey, and which since the creation of man, the pencil has seldom been able to depict. (*NSW* VIII 304)

This painting, juxtaposing the Madonna's joy with King Herod's guilty mass murder of the Innocents, evokes Mary Shelley's deep ambivalence over Harriet Shelley's suicide, a tragedy linked, inseparably, to her deepest joy. Ironically, the same act that left Harriet's children motherless made possible the marriage and children Mary Shelley adored. Moreover, she had not waited for Harriet Shelley's death to become pregnant, for the baby girl who lived only a few days was born in 1815, well before Harriet Shelley's death in 1816; unlike the other pregnancies, this one was probably not welcome. After Harriet's death, both Shelleys blamed Mary for the break-up of the first marriage. During the custody battle for Ianthe and Charles, P. B. Shelley wrote to Harriet's sister that she "may excusably regard [Mary] as the cause of [her] sister's ruin" (*PBSL* I 523).[29] Years later, Mary Shelley joined him in blaming herself, writing in 1839 of "Poor Harriet to whose sad fate I attribute so many of my own heavy sorrows as the atonement claimed by fate for her death" (*J* II 560).

Indeed, these "heavy sorrows" fill the background of Ghirlandaio's *Adoration*; the vengeful Harriet claiming atonement takes the visual form of Herod's soldiers slaughtering babies, a link reinforced by the similarity of names (Harriet/Herod). "[O]n each side of the Virgin," however, "kneel two children, the souls of the innocents who died" (*NSW* VIII 304). This restoration suggests the outcome Mary Shelley might hope for after expiating her guilt, receiving back her dead children, "innocent" of any guilt in their parents' doings. The relief afforded by this outcome is registered obliquely: "There is another picture of this age, which to see, is to feel the happiness which the soul receives from [worthy] objects."

Like most accounts of pilgrimages, Mary Shelley's does not include an account of the journey home. It does, however, include a coda of a couple of chapters after the trip to Rome, which recount a visit to Sorrento. In venturing there, Mary Shelley participated in a revision of the Grand Tourist's routes: as historian Jeremy Black notes, eighteenth-century travelers generally went no farther south then Naples due to poor accommodations and bad roads.[30] This picture changed with the excavation of the city of Pompeii, buried by an eruption of Vesuvius in 79 AD and rediscovered in 1748. About a fourth of Pompeii had been excavated by the mid-nineteenth century, "the greatest progress having been made by the French during the first sixteen years of this century,"[31] and excavation continued sporadically after the war. Though a children's book on Pompeii appeared in 1826, the rage to visit Pompeii was ignited by Sir Edward Bulwer-Lytton's novel, *The Last Days of Pompeii* (1834), popularized in its turn by playwright Louisa Medina (?1814–38). The increasing crowds of tourists inspired locals to improve conditions nearby; as Mary Shelley notes (*NSW* VIII 370), famed traveler Mariana Starke and American novelist James Fenimore Cooper preceded her in visiting and writing about Sorrento, which she describes as follows:

> The Cocumella has become a home – it is a joy to return to our terrace, to breathe the fragrance of the orange-flowers – to see the calm sea spread out at our feet, as we look over the bay to Naples – while above us bends a sky – in whose depths ship-like clouds glide – and the moon hangs luminous, a pendant sphere of silver fire. (*NSW* VIII 386)

Here "home," having been ruptured by deaths of P. B. Shelley, William, and Clara, is restored, as is the calmness of the once-murderous sea. Moreover, the reciprocity between the calm Tyrrhenian Sea and the oceanic sky, full of cloud-ships gliding across its surface (not sinking, as her husband's had) obliquely assert that the journey has does its work of expiation. Mary Shelley, once blamed by her husband as "the cold chaste Moon," is reborn as "a pendant sphere of silver fire."

This posited rebirth crystallizes Mary Shelley's lifelong self-presentation as an author and as the wife of P. B. Shelley. In her first production, she wrote anonymously and as part of a joint project with her husband, with some evidence that she subordinated her contributions to his. In her last, the title page proclaims her as "Mrs. Shelley," the much-published author. Complicating her assertion that she is the "pendant" one, *Rambles* plots Percy Bysshe Shelley's constant presence, not so much an author in his own right, but as a supporting actor in Mary Shelley's vividly unfolding psychological drama. The authority and author-appeal of *Rambles* come from a lifetime of excitement, suffering, and literary production; it gives an author's seasoned reflections on themes she visited earlier, such as the wrenching death of one's children (in *The Last Man*) and the need for a maternal figure in religion (broached in *Valperga*). *Rambles*, in particular, helps scholars to reveal Mary Shelley's narrative power, political astuteness, and psychological depth.

NOTES

The author thanks Ivy Rudd Barger, Doucet Devin Fischer, and Kristen Tate for their comments on previous drafts of this chapter.

1 Pierre Bourdieu, *Outline of the Theory of Practice*, trans. Richard Nice (Cambridge: Cambridge University Press, 1977), pp. 171–83. For the Grand Tour, see Jeremy Black, *The British and the Grand Tour* (Beckenham, Kent: Croom Helm, 1985); and Gerald Newman, *The Rise of English Nationalism*, 2nd edn. (New York: St. Martin's Press, 1997), pp. 42–44.

2 See Charles Batten, *Pleasurable Instruction: Form and Convention in Eighteenth-Century Travel Literature* (Berkeley: University of California Press, 1978); and Percy G. Adams, *Travelers and Travel Liars, 1660–1800* (Berkeley: University of California Press, 1962).

3 Donald H. Reiman, ed., *Shelley and his Circle, 1773–1822*, 8 vols. (Cambridge, MA: Harvard University Press, 1986), VII 41. Jonathan Wordsworth disagrees about the volume's intentionality; see the Introduction to *History of a Six Weeks' Tour* by Mary Shelley and Percy Bysshe Shelley (Oxford: Woodstock Books, 1991), n.p. In this chapter, I use J. Wordsworth's edition of *History of a Six Weeks' Tour* (*HSWT*) for P. B. Shelley's contributions, cited in the notes. Quotations from Mary Shelley's contribution to *HSWT* and *Rambles* are drawn from *Travel Writing*, ed. Jeanne Moskal, vol. VIII in *NSW*; see also Moskal, "'To speak in Sanchean phrase': Cervantes and the Politics of Mary Shelley's *History of a Six Weeks' Tour*," *MST* 18–37; and Moskal, "Introductory Note" to *HSWT*, *NSW* VIII 1–6. For further discussion, see citations in "Further reading" to works by Angela Jones, Benjamin Colbert, and Jacqueline M. Labbe.

4 Moskal, "Introductory Note" to *HSWT*, *NSW* VIII 2.

5 Throughout this paragraph I rely on John Mee, "Rousseau," in *An Oxford Companion to the Romantic Age: British Culture 1776–1832*, gen. ed. Iain McCalman (Oxford: Oxford University Press, 1999), pp. 684–85; and on Gregory Dart, *Rousseau, Robespierre and English Romanticism* (Cambridge: Cambridge University Press, 1999), pp. 1–9.

6 Mary Wollstonecraft, *The Wrongs of Woman; or, Maria*, in *Works of Mary Wollstonecraft*, eds. Janet Todd and Marilyn Butler, 7 vols. (London: William Pickering, 1989), I 96.

7 *HSWT*, ed. Jonathan Wordsworth, p. 128.

8 Dart, *Rousseau*, p. 2.

9 David Duff, *Romance and Revolution: Shelley and the Politics of a Genre* (New York: Cambridge University Press, 1994), p. 3.

10 William Blake, *Jerusalem*, plate 95, l. 20, *The Complete Poetry and Prose of William Blake*, ed. David V. Erdman, newly rev. edn. (New York: Doubleday, 1988), p. 255.

11 Esther H. Schor, "Mary Shelley in Transit," *OMS* 236.

12 Emily W. Sunstein, *Mary Shelley: Romance and Reality* (Boston: Little, Brown, 1989), pp. 360–71; on Gatteschi, see *L* III 85, n. 8. On *Rambles*, see citations in "Further reading" to Elizabeth Nitchie, Jean de Palacio, Shirley Foster, Esther Schor, Beth Dolan Kautz, Clarissa Campbell Orr, Nora Crook; Jeanne Moskal, "Speaking the Unspeakable: Art Criticism as Life-Writing in Mary Shelley's *Rambles in Germany and Italy*," in *Mary Wollstonecraft and Mary Shelley: Writing Lives*, eds. Helen Buss, D. L. Macdonald, and Anne McWhir (Waterloo, Ont.: Wilfrid Laurier University Press, 2001), pp. 189–216; and Moskal, "Introductory Note" to *Rambles*, *NSW* VIII 49–54.

13 See also Moskal, "Introductory Note," *NSW* VIII 49, 54.

14 See Nora Crook, " 'Meek and Bold': Mary Shelley's Support for the Risorgimento," in *Mary versus Mary*, eds. Lilla Maria Crisafulli and Giovanna Silvani (Naples: Liguori, 2001), pp. 84, 86.

15 Betty T. Bennett and Charles E. Robinson, *The Mary Shelley Reader* (New York: Oxford University Press, 1990), pp. 382–86.

16 See Jeanne Moskal, "Gender, Nationality, and Textual Authority in Lady Morgan's Travel Books," in *Romantic Women Writers: Voices and Countervoices*, eds. Paula R. Feldman and Theresa M. Kelley (Hanover, NH: University of New England Press, 1995), pp. 171–93 and 298–302.

17 Giovanni Battista Niccolini, *Arnold of Brescia, A Tragedy*, trans. Theodosia Garrow (London: Longman, Brown, Green, and Longman, 1846).

18 *The Morning Chronicle*, August 23, 1844, p. 3; *The Spectator*, August 18, 1844, p. 782; *The Critic*, September 2, 1844, p. 36; *The Morning Post*, August 19, 1844, p. 7; *The Observer*, August 11, 1844, p. 3.

19 See Sunstein, *Mary Shelley*, pp. 370–71, and L III 204–14, 230–43.

20 Mary Shelley's disrepute may have sabotaged her romance with Aubrey Beauclerk, an MP who, despite his affection for Mary Shelley, married into the eminent Goring family in 1833 and, after his first wife's death, became engaged to Rosa Robinson shortly after Mary Shelley left for Italy. His career would have been helped by these matches, rather than tarnished by the association with Mary Shelley. See Sunstein, *Mary Shelley*, p. 347.

21 See *ibid.*, pp. 267–68, 398.

22 Mary Jean Corbett, "Literary Domesticity and Women Writers' Subjectivities," in *Representing Femininity: Middle-Class Subjectivity in Victorian and Edwardian Women's Autobiographies* (New York: Oxford University Press, 1992), p. 97.

23 See Leo Eitinger and Robert Krell with Miriam Rieck, *The Psychological and Medical Effects of Concentration Camps and Related Persecutions on Survivors of the Holocaust: A Research Bibliography* (Vancouver: University of British Columbia Press, 1985), p. 5.

24 As per the *Oxford Classical Dictionary* (1996), the modern spelling is "Gaius."

25 Beth Dolan Kautz, "Spas and Salutary Landscapes: The Geography of Health in Mary Shelley's *Rambles in Germany and Italy*," in *Romantic Geographies: Discourses of Travel 1775–1844*, ed. Amanda Gilroy (Manchester: Manchester University Press, 2000), pp. 169–70, 176.

26 Esther Schor, "Mary Shelley in Transit," OMS 244.

27 *History of a Six Weeks' Tour*, ed. Wordsworth, p. 122.

28 Moskal, "Speaking the Unspeakable," pp. 189–216.

29 Percy Bysshe Shelley writes of "the lady whose union with me you may excusably regard as the cause of your sister's ruin" (*PBSL* I 523).

30 Black, *The British and the Grand Tour*, pp. 22–23.

31 John Murray [publisher], *Handbook for Travellers in Southern Italy*, quoted in Moskal, notes to NSW VIII 376, n.1.

16

TIMOTHY MORTON

Mary Shelley as cultural critic

> the voice of dead time, in still vibrations, is breathed from these dumb things . . .
>
> (Mary Shelley, *The Last Man*, III x 336)

The word "culture" is a contested term. It hesitates between "nature" and "nurture," an insoluble conundrum.[1] It can, for instance, mean a corporation's management structures or the medium in which people come to discover their existence. Mary Shelley engaged with varied forms of what we might call "culture." She worked on the journal *The Liberal*, a collaboration amongst the Shelley–Godwin–Hunt circle in England and Italy (*J* II 431). She published at least a dozen essays of the genre that we now call "review essays"[2] and dozens more stories and sketches for the annuals. Shelley also edited and wrote the prefaces and notes to two editions of her late husband's poetry and edited his essays, letters, and translations. In addition to her novels and novella, she wrote poems and plays and translated works from Italian and German. A scholarly edition of her biographies is now available and her travelogues are at last back in print.[3] In all these works, Shelley demonstrated her special awareness and intelligence concerning culture, both specifically as the literary productions and values of her era, and generally as notions of culture as a whole way of life (as the critic Raymond Williams, author of *Culture and Society*, would have phrased it).[4]

This chapter is divided into four sections. The first closely reads several of Shelley's review essays, which provide a strong sense of her views of culture. The second investigates notions of culture available to her. The third focuses upon one aspect of Shelley's ideas about culture, that of the space of contact among people, and the fourth closely traces this aspect through her essays. The result is a picture of Mary Shelley as cultural critic: not only contributing to culture at large through production, but actively participating in a debate that was key to discussions about society and politics in the nineteenth century.

Mary Shelley's cultural work

Mary Shelley's essays, published in a variety of venues, exemplify the ways in which this genre can encompass wide cultural spaces, bounded in the nutshell of its form. Many of her essays appeared in *The Liberal* and James Mill's *Westminster Review*. The latter journal was not radical like some of the underground journals of Shelley's day, such as Thomas Wooler's *Black Dwarf*, but it was a good way left of the *Quarterly Review*, which had attacked the Shelleys' doctor, the materialist William Lawrence. Shelley also wrote for the *London Magazine* and *Blackwood's*; both engaged the liberal and radical thought of the Romantics. Shelley's work demonstrates her mastery in the art of the essay: each essay is replete with balanced, antithetical prose of vigor and gravity that searches for the deeper implications of her topics. Upon close reading, these essays reveal an expansive critical mind engaging with issues crucial to her contemporaries: the nature of poetry, the workings of the human mind, the idea of culture itself.

Shelley knew too well what it was to be a cultural alien, staying too long in a foreign country to be classified as a tourist, too short to become naturalized, even if that had been her inclination. In her review essay, "The English in Italy" (1826), she looks for general cultural patterns in the behavior of Anglo-Italians. It begins by grouping expatriots and the reader together under the sign of a knowing "we." Shelley displays her knowledge that culture constitutes an environment, a set of unwritten rules that literally demarcate social positions. Her example is marriage. The "laws" of constraint and propriety recorded by Lord Normanby in his collection of Anglo-Italian stories "are the music, the accompaniment by which [women] regulate their steps until they cannot walk without it." The description of Tuscan farms later in the essay seems to incarnate this idea of culture as a surrounding aesthetic dimension: "[T]he loud cicale, with ceaseless chirp, fills the air with sound, and in the evening the fire-flies come out from the myrtle hedges, and form a thousand changing and flashing constellations on the green corn-fields, which is their favourite resort." As we shall see, this idea of all-pervasive ambient culture had significant theoretical overtones for Shelley. Let us note here in passing that Shelley is not quite rooting us to the soil of a particular region: the fire-flies disorientate the sense of heaven and earth by looking like stars on the fields; earlier in the same paragraph the smell of the myrtle is a "spicy odour" that "gives a taste of Indian climes."[5] The ambience is vivid, yet strange: particular, yet disorientating. In studying Shelley's sense of culture, we encounter this structure of feeling again and again.

In an essay on Rousseau's lover, Madame d'Houdetôt, her theme is the reclamation of a woman lost to patriarchal history. Shelley uses a republican rhetoric of Enlightenment pedigree, of a chain of illuminating continuity between present and past. History is memory; culture shines a light in the darkness. To break the chain is to fall into the so-called dark ages, an Enlightenment-period construct for pre-Renaissance Europe. Shelley, however, extrapolates the meaning of "dark ages" to feminist effect, implying that if we forget such women, we ourselves fall into the dark ages. "[D'Houdetôt] was," writes Shelley, "a witness of those tremendous vicissitudes that shook our moral world as an earthquake"; she contributed to her era as a woman writer, sitting "over her embroidery frame."[6]

Reviewing Prosper Mérimée's *Illyrian Poems*, Shelley admired Mérimée for his republican hostility to feudal power: his simulated poetry from an imagined Bohemia, she writes, presents "a new and terrible page of human experience." Such poetry is historically significant, depicting "the peasantry, long trampled on by the iron heel of feudal tyranny," but the writer himself is a kind of Columbus, a discoverer of new worlds. Shelley suggests here, as her husband did in *A Defence of Poetry* and *A Philosophical View of Reform*, that poetry, in its very nature, cuts through hierarchical structures: "Columbus, anticipating the discovery of the unknown shores that pale over western progress over the wild and distant waves of the Atlantic, felt the old world, extended in latitude and longitude so far and wide, a narrow prison."[7] Such is the utopian edge of capitalist ideology. Moreover, uninterested in fostering a concept of Englishness limited to the study and embellishment of works of English literature, Shelley reveals her cosmopolitanism.

Shelley's review of Anna Brownell Jameson's *Loves of the Poets* extends her poetics further. Here, she takes a utilitarian view of poetry in a Marxian sense, insisting that artistic endeavor finds its basis in "satisfaction and enjoyment to our senses and our physical wants." A class distinction instantly appears between "the rich," who enjoy "much of these" "[i]n this Northern clime," while the relatively poor enjoy those activities (or non-activities) associated with pauses from labor: food, sleep, rest. Ultimately, however it is "love" that takes the sting from life, for rich and poor alike; this is the fulcrum of the essay.[8] Here she quotes Percy Bysshe Shelley's fragment, "On Love": love is "when we find within our own thoughts the chasm of an [insufficient] void, and seek to awaken in all things that are, a community with what we experience within ourselves" (*SPP* 503). (Shelley substituted "inefficient" for her late husband's "insufficient," a slip to which we will return.) For both Shelleys, the social field is constituted through a compassionate extension of one's sympathies, conceived in the terms of contemporary neurophysiology: a spreading-out of mental (and emotional) feelers into an otherwise "indifferent void."[9] "Community" is contact across an empty gulf, like a spark of electricity in space; the medium is empty, but it can flash with energy. Here Shelley oscillates between individualist (Romantic) and collectivist (sentimentalist) views of social being.

Thus Shelley clinches her argument, returning to her utilitarian opening with renewed depth and clarity: "is not a poet an incarnation of the very essence of love?" In Mary Shelley's defense of poetry – "Is [the poet] not that which wakens melody in the silent chords of the human heart?" – the poet is an energetic principle rather than a metaphysical being. Shelley is here neither a humanist nor a strict anti-humanist, neither a strict materialist nor a strict idealist. It is love rather than sleep and bread which finally soothes the world, but love itself is a vibration, a thrill of matter. On the other hand, the way poetry reflects reality is as a utopian, idealizing concentration of energy: "[The poet's] soul is like one of the pools in the Ilex woods of the Maremma, it reflects the surrounding universe, but it beautifies, groupes [sic], and mellows their tints, making a little world within itself, the copy of the outer one; but more entire, more faultless."[10] For Shelley, simply copying the universe establishes a critical difference. Theodor Adorno, the Frankfurt School theorist, would perhaps agree, having declared that the very form of art, howsoever reactionary its aims, opens up the possibility that things might have been otherwise. For Adorno, art is the negative knowledge of reality, in that its beauty and sublimity provoke us to reflect upon why our world is so full of pain and suffering.[11]

Mary Shelley's view was always complex, always plying between worlds. Having been a participant-observer in the culture of Italy, and having been a professional woman of letters in a field dominated by male writers, Shelley knew well the condition of "betweenness." Shelley's "betweenness" made her reluctant to decide between the individual and the group, and between collectivist and individualist ideas of how we live among others. Typically, in the process of delimiting the argument toward the particular condition of being a woman poet, which is where the essay on Jameson closes, Shelley includes the whole world. On the one hand, the "betweenness" which Shelley articulates is a useful cultural-critical tool. At the same time, it belongs to a long tradition of playful speculation in the genre of essay writing. From Montaigne to Hazlitt, the essay has been a mode that has stressed openness over closure (essai, "attempt"). Within the neat bounds but open contours of the essay genre, Shelley's intellect boldly leaps.

Ideas of culture

Critics have not perceived Shelley to have participated directly in the "culture and society" debate that preoccupied many nineteenth-century British writers, from Samuel Taylor Coleridge and Thomas Carlyle to Matthew

Arnold and J. S. Mill. As Raymond Williams has demonstrated, these writers sought in various ways to establish an idea of cultural criticism, or critique, that would mitigate the ravages of the Industrial Revolution, utilitarianism and other symptoms of the modern age. Shelley's slight use of the word "culture" is generally characteristic of her period and her intellectual circles. When Shelley does use the word "critique" – for instance when she asks John Bowring of the *Westminster Review*, "Is it now too late to write the critique I promised?" (*L* II 45) – she uses it to mean an essay examining a literary or artistic work. But in Shelley's day, this word would expand to its more philosophically engaged, originally Marxist, definition, that used by the Frankfurt School and currently by Anglo-American cultural studies.[12] Shelley's sense in the quotation is surely the former.

Might the very slightness of Shelley's use of "culture" be a clue to her view of collective social being? In other words, the rarely used word might be like Sherlock Holmes's non-existent barking dog, whose non-barking is precisely the vital evidence.[13] My contention here is that Shelley nudged the idea of culture away from what reactionary writers such as Edmund Burke depicted in his 1790 *Reflections on the Revolution in France*: the all-encompassing, grave, and aestheticized authority of layers upon layers of tradition, an organicism so popular with a strain of cultural critics from Coleridge to T. S. Eliot. Such theories of culture look back; but after a brief survey of several ideas of culture available to Shelley, I will argue that, to some extent, Mary Shelley's theory looks forward.

The medicinal, even salvific, Germanic Romantic ideas of *Kultur* and *Gemeinschaft* are warmer, more concretely embodied versions of the organicist idea. Emerging in the writings of such eighteenth-century thinkers as Alexander von Humboldt, who had invoked the idea of culture as rooted in climate or local atmosphere, these terms evoke a touchy-feely sense of community, a realm of intimate contact and traditions, similar to the English nationalist notion of "organic community" propagated by the twentieth-century Cambridge critic, F. R. Leavis. Leavis's ideal society was a village-like space in which face-to-face contact guaranteed the stability of representation, and in which intellectual ideas were felt on the pulses. Jürgen Habermas's late twentieth-century theory of the "public sphere" of the bourgeoisie, embodied in the seventeenth- and eighteenth-century coffee house and stock exchange, offers an alternative view that is less utopian, more pragmatic; it is focused upon the idea of culture as a conversation between equal participants. By contrast, the Francophone, republican idea of *civilisation* is a more bracing, rationalist model of social space.[14] Like American republicanism, it rejects antiquated feudal hierarchies while strengthening the idea that private property guarantees access to the new world of open communication (or *conversazione*, as the eighteenth-century radical John Thelwall called it), leaving unresolved the issue of who exactly has access.

Since Burke's *Reflections*, with its notion of culture as inherited prejudice, or "second nature," English ideas of culture have oscillated between the nestling warmth of Coleridge's early depictions of the nook or dell in which poetry can be made, and the class of the "clerisy," who would temper opposing classes to suit the needs of the whole, on to the cooling liquid of Matthew Arnold's mid-Victorian idea of culture as expressed in *Essays in Criticism*. Arnold consistently imagines culture as a refreshing stream of the "best" that has been thought and said, intuitively available through miniaturized "touchstones" that may consist in a mere few lines of verse. Such views have in general been established in opposition to crass utilitarianism and industrial capitalist society: they are more like *Gemeinschaft* than *civilisation*. Where did Shelley fit in?

Ambience and the fantasy of contact

Shelley was fascinated by one of anthropology's founding myths, that of "first contact" between humans from different cultures, taking place upon a supposedly neutral ground, like a chance encounter in a forest or a meeting on a deserted beach. Stories of such encounters had developed since the early-modern recording of tales of wonder, Othello's "anthropophagi," toward something more scientific, though still invested with a provoking sense of otherness.[15] *Frankenstein*, in part, is a thought-experiment in which the Creature's cultural environment is severely attenuated, a kind of laboratory condition: at one point, it is just a kennel, a pile of books, and an adjacent household. Sometimes Shelley placed such moments in her fiction as a sort of message in a bottle from the future: consider, for example, the discovery of the Sybil's prophetic leaves by the "editor" in the "Author's Introduction" to *The Last Man* (see chapter 7).

In these moments, self and other, reader and text, scientist and object, come together in a neutral-seeming medium. The image of the idyllic meeting between equals is both the fantasy object of an anthropological gaze, and the basis of models of society such as Rousseau's theory of the social contract. What this idyll emphasizes is the supposed neutrality of the space of contact. Just as actors might appear on a bare stage and improvise a play, the social appears to be generated by agents who have somehow existed *before* its constitution. Furthermore, the numerous feral children reported in the eighteenth century suggested that humans could live outside society – raised by wolves, for instance – and could then be brought in to human culture and exist in some (marginal) way. Frankenstein's creature deserves some kindness and recognition (and perhaps nurturing? education?) because he is already a part of culture, insofar as culture emerges out of what is natural. The satirical force of the Creature's innocence, reminiscent of Lemuel Gulliver's in Swift's *Gulliver's Travels*, also comments upon notions of culture that are, in Shelley's view, "unnatural." The creature is able spontaneously to differentiate among types of birds and plants, but cannot make sense of the kinds of suffering wrought by humans upon each other in the texts that he reads in the kennel outside the De Laceys' house.

To help elaborate the idea of culture as neutral medium, let us explore the simple and abstract structuralist notion of "contact." In Roman Jakobson's "Closing Statement," six parts of communication make up any message: the addresser, the addressee, the context, the contact, the code, and the message itself. All messages foreground one of these parts.[16] In the traditional structuralist view a "poetic" message foregrounds the message itself at the expense, say, of its referential context or an immediate addressee. Those statements which foreground the "contact" or medium of communication are "phatic": for example, complaining about a crackly telephone line, or the opening declaration of a radio host to her guest – "You're on the air."

What if there were a poetics which foregrounded the contact *as* message? Mary Shelley elaborates images of *contact as content*. When she calls the void "inefficient" in her misquotation of Percy Shelley on love (see the earlier citation), there is a hint of this: that the void is an inefficient medium that has become detectable in its very inadequacy. Shelley's images of space, whether collective or encountered by an alien, are not Germanic and heavy but light and airy. Shelley uses the word "dilate" – to meditate upon or consider – in the 1831 Introduction to *Frankenstein*, noting that she was asked "How I came to think of, and dilate upon, so hideous an idea . . ." In the light of her spacious imagery of collective experience, "dilate" may thus have cultural and political resonances in addition to biographical and obstetric ones. For Shelley, culture should be a liberal, dilating space which opens to encompass as many participants as possible.

Contact in Shelley's essays

The question arises: to what extent is the apparently neutral medium in fact *stained*? Is its neutrality either a disguise for ideological orientations, and/or is that neutrality *itself* a form of ideological orientation? Culturally speaking, is the collective space we inhabit really unmarked by any particular (political) interest? By the 1840s, this notion of a neutral social space comes in for negative criticism when Marx, writing on Rousseau, undermines the idea of "culture" as "natural." He discovers that the supposedly neutral medium of contact is none other than the notion of abstract value, crucial to the function of capitalism and its ideological forms. Two decades earlier, Shelley also contemplates the question of neutrality in her essay "Giovanni Villani" (1823), but for her, the nemeses of neutrality are loosely grouped in the category of "incursions": Shelley notes "a frequent fault among modern authors, and peculiarly among those of the present day, to introduce themselves, their failings and opinions, into the midst of works dedicated to objects sufficiently removed, as one might think, from any danger of such an incursion." But while the "incursive" ego is one liability, "incursions" may also come about when the accretions of the social space diminish the space for people. As we look more closely at Shelley's essays, we find her exploring "incursions" on the space of contact in three contexts: the drama, history, and the city.

In her essay on Florentine historian Giovanni Villani, Shelley uses the drama to think through the space of culture. Shelley herself wrote two mythological dramas (see chapter 11); Percy Shelley so admired them that he turned to her for a play about the Cenci family, which she refused to write. Alluding to the *Spectator* for March 16, 1711, she writes of the ego's incursions:

> This has sometimes the effect of a playhouse anecdote I once heard, of a man missing his way behind the scenes, in passing from one part of the house to the other, and suddenly appearing in his hat and unpicturesque costume, stalking amidst the waves of a frightful storm, much to the annoyance of the highly-wrought feelings of the spectators of the impending catastrophe of a disastrous melodrame.[17]

In the "disastrous" melodrama in the anecdote, the content is *too* immersive; presumably, the storm entails the use of ambient sound-effects like cinema "surround sound" and when the man appears "amidst" the artificial waves, there is some illusion of three-dimensionality. But the disruptive appearance of the man in "unpicturesque" costume, jolts the audience out of the suspension of disbelief, out of the paralysis of thought, and into the more uncertain, open space of the theatre itself, in which thinking can resume.

Shelley conceives of the historian as one who wanders about history as if it were a concrete, fixed dimension, like the Last Man wandering around Rome. Her description of the "wandering" planets (for "wandering" is the meaning of the Greek *planetes*) in her essay on Villani rewrites her idea of history as a Miltonic, republican cosmology: "The fixed stars appear to aberrate; but it is we that move, not they. The regular planets make various *excursions* into the heavens, and we are told that some among them never return to the point whence they departed, and by no chance ever retrace the same path in the pathless sky (my emphasis)."[18] The sky is "pathless": here,

Shelley's notions of contact align with republican political theory, which tends to displace the figure of the monarch central to feudal thinking. In republican forms of representation, instead of the throne and the people beneath it, we find an assembly hall – perhaps a round one – with equal participants joining in conversation across its more open space. The notion of a single solid ruler has been undermined. Thus, while Shelley never took up her father's suggestion to write a history of the Commonwealth, she was keen to demonstrate again and again that she understood the radical forms of representation thrown up in the English Revolution. These survive in her cultural-critical prose, having been almost lost under the weight of reactionary and Whiggish interpretations of British literary tradition.[19] When Frankenstein, traveling through Oxford, visits the tomb of the republican hero Hampden, he contemplates "the divine ideas of liberty and self-sacrifice" and dares for a moment to "shake off [his] chains, and look around [him] with a free and lofty spirit" (F III ii III).[20] This is not to mention the republican intensity of *Valperga*, for which Shelley's reading of Villani was a preparation (see chapter 6).[21]

In the passage on planets quoted above, Shelley alludes to John Milton, whose works have recently been read by David Norbrook and Nigel Smith as significant examples of republican poetics. In Milton's narrative of the creation of the earth and its creatures in Book VIII of *Paradise Lost*, the angel Raphael criticizes those false future astronomers who "contrive to save appearances" (PL VIII 81) – those feudal ones, for instance, who asserted that the earth is the center of the universe. Against these scribblings, Milton and Shelley assert a cooler, more Neoplatonic and mathematical form of beauty, deriving an apt image of culture not as thick, maximalist *Kultur* but as determinate yet spacious minimalist ambience:

> Let us, applying the rules which appertain to the sublimest objects in nature, to the sublimest work of God, a Man of Genius, – let us, I say, conclude, that though one of this species appear to err, the failure is in our understandings, not in his course; and though lines and rules, "centric and eccentric scribbled o'er," have been marked out for the wise to pursue, that these in fact have generally been the leading-strings and go-carts of mediocrity, and have never been constituted the guides of those superior minds which are themselves the law, and whose innate impulses are the fiats, of intellectual creation.[22]

In a review essay of 1826, "The English in Italy," Shelley spells out her republican conviction that the prerogatives of rank can also trespass on genius, chiding Lord Normanby for his patronizingly aristocratic tone: "His lordship has too much real talent," she writes, "not to feel and appreciate the nobility of nature as well as that of birth, and some indication of such a feeling would give a grace to his productions, in which, at present, they are deficient."[23]

In her 1826 essay, "A Visit to Brighton," Shelley explores urban space as a concrete embodiment of ideas of culture. Here, Shelley engages the ideology of consumerism elliptically, via an analogy with a dandy who prefers to wander around London out of season because commodities are more readily available, without the interference of crowds. Shelley claims to prefer London maximalist and busy, and the countryside minimalist and quiet, as a sequence of near-empty spaces, or potentially (but not quite) populated ones: "the verdant meadow – the undulating park – the deep embowered wood – the murmur of streams – the flowery hedge, shady lane, and neat latticed cottage," she writes, miming a progress like that of the Creature in *Frankenstein*. In this passage, Shelley's spacious parataxis – the spare placing of phrases and clauses in parallel – contrasts with the complex construction describing London as "blocked up with carriages."[24] Thus the natural world, as in *Frankenstein*, becomes the basis of a truer kind of culture than the cluttered world of sedimented tradition (second nature) symbolized by London. In that novel, the spaces grow vaster, more neutral and more uninhabited, a point made in at least one ecocritical reading.[25] The Creature and his creator finally confront each other as equals (though they both die) in the blank space of the Arctic ocean. For a more positive example, we might consider the potent, shimmering descriptions of nature in *Valperga*, analogues for the kind of neutral but effervescent medium that Shelley construed culture itself to be. This is not to say that here she is understanding culture as a "second nature" in the manner of Edmund Burke. In some sense, indeed, she is doing the reverse: enculturing nature, turning the world into a place where potent political conversation can take place. Guinigi's description of the countryside around Monte Selice is a case in point, an object-lesson in how fertile places and fertile ideas can go together.

Shelley does not want her notion of nature to appear to be rooted in an idea of a particular place, another blow to a notion of culture as that which is traditional and customary. Instead, she judges from a cosmopolitan perspective: "Do not imagine . . . that I am a mere Londoner; I am . . . a traveller." She has been everywhere, like a good transparent narrator, and so is in a perfect position to inform us that Brighton is full of – nothing. For Shelley, Brighton does not feel inhabited:

> grass would spring up rank in the streets, if grass grew any where in the neighbourhood of Brighton; neither man or dog is to be seen, or any sound heard, save the melancholy roar of the near ocean. Meanwhile the houses sparkle in all the freshness of youth. So far was the mania of speculation carried, that

over one gate, innocent of a guest, is inscribed "Tea Gardens" . . . while in mockery of the solitude around, every gate was open to afford easy ingress to the traveller; nay, the ready waiter stood at the door – the only inhabitant he of the whole place – and the lamp suspended in the hall was alight, for I had rode thither in the evening, and the gathering twilight added to the desolation. Was he waiting for the advent of some shipwrecked sailor . . . or is that the retreat of the "Last Man"?

Here, Brighton is a symbol of rash "speculation," revolutionary capitalist energy transforming the social and natural worlds, a corrupted, cast-off version of public space permeated with loneliness and strange beauty. The almost military readiness of the waiter to serve suspends his body in (non)labor. The parades and rooms to which Shelley hastens are no respite from the built-in loneliness of a commodified landscape. In Shelley's austere description, a man stands at the end of each bench "vociferating" a series of mere numbers to a "ghost of a tune," a "tuneless tune." In "A Visit to Brighton," Shelley's minimalist view of culture is not so much traditionally Romantic as it is strikingly modern.

In Brighton, the background has become the foreground; Shelley reduces and even undermines the difference between the two. As a rainy day attenuates Brighton to its monotony of "sea, sea, sea," Shelley complains that the sea itself, usually "called immense, sublime – the best created image of space and eternity," has been flattened to "a Russian steppe," "a very dull object." But this unpromising ground becomes the very figure of the picturesque and sublime as it is suffused with moonlight: "Moonlight is to the sea what colour is to the rainbow." Everywhere, Brighton's beauty stems from the displaced, the exotic, and the nonfunctional. She praises the Regent's orientalist Pavilion: "Its chief defect is that it is situated in Brighton." It would have looked picturesque in Lucknow or Isfahan, Indian and Persian cities, "this groupe of domes, minarets, and other unnamed lantern-like spires, rising from the little grove that surrounds it, and sleeping placidly in the star-light"; even the pier looks fragile and "bending," "seemingly not sea-worthy," which "constitutes its strength."[26] As Shelley disturbingly observed in "Modern Italy," "To render Rome really a Roman scene . . . every inhabitant should be dismissed."[27] This is surely the plot of *The Last Man*, turned into a meditation on what counts as culture.

From these ghostly places, it is a small step to Shelley's essay "On Ghosts" (1824), published in the *London Magazine*. In "On Ghosts," grief provides the basis for a renewed understanding of what it means to share a community, a phenomenon also felt by Frankenstein's Creature: "The sun drawing up the vaporous air makes a void, and the wind rushes in to fill it, – thus beyond our

soul's ken there is an empty space; and our hopes and fears, in gentle or ter-
rific whirlwinds, occupy the vacuum." We have returned to the intellectual
framework of Shelley's writing on love and poetry. Shelley's startling description of her own haunting offers a poetics of ambience: metonymy, parataxis
(which accelerates through the passage), the *vraisemblable*, apophasis (nega-
tion), use of an intrinsically unreliable first person narrator, the interleaving
of inside and outside:

> [The house where I had last seen him] was deserted, and though in the midst
> of a city, its vast halls and spacious apartments occasioned the same sense
> of loneliness as if it had been situated on an uninhabited heath. I walked
> through the vacant chambers by twilight, and none save I awakened the echoes
> of their pavement. The far mountains (visible from the upper windows) had
> lost their tinge of sunset; the tranquil atmosphere grew leaden coloured as the
> golden stars appeared in the firmament; no wind ruffled the shrunk-up river
> which crawled lazily through the deepest channel of its wide and empty bed;
> the chimes of the Ave Maria had ceased, and the bell hung moveless in the
> open belfry . . . I walked through the rooms filled with sensations of the most
> poignant grief. He had been there; his living frame had been caged by those
> walls, his breath had mingled with that atmosphere, his step had been on those
> stones, I thought: – the earth is a tomb, the gaudy sky a vault, we but walking
> corpses. The wind rising in the east rushed through the open casements, making
> them shake; – methought, I heard, I felt – I know not what – but I trembled.[28]

The "spacious apartments" take on the "loneliness" of "an uninhabited
heath" – inside and outside, empty culture and barren nature are equated.
Shelley's skillful handling of apophasis – saying something by not saying it –
creates ghosts that haunt her prose, if not the "vacant chambers" themselves. "None save I awakened the echoes": the language invokes a present
absence, implying that someone (or more) is positively not there, or there
but somewhere else, lurking in the shadow of our (readerly) sense of ambiguity. The following sentence lays out descriptive language in parallel phrases
(parataxis), a cumulative effect. Shelley notes the contact, the atmosphere,
changing to a "leaden" color. Apophasis returns with "no wind"; the river
itself is less visible than its bed – another reversal of figure and ground, repeated by the following image of the "moveless" bell in its "open belfry."
As readers we hear the "chimes of the Ave Maria" before we are told that
they have "ceased": language is haunting us, and silence becomes tinted with
sound.

The passage closes with an unnamed sensation ("I know not what")
that bisects the discourse with dashes, making it tremble and enact its own
meaning: "methought, I heard, I felt . . . I trembled." As the verbs become

less mental and more physical (hearing is often placed above feeling in the hierarchy of the senses), Shelley's sense of present absence becomes embodied in her own reaction: she is modeling how a reader should thrill to her prose. In this paradoxical way, Shelley obtains the consciousness depicted in that very modern (anti-feudal) play *Hamlet*: "the earth is a tomb, the gaudy sky a vault, we but walking corpses." A sense of artificiality and constriction mark the state of grief. But she obtains this not through a Hamlet-like separation of mind and body – hiding in a nutshell while counting oneself king of infinite space – but in an ever-more embodied *idea* that grows strangely less tangible the more we thrill to the prose effects. "On Ghosts" is a masterpiece of sensational writing; through a series of sophisticated rhetorical devices, Shelley renders the concrete but slippery experience of the void where love and poetry are free to move, and move us.

Shelley's representation of culture as an open, yet pregnant, space argues against those who perceive an increasing conservatism in her career. In her essays, we discover her fascination with republican forms of poetics, sidestepping those concerns we have traditionally associated with the aesthetic.[29] Mary Shelley added her own language to the congeries of figurative, political, and philosophical criticisms of commodified life. Precisely insofar as we are slightly cynical toward the surrounding cultural world – and in particular, a world of commodities; precisely because we have a distance toward it, we are able to take up various positions within that world beyond mute or crude belief. Culture, for Shelley, is not the suspension of disbelief. It is, in fact, believing in the power of suspension.

NOTES

I am indebted to Esther Schor for her valuable comments on this chapter.

1 On the "debate" between environment and self as causal factors, see David Simpson, *Situatedness, or, Why We Keep Saying Where We're Coming From* (Durham, NC: Duke University Press, 2002).

2 One of these, an essay on Mérimée's *Chronique du Temps de Charles IX*, is a conjectural attribution; see Pamela Clemit's remarks in *NSW* II 115.

3 *LL* and *NSW* VIII.

4 Raymond Williams, *Culture and Society: Coleridge to Orwell* (London: Chatto and Windus, 1958; rpt. Hogarth Press, 1987).

5 Mary Shelley, "[The English in Italy]," *Westminster Review* 6 (October 1826), 326, 329, 335, 334.

6 Mary Shelley, "Madame d'Houtetôt," *The Liberal* 2.3 (1823), 68, 82–83.

7 Mary Shelley, "[Illyrian Poems – Feudal Scenes]," *Westminster Review* 10 (January 1829), 78, 78, 80.

8 Mary Shelley, "[Loves of the Poets]," *Westminster Review* 11 (October 1829), 472, 472.

9 See Alan Richardson, *British Romanticism and the Science of the Mind* (Cambridge: Cambridge University Press, 2001), chapters 1 and 6, especially pp. 6–8, 36–37, 151, 160–63, 177–78.

10 Mary Shelley, "[Loves of the Poets]," 473, 473, 473.

11 Theodor W. Adorno, *Aesthetic Theory*, trans. and ed. Robert Hullot-Kentor (Minneapolis: University of Minnesota Press, 1997), pp. 19, 67, 78.

12 See for example Theodor W. Adorno, "Cultural Criticism and Society," in *Prisms*, trans. Samuel and Shierry Weber (Cambridge, MA: MIT Press, [1967], rpt. 1997), pp. 17–34; Raymond Williams, *Culture and Society*. See also *Oxford English Dictionary*, "critique," sb. 1, 2.

13 The dog makes its non-appearance in the story "Silver Blaze."

14 See Geoffrey Hartman, *The Fateful Question of Culture* (New York: Columbia University Press, 1997), p. 211; Terry Eagleton, *The Idea of Culture* (Oxford: Blackwell, 2000), p. 9.

15 See Stephen Greenblatt, *Marvelous Possessions: The Wonder of the New World* (Chicago: University of Chicago Press, 1991).

16 Roman Jakobson, "Closing Statement: Linguistics and Poetics," in *Style in Language*, ed. Thomas A. Sebeok (Cambridge, MA: MIT Press, 1960), pp. 350–77; 355–56.

17 Mary Shelley, "Giovanni Villani," *The Liberal* 2.4 (1823), 281–97, in *Matilda, Dramas, Reviews and Essays, Prefaces and Notes*, ed. Pamela Clemit, *NSW* 11 128–39; 282, 282. (I use the original pagination of Shelley's essays, provided by Clemit.)

18 *Ibid.*, 281–82. For Shelley's understanding of *planetes*, see the "Note on Prometheus Unbound," in *PW* 11 136–37.

19 For accounts of the tentativeness of republican history and Shelley's figurative language, see Tilottama Rajan, "Between Romance and History: Possibility and Contingency in Godwin, Leibniz, and Mary Shelley's *Valperga*," *MST* 88–102, esp. 99; and Michael Rossington, "Future Uncertain: The Republican Tradition and its Destiny in *Valperga*," *MST* 108–09.

20 For a strong analysis of Victor's egotism and the reactionary science in which he invests, see Marilyn Butler, "Introduction," to Mary Shelley, *Frankenstein, or, the Modern Prometheus; the 1818 Text* (Oxford: Oxford University Press, 1994), especially pp. xv–xxi.

21 See Timothy Morton and Nigel Smith, "Introduction," in *Radicalism in British Literary Culture, 1650–1830: From Revolution to Revolution* (Cambridge: Cambridge University Press, 2000), pp. 1–26; 5–6.

22 Mary Shelley, "Giovanni Villani," 282.

23 Mary Shelley, "[The English in Italy]," 341.

24 Mary Shelley, "A Visit to Brighton," *London Magazine* 16 (December 1826), 460–66, in *Matilda, Dramas, Reviews and Essays, Prefaces and Notes*, ed. Pamela Clemit, *NSW* 11 164–71; 460, 462, 461.

25 See Jonathan Bate, *The Song of the Earth* (Cambridge, MA: Harvard University Press, 2000), pp. 54–5.

26 Mary Shelley, "A Visit to Brighton," 462, 464, 465, 465, 465, 465–66.

27 Mary Shelley, "[Modern Italy]," in *Matilda, Dramas, Reviews and Essays, Prefaces and Notes*, ed. Pamela Clemit, *NSW* II 182–94; 130.
28 Mary Shelley, "On Ghosts," *London Magazine* 9 (March 1824), 253–56; 254, 254.
29 See Paul Hamilton, "The Republican Prompt," in *Radicalism in British Literary Culture*, eds. Morton and Smith, esp. pp. 204, 214.

FURTHER READING

Editions

Frankenstein, Susan J. Wolfson (ed.), New York: Longman, 2002.

Frankenstein: The 1818 Text, J. Paul Hunter (ed.), New York: Norton, 1996.

Frankenstein, or The Modern Prometheus, Maurice Hindle (ed.), Harmondsworth: Penguin, 1985.

Frankenstein; or, The Modern Prometheus: The 1818 Version, D. L. Macdonald and Kathleen Scherf (eds.), Peterborough, Ontario: Broadview, 1994.

The Journals of Mary Shelley, 1814–44, Paula R. Feldman and Diana Scott-Kilvert (eds.), 2 vols., Oxford: Oxford University Press, 1987.

The Last Man, Hugh J. Luke, Jr. (ed.); Anne K. Mellor (intro.), Lincoln: University of Nebraska Press, 1993.

The Letters of Mary Wollstonecraft Shelley, Betty T. Bennett (ed.), 3 vols., Baltimore: Johns Hopkins University Press, 1980–83.

Lives of the Most Eminent Literary and Scientific Men of France, 2 vols., London: Longman, 1838, 1839.

Mary Shelley: Collected Tales and Stories, Charles E. Robinson (ed.), Baltimore: Johns Hopkins University Press, 1976.

Mary Shelley's Literary Lives and Other Writings, Nora Crook (ed.), 4 vols., London: Pickering and Chatto, 2002.

The Mary Shelley Reader, Betty T. Bennett and Charles E. Robinson (eds.), New York: Oxford University Press, 1990.

Maurice, or the Fisher's Cot, Claire Tomalin (ed. and intro.), London: Viking Penguin, in association with the Keats–Shelley Memorial Association, 1998.

The Novels and Selected Works of Mary Shelley, Nora Crook (gen. ed.) with Pamela Clemit, Betty T. Bennett (cons. ed.), 8 vols., London: William Pickering, 1996.

Valperga: or, The Life and Adventures of Castruccio, Prince of Lucca, Stuart Curran (ed.), New York: Oxford University Press, 1997.

Biographies

St. Clair, William, *The Godwins and the Shelleys: The Biography of a Family*, London: Faber and Faber, 1989.

Seymour, Miranda, *Mary Shelley*, London: John Murray, 2000.

Spark, Muriel, *Mary Shelley*, New York: Dutton, 1987.
Sunstein, Emily, *Mary Shelley: Romance and Reality*, Boston: Little, Brown, 1989.

Early reviews

Frankenstein

The British Critic n.s. 9 (April 1818), 432–38.
[Croker, John Wilson], *Quarterly Review* 18 (Jan. 1818), 379–85.
The Edinburgh Magazine, and Literary Miscellany 2 (1818), 249–53.
[Scott, Walter], "Remarks on *Frankenstein, or the Modern Prometheus*, a Novel," *Blackwood's Edinburgh Magazine* 2 (1818), 613–20.

The Last Man

The Literary Gazette and Journal of Belles Lettres, Arts, Sciences, &c. (February 18, 1826), 102–03.
The Monthly Review, or Literary Journal n.s. 1 (March 1826), 333–35.
The Panoramic Miscellany, or Monthly Magazine and Review of Literature, Sciences, Arts, Inventions, and Occurrences 1 (March 1826), 380–86.
The Panoramic Miscellany, or Monthly Magazine and Review of Literature, Sciences, Arts, Inventions, and Occurrences 1 (March 1826), 380–86.

Lodore

The Athenaeum (March 28, 1835), 238–39.
The Examiner (May 24, 1835), 323–24.
Fraser's Magazine for Town and Country 11 (May 1835), 600–05.

Valperga

[Lockhart, John Gibson], *Blackwood's Edinburgh Magazine* 13 (1823), 283–93.

Bibliographies

Lyles, W. H., *Mary Shelley: An Annotated Bibliography*, New York: Garland, 1975.

Criticism

Essay collections

Behrendt, Stephen C. (ed.), *Approaches to Teaching Shelley's "Frankenstein,"* New York: MLA, 1990.
Bennett, Betty T. and Curran, Stuart (eds.), *Mary Shelley in Her Times*, Baltimore: Johns Hopkins University Press, 2000.
Conger, Syndy M., Frank, Frederick S., and O'Dea, Gregory (eds.), *Iconoclastic Departures: Mary Shelley after "Frankenstein": Essays in Honor of the Bicentenary of Mary Shelley's Birth*, Madison, NJ: Fairleigh Dickinson University Press, 1997.
Crisafulli, Lilla Maria and Silvani, Giovanna (eds.), *Mary Versus Mary* (Naples: Liguori, 2001). [In Italian and English]

Eberle-Sinatra, Michael (ed.), *Mary Shelley's Fictions: From "Frankenstein" to "Falkner,"* New York: St. Martin's Press, 2000.

Fisch, Audrey A., Mellor, Anne K., and Schor, Esther H. (eds.), *The Other Mary Shelley: Beyond "Frankenstein,"* New York: Oxford University Press, 1993.

Knoepflmacher, U. C. and Levine, George (eds.), *The Endurance of "Frankenstein": Essays on Mary Shelley's Novel,* Berkeley: University of California Press, 1979.

Articles, chapters in books, books, hypertext

Aaron, Jane, "The Return of the Repressed: Reading Mary Shelley's *The Last Man,*" in *Feminist Criticism: Theory and Practice,* Susan Sellers (ed.), New York: Harvester Wheatsheaf, 1991, pp. 9–21.

Abbott, Joe, "The 'Monster' Reconsidered: *Blade Runner*'s Replicant as Romantic Hero," *Extrapolation* 34 (1993), 340–50.

Austin, Margaret, "An Integral Relationship: Mary Shelley's Use of the Persephone Myth," Ph.D. dissertation, Washington State University, 1996.

Baldick, Chris, *In Frankenstein's Shadow: Myth, Monstrosity, and Nineteenth-Century Writing,* Oxford: Oxford University Press, 1987.

Bann, Stephen (ed.), *"Frankenstein": Creation and Monstrosity,* London: Reaktion, 1994.

Beckman, Karen, *Vanishing Women,* Durham, NC: Duke University Press, 2002.

Bennett, Betty T., "Machiavelli's and Mary Shelley's Castruccio: Biography as Metaphor," *Romanticism* 3.2 (1997), 139–51.

Mary Wollstonecraft Shelley: An Introduction, Baltimore: Johns Hopkins University Press, 1998.

"The Political Philosophy of Mary Shelley's Historical Novels: *Valperga* and *Perkin Warbeck,*" in *The Evidence of the Imagination,* Betty T. Bennett, Michael C. Jay, and Donald H. Reiman (eds.), New York: New York University Press, 1978, pp. 354–71.

Bewell, Alan, "An Issue of Monstrous Desire: *Frankenstein* and Obstetrics," *The Yale Journal of Criticism* 2.1 (1988), 105–28.

Romanticism and Colonial Disease, Baltimore: Johns Hopkins University Press, 1999.

Blumberg, Jane, *Mary Shelley's Early Novels: "This Child of Imagination and Misery,"* London: Macmillan, 1993.

Bohls, Elizabeth A., "Standards of Taste, Discourses of 'Race,' and the Aesthetic Education of a Monster: Critique of Empire in *Frankenstein,*" *Eighteenth-Century Life* 18.3 (1994), 23–36.

Botting, Fred, *Making Monstrous: "Frankenstein," Criticism, Theory,* New York: St. Martin's, 1991.

Bush, Ronald, "Monstrosity and Representation in the Postcolonial Diaspora: *The Satanic Verses, Ulysses,* and *Frankenstein,*" in *Borders, Exiles, Diasporas,* Elazar Barkan and Marie-Denise Shelton (eds.), Stanford, CA: Stanford University Press, 1998.

Buss, Helen, Macdonald, D. L., and McWhir, Anne (eds.), *Mary Wollstonecraft and Mary Shelley: Writing Lives,* Waterloo, Ont.: Wilfrid Laurier University Press, 2001.

Cantor, Paul, "Mary Shelley and the Taming of the Byronic Hero: 'Transformation' and *The Deformed Transformed*," *OMS* 89–106.

Carlson, Julie, "Coming After: Shelley's *Proserpine*," *Texas Studies in Literature and Language* 41.4 (1999), 351–72.

Chandler, James, *England in 1819: The Politics of Literary Culture and the Case of Romantic Historicism*, Chicago: University of Chicago Press, 1998.

Chevigny, Bell Gale, "Daughters Writing: Toward a Theory of Women's Biography," *Between Women: Biographers, Novelists, Critics, Teachers and Artists Write about Their Work on Women*, Carol Ascher, Louise DeSalvo, and Sara Ruddick (eds.), Boston: Beacon Press, 1994, pp. 357–79.

Clemit, Pamela, "From *The Fields of Fancy* to *Matilda*: Mary Shelley's Changing Conception of her Novella," *MST* 64–75.

The Godwinian Novel: The Rational Fictions of Godwin, Brockden Brown, Mary Shelley, New York: Oxford University Press, 1993, rpt. 2001.

Clery, E. J., *The Rise of Supernatural Fiction 1762–1800*, Cambridge: Cambridge University Press, 1995.

Women's Gothic: From Clara Reeve to Mary Shelley, Plymouth: Northcote House, 2000.

Colbert, Benjamin, "Contemporary Notice of the Shelleys' *History of a Six Weeks' Tour*: Two New Early Reviews," *KSJ* 48 (1999), 22–29.

Cox, Jeffrey N., "Staging Hope: Genre, Myth, and Ideology in the Dramas of the Hunt Circle," *Texas Studies in Language and Literature* 38 (Fall/Winter 1996), 245–64.

Crook, Nora, "Germanizing in Chester Square: Mary Shelly, *Cecil* and Ida von Hahn-Hahn," *TLS* June 6, 2003, p. 14.

"'Meek and Bold': Mary Shelley's Support for the Risorgimento," in *Mary Versus Mary*, Lilla Maria Crisafulli and Giovanna Silvani (eds.), Naples: Liguori, 2001, pp. 73–88.

Desser, David, "The New Eve: the Influence of *Paradise Lost* and *Frankenstein* on *Blade Runner*," in *Retrofitting "Blade Runner": Issues in Ridley Scott's "Blade Runner" and Philip K. Dick's "Do Androids Dream of Electric Sheep?*," Judith B. Kerman (ed.), Bowling Green, OH: Bowling Green State University Popular Press, 1991, pp. 53–65.

Dixon, Wheeler Winston, "The Films of Frankenstein", in *Approaches to Teaching Shelley's "Frankenstein,"* Stephen C. Behrendt (ed.), New York: Modern Language Association, 1990, pp. 166–79.

Duff, David, *Romance and Revolution: Shelley and the Politics of a Genre*, New York: Cambridge University Press, 1994.

Dunn, Richard J., "Narrative Distance in *Frankenstein*," *Studies in the Novel* 6 (1974), 408–17.

Eagleton, Terry, *The Idea of Culture*, Oxford: Blackwell, 2000.

Eilenberg, Susan, "Nothing's Namelessness: Mary Shelley's *Frankenstein*," in *Faces of Anonymity: Anonymous and Pseudonymous Publication from the Sixteenth to the Twentieth Century*, Robert Griffin (ed.), New York: Palgrave, 2002, pp. 167–92.

Ellis, Kate Ferguson, *The Contested Castle: Gothic Novels and the Subversion of Domestic Ideology*, Urbana: University of Illinois Press, 1989.

"Monsters in the Garden: Mary Shelley and the Bourgeois Family," *EF* 123–42.

Favret, Mary, "Mary Shelley's Sympathy and Irony: The Editor and Her Corpus," *OMS* 17–38.

Feldman, Paula, "Biography and the Literary Executor: The Case of Mary Shelley," *The Papers of the Bibliographical Society of America* 72 (1978), 287–97.

Fisch, Audrey A., "Plaguing Politics: AIDS, Deconstruction, and *The Last Man*," *OMS* 267–86.

Fleck, P. D., "Mary Shelley's Notes to Shelley's Poems and *Frankenstein*," *SiR* 6 (1967), 226–54.

Forry, Steven Earl, *Hideous Progenies: Dramatizations of "Frankenstein" from Mary Shelley to the Present*, Philadelphia: University of Pennsylvania Press, 1990.

Foster, Shirley, *Across New Worlds: Nineteenth-Century Women Travellers and their Writings*, New York: Harvester/Wheatsheaf, 1990, pp. 3–68.

Fraistat, Neil, "Illegitimate Shelley: Radical Piracy and the Textual Edition as Cultural Performance," *PMLA* 109 (May 1994), 409–23.

Gaull, Marilyn, "The Theatre," in *English Romanticism: The Human Context* (New York: Norton, 1988), pp. 81–105.

Gigante, Denise, "Facing the Ugly: The Case of *Frankenstein*," *ELH* 67.2 (2000), 565–87.

Gilbert, Sandra and Gubar, Susan, *The Madwoman in the Attic: The Woman Writer and the Nineteenth-Century Literary Imagination*, New Haven: Yale University Press, 1979.

Gould, Stephen Jay, "The Monster's Human Nature," *Natural History* 103 (July 1994), 14–21.

Gubar, Susan, "Mother, Maiden and the Marriage of Death: Woman Writers and an Ancient Myth," *Women's Studies* 6 (1979), 301–15.

Harpold, Terence, "'Did You Get Mathilda from Papa?': Seduction Fantasy and the Circulation of Mary Shelley's *Mathilda*," *SiR* 28 (1989), 49–67.

Heffernan, James A. W., "Looking at the Monster: *Frankenstein* and Film," *Critical Inquiry* 24.1 (1997), 133–58.

Hodges, Devon, "*Frankenstein* and the Feminine Subversion of the Novel," *Tulsa Studies in Women's Literature* 2.2 (1983), 155–64.

Hoeveler, Diane Long, "Fantasy, Trauma, and Gothic Daughters: *Frankenstein* as Therapy," *Prism(s)* 8 (2000), 7–28.

   Gothic Feminism: The Professionalization of Gender from Charlotte Smith to the Brontës, University Park: Pennsylvania State University Press, 1998.

Hofkosh, Sonia, "Disfiguring Economies: Mary Shelley's Short Stories," *OMS* 204–19.

Homans, Margaret, "Bearing Demons: *Frankenstein*'s Circumvention of the Maternal," in *Bearing the Word: Language and Female Experience in Nineteenth-Century Women's Writing*, Chicago: University of Chicago Press, 1986.

Hopkins, Lisa, "Memory at the End of History: Mary Shelley's *The Last Man*," *Romanticism on the Net* 6 (May 1997). http://users.ox.ac.uk/~scato385/lastman.html.

Jackson, Shelley, *Patchwork Girl; or, A Modern Monster by Mary/Shelley, and Herself*, CD-ROM, Watertown, MA: Eastgate Systems Inc., 1995.

Jacobus, Mary, "Is There a Woman in This Text," *New Literary History* 14.1 (1982), 117–54.

Johnson, Barbara, "My Monster/My Self," *Diacritics* 12.2 (1982), 2–10.

Jones, Angela D., "Lying Near the Truth: Mary Shelley Performs the Private," *ID* 19–34.

Kautz, Beth Dolan, "Spas and Salutary Landscapes: The Geography of Health in Mary Shelley's *Rambles in Germany and Italy*," in *Romantic Geographies: Discourses of Travel 1775–1844*, Amanda Gilroy (ed.), Manchester: Manchester University Press, 2000, pp. 165–81.

Knoepflmacher, U. C., "Thoughts on the Aggression of Daughters," *EF* 88–119.

Komisaruk, Adam, "'So Guided by a Silken Cord': *Frankenstein*'s Family Values," *SiR* 38.3 (1999), 409–41.

Kucich, Greg, "Mary Shelley's *Lives* and the Reengendering of History," *MST* 198–213.

Labbe, Jacqueline M., "A Family Romance: Mary Wollstonecraft, Mary Godwin, and Travel," *Genre* 25 (1992), 211–28.

Langan, Celeste, "Understanding Media in 1805: Audiovisual Hallucination in *The Lay of the Last Minstrel*," *SiR* 40.1 (2001), 49–70.

LaValley, Albert J., "The Stage and Film Children of *Frankenstein*," *EF* 243–89.

Lew, Joseph W., "The Deceptive Other: Mary Shelley's Critique of Orientalism in *Frankenstein*," *SiR* 30.2 (1991), 255–83.

"God's Sister: History and Ideology in *Valperga*," *OMS* 159–81.

Linton, Simi, *Claiming Disability: Knowledge and Identity*, New York: New York University Press, 1998.

London, Bette, "Mary Shelley, *Frankenstein*, and the Spectacle of Masculinity," *PMLA* 108.2 (1993), 256–67.

Markley, A. A., "'The Truth in Masquerade': Cross-Dressing and Disguise in Mary Shelley's Short Stories," in *Mary Shelley's Fictions: From "Frankenstein" to "Falkner*," Michael Eberle-Sinatra (ed.), New York: St. Martin's Press, 2000, pp. 109–26.

Mellor, Anne K., "*Frankenstein*: A Feminist Critique of Science," in *One Culture: Essays in Science and Literature*, George Levine (ed.), Madison: University of Wisconsin Press, 1987, pp. 287–312.

"*Frankenstein*, Racial Science, and the Yellow Peril," *Nineteenth-Century Contexts* 23.1 (2001), 1–28.

Mary Shelley: Her Life, Her Fiction, Her Monsters, New York: Methuen, 1988.

Miles, Robert, *Gothic Writing 1750–1820: A Genealogy*, London: Routledge, 1993.

Moers, Ellen, *Literary Women*, Garden City, NY: Doubleday, 1976.

Morton, Timothy, *The Poetics of Spice: Romantic Consumerism and the Exotic*, Cambridge: Cambridge University Press, 2000.

"The Pulses of the Body: Romantic Vegetarian Rhetoric and its Cultural Contexts," in *1650–1850: Ideas, Aesthetics, and Inquiries in the Early Modern Era*, vol. IV, Kevin Cope (ed.), New York: AMS Press, 1998, pp. 53–87.

Morton, Timothy and Smith, Nigel (eds.), *Radicalism in British Literary Culture, 1650–1830: From Revolution to Revolution*, Cambridge: Cambridge University Press, 2002.

Moskal, Jeanne, "Gender and Italian Nationalism in Mary Shelley's *Rambles in Germany and Italy*," *Romanticism* 5.2 (1999), 188–201.

"Speaking the Unspeakable: Art Criticism as Life-Writing in Mary Shelley's *Rambles in Germany and Italy*," in *Mary Wollstonecraft and Mary Shelley: Writing*

Lives, Helen Buss, D. L. Macdonald and Anne McWhir (eds.), Waterloo, Ont.: Wilfrid Laurier University Press, 2001, pp. 189–216.

" 'To speak in Sanchean phrase': Cervantes and the Politics of Mary Shelley's *History of a Six Weeks' Tour*," *MST* 18–37.

Mulvey-Roberts, Marie, "The Corpse in the Corpus: *Frankenstein*, Rewriting Wollstonecraft and the Abject," in *Mary Shelley's Fictions: From "Frankenstein" to "Falkner,"* Michael Eberle-Sinatra (ed.), New York: St. Martin's Press, 2000, pp. 197–210.

Nestrick, William, "Coming to Life: *Frankenstein* and the Nature of Film Narrative," *EF* 290–315.

Nitchie, Elizabeth, "Mary Shelley, Traveller," *KSJ* 10 (Winter 1961), 22–90.

Norbrook, David, *Writing the English Republic: Poetry, Rhetoric and Politics 1627–1660*, Cambridge: Cambridge University Press, 1999.

Norman, Sylva, *Flight of the Skylark: The Development of Shelley's Reputation*, Norman: University of Oklahoma Press, 1954.

O'Brien, Karen, *Narratives of Enlightenment: Cosmopolitan History from Voltaire to Gibbon*, Cambridge: Cambridge University Press, 1997.

O'Dea, Gregory, " 'Perhaps a Tale You'll Make it': Mary Shelley's Tales for the *Keepsake*," *ID* 62–78.

O'Flinn, Paul, "Production and Reproduction: The Case of *Frankenstein*," *Literature and History*, 9.2 (1983), 194–213.

O'Neill, Michael, " 'Trying to Make It as Good as I Can': Mary Shelley's Editing of P.B. Shelley's Poetry and Prose," *MST* 185–97.

Orr, Clarissa Campbell, "Mary Shelley's *Rambles in Germany and Italy*, the Celebrity Author, and the Undiscovered Country of the Human Heart," *Romanticism on the Net* 11 (1998). http://www.users.ox.ac.uk/~scat0385/rambles.html.

O'Sullivan, Barbara Jane, "Beatrice in *Valperga*: A New Cassandra," *OMS* 140–58.

Palacio, Jean de, "Mary Shelley, *The Last Man*: A Minor Romantic Theme," *Revue de Littérature Comparée* 42 (1968), 37–49.

Paley, Morton, "*The Last Man*: Apocalypse without Millennium," *OMS* 107–23.

Pascoe, Judith, "Poetry as Souvenir: Mary Shelley in the Annuals," *MST* 173–84.

Peckham, Morse, "Dr. Lardner's *Cabinet Cyclopaedia*," *The Papers of the Bibliographical Society of America* 45 (1951), 37–58.

Petronella, Vincent F., "Mary Shelley, Shakespeare, and the Romantic Theatre," in *Jane Austen and Mary Shelley and Their Sisters*, Laura Dabundo (ed.), Lanham, MD: University Press of America, 2000, pp. 121–34.

Phillips, Mark Salber, *Society and Sentiment: Genres of Historical Writing in Britain: 1740–1820*, Princeton: Princeton University Press, 2000.

Poovey, Mary, *The Proper Lady and the Woman Writer: Ideology as Style in the Works of Mary Wollstonecraft, Mary Shelley, and Jane Austen*, Chicago: University of Chicago Press, 1984.

Purinton, Marjean D., "Polysexualities and Romantic Generations in Mary Shelley's Mythological Dramas *Midas* and *Proserpine*," *Women's Writing* 6.3 (1999), 385–411.

Rajan, Tilottama, "Between Romance and History: Possibility and Contingency in Godwin, Leibniz, and Mary Shelley's *Valperga*," *MST* 88–102.

Rauch, Alan, "The Monstrous Body of Knowledge in Mary Shelley's *Frankenstein*," *SiR* 34.2 (1995), 227–53.

Reiman, Donald H., *Romantic Texts and Contexts*, Columbia: University of Missouri Press, 1987.

Richardson, Alan, "*The Last Man* and the Plague of Empire," *Romantic Circles* MOO Conference, September 13, 1997. http://www.rc.umd.edu/villa/vc97/richardson.html.

"*Proserpine* and *Midas*: Gender, Genre, and Mythic Revisionism in Mary Shelley's Dramas," *OMS* 124–39.

Rosenthal, Peggy, "Feminism and Life in Feminist Biography," *College English* 36 (1974), 180–88.

Rossington, Michael, "Future Uncertain: The Republican Tradition and its Destiny in *Valperga*," *MST* 103–18.

St. Clair, William, "The Impact of Frankenstein," *MST* 38–63.

Schor, Esther H., "Mary Shelley in Transit," *OMS* 235–57.

Scott, Joan Wallach, *Gender and the Politics of History*, New York: Columbia University Press, 1988.

Shapiro, Ann Louise, ed., *Feminists Revision History*, New Brunswick, NJ: Rutgers University Press, 1994.

Smith, Bonnie, *The Gender of History: Men, Women, and Historical Practice*, Cambridge, MA: Harvard University Press, 1998.

Smith, Johanna, *Mary Shelley*, New York: Twayne, 1996.

Smith, Nigel, *Literature and Revolution in England, 1640–1660*, New Haven: Yale University Press, 1994.

Snyder, Robert Lance, "Apocalypse and Indeterminacy in Mary Shelley's *The Last Man*," *SiR* 17 (1978), 435–52.

Spatt, Hartley S., "Mary Shelley's Last Men: The Truth of Dreams," *Studies in the Novel* 7 (1975), 526–37.

Spivak, Gayatri Chakravorty, "Three Women's Texts and a Critique of Imperialism," *Critical Inquiry* 12 (1985), 243–61.

Sterrenburg, Lee, "*The Last Man*: Anatomy of Failed Revolutions," *Nineteenth-Century Fiction* 33 (1978), 324–47.

"Mary Shelley's Monster: Politics and Psyche in *Frankenstein*," *EF* 143–71.

Stryker, Susan, "My Words to Victor Frankenstein above the Village of Chamounix: Performing Transgender Rage," in *States of Rage: Emotional Eruption, Violence, and Social Change*, Renée R. Curry and Terry L. Allison (eds.), New York: New York University Press, 1996, pp. 195–215.

Tropp, Martin, *Mary Shelley's Monster*, Boston: Houghton Mifflin, 1976.

Veeder, William, *Mary Shelley & Frankenstein: The Fate of Androgyny*, Chicago: University of Chicago Press, 1986.

Vlasopolos, Anca, "*Frankenstein*'s Hidden Skeleton: The Psycho-Politics of Oppression," *Science-Fiction Studies* 10 (1983), 125–36.

Wake, Ann M. Frank, "Women in the Active Voice: Recovering Female History in Mary Shelley's *Valperga* and *Perkin Warbeck*," *ID* 235–59.

White, Daniel E., " 'The God Undeified': Mary Shelley's *Valperga*, Italy, and the Aesthetic of Desire," *Romanticism on the Net* 6 (May 1997). http://www.sul.stanford.edu/mirrors/romnet/valperga.html.

Williams, Anne, *The Art of Darkness: A Poetics of Gothic*, Chicago: University of Chicago Press, 1995.

Winnett, Susan, "Coming Unstrung: Women, Men, Narrative, and Principles of Pleasure," *PMLA* 105.3 (1990), 505–18.

Wolfson, Susan, "Editorial Privilege: Mary Shelley and Percy Shelley's Audiences," *OMS* 39–72.

Youngquist, Paul, "*Frankenstein*: The Mother, the Daughter, and the Monster," *Philological Quarterly* 70.3 (1991), 339–59.

Zakharieva, Bouriana, "Frankenstein of the Nineties: The Composite Body," *Canadian Review of Comparative Literature* 23.3 (1996), 739–52.

Zizek, Slavoj, *Looking Awry: An Introduction to Jacques Lacan through Popular Culture*, Cambridge, MA: MIT Press, 1992.

SELECT FILMOGRAPHY

1910 *Frankenstein*, dir. J. Searle Downey
1931 *Frankenstein*, dir. James Whale
1935 *Bride of Frankenstein*, dir. James Whale
1948 *Abbott and Costello Meet Frankenstein*, dir. Charles T. Barton
1957 *The Curse of Frankenstein*, dir. Terence Fisher
1958 *The Revenge of Frankenstein*, dir. Terence Fisher
1958 *Frankenstein – 1970*, dir. Howard W. Koch
1965 *Frankenstein Conquers the World*, dir. Inoshiro Honda (Japanese)
1973 *El Espíritu de la Colmena*, dir. Victor Erice (*Spirit of the Beehive*; Spanish)
1974 *Young Frankenstein*, dir. Mel Brooks
1974 *Flesh for Frankenstein* (*Andy Warhol's Frankenstein*), dir. Paul Morrissey
1975 *Rocky Horror Picture Show*, dir. Jim Sharman
1982 *Blade Runner*, dir. Ridley Scott; director's cut, 1992
1986 *Gothic*, dir. Ken Russell
1987 *Making Mr. Right*, dir. Susan Seidelman
1987 *Remando al viento/Rowing with the Wind*, dir. Gonzalo Suárez
1988 *Haunted Summer*, dir. Ivan Passer
1994 *Mary Shelley's Frankenstein*, dir. Kenneth Branagh
1998 *Gods and Monsters*, dir. Bill Condon
2001 *A.I.: Artificial Intelligence*, dir. Steven Spielberg

INDEX

Note: Mary Shelley's books (including novels, collections of biographies and travel writings) and plays are listed alphabetically. Her biographies, stories, poems, reviews, and essays are listed under her name. All other works are listed under author or director.

CAMBRIDGE COMPANIONS TO LITERATURE

Lightning Source UK Ltd.
Milton Keynes UK
UKOW04f0859290116

267378UK00001BA/163/P

9 780521 007702